RACIALLY MIXED PEOPLE IN AMERICA

RACIALLY MIXED PEOPLE IN AMERICA

EDITED BY

Maria P. P. ROOT

SAGE PUBLICATIONS
International Educational and Professional Publisher
Newbury Park London New Delhi

Cover photos courtesy of Maria P. P. Root.

For information address:

SAGE Publications, Inc.
2455 Teller Road
Newbury Park, California 91320

SAGE Publications Ltd.
6 Bonhill Street
London EC2A 4PU
United Kingdom

SAGE Publications India Pvt. Ltd.
M-32 Market
Greater Kailash I
New Delhi 110 048 India

Printed in the United States of America

Library of Congress Cataloging-in-Publication Data

Racially mixed people in America / edited by Maria P.P. Root.
p. cm.
Includes bibliographical references and index.
ISBN 0-8039-4101-3. — ISBN 0-8039-4102-1 (pbk.)
1. Racially mixed people—United States. 2. United States—Population. 3. United States—Race relations. I. Root, Maria P. P.
E184.A1R324 1992
305.8'00973—dc20 91-38114
CIP

92 93 94 95 10 9 8 7 6 5 4 3

Sage Production Editor: Judith L. Hunter

Contents

Part IV: Challenging the Census

Dedication

For the children of all colors of the present and future. I hope the journey to finding your place in this world is made easier by our collaboration on this volume and our work toward multiracial understanding in our communities, institutions, and homes.

For the collaborators of this volume, many of whom might be characterized as innovative nonconformists. This collaboration was made possible only by the adventurous and inquisitive spirit that led many of the contributors to research, write, and teach on multiraciality when there was little support. Knowing that this volume has been a glint in the mind's eye of many of the contributors to this volume, it is encouraging to know that dreams can come true.

For my parents, Robert Norman Newhouse and Milagros Alejandra Newhouse, for opting to take the harder path in life during a time when interracial and international marriages were discouraged and punished. I especially am grateful to my mother for instilling in me a pride in my heritage, for encouraging me to question what is considered "fact," and for teaching me how to take care of myself in a color-conscious society.

PART I

Racial Ecology

1

Within, Between, and Beyond Race

MARIA P. P. ROOT

The "biracial baby boom" in the United States started about 25 years ago, around the time the last laws against miscegenation (race mixing) were repealed in 1967. The presence of racially mixed persons defies the social order predicated upon race, blurs racial and ethnic group boundaries, and challenges generally accepted proscriptions and prescriptions regarding intergroup relations. Furthermore, and perhaps most threatening, the existence of racially mixed persons challenges long-held notions about the biological, moral, and social meaning of race.

The emergence of a racially mixed population is transforming the "face" of the United States. The increasing presence of multiracial[1] people necessitates that we as a nation ask ourselves questions about our identity: Who are we? How do we see ourselves? Who are we in relation to one another? These questions arise in the context of a country that has held particular views of race—a country that has subscribed to race as an immutable construct, perceived itself as White, and been dedicated to preserving racial lines. Thus such questions of race and identity can only precipitate a full-scale "identity crisis" (Fernández, Chapter 10, this volume) that this country is ill equipped to resolve. Resolving the identity crisis may force us to reexamine our construction of race and the hierarchical social order it supports.

The "racial ecology" is complex in a phenotypically heterogeneous society that has imbued physical differences with significant meaning in a convention that benefits selective segments of the society. At a personal level, race is very much in the eye of the beholder; at a political level, race is in the service of economic and social privilege. Similarly, ethnic identity is relevant only in an ethnically heterogeneous environment. Whereas race can contribute to ethnicity, it is neither a sufficient nor necessary condition for assuming one's ethnicity, particularly with multiracial populations (see works in this volume by Hall, Chapter 18; Mass, Chapter 19; Stephan, Chapter 5). Our confusion of race and ethnicity indicates that it will be difficult to abandon the smoke screen that hides our "caste system" surrounding theory, politics, health care, education, and other resources.

Our tendency to think simplistically about complex relationships has resulted in dichotomous, hierarchical classification systems that have become vehicles of oppression. The way in which we have utilized the construction of race has placed the multiracial person "betwixt and between" (G. R. Daniel, personal communication, 1991) in the racial ecology since colonial times. The publication of this volume suggests that the emerging critical mass of multiracial persons, catalyzing a national identity crisis, might enable us to disassemble the vehicle of oppression.

Although oppression takes different forms, it is consistently characterized by the hierarchical interpretation of differences. Sandoval (1990) provides an insightful four-tier model for examining the development of social oppression by gender and racial group social status, which affect and order economic power:

> Most definitions of "freedom" in the U.S. are activated in relation to a primary category most easily embodied by the white, capitalist and male reality. White males who move into this power nodule do so by defining themselves in opposition to white women and to third world women and men who are cast as "others." White women inhabit the second category in this hierarchy through the very definition of a primary white male position. Interestingly, even though white women experience the pain of oppression they also experience the will-to-power. For while white women are "othered" by men and feel the pain of objectification, within this secondary category they can only construct a solid sense of "self" through the objectification of people of color. Within the dialectic of this power construct no one can deny the oppression of third world men. However, men of color can call upon the circuits which charge the

> primary category with the gendered aspect of its privileges and powers, even without the benefit of race or class privileges. This kind of identification with the powerful stratum/caste of "male" for the construction of a solid sense of self has been utilized as an effective weapon for confronting the oppressions they experience. Ironically, however, women of color are cast into the critical category against which third world "male" subjectivity becomes constituted. The final and fourth category belongs to women of color who become survivors in a dynamic which places them as the final "other" in a complex of power moves. (p. 64)

Extending this model, racially mixed men and women would occupy the fifth and sixth tiers in this model, respectively, because of the rigidity of the dichotomy between White and non-White. Subsequently, multiracial people experience a "squeeze" of oppression *as* people of color and *by* people of color. People of color who have internalized the vehicle of oppression in turn apply rigid rules of belonging or establishing "legitimate" membership. The internalization of either/or systems of thinking operates even between communities of color, such as Asian American and African American communities. As Paulo Freire (1970) suggests, marginal status is created by the society and structures and rules that order it. Anzaldua (1990) challengingly observes:

> The internalization of negative images of ourselves, our self-hatred, poor self-esteem, makes our own people the *Other*. We shun the white-looking Indian, the "high yellow" Black woman, the Asian with the white lover, the Native woman who brings her white girl friend to the Pow Wow, the Chicana who doesn't speak Spanish, the academic, the uneducated. Her difference makes her a person we can't trust. Para que sea "legal," she must pass the ethnic legitimacy test we have devised. And it is exactly your internalized whiteness that desperately wants boundary lines (this part of me is Mexican, this Indian) marked out and woe to any sister or any part of us that steps out of our assigned places. (p. 143)

The mechanisms that have historically evolved to suppress multiple heritage identification have largely benefited White society. The rules of hypodescent enlist simplistic, dichotomous rules of classification (e.g., White versus non-White) and have been obviously employed in our historical amnesia. These strategies have fueled the oppression of America's people of color (Allen, 1988) and definitely that of the multiracial people of our country. In fact, attempts by racially mixed persons to move back and forth between color lines have been viewed pejoratively rather than as creative strategies in a multiracial reality (see, in this volume, Bradshaw, Chapter 7; Daniel, Chapter 8; Nakashima, Chapter 12). Furthermore, persons of color mixing with other persons of color—such as American Indians and Blacks, Filipinos and Native Americans, Latinos and Blacks—has been given little attention in the literature. This mixing does not conventionally threaten the border between White and non-White. The racial mixes over which there has been the most concern are those between groups that are most distant culturally and socially—Blacks and Whites, Japanese and Blacks, and Japanese and Whites. Furthermore, this concern has involved groups that are most convinced of the immutability of race and most wedded to preserving "purity" of race: Whites and Asians.

The simplicity and irrationality of our basis for conceptualizing race affects how we subsequently think about social identity. Linear models of social relations have provided the basis for many social psychological theories about racially mixed persons. The monoracial and monocultural bias of these theories is evident in constructions of assimilation and acculturation models (see Phinney, 1990) and many early theories addressing identity issues for persons with mixed heritages (Park, 1928; Stonequist, 1937). The theories, like our racial classification system, are characterized by dichotomous or bipolar schemes and as such can only marginalize the status of racially or ethnically mixed persons.

The recent consideration of multidimensional models has allowed the possibility that an individual can have simultaneous membership and multiple, fluid identities with different groups (e.g., Duffy, 1978; see also, in this volume, Hall, Chapter 18; Stephan, Chapter 5; Williams, Chapter 20). These models abolish either/or classifications systems that create marginality. Multidimensional models of identity will not be perplexed that phenotype, "genotype," and ethnicity do not necessarily coincide with or reliably predict identity. Several studies illustrate this phenomenon. A person of Black-Japanese heritage may look Filipino and may identify as both African American and Asian American. Similarly, a person of White-Asian background may phenotypically appear more similar to someone of European than Asian descent but may identify as a first-generation Japanese American. It is confusing to our linear models of identity to consider that a multiracial Black-Indian-European person who looks African

American self-identifies as multiracial, when someone of a similar heritage identifies as a monoracial African American. Moreover, the difference is more likely to be pathologized in a linear model. Many persons will be challenged to consider that the multiracially identified person is liberated from oppressive rules of classification rather than confined by them if they do not fit his or her experience.

Why has the United States suppressed the historical reality that a significant proportion of its citizenry has multigenerational multiracial roots? On one hand, it might be suggested that we have manufactured a media image. Winterson (1987) observes: "Very often history is a means of denying the past. Denying the past is to refuse to recognize its integrity. To fit it, force it, function it, to suck out the spirit until it looks the way you think it should" (pp. 93-94). On the other hand, this tendency may be seen as simply consistent with social models of assimilation (Phinney, 1990) that encourage a casting off of cultural ties and roots (Allen, 1988) to blend into the mythical "melting pot." It is more likely, however, that this tendency is largely tied to economic motives and class privileges (J. D. Forbes, 1990) and to ideas of supremacy that guide rules of hypodescent (assignment to the racial group with lower status). An ethnic past remains relevant to the extent that it is physically visible, such as with people of color and multiracial people.

The silence on the topic of multiraciality must be understood in context. In the not-so-distant past—in the lifetimes of almost all the contributors to this volume—antimiscegenist sentiments were profound. These attitudes were supported by legislation in most states, ruling these interracial unions and marriages illegal until a U.S. Supreme Court ruling in 1967 (see Spickard, 1989). The history of antimiscegenist laws and attitudes combined with rules of hypodescent, a pseudoscientific literature on race mixing (e.g., Provine, 1973), and the internalized oppression still evident in communities of color have unquestionably contributed to the silence on this topic.

Whereas one of the breakthroughs of the civil rights movement was empowerment of American racial minority groups by self-naming (Helms, 1990), this process is just beginning among multiracial persons. In essence, to name oneself is to validate one's existence and declare visibility. This seemingly simply process is a significant step in the liberation of multiracial persons from the oppressive structure of the racial classification system that has relegated them to the land of "in between." A confluence of factors has prevented this form of empowerment until now:

(1) The social understanding of race has allowed only one category of racial identification (a practice supported by the U.S. Census Bureau).
(2) Recent pride in being a person of color has demanded full-fledged commitment to the racial and ethnic minority group in order to pass "legitimacy tests."
(3) Epithets, which have been multiracial persons' only "universal" labels, have discouraged pride in self-identification.
(4) Isolation of interracial families, in part because of antimiscegenist legislation, has kept many multiracial families and individuals from meeting and accumulating a critical mass, a catalyst for empowerment.
(5) Race and ethnicity have been confused such that many multiracial people may identify monoculturally, as in the case of many Latinos, American Indians, and African Americans.

The biracial baby boom forces us to confront the meaning of race and the social order predicated upon it. *Race*, as constructed by social Darwinism (see Spickard, Chapter 2, this volume) and government construction by *blood quantum*, is more an artifice of the mind than a biological fact. Cooper and David (1986) observe that although the scientific construction of race was intended to provide a means of understanding and interpreting human variation, uncritical acceptance of the biological concept of race and lack of consistent definition by phenotypical markers is a problem even in biological arenas. Furthermore, a significant number of people around the world are not classifiable by such a system, including multiracial people (see Spickard, Chapter 2, for an in-depth discussion of race). Unfortunately, this problematic taxonomy has been transformed into a sociopolitical system that has been deeply imprinted in our psyches. Subsequently, race has become insidiously enmeshed with our social structure, determining the distribution of resources among social groups and even influencing the methodologies and theories of social science research.

Nowhere is the validity or reliability of race more questionable than in government policies. For example, blood quantum, used to operationalize the definition of race biologically, has been used liberally to justify the dislocation of American Indians and Native Hawaiians off their native lands, to intern Japanese Americans during World War II, to determine immigration quotas (see Thornton, Chapter 6, this volume), and to determine African Americans' racial identity and subsequent limits of access to resources. Generally, small blood quantum have been used to deprive people of color of their civil rights. Conversely, in more recent years conservatives have used blood quantum—that is, proportions of heritage—to determine allocations of lands to Native Americans (including Native Hawaiians) or qualification for government funding (Wilson, Chapter 9). Race cannot be a scientific construct if it has changing boundaries mitigated by laws, history, emotions, or politics (see, in this volume, Daniel, Chapter 8; Nakashima, Chapter 12; Wilson, Chapter 9).

Despite the significant number of people of all colors who have questioned the validity of race and the way it is abused in this country, taxonomies and institutions, like attitudes, are slow to change. Nowhere is this illustrated better than in how the U.S. Census Bureau has insisted on distinct monoracial categories. When Hawaii became the fiftieth state, the U.S. Census Bureau imposed its categories on a population that up until then had recorded its population according to categories and mixtures that reflected its multiracial reality (Lind, 1980). The Census Bureau does not acknowledge multiple heritages, despite the following facts: Currently, it is estimated that 30-70% of African Americans by multigenerational history are multiracial (Clifton, 1989); virtually all Latinos (Fernández, Chapter 10, this volume) and Filipinos (Cordova, 1973) are multiracial, as are the majority of American Indians (Wilson, Chapter 9, this volume) and Native Hawaiians (Pacheco, 1990). Even a significant proportion of White-identified persons are of multiracial origins (Alba & Chamlin, 1983). The way in which the Census Bureau records data on race makes it very difficult to estimate the number of biracial people, let alone multiracial persons, in the United States. Any estimates that have been made are conservative.

Now that we have almost 25 years' distance from the 1967 Supreme Court ruling that required the last 14 states holding antimiscegenist laws to repeal them, perhaps we can reconsider the subject of racially mixed persons in a less biased and less hostile context. It is likely that in the next decade, many persons previously identified as monoracial will begin to identify as multiracial, as they experience the dynamic nature of identity. As time evolves we will have more and more difficulty "judging the book by its cover." If we are truly to attempt constructive answers to the questions offered earlier (Who are we? How do we see ourselves? Who are we as a nation in relation to one another?), we will need to perform several social, political, and psychological "surgeries" to remove the deeply embedded, insidious, pseudoscientific construct of race from our social structure.

Initially, I thought my interest in exploring this topic was too personal. However, after a decade of contemplation, reading, writing, doing therapy, teaching, and finally a year of living in Honolulu, Hawaii, I think there is much to say. The topic of racially mixed persons provides us with a vehicle for examining ideologies surrounding race, race relations, and the role of the social sciences in the deconstruction of race. To this end, a progressive group of 28 interdisciplinary scholars, teachers, mentors, activists, administrators, and psychotherapists have collaborated to publish this first collection of contemporary American descriptive, empirical, conceptual, and theoretical studies on racially mixed persons since the repeal of antimiscegenist laws. The chapters are intellectually and personally challenging. An array of methodologies and twists to conventional research are described; some of the multiracial history of the United States is summarized; conventional constructs such as identity and passing are reexamined in the light of a multiracial ecology. The authors repeatedly and independently break with the characterization of the racially mixed person as a tragic figure relegated to a marginal, anomic existence as they offer multidimensional theories as contexts within which to examine multiracial phenomenology. It is suggested that the multiracial person's understanding of her- or himself can enhance society's understanding of intra- and intergroup relations, identity, and resilience.

Confusion may be a necessary element in the deconstruction and subsequent reconstruction of our social relationships in a qualitatively different way; thus the intent of this four-part volume is to both educate and confuse the reader. Part I, Racial Ecology, provides a context for examining the logic or illogic about race, variables affecting the formation of identity, and trends that will affect the future complexion of the United States. Part II, Recovering the Multiracial Past, provides historical information and analyses that are neither readily accessible nor common knowledge, from a multigenerational foundation for much of America of color. The mythology around multiraciality is examined. Classic and contemporary pieces of research on multiracial identity, adjustment, and relationships are summarized in Part III, What of the Children? The developmental periods span from preschool to adulthood; different multiple heritages are researched. Finally, Part IV, Challenging the Census, encourages the reader to digest the challenge of this volume and imagine how the resolution to our impending national identity crisis will unfold through a reconsideration of the roles of labels, classification, and stereotypes.

Collectively, these chapters take us full circle, beginning with the questions that have been posed to racially mixed persons for decades: What are you? Which one are you? With which group do you identify most? How do you see yourself? Then, questions are posed that we must attempt to answer as a nation in order to resolve a developing national identity crisis: Who are we? How do we see ourselves? Who are we as a nation in relation to one another? The answers are not likely to be found in a new system of classification, but in deconstruction, synthesis, and evolution.

Note

1. In this volume the terms *biracial* and *multiracial* are sometimes used interchangeably. *Biracial* refers to someone with two socially and phenotypically distinct racial heritages—one from each parent. However, this term can also refer to a multigenerational history of prior racial blending. For example, someone may have a parent or grandparent who was biracial and may acknowledge this heritage through self-identification as biracial. In this "looser" definition, one moves away from the notion of "halves"—half Black, half White. *Multiracial* includes the case of the biracial person and persons synthesizing two or more diverse heritages, such as the person with African, Indian, and European heritages. It also is a term that acknowledges that the suppression of multiracial heritage in this country may limit people's knowledge about their "racial" roots; subsequently, *multiracial* may be a more accurate term than *biracial*. This term is inclusive of all racially mixed persons.

Acknowledgment

I wish to express appreciation to G. Reginald Daniel for helpful feedback on an earlier draft of this chapter.

2

The Illogic of American Racial Categories

PAUL R. SPICKARD

The Mulatto to His Critics

Ashamed of my race?
And of what race am I?
I am many in one.
Thru my veins there flows the blood
Of Red Man, Black Man, Briton, Celt and Scot
In warring clash and tumultuous riot.
I welcome all,
But love the blood of the kindly race
That swarthes my skin, crinkles my hair
And puts sweet music into my soul.

JOSEPH COTTER (1918/1990).
From *Joseph Seamon Cottor, Jr.: Complete Poems*,
edited by James Robert Payne. © 1990 by
The University of Georgia Press. Used by permission.

This poem by Joseph Cotter, a promising African American poet who died young early in this century, highlights several of the ways Americans think about race. What is a race? And, if we can figure that out, what is a person of mixed race? These are central questions of this essay and this book.

In most people's minds, as apparently in Cotter's, race is a fundamental organizing principle of human affairs. Everyone has a race, and only one. The races are biologically and characterologically separate one from another, and they are at least potentially in conflict with one another. Race has something to do with blood (today we might say genes), and something to do with skin color, and something to do with the geographical origins of one's ancestors. According to this way of thinking, people with more than one racial ancestry have a problem, one that can be resolved only by choosing a single racial identity.

It is my contention in this essay, however, that race, while it has some relationship to biology, is not mainly a biological matter. Race is primarily a sociopolitical construct. The sorting of people into this race or that in the modern era has generally been done by powerful groups for the purposes of maintaining and extending their own power. Not only is race something different from what many people have believed it to be, but people of mixed race are not what many people have assumed them to be. As the other essays in this volume amply demonstrate, people with more than one racial ancestry do not necessarily have a problem. And, in contrast to Cotter's earlier opinion, these days people of mixed parentage are often choosing for themselves something other than a single racial identity.

Race as a Biological Category

In the thinking of most Europeans and Americans (and these ideas have spread around the world in the last century), humankind can be divided into four or five discrete races. This is an extension of the admittedly artificial system of classification of all living things first constructed by Swedish botanist and taxonomist Carolus Linnaeus in the eighteenth century. According to the Linnaean system, human beings are all members of the kingdom *Animalia*, the phylum *Chordata*, the class *Mammalia*, the order *Primates*, the family *Homididae*, the genus *Homo*, and the species *Homo sapiens*. Each level of this pyramid contains subdivisions of the level above. In the nineteenth century, pseudoscientific racists such as Johann Friedrich Blumenbach (1865/1973) and Joseph Arthur, comte de Gobineau (1915/1967), tried to extend the system down one more level to human *races*, on the basis of geography and observed physical differences. Details of the versions differed, but most systems of categorization divided humankind up into at least red, yellow, black, and white: Native Americans, Asians, Africans, and Europeans. Whether Australian aborigines, Bushmen, and various brown-skinned peoples—Polynesians and Malays, for example—constituted separate races depended on who was doing the categorizing.

There has been considerable argument, in the nineteenth century and since, over the nature of these "races." The most common view has been to see races as distinct *types*. That is, there were supposed to have been at some time in the past four or five utterly distinct and pure races, with physical features, gene pools, and character qualities that diverged entirely one from another. Over millennia there had been some mixing at the margins, but the observer could still distinguish a Caucasian type (light of skin, blue-eyed, possessing fine sandy hair, a high-bridged nose, thin lips, and so on), a Negroid type (dark brown of skin, brown-eyed, with tightly curled black hair, a broad flat nose, thick lips, and so on), an Asian type, and so on. There was debate as to whether these varieties of human beings all proceeded from the same first humans or there was a separate genesis for each race. The latter view tended to regard the races as virtual separate species, as far apart as house cats and cougars; the former saw them as more like breeds of dogs—spaniels, collies, and so forth. The typological view of races developed by Europeans arranged the peoples of the world hierarchically, with Caucasians at the top, Asians next, then Native Americans, and Africans at the bottom—in terms of both physical abilities and moral qualities.[1]

Successors in this tradition further subdivided the races into subunits, each again supposed to carry its own distinctive physical, genotypical, and moral characteristics. Madison Grant (1918/1970) divided the Caucasian race into five subunits: the Nordic race, the Alpine race, the Mediterranean race, the extinct races of the Upper Paleolithic period (such as Cro-Magnon humans), and the extinct races of the Middle Paleolithic period (including Neanderthal humans).[2] Each of the modern Caucasian subunits, according to Grant, included at least five further subdivisions. Each of the major subunits bore a distinctive typical stature, skin color, eye color, hair color, hair texture, facial shape, nose type, skull shape, and cephalic index.[3] Each was also supposed to carry distinctive intellectual and moral qualities, with the Nordic being the highest type. According to Henry Fairfield Osborn (1924; cited in Barzun, 1937/1965, p. 224), even where there was achievement of distinction in non-Nordic peoples, it came from a previous infusion of Nordic genes. He contended in a *New York Times* article that Raphael, Cervantes, Leonardo, Galileo, Titian, Botticelli, Petrarch, Columbus, Richelieu, Lafayette, Joffre, Clemenceau, Rodin, Racine, Napoleon, Garibaldi, and dozens of other Continentals were all actually of Nordic origin—hence their genius. In similar fashion, pseudoscientific racists saw White bloodlines as the source of the evident capabilities of Booker T. Washington, Frederick Douglass, and George Washington Carver.[4]

In the twentieth century, an increasing number of scientists have taken exception to the notion of races as types. James C. King (1981), perhaps the foremost American geneticist on racial matters, denounces the typological view as "make-believe" (p. 112).[5] Biologists and physical anthropologists are more likely to see races as *subspecies*. That is, they recognize the essential commonality of all humans, and see races as geographically and biologically diverging populations. Thus physical anthropologist Alice Brues (1977) sees a race as "a division of a species which differs from other divisions by the frequency with which certain hereditary traits appear among its members" (p. 1). They see all human populations, in all times and places, as mixed populations. There never were any "pure" races. Nonetheless, there are populations in geographical localities that can be distinguished from each other by statistically significant frequencies of various genetic or physical traits, from blood type to hair color to susceptibility to sickle-cell anemia. Most such thinkers have agreed, however, that the idea of race is founded in biology. Nineteenth-century Europeans and Americans spoke of blood as the agent of the transmission of racial characteristics. More recently, genes have been accorded the same role once assigned to blood.

The most important thing about races was the boundaries between them. If races were pure (or had once been), and if one were a member of the race at the top, then it was essential to maintain the boundaries that defined one's superiority, to keep people from the lower categories from slipping surreptitiously upward. Hence U.S. law took pains to define just who was in which racial category. Most of the boundary drawing came on the border between White and Black. The boundaries were drawn on the basis not of biology—genotype and phenotype—but of descent. For purposes of the laws of nine southern and border states in the early part of this century, a "Negro" was defined as someone with a single Negro great-grandparent; in three other southern states, a Negro great-great-grandparent would suffice. That is, a person with 15 White ancestors four generations back and a single Negro ancestor at the same remove was reckoned a Negro in the eyes of the law (Spickard, 1989, pp. 374-375; Stephenson, 1910, pp. 12-20).

But what was a "Negro"? It turned out that, for the purposes of the court, a Negro ancestor was simply any person who was socially regarded as a Negro. That person might have been the descendant of several Caucasians along with only a single African. Thus far less than one-sixteenth actual African ancestry was required in order for an individual to be regarded as an African American. In practice—both legal and customary—anyone with *any* known African ancestry was deemed an African American, while only those without any trace of known African ancestry were called Whites. This was known as the "one-drop rule": One drop of Black blood made one an African American. In fact, of course, it was not about blood—or biology—at all. People with no discernible African genotype or phenotype were regarded as Black on the basis of the fact that they had grandfathers or other remote relatives who were socially regarded as Black, and they had no choice in the matter (see, elsewhere in this volume, essays by Daniel, Chapter 8; Hall, Chapter 18; Williams, Chapter 20). The boundaries were drawn in this manner to maintain an absolute wall surrounding White dominance.

This leads one to the conclusion that race is primarily about culture and social structure, not biology. As geneticist King (1981) admits:

> Both what constitutes a race and how one recognizes a racial difference are culturally determined. Whether two individuals regard themselves as of the same or of different races depends not on the degree of similarity of their genetic material but on whether history, tradition, and personal training and experiences have brought them to regard themselves as belonging to the same group or to different groups. . . . there are no objective boundaries to set off one subspecies from another. (pp. 156-157)

The process of racial labeling starts with geography, culture, and family ties and runs through economics and politics to biology, and not the other way around. That is, a group is defined by an observer according to its location, its cultural practices, or its social connectedness (and their subsequent economic, social, and political implications). Then, on looking at physical markers or genetic makeup, the observer may find that this group shares certain items with greater frequency than do other populations that are also socially defined. But even in such cases, there is tremendous overlap between racial categories with regard to biological features. As King (1981) writes, "Genetic variability within populations is greater than the variability between them" (p. 158).

Take the case of skin color. Suppose people can all be arranged according to the color of their skin along a continuum:

darkest 2 3 4 5 6 7 lightest

The people Americans call Black would nearly all fall on the darker end of the continuum, while the people we call White would nearly all fall on the lighter end:

```
                darkest  2   3   4   5   6   7   lightest
Blacks           |------------------------|
Whites                   |--------------------|
```

On the *average*, the White and Black populations are distinct from each other in skin color. But a very large number of individuals who are classified as White have darker skin color than some people classified as Black, and vice versa. The so-called races are not biological categories at all; rather, they are primarily social divisions that rely only partly on physical markers such as skin color to identify group membership.

Sometimes, skin color and social definitions run counter to one another. Take the case of Walter White and Poppy Cannon (Cannon, 1952). In the 1930s and 1940s, White was one of the most prominent African American citizens in the United States. An author and activist, he served for 20 years as the executive secretary of the NAACP. Physically, White was short, slim, blond, and blue-eyed. On the street he would not have been taken for an African American by anyone who did not know his identity. But he had been raised in the South in a family of very light-skinned Blacks, and he was socially defined as Black, both by others and by himself. He dedicated his life and career to serving Black Americans. In 1949, White divorced his African American wife of many years' standing and married Cannon, a White journalist and businesswoman. Although Cannon was a Caucasian socially and ancestrally, her hair, eyes, and skin were several shades darker than her new husband's. If a person were shown pictures of the couple and told that one partner was Caucasian and the other Black, without doubt that person would have selected Cannon as the Afro-American. Yet, immediately upon White's divorce, there was an eruption of protest in the Black press. White was accused of having sold out his race for a piece of White flesh, and Cannon of having seduced one of Black America's most beloved leaders. White segregationists took the occasion to crow that this was what Black advocates of civil rights really wanted: access to White women. All the acrimony and confusion took place because Walter White was socially Black and Poppy Cannon was socially White; biology—at least physical appearance—had nothing to do with it.

All of this is not to argue that there is no biological aspect to race, only that biology is not fundamental. The origins of race are sociocultural and political, and the main ways race is used are sociocultural and political. Race can be used for good as well as for ill. For example, one may use the socially defined category Black to target for study and treatment a population with a greater likelihood of suffering from sickle-cell anemia. That is an efficient and humane use of a racial category. Nonetheless, the origins of racial distinctions are to be found in culture and social structure, not in biology.

Race as a Social Category

Race, then, is primarily a social construct. It has been constructed in different ways in different times and places. In 1870, the U.S. Bureau of the Census divided up the American population into races: White, Colored (Blacks), Colored (Mulattoes), Chinese, and Indian (U.S. Department of Interior, 1872, pp. 606-609). In 1950, the census categories reflected a different social understanding: White, Black, and Other. By 1980, the census categories reflected the ethnic blossoming of the previous two decades: White, Black, Hispanic, Japanese, Chinese, Filipino, Korean, Vietnamese, American Indian, Asian Indian, Hawaiian, Guamanian, Samoan, Eskimo, Aleut, and Other. In England in 1981, the categories were quite different: White, West Indian, African, Arab, Turkish, Chinese, Indian, Pakistani, Bangladeshi, Sri Lankan, and Other—because the sociopolitical landscape in England demanded different divisions (Banton, 1983, pp. 56-57). (The fact that some of these are also nationality labels should not obscure the fact that many in the United States and Great Britain treat them as domestic racial units.) In South Africa, there are four racial categories: White, African, Coloured, and Asian (Fredrickson, 1981). In Brazil, the gradations between Black and White are many: *preto, cabra, escuro, mulato escuro, mulato claro, pardo, sarará, moreno,* and *branco de terra* (Degler, 1971, p. 103). Each of these systems of racial classification reflects a different social, economic, and political reality. Such social situations change, and so do racial categories.

Social distinctions such as race and class come about when two or more groups of people come together in a situation of economic or status competition. Frequently such competition results in stratification—in the domination of some groups by others. People in Africa did not experience their lives as Africans or as Blacks; they were Hausa or Ibo or Fon, or members of any of several other groups. But when they were brought to America they were defined as a single group by the Europeans who held power over their lives. They were lumped together as Africans or Negroes or Blacks, partly because they shared certain physical similarities, especially when contrasted with Europeans, and partly because they shared a common status as slaves (W. D. Jordan, 1969).

From the point of view of the dominant group, racial distinctions are a necessary tool of dominance. They serve to separate the subordinate people as Other. Putting simple, neat racial labels on dominated peoples—and creating negative myths about the moral qualities of those peoples—makes it easier for the dominators to ignore the individual humanity of their victims. It eases the guilt of oppression. Calling various African peoples all one racial group, and associating that group with evil, sin, laziness, bestiality, sexuality, and irresponsibility, made it easier for White slave owners to rationalize holding their fellow humans in bondage, whipping them, selling them, separating their families, and working them to death (Fredrickson, 1971; W. D. Jordan, 1969). The function of the one-drop rule was to solidify the barrier between Black and White, to make sure that no one who might possibly be identified as Black also became identified as White. For a mixed person, then, acceptance of the one-drop rule means internalizing the oppression of the dominant group, buying into the system of racial domination.

Race is by no means only negative, however. From the point of view of subordinate peoples, race can be a positive tool, a source of belonging, mutual help, and self-esteem. Racial categories (and ethnic categories, for they function in the same way)[6] identify a set of people with whom to share a sense of identity and common experience. To be a Chinese American is to share with other Chinese Americans at least the possibility of free communication and a degree of trust that may not be shared with non-Chinese. It is to share access to common institutions—Chinese churches, Chinatowns, and Chinese civic associations. It is to share a sense of common history—immigration, work on the railroads and in the mines of the West, discrimination, exclusion, and a decades-long fight for respectability and equal rights. It is to share a sense of peoplehood that helps locate individuals psychologically, and also provides the basis for common political action. Race, this socially constructed identity, can be a powerful tool, either for oppression or for group self-actualization.

At the Margins: Race as Self-Definition

Where does this leave the person of mixed parentage? Such people have long suffered from a negative public image. In 1912, French psychologist Gustave LeBon contended that "mixed breeds are ungovernable" (quoted in Barzun, 1937/1965, p. 227). American sociologist Edward Reuter (1931/1969) wrote that "the mixed blood is [by definition] an unadjusted person" (p. 216). Writers and filmmakers from Thomas Nelson Page to D. W. Griffith to William Faulkner have presented mixed people as tormented souls (Spickard, 1989, pp. 329-339). Yet, as the other essays in this volume make clear, even if such a picture of pathology and marginal identity has ever been partially accurate, it certainly is no longer the case.

What is a person of mixed race? Biologically speaking, we are all mixed. That is, we all have genetic material from a variety of populations, and we all exhibit physical characteristics that testify to mixed ancestry. Biologically speaking, there never have been any pure races—all populations are mixed.

More to the point is the question of to which socially defined category people of mixed ancestry belong. The most illogical part of all this racial categorizing is not that we imagine it is about biology. After all, there *is* a biological component to race, or at least we identify biological referents—physical markers—as a kind of shorthand to stand for what are essentially socially defined groups. What is most illogical is that we imagine these racial categories to be exclusive. The U.S. Census form says, "Check one box." If a person checks "Other," his or her identity and connection with any particular group is immediately erased. Yet what is a multiracial person to do?

Once, a person of mixed ancestry had little choice. Until fairly recently, for example, most Americans of part Japanese or part Chinese ancestry had to present themselves to the world as non-Asians, for the Asian ethnic communities to which they might have aspired to be connected would not have them.[7] For example, in the 1920s, 7-year-old Peter fended for himself on the streets of Los Angeles. He had been thrown out of the house shortly after his Mexican American mother died, when his Japanese American father married a Japanese woman, because the stepmother could not stand the thought of a half-Mexican boy living under her roof. No Japanese American individual or community institution was willing to take him in because he was not pure Japanese (Spickard, 1989, pp. 110-117).

On the other hand, the one-drop rule meant that part-Black people were forced to reckon themselves Black. Some might pass for White, but by far the majority of children of African American intermarriages chose or were forced to be Black. A student from a mixed family described his feelings in the 1970s: "At home I see my mom and dad and I'm part of both of them. But when I walk outside that door, it's like my mom doesn't exist. I'm just Black. Everybody treats me that way." When he filled out his census form, this student checked the box marked "Black" (Spickard, 1989, pp. 329-339, 360-361).

The salient point here is that once, before the last third of the twentieth century, multiracial individuals did not generally have the opportunity to choose identities for themselves.[8] In the 1970s and particularly the 1980s, however, individuals began to assert their right to choose their own identities—to claim belonging to more than one group, or to create new identities (see essays in this volume by Kich, Chapter 21; Thornton, Chapter 22; Williams, Chapter 20). By 1990, Mary Waters could write, "One of the most basic choices we have is whether to apply an ethnic label to ourselves" (p. 52). She was speaking of a choice of ethnic identities from among several White options, such as Italian, Irish, and Polish. Yet the concept of choice began to apply to mixed people of color as well.

Some even dared to refuse to choose. In 1985 I observed a wise Caucasian-Chinese 5-year-old. Dining with her family in Boston's Chinatown during Chinese New Year, she was asked insistently by an adult Chinese friend of the family, "Which are you really—Chinese or American?" It was clear the woman wanted her to say she was really Chinese. But the girl replied simply, "I don't have to choose. I'm both." And so she was.

This child probably could not have articulated it, but she was arguing that races are not types. One ought not be thrust into a category: Chinese or American, White or Black. Her answer calls on us to move our focus from the boundaries between groups—where we carefully assign this person to the White category and that person to the Black category—to the centers. That is, we ought to pay attention to the things that characterize groups and hold them together, to the content of group identity and activity, to patterns and means of inclusiveness and belonging. A mixed person should not be regarded as Black *or* White, but as Black *and* White, with access to both parts of his or her identity. In the poem presented at the outset of this essay, Joseph Cotter's mulatto felt the pull of the various parts of his heritage, but felt constrained to choose only one. In the 1990s, that choice is still available to mixed people, but it is no longer *necessary*. Today a person of mixed ancestry can choose to embrace all the parts of his or her background. Many of the essays in this volume are about the issues attendant upon such a choice of a multiethnic identity. As the essays attest, the one-drop rule no longer applies.

Notes

1. There were two ways of conceiving this hierarchy, depending on which side of the Darwinian divide one inhabited. Pre-Darwinians thought of Adam and Eve as Caucasians, with Asians, Africans, and Native Americans representing degenerated descendants in separate lines. Those who came after Darwin and embraced the evolutionary view conceived of the human races as part of a continuum of ever-improving species and races, with great apes succeeded by chimpanzees, then by Africans, Asians, and Caucasians. The last were seen as the most complex and perfect of evolution's products (King, 1981, pp. 125-126).

2. The Nordics were people who could trace unmixed ancestry from Scandinavia, northern Germany, or the British Isles. Alpines were most minority peoples of Europe (Bretons, Basques, Walloons, and so on), French, southern Germans, northern Italians, Swiss, Russians, other East Europeans, and so on. Mediterraneans included Iberians, southern Italians, northern Africans, Hindus, Persians, and many Middle Easterners.

3. The cephalic index was the ratio of the breadth of the head to its length, expressed as a percentage.

4. Lest the reader think that these are all outdated ideas that no longer have impact, it should be noted that John R. Baker published a massive volume of pseudoscientific racism in 1974 that echoed the ideas of Blumenbach, Gobineau, and Grant. In addition, the 1982 edition of the Bartholomew *World Atlas* contains a map that divides up the world by skin color:

- Light Skin Colour (Leocodermi)
  - Indo-European: White skin, straight to wavy hair
  - Indo-European: Light brown skin, wavy hair
  - Hamitic-Semitic: Reddish brown skin, wavy hair
  - Polynesian: Light brown skin, wavy hair
- Yellow Skin Colour (Xanthodermi)
  - Asiatic or Mongolian: Yellow skin, straight hair
  - Indonesian: Yellow brown skin, straight hair
  - American Indian: Reddish yellow skin, straight hair
- Dark Skin Colour (Melanodermi)
  - African Negro: Dark brown skin, kinky hair
  - Pigmy Negro: Brown skin, kinky hair
  - Melanesian: Dark brown skin, kinky hair
  - Australo-Dravidian: Brown to black skin, wavy to kinky hair

There is also a map dividing the world by cephalic index:

Dolichocephalic (Long-headed)—primarily the peoples of Africa, Arabia, India, and Australia

Mesocephalic (Medium-headed)—Northwest Europe, North America, China, Japan, Persia

Brachycephalic (Broad-headed)—rest of Europe, Latin America, rest of Asia

Hyperbrachycephalic (Very broad-headed)—Russia

What the mapmakers imagine they are measuring and classifying is unclear, but it is clear that pseudoscientific racism is alive.

5. One must be careful of even this appeal to argument by scientists. Much of the allure of the Blumenbach argument was that it was put forth on the supposed basis of science. Since some people regard science with a kind of ritual awe, they are unable to think critically about any idea, however preposterous, put forth in the name of science.

6. Since both are defined on the basis of social and not biological criteria, a race and an ethnic group are in essence the same type of group. They reckon (real or imagined) descent from a common set of ancestors. They have a sense of identity that tells them they are one people. They share culture, from clothing to music to food to language to child-rearing practices. They build institutions such as churches and fraternal organizations. They perceive and pursue common political and economic interests (Cornell, 1985; Spickard, 1989, pp. 9-17).

7. This was true for people of mixed Jewish and Gentile background as well: They were shunned by Jewish people and institutions and typically had to adopt Gentile identities.

8. Sometimes the assignments were a bit arbitrary. Anthropologist Max Stanton tells of meeting three brothers in Dulac, Louisiana, in 1969. All were Houma Indians, had a French last name, and shared the same father and mother. All received their racial designations at the hands of the medical people who assisted at their births. The oldest brother, born before 1950 at home with the aid of a midwife, was classified as a Negro, because the state of Louisiana did not recognize the Houma as Indians before 1950. The second brother, born in a local hospital after 1950, was assigned to the Indian category. The third brother, born 80 miles away in a New Orleans hospital, was designated White on the basis of the French family name (M. Stanton, personal communication, 1990; see Stanton, 1971).

Acknowledgments

I am grateful to Sharlene Furuto and Max Stanton for helpful comments on an earlier version of this essay.

3

The Human Ecology of Multiracial Identity

ROBIN L. MILLER

Cross

My old man's a white old man
And my old mother's black.
If ever I cursed my white old man
I take my curses back.

If ever I cursed my black old mother
And wished she were in hell,
I'm sorry for that evil wish
And now I wish her well.

My old man died in a fine big house.
My ma died in a shack.
I wonder where I'm gonna die,
Being neither white nor black?

LANGSTON HUGHES
From *Selected Poems by Langston Hughes*,

The first question many biracial Black-White people are asked is, "Which one are you?" The importance of the question for the speaker stems from the societal belief that one cannot have multiple racial group affiliations and that the interracial person must inevitably choose to align him- or herself with one racial group. Yet, as the Langston Hughes poem above illustrates, many interracial people feel they are members of both, but at the same time neither, of the groups from which they take their heritage.

Racial and ethnic identity are fundamental parts of the psychological profile of any individual who is a member of a racially or ethnically heterogeneous society (Rotheram & Phinney, 1987). Understanding the process by which individuals develop racial and ethnic identities is therefore an important part of understanding the total person. Additionally, theory that accurately describes racial and ethnic identity development can provide a guide to creating environments that best facilitate healthy identification. Accurate theory also permits the identification of problems in development and the creation of useful corrective intervention.

As multiracial and multiethnic people become more prevalent in society, the need for theory that can describe their experiences becomes increasingly important. Historical, cross-cultural, regional, and social group variations in the accommodation of multiethnic and multiracial people indicate that the identity development process is ecologically anchored. There are several social-ecological factors a theory would have to describe, therefore, in order to be relevant to and accommodate multiracial or multiethnic experiences. In this chapter the experiences of African American-White biracial people will be discussed to illustrate the social ecological factors shaping identity.

Group Relations

A theory that accommodated multiethnic or multiracial people would describe a developmental process embedded in a system of intergroup relations (Christian, Gadfield, Giles, & Taylor, 1976; Tajfel, 1978), with attention to economics, population ratios, societal images, socialization by the collective, and rules for intergroup relations. When groups are of relatively equal status in society, the boundaries between them may be less rigid than the boundaries between groups of unequal status (Blau, Blum, & Schwartz, 1982; van den Berghe, 1967). Mobility between two groups of relatively equal status may have few implications in terms of social and economic resources, making integration of these groups relatively nonthreatening for members of both groups. When there is little tension between groups, there is likely to be acceptance; crossing the boundary between the groups will be common, there will be people who claim their heritage from both groups, and the notion that it is acceptable to claim heritage from more than one group will be widespread. For example, African American slaves and members of American Indian tribes have blended to form new groups, such as the Lumbees of North Carolina (see B. Berry, 1963). The nature of the relationships among groups also describes the commonly held attitudes toward those groups, attitudes that the multiethnic or multiracial individual will have to accommodate and that will have direct implications for the meaning of having multiple group affiliations (A. Wilson, 1984).

ECONOMICS

Whether or not groups are economic competitors and economically interdependent, dependent, or independent affects the degree to which group relations are adversarial or cooperative (Deschamps, 1982; Tajfel, 1978; van den Berghe, 1967). When one group controls the economic well-being of another, it is likely that the dependent group will be stigmatized. The controlling group will determine the other group's access to housing, employment, and basic resources, and can therefore determine the arenas in which intergroup contact is appropriate, the nature of acceptable group contacts, and rules and norms governing interaction (Gibbs, 1989). Affiliation with the controlling group under these circumstances would bring elevated social status. In order to guard that status, membership rules for the controlling group will likely be rigid. The status of African Americans in White America during slavery and postemancipation illustrates this relationship. Part of the function of the "one-drop rule" (which stated that one drop of Black blood in a person's heritage made him or her Black) was to preserve the "purity" of White society, and thereby limit access to economic (and political) control by people other than Whites. When a relationship exists of economic dependency by one group on another group, an interracial or interethnic background may be stigmatized because it represents a threat to the controlling group's power.

When groups are economic competitors, group relations will be tense. The adversarial nature of group relations will make personal intergroup contacts undesirable. When groups are economically competitive, interracial or interethnic people may be pressured to adopt but one identity, because multiple affiliations represent a threat to both groups. The importance of affiliating with only one group will increase as competition increases. An illustration of this principle can be seen in the view adopted of Blacks when the economic relationship between Blacks and unskilled White laborers shifted toward competition following emancipation. Segregation became the primary mechanism for maintaining social distance between African Americans and White Americans, because economic relationships alone could no longer maintain that distance (Frazier, 1948). Paralleling these trends, biracial people began to be viewed as shifty and untrustworthy, where they once had been viewed as having greater potential than full-blooded Blacks (Mencke, 1979; van den Berghe, 1967).

Finally, when groups are economically independent or cooperative, strain between them will be minimal. In such a relationship, involvement with members of other groups represents no significant threat to the economic well-being of either group, and may even facilitate cooperation. A multiracial or multiethnic person may be viewed as an individual with unique heritage who has combined harmonious elements into a new whole.

POPULATION RATIOS

The frequency and probability of interracial contact will influence how often society will confront multiracial issues and how many multiracial people society will have to accommodate (Blau, Becker, & Fitzpatrick, 1984; Blau et al., 1982). If one group is very small or very segregated, the likelihood that many people in other groups will have contact with that group is remote, limiting the probability of interethnic or interracial contact. At the same time, a small, geographically dispersed group would have to outmarry frequently. Thus multiethnic or multiracial combinations of certain types will be more or less rare, given the probability of group contact and the ratio of group members to one another. Vermont, for example, has one of the highest rates of African American to White marriages in the country. In a state where Blacks are less than one-fourth of 1% of the total population, Black Vermonters have many across-group marriage opportunities and few within-group marriage opportunities available to them (Monahan, 1976).

The ratio of men to women in each group is also an important determinant of how common multiethnic or multiracial unions are between groups and what those unions mean in society (Degler, 1971).

If group X is composed largely of males and group Y of females, X and Y might have to unite in order to continue both groups' existence. If the ratios of men to women within both groups are reasonably balanced, unions outside the groups are less permanent. Early Portuguese settlers in Brazil were primarily single men, so interracial unions with African slaves were a common and necessary means of increasing the population; in the United States, settlers came in family units, so although interracial unions did occur in the United States, their frequency and meaning were quite different from in the Brazilian case (Degler, 1971; van den Berghe, 1967).

Depending upon the likelihood of contact and population ratios of groups, multiethnic or multiracial people will be: (a) so rare that issues of affiliation are flexible and no widespread social rules exist regarding affiliation, as was the case in the United States prior to the implementation of antimiscegenation laws; (b) sufficiently prevalent that they threaten to alter the nature of group relations unless somehow prohibited, as was the case in the United States when antimiscegenation laws were enacted; or (c) sufficiently prevalent that they are considered a legitimate new group, such as the mestizos in Mexico, or force society to change the means by which it stratifies people, as in Brazil, with its continuum of colors.

SOCIETAL IMAGES

A group's status in society is reflected in popular images. The balance or imbalance of positive images of groups in society, a byproduct of group relationships, affects multiracial or multiethnic experiences by communicating a sense of the value of the groups and by providing (or failing to provide) access to role models. Theory would therefore need to account for the desirable and undesirable social images of each group. For example, in the United States attractiveness has long been projected as Caucasian (Gibbs, 1989), as have other traits considered desirable by mainstream culture. African American images have traditionally been rare in popular culture, except to confirm widely accepted negative stereotypes. This imbalance in available positive images influences biracial Black-White identification by making one affiliation appear more desirable or of greater status than another and making positive role models more or less available from one group, potentially engendering conflict for the biracial individual.

SOCIALIZATION BY THE COLLECTIVE

A common African adage holds, "I am because we are and because we are, therefore I am," emphasizing the significance of the collective for individual identity (see Mbiti, 1970). A theory of multiethnic or multiracial identification would need to account for the behavior of the collectives representing the multiethnic or multiracial individual in fostering group membership. The extent to which one group might actively socialize individuals into the collective and pass on the values and culture of the group while another group might be passive, disinterested, or even rejecting will influence the individual's process of identification. Traditionally, biracial Black-White people have been actively socialized as Black and considered part of the spectrum of the community, increasing the likelihood of identification with Black experiences. If all involved groups encourage a sense of belonging and acceptance, a multiracial or multiethnic identity might be easily achieved, as has occurred in the case of Hawaii, where native Hawaiians, Japanese immigrants, Chinese immigrants, and others have blended together in a climate of mutual acceptance to create a new multiethnic identity. If the groups do not actively foster affiliation, marginalization might occur, as happened to many Amerasian children following the wars in Korea and Vietnam. Thus the collectives' behavior toward an individual, particularly toward ambiguous individuals, would have to be described adequately in any theory (Hutnik, 1986).

HISTORICAL LEGACIES

Individuals and groups live their lives in historical space. Both historical relations and alterations in present relations will be important aspects of understanding multiracial identity. Historically, White Americans have oppressed African Americans; children of mixed African American and White American parentage must cope with that historical relationship in resolving their identities. At the same time, the relationship between African Americans and White Americans continues to evolve, and will do so across the life span of the individual. An African American-White individual born in 1960 would by his or her thirtieth birthday have witnessed the assassinations of Martin Luther King and Malcolm X, the abolition of laws restricting interracial marriage as unconstitutional, the elections of David Dinkins and David Duke, and the disintegration of civil rights legislation under

Presidents Reagan and Bush. The historical space spanning 1960 to 1990 offered quite a different emerging picture of the relationships between Blacks and Whites than did the space between 1930 and 1960 or that between 1860 and 1890. Changes across their life spans will require multiracial persons to realize the meaning of their identities repeatedly over time.

RULES FOR INTERGROUP BOUNDARIES

Finally, a theory of ethnic identity development that could accommodate multiethnic or multiracial people would need to incorporate rules governing the rigidity or fluidity of boundaries surrounding social groups, principles for accommodating structural change, and rules to describe situational views of self. Rules regarding boundaries influence opportunities for selecting group affiliation, as well as how easy it is to gain group acceptance; choice making and shifting group boundaries may influence structural change, which will in turn alter the choices available. For example, the American rule that one drop of African heritage was sufficient to label a person Black set strict criteria for "Whiteness." Under the one-drop rule, it was difficult for biracial Black-White people to gain acceptance for their total identities. As it became difficult to enforce, and was increasingly rejected as arbitrary, and as multiracial labels such as *mulatto* persisted, the one-drop rule became necessarily less rigid.

More immediately, identities may not be invariant properties, but may instead alter according to the social context. Individuals' perceptions of self shift with the specific social situations they experience (Root, 1990; A. Wilson, 1984). At home a biracial person may experience him- or herself as biracial; with his or her White grandparents he or she is still biracial but may experience him- or herself as a descendant of Ireland, Scotland, or Sweden. In an all-White classroom, the biracial person may filter experience through a self-view of Black. In this way, social context may influence the multiracial individual's experience of him- or herself.

SUMMARY

Thus a developmental theory that could account for the multiracial or multiethnic experience would contain the following social-ecological elements: the nature of the relationship between relevant groups, the level of economic strain between relevant groups, the likelihood of intergroup contact and the ratio of group populations, the balance of group images in larger society and the availability of role models, the behavior of groups toward potential members, the historical and evolutionary relationship between groups, the structure of social categories, and the situational experience of self. These elements shape the human environment in which multiethnic or multiracial identity development occurs and the identification process itself.

Common Theoretical Models

Current models of ethnic identity development are often inadequate to address the experiences of multiracial individuals. The criteria outlined above, so critical to a contextual understanding of the multiracial person, are largely absent in commonly applied theoretical models. Largely ahistorical and acontextual, developmental models minimize the social-ecological aspect of racial and ethnic classification. In this section commonly applied theoretical models will be examined in light of the criteria outlined in the first half of the chapter. Attention will be given to the assumptions underlying widely used models, particularly assumptions regarding universality and linearity of process.

UNIVERSALITY

Eriksonian-based models of ethnic identity development assume that the developmental process is universal (i.e., that the content of identity development is immaterial for understanding the psychological process of coming to feel that one is a member of a social group). Similarly, social psychological theories of group affiliation assume that the process itself is always the same, regardless of the specific self-to-other comparisons one makes. Yet, by the criteria established for accommodating multiethnic or multiracial people, the daily life experience of any ethnic or racial group in a given society will be unique, and these differences in daily life experience will contribute directly to identity (Gibbs, 1989; Spencer, 1987) by influencing the meaning of group membership and the environmental constraints on the process of identification. How common interracial families are in a given area, how the family is treated by the community, the level of discrepancy in the way each parent is dealt with by others, and so on, will indicate to family members their immediate social position, level of social acceptance, and opportunity for affiliation.

The acceptance of universality of process inhibits consideration of the influence of specific relevant social relationships and structures on identity development. In racially and/or ethnically homogeneous societies, for example, the development of racial or ethnic identity may never occur, since race or ethnicity cannot be an important means of ordering people within the social structure. Thus assuming universality ignores social reality—these theories are derived from White Eurocentric models, in which the ideal society is homogeneous and unchanging (Murayama, 1983).

Biracial Black-White children will experience the development of an ethnic identity that is heavily influenced by content. It is social content that will inform whether an individual becomes marginalized or unaffiliated, have a unique role in several social groups, adopt a monoracial social label, or create a new group label. Parent, peer, and community socialization influences will guide the content of available identity options for the interracial individual. The Black-White child raised by the Black parent in the Black community may be socialized almost exclusively toward a Black identity; this child's developmental experience may mirror the experiences described in models of Black identity development. The same child raised by both parents in a multiracial community may be socialized toward a multiracial identity, experiencing a developmental process that is not reflected in current models.

Eriksonian-based models do not describe roles for the group(s) to which a person belongs, while social models discuss the larger group in passive terms. As previously discussed, the degree to which affiliation is fostered, encouraged, or pressed upon an individual will vary, given the actions of the collective networks and their value systems. The process of developing an affiliation within some networks will occur more quickly and easily than in others. The interracial child who is included and validated by a collective may experience an easy transition to an internalized identity. The collective may foster that identity as monoracial or multiracial, but the active inclusion by a collective will encourage feelings of group comfort and acceptance. The collective's behavior shapes the life content of the individual.

LINEARITY

Many Eriksonian and social theories of development speak of the process in linear terms, assuming an end state. Particularly for the multiracial individual, the identification process may be far from linear (Hutnik, 1986; Poussaint, 1984; Root, 1990). While some multiracial people may select a single identity that is invariant with social context, it is probable that many have fluid identities that adjust to their immediate surroundings (Root, 1990; A. Wilson, 1984). The multiracial person may select behavior, labels, and perspectives based on their immediate utility in a given context. The identity process is linear only to the extent that multiculturalism itself is an end state.

The assumption that identity development is linear ignores the criterion of existence in historical space. Within the life space of any one individual, the relationships between his or her social groups and other groups might change: The yardstick by which a person determines his or social fit may change over time. Social identity will change concomitantly. As relationships between the groups from which a multiracial person claims his or her ancestry change, so might the person's sense of self. Despite the persistence of racism and discrimination, the relationship between Blacks and Whites in the United States has undergone repeated change. These changes have significantly altered the self-perceptions of members of both groups, and have also affected the self-views of multiracial people with Black and White ancestry. Any individual who witnesses the evolution of social change may also witness change in his or her own self-view.

The reality of behavioral and cultural variations among groups requires that multiracial people successfully negotiate these behavioral and cultural variants through a flexible experience of self. Just as the multilingual person thinks in French when speaking French and thinks in English when speaking English, the multiracial person may shift in self-perception in appropriate contexts.

ASCRIPTION AND DUALITY

Eriksonian and social theories assume that the ascribed racial or ethnic identity and heritage of an individual match. Most theories cope with the possibility that some people's heritages might not match their ascribed identities by the qualification that one can only develop an identity that is legitimate within the social structure. Thus these theories were developed with the monoracial case in mind. By not describing the process of identification for persons whose backgrounds do not match the ascribed categories well, the theories fail to explain how a multiracial person develops an identity. These assumptions also often lead to the belief that multiracially identified people are "mixed up" or maladjusted. What is the nature of the process of exploring self when self is not neatly reflected in the labels others assign to you? How does the process develop when others cannot generate a label for you at all? How does a person create a new label, one that is not reflected in the existing social structure? Is the process limited to include only those categories that are socially legitimate?

Eriksonian and social identity theories suggest that an individual cannot view him- or herself concurrently as a member of two groups (Rotheram & Phinney, 1987). Thus a person cannot see him- or herself as Canadian and American in the same instance, or as Catholic and Jewish, Black and White, or male and female. This assumption applies only to monoracial individuals, about whom these theories were formulated and for whom the process is one of accepting oneself as part of an ascribed group.

Conclusion

Eurocentric, individualistic models are clearly inadequate to describe biracial identity development. Additionally, these models contribute to the perpetuation of an oppressive psychology (Root, in press-b). By using Eurocentric, individualistic perspectives to understand multiracial people, the realities of society are ignored, realities that shape the life and identity of the multiracial individual. Bronfenbrenner (1977) describes the greatest limitation of the study of human development as the failure to go beyond the focus on the individual; he suggests that a full understanding of individual development requires an examination of the larger social ecology. Specifically, Bronfenbrenner stresses the importance of describing the process of development as it occurs within settings that are embedded within successively larger social systems. Similarly, Katz and Kahn (1978) and Seidman (1983) describe the importance of social systems in structuring events, roles, norms, thoughts, and values, and thereby individual and group behavior. It would seem appropriate, given the role of social systems in shaping individual outcomes, that ethnic or racial identity development be understood through the larger ecology.

Values regarding race and social identity are transmitted through institutional structures (Bronfenbrenner, 1977); social status, resource distribution, economic attainment, and residential patterns, for example, are managed at this level. These systems mediate social interactions, strongly influencing the nature of schools, families, and other arenas of immediate contact with the individual. As the individual moves through these systems, he or she encounters the normative and subcultural values communicated by social systems; as the social structure changes or as patterns of interaction in subsystems of the social structure change in character and form, so do the individual's interactions. It is within such a sociostructural context that the individual begins to develop an identity. Additionally, each ethnic and racial minority group has a unique history that has implications for the social position of the group, social attitudes toward the group, stereotypes of the group, and so on. The social artifacts of these histories not only inform the course of current social interactions, but also play a role in an individual's commitment to and feelings about his or her ethnic or racial group.

Biracial individuals directly highlight the structure of racial dichotomization because they do not belong to either of two mutually exclusive social groups, yet lack a socially legitimated group that describes their biracial origins. The ambiguity of their belongingness from a sociostructural perspective illuminates the role of ecological forces (e.g., community demographics, economic status) in shaping individual outcomes.

Biracial people achieve a variety of ethnic identities, despite society's difficulty in placing them easily in prescribed groups. As one biracial adult noted, "I know what and who I am, even if you don't, even if you devise categories for me to jump into that I don't find fit me at all." It is perhaps this phenomenon, because it defies the principles of ascriptive identity, that best highlights the variety of ecological factors operating to influence identity and serves to develop a model that is readily generalizable to other groups.

Acknowledgments

I am grateful to Maria P. P. Root, Martin Manalansan, Barbara Miller, Sutherland Miller, Edward Seidman, Marybeth Shinn, Diane Hughes, Bruce Rapkin, Dorothy Chin, James Sidanius, and my NYU peers for their feedback on earlier drafts of this chapter.

4

Developmental Pathways: Toward an Ecological Theoretical Formulation of Race Identity in Black-White Biracial Children

DEBORAH J. JOHNSON

The study of identity development among biracial children in early childhood is literally a study of development in context. The interest in and importance of distinguishing biracial children as a group is not due to the biological fact of their racial parentage. This factor alone holds no unique consequences for the developmental milestones biracial children encounter en route to acquiring racial identity. Biracial children, like children of monoracial (same-race) parentage, must endure passage through a process replete with developmental markers, such as color differentiation, racial awareness, self- and race identification, and self-evaluation (both personal and group). In this chapter I argue that social meaning, sociocognition, and socialization are at the crux of the unique developmental pathways possible for biracial children. I have attempted to structure the groundwork for an expanded framework based on Boykin's (1985; Boykin & Toms, 1985) theory that will then have maximal utility for identity formation in biracial children. While the argument and perspective presented have broader applications, I limit the focus of my discussion here to Black-White children and their families.

Background

Several authors in this volume note the increase in interracial marriage and subsequent rise in the number of biracial children who currently reside in the United States. Intermarriages of Euro-Americans with Asians and Asian Americans make up the largest proportion of those statistics. Black-White marriages, which totaled an estimated 121,000 in 1980, still make up the smallest percentage of interracial unions, at about 3.4% of first marriages involving Blacks or Whites (P. C. Glick, 1988). Yet these unions, along with the general trend, are increasing at a fairly rapid rate, with significant increases in outmarriage among Black women. According to Tucker and Mitchell-Kernan (1990), regional statistics for females ranged from .5% to 2.1% in 1970 and from .6% to 3.1% in 1985. Concurrently, we are witnessing an increase in biracial offspring of these unions (Gibbs, 1989). The usual estimates are likely to underrepresent these children, particularly children born to unwed mothers, who may then be identified by records that likely label the children monoracially.

Assimilating Social Meaning Through Self-Definition

Despite our inability to reflect the increased numbers of biracial children accurately, the data currently available indicate continued social change. Social change is an integral part of the context within which children's identities develop. Social change has had an impact on the ever-increasing numbers of multiracial families. Changes in racial attitudes, affirmative action policies, and greater mobility within the society have served to bring people of varying backgrounds into closer contact with one another through vehicles of thought and social institutions such as school, work, and community. Yet the phenomenon of interracial and multiracial families and their children is itself a social change factor affecting other American families. Contact and, more important, interaction with biracial individuals and multiracial families offer important challenges to other individuals and to social institutions to rethink and broaden definitions of race and social meaning. Schools in particular are facing the growing challenges of identifying and sensitizing themselves to some unique needs of biracial children.

Society has its own ways of categorizing individuals that have meaning and provide order for its members. Terms used to categorize racial and cultural boundaries often reflect the current political climate and serve to exercise the cultural worldview of the dominant members of that society. A. Wilson (1987) suggests that English children of mixed race, Anglo-African/West Indian, are recognized as such; however, this category is subsumed under the larger rubric of Black or African. That is, they are primarily considered categorized as though they were monoracial persons of African descent and secondarily considered as mixed race. In South Africa the classification *Coloured,* usually referring to persons of Euro-African descent, is a separate category unto itself, not subsumed under any other group, which carries its own separate political standing and clout distinct from both Whites and Africans (Burman & Reynolds, 1986). As a nation, the United States has historically conceptualized biracial persons of Euro-African descent in ways similar to those used in Great Britain. The history of our miscegenation laws clearly exemplifies this point. The last of these laws, which were removed as recently as 1967, centered on the determination of a dichotomous boundary line that distinguished "pure White" from non-White and, therefore, Black as well (Spickard, 1989).

Multiracial families, parents and children, are challenging the societal construction of race and its meaning for them ("No Place for Mankind," 1989; Wardle, 1990). At the level of the family, they are taking active and assertive roles in dismantling accepted social definitions of biracial children and interracial families, and are seeking to be self-defining. White fathers of biracial children are increasingly articulating desires for their children to express non-Black aspects of their identities (Wardle, 1990). From these racial identity struggles come terms that are slowly entering the American vocabulary—such as *mixed race, biracial,* and *multiracial*—that speak to these efforts at self-definition. These efforts come at a time when other non-White racial and cultural groups have recently struggled with general acceptance of self-redefinitions; for instance, the terms *Chicano, Asian American, Black* and *African American, Native American,* and the like have begun to replace other less acceptable terms, such as *Mexican, Oriental,*

Negro, and *Indian*. Yet variation and diversity continue to exist among these families and individuals regarding self-definition and social meaning.

What are the unique ecological factors influential in a biracial child's development that support the adoption of an identity, perhaps biracial, and its encumbered label? Investigation into the identities and race attitudes of biracial children provides an important opportunity to discover how differing outcomes regarding racial identity are linked to child and family characteristics that, ostensibly, are no different from those found in monoracial families.

Social Cognition, Racial Preference, and Biracial Identity

Race classification, preference, and social meaning are concepts related to identity that develop at various stages in the life course of the young child. Identity formation is an ongoing process reaching beyond the experiences of early childhood. In this section I will discuss those concepts that may distinguish Black-White biracial children from their monoracial Black and White cohorts.

Currently we lack empirical evidence that identifies the average age at which biracial children move from color differentiation to race awareness. According to Goodman (1964) and others (e.g., Aboud, 1988; Stevenson & Stewart, 1958), Black children acquire race awareness 6 months to 1 year earlier than do White children. Estimating the point at which this milestone might occur for biracial children is difficult; the simplest model, and perhaps the correct one, is that biracial children fall somewhere in between. However, since most mothers of biracial children are White (due to the higher rates of outmarriage among Black men) and these mothers may have specific views about race, perhaps the humanistic view or deemphasis of race altogether, biracial children may develop race awareness later than both Black and White children. Other alternatives exist as well. Nevertheless, somewhere between the ages of 3 and 4½, these children develop race awareness.

Racial self-identification among White children is highly accurate when the stimuli used are dolls or pictures. Among Black children accuracy is lower. In the past, researchers have accounted for this consistent finding among Blacks as related to variations in skin color that placed some Black children physically closer to the White stimuli (Greenwald & Oppenheim, 1968; Payne, 1977). Among Black children in some studies, identification declined as skin color darkened (Clark & Clark, 1947; Greenwald & Oppenheim, 1968; Morland, 1966). Greenwald and Oppenheim (1968) increased the accuracy of response among Black children by offering a third, intermediary doll. Findings from the Payne (1977) study indicate a relationship between skin color and choice of doll, as in the earlier Clark and Clark (1947) study.

Gunthrope (1977/1978) sampled 25 biracial children ages 3 through 5, matching each with a White and Black cohort. Comparisons were made on the responses of children with those in the Greenwald and Oppenheim study. As with findings in the Payne study, biracial children achieved accuracy in racial self-identification irrespective of variations in skin tone. Gunthrope reported that, overall, children were able to recognize racial differences as depicted by skin color, although he found no significant differences in skin color preferences.

In the formation of racial attitudes two factors are of particular importance to biracial children: time (or developmental stage) and race of mother. In a recent study of biracial preschoolers using measures developed by Williams, Best, Boswell, Mattson, and Graves (1975a, 1975b), I found that, overall, racial preference scores fell somewhere between those of monoracial children of Black and White parentage (D. J. Johnson, in press). Despite the significant difference between the racial preference scores of Black and White children in the study, the preference scores of biracial children were not significantly different from those of their White or Black cohorts. However, when analyses were conducted by race and age patterns, the three groups were statistically distinguishable. An important aspect of the racial preferences of biracial children was revealed by certain age trends compared with those of Black and White children. Biracial children were represented in the no-preference range more than any other group at age 3. Although 4-year-old biracial children had a greater preference for White, they displayed dramatically less preference for White than did monoracial children in the same age group. The preferences of 5-year-old biracial children paralleled those of White children, who showed a strong pro-White bias.

Two plausible interpretations can be articulated regarding these findings. One is that racial awareness develops more slowly in biracial children, possibly because their parents less often stress the social dominance of one race over another. This interpretation is partially supported by the finding that biracial children were less likely than White children to offer racial reasons for their choices. Alternatively, perhaps biracial children remain balanced in their preferences for a longer span of time simply because they have more exposure to the racial and/or cultural groups of their parents. Thus, as they move toward greater understanding of their school, peer, and community environments, their preferences shift, given cultural influences and various reinforcement strategies of their primary caregivers (Boykin, 1982, 1985).

A second alternative, or third interpretation, may be offered in light of Jacobs's (1977) stage theory. Jacobs is concerned with the development of boundaries that might indicate the permanence of racial categorization. He suggests that mixed-race children in the "transitional" stage may internalize the biracial label. He builds this assertion upon such responses as "I'm brown," "I'm tan," "I'm both Black and White," or "I'm interracial." The lag in White preference shown by biracial children between 3 and 5 years old may be linked developmentally to the difficulty associated with acquiring a "biracial" label. Labels for Black and White children are common and easily accessible, even reinforced, in the broader society. Fundamental research in this area has shown that self-identity is no less than concomitant with racial preference and perhaps precedes the preference (Cross, 1981, 1985; Goodman, 1964; Phinney & Rotheram, 1987; Semaj, 1979; Spencer, 1984). It is certain that even the rudiments of social meaning attached to preference must build upon self-identification (Alejandro-Wright, 1985; Semaj, 1980; Spencer, 1983, 1985; Williams & Morland, 1976).

Race of the mother is a second factor thought to be of significance in the developing race attitudes of biracial children (D. J. Johnson, in press; Payne, 1977). The trends found in the D. J. Johnson study, cited above, indicated that race of mother is associated with differing preference patterns among biracial children. In a sample of 16, children of White mothers ($n = 11$) averaged scores in the pro-White range and children of Black mothers ($n = 5$) averaged in a no-preference range. Obviously, this is not conclusive evidence, but it is intriguing enough to warrant further systematic investigation.

Payne (1977) grouped biracial children in a sample according to race of the mother. The methods developed by Clark and Clark (1939, 1940) were employed in the study, with one important modification: Payne added two dolls to the stimulus choices that represented skin tones intermediate to the extremes of the very dark brown and very light pinkish tones of the primary dolls. Interestingly, race of the mother had a significant effect on doll choice and color preference. The level of racial awareness for biracial children was significantly higher than that for White children. When asked about racial preferences in the negative (e.g., Is there a doll you do not want to be?), mixed-race children with Black mothers chose the dark brown doll and mixed-race children with White mothers chose the medium brown or light dolls. By comparison, in the monoracial groups, White children chose the dark brown doll and Black children chose the medium brown or light doll.

Research on biracial children has generally shown an overall preference for White, but the findings are more complex than previously indicated. In general, the results of studies on biracial children appear similar to studies of Black children who were categorized by skin color. However, within-group scores of biracial children generally resemble those of White children in studies where no biracial group was established (i.e., Goodman, 1964; Williams & Morland, 1976). These seemingly conflicting findings are unique to biracial children.

The data currently available suggest that children's personal characteristics have been considered in research on identity development. Specifically, aspects of physiognomy (such as skin color) have been focused on in the preference literature. Likewise, some researchers have attempted to illuminate socialization influences on the identity development and developing racial cognitions of biracial children. In the following section I begin to articulate a model of developmental pathways that both incorporates and expands on the centrality of these factors and others for biracial identity formation.

Toward a Model of Biracial Identity

The increased potential for and complexities of race dissonance (Spencer, 1985) among biracial children are to be considered in developing an appropriate theoretical framework. Spencer defined race dissonance as a basic nonfit between personal identity (self-esteem) and group identity (racial group membership or orientation). Each perspective or vantage point carries a component of social cognition, the ability to see oneself from the perspective of others, and cultural cognition, the evolving knowledge of race as a biological and social phenomenon (pp. 217-220). The expected course of a Black child's life, according to Spencer, is toward race imbalance—that is, without psychological and sociocultural intervention.

The question for biracial children becomes, Who is my reference group? Race dissonance, as defined, is likely experienced at this point. If, as Semaj (1985) points out, the individual's self-concept is a combined personal self-view and extended self-view, is the extended self other biracial or multiracial children? Is it Blacks or Whites? How can a child choose both when the most rudimentary social knowledge indicates conflict between these groups? As an extended self option, the biracial group is most often not available; given relative size of the population, access to a group of biracial children is unusual without focused effort on the part of families or schools. Moreover, there are no cultural rituals, values, or artifacts with which to identify. The intangibility of the "group" makes identification much more difficult. At the preschool age, early identification may therefore be relegated to the choice of the closest, most involved image of the primary caregiver, usually the mother, who in most of these instances is White.

The Theory of Triple Quandary: Developmental Trajectories for Biracial Children

Boykin (1982, 1985; Boykin & Toms, 1985) has developed a framework from which we might begin to understand differing developmental pathways to racial identity and attitudes among biracial children in early childhood. Boykin proposes a tricultural view of Black children's experiences in the society and the important influences of these experiences on development. Three "realms of negotiation"—the distinct but overlapping contexts of values, expectations, and rituals in which individuals and families may be simultaneously involved or aware—are articulated. Boykin's analysis describes theoretically the negotiation process for Black Americans. He suggests that experiences of this group include the mainstream, minority versus majority, and Euro-American versus African American cultural experiences. For Euro-Americans he observes that mainstream, majority, and Eurocultural realms are fairly consistent experiences, overlapping in values, expectations, and rituals. For African Americans, however, tensions and inconsistencies exist among these three realms.

The model holds interesting complexities, particularly for biracial children of Black-White parentage. Most Americans have access to mainstream experiences to the extent that the media and critical institutions, such as schools, have influence in our lives. Biracial children are no less likely than others to have these experiences. However, the minority/majority realm offers other considerations for the biracial child. The interracial family environment is more likely to offer the biracial child a majority socialization context as regards parental social status. The minority experience is likewise apparent in the socialization context, but has multiple dimensions. First, owing to the potential availability of a minority-status member within the family configuration, the child may identify with the influential experiences of that member, through his or her personal history, the values shaped by the experiences of a minority-status ecology, and the characteristics of that ecology that impinge on the socialization context.

Second, the family itself has undergone a minority-status transition. From society's view, the social status of the more valued member has been compromised. Thus, while the individual may continue to be valued in the society when viewed alone, as a member of a minority-status family his or her value is compromised. The biracial child is therefore a member of a minority-status family, which has its own unique characteristics.

Finally, the biracial child has a dual minority status both within the larger society as a member or partial member of a devalued racial group and often within the African American community due to perceived lack of "full" affiliation. The African American community may marginalize the biracial child because his or her allegiance cannot be readily assessed. This marginalization process is twofold: (a) the threatening perception that partial membership in a valued racial group may offer choices regarding loyalty and affiliation, and (b) historical hostility toward African Americans and multiracial people of African descent who, through the exploitation of their ambiguous phenotype, sought to take advantage of White society by denying, mystifying, or concealing their heritage (Spickard, 1989).

Biracial children may experience both cultural realms as well as the conflicts between the unique characteristics of those cultures. Among monoracial groups, Black or White, there exists the potential to span the cultural continuum between the two groups. Whether a biracial child chooses to integrate and balance Euro-American and African American cultural characteristics or embed the self in one or the other is dependent upon a multiplicity of factors yet unstudied. In whatever ways the cultural continuum does not distinguish the biracial child, certainly the nature of that access and the constraints exerted by virtue of the socialization contexts offer their unique influences on the child's cultural referent.

The interface of the biracial experience with the cultural realm has particular importance to the development of identity and self-definition. Most Americans can claim multiethnicity, and many may purport multiracial heritage if the family tree is traced sufficiently, three, four, five generations or more (Poussaint, 1984). Given these possibilities, how does the "first-generation" (Buttery, 1987) biracial individual distinguish self and experience from other more distal multiethnic and multiracial heritages?

Boykin's framework lacks some dynamic considerations that might be included as part of a developmental focus. Dynamism is particularly important given the low predictability of children's racial attitudes and the variation in factors influencing identity formation from one developmental period to the next or later periods.

Boykin's framework provides an excellent shell within which to establish pathways. In order to address the differential experiences of biracial children and their families, two tasks must be accomplished: (a) Boykin's model must be broadened to incorporate dynamic aspects of child development, and (b) the developmental view must be expanded to include an ecological perspective (Bronfenbrenner, 1979) that captures not only the influences of families, but those of peers and the community. Boykin's three realms of negotiation are the domains that impinge on concentric circles of the child's ecology, at the micropersonal level, the family, the community, and ultimately, the society.

CHILD FACTORS

The child brings to any situation or set of experiences his or her own unique characteristics. These characteristics, in part, interact with events and determine how subsequent events are perceived and interpreted by both the child and others interacting with the child. In this framework we must particularly consider the child's physiognomy, personality (i.e., aptitude, self-esteem, perceptual skills, coping orientation), and individual experiences. Skin color, facial and hair features, and physique contribute in shaping the child's experiences. These may have particular salience in the child's relationships with family and friends, in perceived racial group membership, and so on.

FAMILY FACTORS

Several aspects of family factors have critical value and importance in the child's development. Three areas are considered especially important: family background, structural factors, and family dynamics and attitudes. Interracial families exist at every socioeconomic level; family background—education, income, occupation—will necessarily be important in shaping children's values. Structural factors will also be influential, particularly living arrangements, family configuration, and extended family contact. Children living in single-parent families may be excluded from access to the cultural and value experiences embodied in the family of the nonresident parent. Biracial children in stepfamilies, blended families, or adoptive families might be confronted with comfortable or uncomfortable relationships with monoracial siblings. Parenting dynamics may be affected by family transformations and may race imbalance. Quality and frequency of contact with extended family members contribute to the development of self-concept as well as to racial self-concepts of children.

Finally, and of great importance, are family attitudes. Extended family acceptance or rejection orientations in connection with frequency of contact are a potentially important component of family attitudes. Extended family contact may have greater significance for biracial children, whose families run the increased risk of rejection by either maternal or paternal grandparents (Buttery, 1987; Root, 1990). Interracial families have varying racial attitudes; these may run the gamut from humanistic and "color-blind" to racially polarized. These attitudes are further influenced by the family's view of itself as marginal (Gibbs, 1987) or more mainstream. Other dimensions of family dynamics and personality may include cultural embeddedness. Wardle (1990) takes the view that interracial families explore their cultural histories in depth; however, some interracial families may view cultural ascription as divisive. These views will necessarily affect family attitudes and the choices and nature of legitimate family activities, as well as interpretation of these and other experiences.

PEER AND COMMUNITY FACTORS

Racial composition of the school and community will determine the degree of comfort and security biracial children experience as they move through their communities and the institutions within them (schools, churches, clubs, stores). These factors also potentially control the racial backgrounds (biracial, other children of color) of available peers. In addition, the racial climate of a community or school may be related to its racial composition, class structure, region of the country (Morland, 1958, 1962), or population density, to name a few. A final element is that of available supports for the child in the community. Organizations or groups that may or may not emphasize the experiences of biracial children or interracial families may have influence on children's identity formation and social or cultural cognitions.

The realms of negotiation interface with components of the model at each level: the child, the family, and the community. The pathways possible are many and complex; they are woven from an interdependent cross section of the aforementioned ecological factors. In addition, the broader society and its dynamism present undulating contexts of social change. G. M. Vaughan (1987) emphasizes the impact of social change contexts as an important consideration in children's identity development.

Conclusions

In this chapter I have sought to elucidate the critical nature of social meaning, sociocognition, and socialization issues relevant to building a model that articulates the potential developmental pathways of identity formation among biracial children. The discussion has been a first step toward the full explication of biracial identity formation. Only a few of the components and factors identified have been tested empirically. I have argued that this lack of research is the consequence of psychological and developmental models that lack dynamism, fluidity, and ecological perspective. Future research in this area must endeavor to use longitudinal designs and to develop frameworks that are ecological. In addition, while the focus here has been primarily on the experiences of mixed-race offspring of Black-White parents, I believe the paradigm can be more broadly applied to incorporate and explain identity development in biracial children of various racial backgrounds. Finally, although as a researcher I cannot advocate categorization of biracial individuals as a unique group, as individual and self-determinism must be preserved. However, given the more-than-adequate evidence presented in this chapter and in others, I can, on scientific grounds, suggest the importance of special grouping for the study of these populations.

5

Mixed-Heritage Individuals: Ethnic Identity and Trait Characteristics

COOKIE WHITE STEPHAN

Many sociologists have argued that the self is composed of two categories of concepts: identities and trait characteristics (e.g., Rosenberg, 1981; Zurcher, 1977). The purpose of this chapter is to use this conception of the self to explore and interconnect three important issues with respect to the ethnic identity of mixed-heritage individuals, those whose ancestry is derived from more than one biological and social group. I will first focus on identities as a way of understanding the content and antecedents of mixed-heritage ethnic identity, and then I will examine trait characteristics to understand the consequences of being of mixed heritage. The specific issues to be addressed are as follows:

- What are the ethnic identities of mixed-heritage individuals?
- What are the antecedents of these ethnic identities?
- What are the consequences of being a mixed-heritage individual?

Throughout this chapter, the term *mixed heritage* is used rather than *race*. While *race* suggests a strict biological division of groups, one that is certainly fictional in our society, *heritage* suggests a combination of biological and cultural factors that are the actual components of our designations of "race" and "ethnicity." In addition, the word *race* implies a biological basis for ethnic identity, an implication that will be shown to be inaccurate.

Identities are meanings that the self acquires through social interaction (McCall & Simmons, 1966; Stone, 1962; Stryker, 1980), and as such are crucial to an understanding of an individual's sense of him- or herself. Identities are thought to stem from a feeling of consciousness of kind that begins with commonalities of culture (e.g., Elkin, 1983; Weber, 1961). Ethnic identity, the identification of an individual or group of individuals with a particular ethnic group or groups, is particularly important to the self because it is a master status, an identity that overrides all others in others' judgments of the self. As such, it is also basic to the establishment of self-meaning. The question of ethnic identity is particularly acute and potentially problematic for people of mixed ancestry.

Characteristics of Ethnic Identity

To laypersons, ethnic identity is generally regarded as an objective process, one determined by biological heritage. For example, on employment forms, census forms, and even passport applications, an individual is asked to state his or her ethnic group. An explanation for the selection is never deemed necessary; ethnic identity is regarded as fact. By contrast, social scientists have found the process of ethnic identity to be anything but objective. Ethnic identity has been shown to be both subjective and unstable (Barth, 1969; Nagata, 1974; Okamura, 1981; van den Berghe & Primov, 1974). Individuals with the same biological heritage often have different ethnic identities. While these identities are often based on biological heritage, some individuals identify with groups from which they are not derived biologically. In addition, some individuals' ethnic identities are situational. These individuals feel a part of one group in one situation, and a part of other groups in other situations. Individuals may also change from one single identity to another as a response to life changes.

The Prevalence of Multiple-Heritage Ethnic Identities

The instability and subjectivity of ethnic identity are particularly likely to be manifest in people of mixed ancestry. The first issue to be addressed concerns the content of mixed-heritage individuals' ethnic identities. The question asked is: Do most mixed-heritage individuals develop stable, single-heritage ethnic identities (e.g., Filipino), or are they more likely to have multiple-heritage ethnic identities (e.g., Filipino-Chinese)?

This question is important not only because ethnic identity is such a critical component both of the self and the way in which the individual is perceived and prejudged by others, but also because it has implications for the likelihood of minority group assimilation in the United States (Alba & Chamlin, 1983; Alba & Golden, 1986; Lieberson & Waters, 1985). Intermarriage rates are increasing in the United States, creating growing numbers of mixed-heritage individuals (Alba & Golden, 1986; Crester & Leon, 1982; Lieberson & Waters, 1985). In addition, mixed-heritage individuals have particularly high rates of intermarriage (Alba & Golden, 1986; Tinker, 1973). If mixed-heritage individuals identify less strongly with their heritage groups than do single-heritage individuals, then intermarriage may reduce the number of individuals who identify themselves as members of single minority groups.

One cannot conclude on the basis of increased intermarriage rates that the incidence of multiple-heritage ethnic identity is increasing, however. An individual whose ancestry is derived from two different groups may identify with one, both, or neither. For example, an individual whose ancestry is Russian and Irish may or may not identify with the people or culture of Russia or Ireland. Since the ethnic identity of mixed-heritage individuals is selected from a number of options, rather than fixed, the best way to determine the ethnic identity of a multiple-heritage individual is to ask him or her (Barth, 1969; Moerman, 1965; T. W. Smith, 1980).

While little research exists on the ethnic identities of mixed-heritage individuals, theorists from both the assimilationist and ethnic pluralist positions have argued that mixed-heritage individuals are most likely to identify with a single ethnic group (Gordon, 1964; Greeley, 1971). This argument has been put to empirical test with three samples of mixed-heritage college students: part-Japanese Americans in Hawaii, a variety of mixed-heritage students in Hawaii, and part-Hispanic Americans in New Mexico (C. W. Stephan, 1991; Stephan & Stephan, 1989). In an open-response format, each respondent was asked to name the ethnic identity he or she used when completing an official form, as well as the ethnic identity he or she took on with family, classmates, and friends; finally, each was asked to name the group with which he or she identified most closely.[1]

In all three samples of students, a multiple-heritage ethnic identity was a common response to one or more of the five identity questions. Multiple-heritage ethnic identities were common even on the final question, which seems to demand a single-heritage answer. Among the Hawaii samples, a majority of students gave multiple-heritage ethnic identities. Only 26% of the part-Japanese Americans and 11% of the multigroup Hawaii sample gave one single-heritage ethnic identity in response to all five questions. The percentage was larger for the part-Hispanic Americans, with 56% giving single-heritage ethnic identities.

The responses of those with multiple-heritage ethnic identities clearly demonstrate the subjective and situational nature of ethnic identity. Respondents with the same biological heritage often had different ethnic identities. As one example of this difference, in the multigroup Hawaii sample about 15% of the respondents identified in part with groups from which they were not biologically derived. In addition, no respondent in the three samples gave a single mixed-heritage ethnic identity to all five questions. Many of these respondents gave both single-heritage and multiple-heritage responses.

Why did a smaller percentage of part-Hispanic respondents have multiple identities than the subjects in the two Hawaii samples? One possible explanation is that the Hawaii samples had biological and cultural ties with more groups than did the part-Hispanic sample. Thus the former groups had a greater number of choices of identity available to them, compared with the part-Hispanic respondents. A second explanation involves locally available mixed-heritage labels. In Hawaii, where intermarriages constitute almost 50% of all marriages (State of Hawaii, Department of Health, 1987), a number of terms are used to designate mixed-heritage people. By contrast, in New Mexico, where intermarriage is less common, such a varied vocabulary for designating mixed-heritage identity is lacking. The availability of ready labels to designate mixed-heritage status may influence the ease with which individuals can identify themselves as being of mixed heritage.

In summary, in three samples of college students, mixed-heritage ethnic identity was found to be common. In addition, mixed-heritage ethnic identity was often associated with situational changes in ethnic identity.

The Antecedents of Ethnic Identity

Having some conception of the content of the ethnic identities of mixed-heritage individuals, we turn now to causal factors. The question to be addressed is: What antecedent factors are most important in the determination of ethnic identity? In the absence of literature on the antecedents of the identity of mixed-heritage individuals, we turn to the literature on identification with a single group. Several theorists have argued that identification with a single ethnic group is caused by a feeling of consciousness of kind that begins with commonalities of culture, such as language, religious beliefs, and styles of living (e.g., economic life, food, clothing, housing, and holiday celebrations) (e.g., Elkin, 1983; Weber, 1961).

Anthropological studies of the ethnic identity of groups suggest that identity is a joint process, in which both the individual and relevant outsiders together agree on ethnic identity (Cohen, 1978; Isaacs, 1975; van den Berghe & Primov, 1974). Thus a second kind of commonality that may lead to identification with an ethnic group is physical appearance (Isaacs, 1975; Weber, 1961). In addition, acceptance by the group probably plays a role in identity with the group. Since identity with a group can confer high or low status on the individual, the groups' statuses or power within a society may also be relevant factors (Blalock, 1967; Schermerhorn, 1978). Psychological identification with the beliefs and values of one parent may also increase identity with the group from which that parent derives (Bandura & Huston, 1961; Sears, 1957). And, of course, percentage of biological heritage from a given group, with identity increasing in proportion to heritage from the group, is likely to be important.

STUDY 1

The above factors thought to be associated with the ethnic identities of single-heritage individuals or groups were examined quantitatively to determine if they also constitute antecedents of mixed-heritage-individuals' ethnic identities. Two of the samples of mixed-heritage college students described above, the Japanese heritage Americans in Hawaii and the Hispanic heritage Americans in New Mexico, were employed in this analysis (Stephan & Stephan, 1989). The respondents completed a questionnaire that included questions on cultural exposure and physical resemblance to their heritage groups, perceived status of the groups and acceptance by the groups, psychological identification with each parent, and, for each group, percentage of heritage of the mother, father, and respondent.

The results showed only a single similarity in significant antecedents between the samples. For both the Japanese and Hispanic heritage respondents, exposure to Japanese or Hispanic customs played a significant role in ethnic identity as Japanese or Hispanic. The relative status of the groups and involvement in Eastern religion were significantly or marginally significantly associated with identity as Japanese. Physical resemblance to the members of a group, percentage of father's Hispanic heritage, and psychological identification with the Hispanic parent were significantly or marginally significantly associated with ethnic identity as Hispanic.

Three factors appear to account for the differences that exist between the specific antecedents of ethnic identity in the two samples. First, some of the significant antecedents appear to distinguish an ethnic group from other ethnic groups in the geographic area. Shintoism and Buddhism distinguish Japanese Americans in Hawaii from most other groups, but Catholicism in New Mexico does not distinguish Hispanics from most other groups in New Mexico. In addition, physical characteristics distinguish Hispanics from other groups in New Mexico but do not distinguish Japanese Americans from other Asian groups in Hawaii.

Second, the fact that status was a significant antecedent in Hawaii but not in New Mexico is probably related to the relative status of these two groups in their localities. The Japanese are considered to be a high-status group in Hawaii, while Hispanics are not considered to be a high-status group in New Mexico. Therefore, claiming an identity as Japanese confers higher status in Hawaii than claiming an identity as Hispanic does in New Mexico.

Third, some antecedents seem to be related to differential socialization into the customs of the group. Because Hispanic identity can be viewed as conferring a status disadvantage, it seems likely that the Hispanic child will be socialized to feel Hispanic only if the father is predominantly of Hispanic heritage, and, because of his greater power in the marriage, the home becomes culturally Hispanic. Because Japanese identity confers a status advantage in Hawaii, children may be socialized to think of themselves as Japanese regardless of parental heritage.

STUDY 2

To determine if the association of cultural exposure and identity would also be found among subjects whose biological heritages derive from many groups, semistructured interviews were conducted with mixed-heritage college students in Hawaii who were descended from two or more of the following groups: Chinese, Caucasian, Japanese, Hawaiian, Portuguese, Filipino, Korean, Vietnamese, Black, Mexican, Samoan, Laotian, and American Indian (C. W. Stephan, 1991). These interviews explored the respondents' experiences when growing up in their families of orientation.

The association of cultural exposure and ethnic identity found among Japanese Americans and Hispanics (Stephan & Stephan, 1989) was also found in this more diverse sample of respondents. When discussing the origins of their ethnic identities, respondents often mentioned various types of cultural exposure. Aspects of material culture mentioned included family furnishings, food, art objects, ways of celebrating festivals, and crafts. Nonmaterial cultural aspects mentioned included music, dance, moral training, holidays, family values, and life-style. Cultural exposure most often took place in the family, but it also occurred in the schools and through neighbors and friends of the respondents' parents.

Other reasons respondents mentioned for their ethnic identities included perceived physical resemblance to members of the group or being identifiable by having a surname associated with the group. In addition, perceived high status of the group was mentioned as being important in some cases. Finally, group acceptance was mentioned by a number of respondents. Not all respondents were accepted by both their fathers' and mothers' relatives, particularly single-heritage relatives from high-status groups.

Implications for necessary and sufficient conditions of ethnic identity. These data indicate that biological heritage is not a necessary condition for identity with a particular group to occur. About 15% of the respondents with multiple-heritage ethnic identities identified with a group from which they were not derived biologically, but to which they had had cultural exposure. In every instance, exposure to friends and their families was the primary reason cited for this identification.

It is also the case that cultural exposure is not a necessary condition for ethnic identity to occur. One-fourth of the respondents who were classified as having multiple-heritage ethnic identities did not have cultural exposure to one or more of the heritage groups with which they identified. Identity with a heritage group without exposure occurred for a variety of reasons, such as the respondent's becoming interested in the group on his or her own, identifying with a group because of a friend or other individual close to him or her, because the group was perceived to be high in status, or because identity with the group was viewed as biologically accurate.

Finally, cultural exposure was not even a sufficient condition for ethnic identity to occur. Approximately 15% of the respondents reported no identification with one or more groups to which they had at least some cultural exposure. There are at least two reasons cultural exposure was not sufficient for ethnic identity to occur. First, cultural exposure can have a number of consequences, not all of which are positive. In fact, some exposure to respondents' heritage groups was experienced as being very negative, and this type of exposure weakened, rather than strengthened, identity with a group. Unpleasant experiences with individual family members, negative group stereotypes, and negative feelings about the political policies of the home country all weakened identity with a group. Second, in some cases cultural exposure to a group was so limited that it did not result in identity with the group.

Single-heritage ethnic identities. What antecedent conditions are associated with the minority of respondents with stable single-heritage ethnic identities? Respondents with single-heritage identities typically had parents who were both derived at least in part from the group and both of whom were identified strongly with it. At the same time that cultural exposure to this group was high, exposure to their other heritage groups was typically very low.

The Consequences of Mixed-Heritage Status

Having some information on the content and antecedents of mixed-heritage ethnic identity, we can now turn to the third issue, the consequences of being a mixed-heritage individual. This section also offers an exploration of the second major component of the self: trait characteristics.

Individuals often categorize themselves, and are categorized by others, in terms of trait characteristics. These trait characteristics stem from our interactions with others in the society, particularly interactions with our significant others (Erikson, 1963). The issue to be explored here is the effect of being of mixed heritage on selected trait characteristics. The question asked is: Is it psychologically advantageous to have a single-heritage background rather than a mixed-heritage background? In order to examine this question systematically, an empirical study was conducted in which two samples of mixed-heritage college students completed a variety of measures of personality, adjustment, and intergroup attitudes and behaviors.

There are at least four reasons one might anticipate differences in personality, adjustment, and intergroup relations between mixed-heritage and single-heritage individuals that favor single-heritage individuals. First, the socialization of children growing up in mixed-heritage families is, to varying degrees, likely to be bicultural. It may thus be inconsistent, and perhaps frustrating and difficult to comprehend. Second, mixed-heritage children have more extensive options in establishing their identities than do children of single-heritage backgrounds. These choices may breed ambivalence and confusion. Third, mixed-heritage children may experience some degree of rejection by their extended families. Fourth, mixed-heritage children may also experience rejection in the larger society.

In fact, an extensive but dated literature based on qualitative data has suggested that intermarriage can have a number of negative effects for the mixed-heritage children of these marriages. These predicted negative effects have included anxiety, insecurity, guilt, anger, depression, and identity conflicts (e.g., Gordon, 1964; Henriques, 1974b; McDermott & Fukunaga, 1977; Piskacek & Golub, 1973). However, very little recent or quantitative literature exists on the consequences of being of mixed heritage. As this is the case, the related literature on cultural assimilation of minority group members was used to suggest the possible effects on individuals of being of mixed heritage. This literature shows that difficulties in assimilating the values, roles, norms, and behaviors of the majority are often a source of stress for minority group members (J. W. Berry, 1980; Griffith, 1984; Ortiz & Arce, 1985). Further, the rejection that minority groups experience may lead them to be alienated from mainstream cultural values. These negative effects have been found in some cases to be associated with symptoms of psychological breakdown (Smither & Rodriguez-Giegling, 1979; Stephan & Stephan, 1971). This literature thus suggests that mixed-heritage individuals may be more alienated, may experience greater stress, and may have lower self-esteem than members of the majority group or members of single-heritage minority groups. In addition, if mixed-heritage individuals are rejected by single-heritage groups, they may have more negative attitudes toward those groups than do individuals who belong to single-heritage groups.

Alternatively, bicultural socialization may have a variety of benefits. It may expose children to a broader range of values, roles, norms, and behaviors than does single-heritage socialization (see Garza & Lipton, 1982). For example, bilingual children have been shown to be more cognitively flexible and less dogmatic than monolinguals (Diaz, 1985; Lambert, 1977) and to have more favorable intergroup attitudes than monolinguals (Lambert, 1969). Similarly, children of mixed heritage who have an opportunity to learn the values, roles, norms, and behaviors of their heritage groups may learn to interact effectively with people from diverse cultures. Minority group members who become bicultural through their exposure to majority group culture have been found to be better adjusted than minority group members who become completely assimilated or who remain monocultural (Griffith, 1984; Szapocznik & Kurtines, 1980). These findings imply that the bicultural experiences of mixed-heritage individuals should lead to more favorable intergroup attitudes and behavior, thereby reducing prejudice, stereotyping, and attributional biases (W. G. Stephan, 1985; Stephan & Stephan, 1985).

The positive and negative effects of bicultural assimilation are not necessarily mutually exclusive. It is possible that mixed-heritage individuals display a combination of positive and negative effects as a consequence of their unique socialization experiences.

To test the above hypotheses, two samples of college students completed measures of personality traits, adjustment, and intergroup relations: one sample of Caucasians, Asian Americans, and students of mixed heritage in Hawaii; and a sample of Caucasians, Hispanic Americans, and mixed-heritage students in New Mexico (Stephan & Stephan, 1991). Each student completed a questionnaire measuring the following: *anomie*, feelings of alienation and normlessness; *attributional complexity*, motivation and ability to interpret others' behaviors in terms of complex causes; *contact with one's heritage groups*, informal voluntary contact in a variety of settings; *dogmatism*, rigid and stereotyped worldview and intolerance of ambiguity; *empathy*, sensitivity to and sympathy toward others; *enjoyment of Caucasian and Hispanic or Asian culture*, measures of liking for music, food, media, and celebrations; *English and Spanish or Asian language facility*, measures of speaking ability; *attitudes toward Caucasians* and *attitudes toward Hispanic Americans or Asian Americans,* overall attitudes toward members of the group; *intergroup anxiety,* anxiety during interactions with unfamiliar out-group members; *intergroup similarity,* similarity between the in-group and an out-group on personality traits, beliefs, attitudes, and customs; *psychophysiological symptoms,* number and frequency of psychosomatic symptoms associated with poor mental health; *quality of life,* life satisfaction and subjective happiness; *self-esteem,* feelings of self-worth; *stereotyping,* overgeneralized beliefs measured by the percentage of members of a particular ethnic group the respondent perceives to possess stereotypical traits of the group; *symbolic racism,* indirect and covert racism, measured by attitudes toward social programs benefiting minorities; *xenophobia,* fear and dislike of foreigners; *socioeconomic status,* measured by occupation, income, and education; and *ethnicity.* In both samples the Caucasians were higher in socioeconomic status than the other two groups, and in the New Mexico sample the students of mixed heritage were higher in socioeconomic status than the Hispanics. For this reason, socioeconomic status was employed as a covariate in the analyses.

The results show some support for the hypothesis that bicultural socialization has positive effects on intergroup contact and attitudes, as well as on abilities. The contact measures indicate that in both New Mexico and Hawaii the single-heritage groups have more informal voluntary contact with members of their own groups than with other groups. In contrast, the mixed-heritage students have more informal voluntary contact with the single-heritage groups than the single-heritage groups have with each other. In addition, while most of the single-heritage groups were ethnocentric, the scores of the mixed-heritage groups fell between those of the single-heritage groups, suggesting that mixed-heritage students were somewhat more tolerant of these groups than the single-heritage groups were of each other. Further, the mixed-heritage students scored higher on enjoyment of Hispanic or Asian American culture than did Caucasians. Finally, these students also scored higher than Caucasians in Spanish or Asian language facility.

This study produced almost no evidence for the hypothesis that being socialized in a bicultural home has negative effects. The only negative effect found was that mixed-heritage students were not as facile in English as Caucasians. The virtual lack of negative findings is somewhat surprising in view of the negative experiences of many minority groups, migrants, and other marginal individuals. One explanation for the lack of support for the deficit approach is that the family setting in which bicultural socialization occurs may buffer these individuals from the negative experiences suffered by single-heritage minority group members or more socially isolated marginal individuals. While some between-sample differences were found, the two samples of mixed-heritage students appeared to experience about an equal number of positive effects from their bicultural socialization.

A Methodological Addendum

Many of the explanations in this chapter are speculative, and are offered primarily as hypotheses for exploration in future research. Further, the generalizability of the findings is limited by the fact that all three samples consist of relatively small numbers from select populations, college students. In addition, these samples are derived from only two geographic locations, and may not be representative of mixed-heritage people overall. More individual-level studies of mixed-heritage people from a variety of groups, ages, regions, and socioeconomic status are needed to validate the finding that multiple ethnic identities are common among mixed-heritage individuals and to explore further the antecedents and consequences of ethnic identity.

One problem in collecting such data is in identifying mixed-heritage individuals. Survey data generally cannot be used for this purpose, for two reasons. First, mixed-heritage individuals are not found in great numbers in most areas of the United States, and thus would not constitute a significant part of the population surveyed. Therefore, it is not cost-efficient to use survey methods to locate them. Also, the secondary analysis of data collected for another purpose is not likely to be useful in the determination of ethnic identity, even if each respondent's ethnicity were collected. Knowledge that an individual is of mixed heritage does not constitute knowledge that he or she has a multiple-heritage identity. The individual might have an identity with one or another of his or her heritage groups, with more than one group, or even with groups from which the individual is not derived biologically or culturally. Thus the study of ethnic identity will almost certainly involve primary data collection. While larger and more representative samples of mixed-heritage individuals would be desirable for purposes of generalization, information on ethnic identity of mixed-heritage individuals will almost necessarily be accumulated through small, unrepresentative samples.

Summary

A review of the issues raised at the beginning of this chapter provides a framework for a summary of results of the various studies. The results will then be placed in theoretical context.

(1) *The ethnic identity of mixed-heritage individuals:* Multiple-heritage ethnic identities are commonly found among mixed-heritage individuals. In addition, the ethnic identity of a mixed-heritage individual depends in part upon the group in question. Whereas a slight majority of mixed-heritage Hispanics did have single-heritage ethnic identities, most respondents from the other samples did not.

(2) *Antecedents of ethnic identity:* Clearly, cultural exposure is extremely important to ethnic identity, although it is neither a necessary nor a sufficient condition for ethnic identity to occur. Other important antecedents include physical appearance, surname, the status of the groups in question, and the individual's acceptance by his or her heritage groups.

(3) *Consequences of mixed-heritage status:* Mixed-heritage individuals do not manifest ill effects from rejection by others, or experience difficulties in establishing identities or in reconciling different cultural norms. In contrast, the data demonstrate that there are benefits of mixed-heritage status, including increased contact with the members of one's heritage groups, enjoyment of the cultures of one's heritage groups, facility in languages spoken by one's heritage groups, and intergroup tolerance.

In addition, the data highlight some of the complexities of the process of ethnic identity formation. They demonstrate the variation in ethnic identity among individuals of the same biological and social heritages. In fact, they show that ethnic identity can take place in the absence of biological or social heritage.

Many sociologists argue that the self is composed of two major categories, identities and trait characteristics. Viewed from this perspective, ethnic identities emerge from individuals' social interactions with members of their (and perhaps others') heritage groups that culminate in their experiencing themselves as members of one or more ethnic groups. For some individuals, ethnic identity changes with changes in roles or situations, while for other individuals ethnic identity is stable. Regardless of number of identities, ethnic identities do not seem to involve conscious selection. One does not experience electing to be Hispanic, for instance, but instead experiences being Hispanic. When asked to explain their ethnic identities, then, individuals render accounts of their identities; they construct justifications for their identities on the basis of their past experiences. For most mixed-heritage individuals, past experiences include being members of more than one group.

Trait characteristics are also products of our interactions with others. The interactions of mixed-heritage individuals with their significant others often include exposure to a broader range of attitudes, values, behaviors, and dispositions than single-heritage individuals' interactions with significant others. That is, most mixed-heritage individuals encounter the distinct constructions of realities of more than one ethnic group. The data on consequences of mixed-heritage identity support the idea that the individual is influenced by exposure to differing conceptions of reality, developing trait characteristics that show the influence of social interaction with each group.

In summary, it appears from these data that the increased rates of intermarriage in our society are producing an increasing number of mixed-heritage individuals who both identify with more than one group and benefit from exposure to more than one group. The mythical American melting pot of individuals who know and respect the cultures of all peoples of the society may have a literal beginning in the experiences of mixed-heritage individuals with cultural exposure to more than one group.

Note

1. Ethnic identity was measured by a combined score on five questions through which the ethnic identity of the respondent in different settings was elicited. The questions were as follows:

If you were completing a form for the State of Hawaii [State of New Mexico], such as an employment form, what would you write down if you were asked to give your ethnic group?

When you are with your parents and brothers and sisters, which ethnic group do you think of yourself as belonging to?

When you are with your classmates at school, which ethnic group do you think of yourself as belonging to?

When you are with your closest friends, which ethnic group do you feel you belong to?

With what ethnic group do you identify most closely? Please list the group that you feel really a part of.

Acknowledgment

I would like to thank Walter G. Stephan for comments on earlier drafts of this chapter.

6

The Quiet Immigration: Foreign Spouses of U.S. Citizens, 1945-1985

MICHAEL C. THORNTON

While contact between people of similar racial and national backgrounds remains the rule, since 1945 world events have conspired to increase tremendously the contacts among diverse populations. As legal restrictions have fallen, and as racist attitudes have become less pronounced, cross-cultural and cross-racial contact has grown in acceptance. For Americans, one consequence of this expanded contact has been the growing phenomenon of intergroup marriage.

The significance of intergroup marriage lies in its challenge to norms of deference and social distance that serve to separate minority groups from the majority. The literature regularly examines how intermarriage relates to issues of assimilation, which is contingent on prior cultural and structural assimilation. Typically, this literature describes interreligious or interracial unions between couples of similar national backgrounds (e.g., American citizens). Following World War II, marriage rates between people of various cultural, national, and racial heritages increased dramatically. However, this trend has received little attention (Cottrell, 1990). Along with a precipitous rise in numbers has been a radical shift in the origins of the foreign spouses involved. Since the 1950s, European spouses have been gradually replaced as a primary source by those from the Third World, Asia in particular. How these relationships will be incorporated into and change American life is perhaps one of the most intriguing questions for the twenty-first century.

Despite 40 years of immigration, we know little about these couples, and what we do know is limited and dated and highlights so-called war bride unions (e.g., Barnett, 1963; Cottrell, 1990; B.-L. C. Kim, 1977) or centers on marriages of American citizens who are foreign residents (e.g., Cottrell, 1990; Imamura, 1986). Perhaps the subject has received little attention because it is a relatively new large-scale phenomenon. It is, however, a significant type of migration, because of its increasing volume, its racial composition, and the potential insights its examination may reveal about the immigration process, intergroup relations, ethnic socialization, and cultural influences on marital adjustment. The study of this increasingly common kind of marriage may provide insight into new family and personality types that reflect and are particularly suited for life in a mobile postmodern world; children from these relationships may provide the prototype of the world citizen of the future.

The cultural and racial heritages of the foreign spouses married to citizens in the United States is closely associated with U.S. immigration policy. Thus the configuration of this phenomenon must be seen within historical, social, and legal contexts. Feelings of antipathy toward non-White peoples have been reflected in statutes making immigration and naturalization eligibility contingent upon geographical location and/or racial heritage. Because of the nature of these immigration policies, spouses of citizens were until recently among the few non-Europeans eligible for entry to U.S. shores. If we are to understand the recent precipitous increase in international marriages, especially involving non-Europeans, we must first explore the influence of legislation on general patterns of immigration. In fact, much of this legislation has focused on keeping non-Europeans out of the United States, and, for most of U.S. history, has affected most directly the presence of Asians in this country.

Immigration Legislation, 1882-1950

In 1882, Congress enacted the first general immigration statute in U.S. history. The Chinese Exclusion Act, also passed that year, suspended Chinese labor immigration for 10 years. Those exclusions were extended for another decade by the Geary Act of 1892 and indefinitely in 1902. Prior to 1850, such laws were unnecessary, for few people of color came to the United States. However, from 1850 to 1882, responding to rising demands for labor in gold mines and famine in Canton, some 200,000 Chinese came to the United States. The passage of anti-Chinese immigration laws was fueled by labor competition and fear of the "yellow peril" (Keely, 1979). While growing numbers of Japanese immigrants followed to fill the vacuum created by the act, they too encountered a backlash when in 1907-1908 Japan was coerced to limit the number of laborers coming to the United States.

The first selective immigration legislation was passed in 1917. The 1917 act included previous grounds for barring certain aliens from entry, but also designated geographical restrictions. This so-called Asiatic barred zone included most Asians and Pacific Islanders. It is clear that while most people of color were unwanted on these shores, immigration legislation until the end of World War I had as a major thrust racial exclusion aimed at Asians (Keely, 1979).

The Immigration Act of 1924 implemented a permanent quota. Because it retained national origin provisions, Northern and Western European nations held relatively large annual quotas (e.g., Germany, 26,000; Great Britain, 65,000) and Eastern European countries relatively small quotas (Poland and Italy had 6,000 each). Although Asian countries typically were assigned quotas of 100, few persons of discernible Asian ancestry were eligible for entry; these slots were filled by Whites born in Asia (Reimers, 1985).

Further legislation enacted during the 1930s closed a loophole that had allowed Filipinos, considered American nationals since 1898, unlimited access to the United States. The new law gave the Philippines an annual quota of 50. The racial slant to this legislation can be seen in subsequent laws passed in 1935 and 1939 promising to pay passage to any Filipino who would return to the Philippines (U.S. Department of Justice, Immigration and Naturalization Service, 1980).

In 1943, China became the subject of the first series of legislation passed to remove racial barriers to immigration and naturalization. These laws repealed the Exclusion Act of 1882, increased the Chinese quota to 105, and made Chinese eligible for naturalization (Riggs, 1950). Subsequent laws extended coverage to other Asians. In 1946, naturalization eligibility included races "indigenous" to India and to all Filipinos, whose quota was increased to 100. Previous laws had allowed only Filipinos who had served in the U.S. armed forces to qualify for naturalization.

Other Asians, however, remained ineligible for immigration. In 1946, Congress changed this by allowing Chinese wives of American citizens to immigrate on a nonquota basis. Liberalized in 1950, the new law gave similar rights to Chinese spouses and minor children of members of the armed forces. The War Brides Act of 1945 facilitated the admission of European spouses and children of armed forces members by waiving visa requirements and some of the excluding provisions of the law. Only in 1953 were these rights extended to include Japanese and Korean spouses.

Immigration Legislation, 1950-1965

The Immigration and Naturalization Act of 1952, better know as the McCarran-Walter Act, while maintaining the policy of numerical restrictions in immigration based on the national origins quota system, removed ostensible racial bars to immigration and naturalization. Japanese residents, previously classified as "aliens ineligible for citizenship," were now eligible for naturalization. The new law had a profound impact on the mostly male Chinese community. With the change in law, 90% of Chinese immigration involved females (Mark & Chih, 1982, p. 173). From 1952 to 1964, more than 30,000 Chinese women immigrated, many joining their husbands after years of separation (Reimers, 1985).

While the 1952 act abandoned the Asiatic barred zones, racial criteria were still integral to the law. Persons of Asian ancestry were not counted against the quota of country of birth, as was the case of all others, but against the quota of the country of Asian forebears. The act stipulated that nations from the Asia-Pacific Triangle, covering most of South and East Asia, would be limited to quotas of 100. To forestall immigration of persons of Asian ancestry from nonquota countries of the Western Hemisphere (e.g., Japanese from Brazil or Chinese from Cuba), the law specified that persons born in the Western Hemisphere whose ancestry was one-half or more Asian would not be nonquota immigrants. Even if they immigrated from nonquota countries, their slots would be charged to the Asian nations of their ancestry, not their countries of birth (Reimers, 1985; U.S. Congress, House Subcommittee on Immigration and Naturalization of the

Committee on the Judiciary, 1948). The quota assigned to Europe was 149,667; Asia's quote was 2,990, and Africa's, 1,400. The differences clearly show that a racial criterion for selection remained embedded in immigration policy (U.S. Bureau of the Census, 1957, p. 91).

Under the National Origin Provision of the Immigration Act of 1924, which remained in effect under the Immigration and Nationality Act of 1952, 2% of the total immigration quota was allotted to Asian countries. Nevertheless, several factors, such as the War Brides Act and nonquota status granted to spouses and children of U.S. citizens, led Asian immigration to far exceed the quotas assigned Asian countries. For example, between 1950 and 1964, 62,000 Japanese immigrants came to the United States, an annual average of 4,479, although Japan had a quota of 185. China, with a quota of 105, averaged more than 3,500 during the same period (Bouscaren, 1963; U.S. Department of Justice, Immigration and Naturalization Service, 1950-1965).

The large U.S. military presence in Asia from 1945 to 1965 is a key factor in explaining most of this spousal immigration to the United States. The occupation of Japan became the major network for postwar Japanese immigration to the United States. Thousands of Chinese entered under the War Brides Act, while others married American citizens after the act expired in 1952, at which time they emigrated as nonquota immigrants under regular immigration laws. Altogether, most of the 17,000 Korean immigrants who came to the United States from 1950 to 1965 were wives of U.S. military personnel (U.S. Department of Justice, Immigration and Naturalization Service, 1950-1966).

The Immigration and Naturalization Act of 1965

The Immigration and Nationality Act was amended by the act of October 3, 1965, which became effective December 1, 1965. It retained a numerical ceiling on immigration, but would in 1968 substitute hemispheric for national quotas. The new system provided an annual ceiling of 170,000 for the Eastern Hemisphere, with no more than 20,000 visas allotted to any single country. Previously unlimited, Western Hemisphere immigration was restricted to 120,000 per year, but without country limitations.

The most visible beneficiaries of the preference provisions of the 1965 act have been Asians. Beginning with a population of approximately 490,000 in 1940, there were about 878,000 Asian Americans in

1960, 3.5 million by 1980, and an estimated 5.1 million in 1985 (Gardner, Robey, & Smith, 1985). Asians from India, the Philippines, and China have benefited most notably from the new law.

After the long history of anti-Asian prejudice, it is ironic that the tremendous influx of Asian immigrants subsequent to the 1965 act appears to be an unplanned artifact of the new law. Reimers (1985) notes in his study of Third World immigration to the United States that legislators believed that the new law would increase Southern and Eastern European immigration and had not anticipated the tremendous growth of Asian immigration in particular. Neither did legislators foresee the influx of other non-European peoples, such as Mexicans and West Indians. The amended law has significantly altered the racial composition of immigration to the United States, making non-Europeans the most significant of all groups migrating to America. One significant subgroup ignored in this discussion has been foreign spouses of U.S. citizens.

Data

Data published since 1945 by the U.S. Immigration and Nationalization Service provide information on the number and country or region of birth of aliens issued visas for entry into the United States. Included are immigrants subject to quota restrictions and those exempt from numerical limitations, such as spouses of U.S. citizens. These data have particular limitations. First, the information obtained pertains to the number of visas issued for a given year. It is unknown if the visas were used in that year or at all. Thus these data are approximations of the number of spouses coming to the United States in a given year. The figures are also limited in that they provide only the sex and country of origin of the foreign spouses; other sociodemographic data, such as age, education, and occupation, are not presented. Finally, by the nature of the data we can only assume that the majority of these relationships are cross-national and or cross-cultural—between two people of different racial and or ethnic heritage. In fact, many of the foreign spouses may indeed be of the same ethnic and/or national heritage as their husbands or wives. While limited in scope, these data do provide a reasonable approximation of national sources and number of spouses who marry U.S. citizens and immigrate to the United States. (For a discussion of some of the limitations of the data, see Kraly, 1979.)

TABLE 6.1 Average Yearly Immigration of Foreign Spouses Married to U.S. Citizens, by Decade

Decade Average	*Yearly Number*
1945-1949	26,345
1950-1959	23,696
1960-1969	30,012
1970-1979	67,308
1980-1985	105,917

SOURCE: All data are from U.S. Department of Justice, Immigration and Naturalization Service (1945-1977, 1978-1985).

As Table 6.1 shows, the number of these unions has increased with each passing decade, quadrupling from the 1940s (with 26,345 immigrant spouses per year) to the 1980s (with 105,917 spouses per year). The greatest change in immigration of international spouses occurred after the passage of the 1968 act and the family reunification component. Recent years have borne witness to a precipitous rise in the number of these relationships. Of the 2 million visas issued to spouses of U.S. citizens since 1945, more than 630,000 (33% of all visas issued for these marriages) were issued in the six years of the 1980s for which data are available. At current rates, almost 48% of all visas issued will have occurred during the 1980s. Interestingly, because general immigration has also increased over these years, the foreign spousal component of total immigration has fluctuated, declining from a high point in the 1940s of 22.2% to 18.3% of total immigration for the first six years of the 1980s. Nevertheless, recent immigration has involved significantly more in actual numbers.

Table 6.2 reveals the changes in the regional sources of foreign spouses for selected years since 1945. Europe and Asia were the primary origins for the years prior to 1970; North America and "other" regions were negligible sources. Since then, while Europe has declined in importance (and in actual numbers), Asia and places such as South America are becoming rich points of origin. Asian participation in this immigration started slowly, picking up speed during the 1950s and then again in the 1970s. North America, Mexico in particular, prior to the 1970s was an insignificant source of foreign spouses, but now has achieved preeminence. Over time the primary conduits of foreign spouses have changed from primarily European, with some

TABLE 6.2 Regional Contributions of International Marriages as Percentage of Total Immigration for 1945-1985

			Region			
Decade	*Europe*	*Asia*	*North America*	*Other*	*International Marriage as % Total Immigration*	*Total Immigration*
1945-1949	108,006	11,720	12,234	12,958	22.2 (144,918)	653,019
1950-1959	146,416	60,921	9,893	4,719	8.9 (221,949)	2,499,268
1960-1969	146,367	97,897	21,465	10,556	8.6 (276,285)	3,213,749
1970-1979	141,939	192,958	230,023	71,175	15.0 (636,095)	4,232,325
1980-1985	106,338	177,272	247,768	89,093	18.3 (620,471)	3,395,045

SOURCE: All data are from U.S. Department of Justice, Immigration and Naturalization Service (1945-1977, 1978-1985).

Asians, to Mexican, Asian, and European; concomitantly, foreign spouses have changed from predominantly White to non-White, representing an increase in interracial marriages. As a proportion of total immigration, foreign spouses during the last decade achieved rates comparable to those of the 1940s.

The 10 most important nations involved in this migration since 1945 are identified in Table 6.3, which shows the numbers of visas issued to spouses during the 1980s, 1970s, and 1960s, and the total number for each country since 1945. The percentages in the table represent the proportion of immigration occurring during the particular era. It is clear that Mexico has contributed the most to this pool. Nevertheless, this is a very recent development. More than 50% of these spouses have arrived since 1980, and almost 98% have come since 1970. Mexico's present rate of migration almost triples that of the nearest competitor, the Philippines.

Although one-half of immigrants are European, most immigrants now come from non-White countries, the biggest change in immigration over the last 20 years. Over time, Asia has become the primary source of spouses of color. Interestingly, except for Mexico, until recently few non-Asian countries of color have contributed many spouses to this pool. The reason for this is unclear. In fact, it remains unclear why these are top sources, although some reasons can be offered. For example, Mexico and Canada are geographically close to the United States. Most of the remainder can be explained by cultural affinity (Great Britain, Italy, Germany) or a significant presence of U.S.

TABLE 6.3 Leading Contributors of Foreign Spouses by Percentage of Individual Country's Immigration for Given Period, 1945-1985

Nation of Origin of Spouse	*1985-1980* N[a]	%[b]	*1979-1970* N	%	*1969-1960* N	%	*1945-1985* N
Mexico	143,594	52.2	125,074	45.5	6,449	2.3	275,117
Germany	23,647	14.2	30,288	18.2	112,478	67.6	166,413
Philippines	52,431	38.1	56,541	41.0	28,810	20.9	137,782
England	28,151	24.6	32,004	32.3	45,532	43.1	105,687
Italy	7,018	6.6	15,488	14.8	82,516	78.6	105,022
Japan	8,672	10.3	17,743	21.1	57,684	68.6	84,099
Korea	25,188	36.9	30,988	45.4	12,120	17.7	68,296
Canada	23,132	36.2	30,538	47.8	10,240	16.0	63,910
China	8,884	15.6	15,605	27.5	32,319	56.9	56,808
Greece	6,882	13.2	31,845	60.9	13,546	25.9	54,273

a. Number of spouses immigrating from that country.
b. Percentage of total immigration from that country.

TABLE 6.4 Leading Contributors of Foreign Spouses, 1980-1985

Country	*Number*
Mexico	143,594
Philippines	52,431
England	28,151
Korea	25,188
Germany	23,647
Iran	23,281
Canada	23,132
Dominican Republic	16,865
Colombia	15,208
Jamaica	13,077

military personal at some point in time (Philippines, Japan, Korea, Italy, and Germany). The Chinese and Greek presences are less clear.

Table 6.4 lists the most frequent sources for spouses during the first six years of the past decade. Many of the countries mentioned above remain popular originating sites, but others have entered the picture, again shifting the regional focus. New to the list are Iran, the Dominican Republic, Colombia, and Jamaica, many of whom have come in part because of economic hardship in the country of origin.

Discussion

The increase in international contact since 1945 has brought about a new millennium in the social landscape of U.S. society. Within the next 50 years one in three Americans will be a person of color. Cultural diversity will be the rule, if not appreciated in practice. This growing kaleidoscope of culture and colors will bring dilemmas to intergroup relationships, and will enrich them as well. While there is a growing awareness of the need for better understanding of multicultural and multiracial factors in our society, this awareness as yet does not include a true appreciation of how immigration may change the dynamics of life in America. This is especially true of international families, particularly those that are interracial, for they will eventually bring about a realignment in the politics of American life and a rethinking of what we mean by race and racial difference.

While these are the best estimates available, they give us little clue as to the number of these unions that are interracial in nature. A better idea of this awaits different data. If we were to exclude spouses from European and predominantly White nations such as Canada (because most of these marriages are between Whites and therefore not interracial), we might have a very rough estimate of interracial unions. As of 1985 approximately 1.2 million spouses from non-White countries had come to the United States. Not all of these necessarily represented interracial unions, of course. For example, many of them may have been the spouses of expatriates, who had left their wives behind in the country of origin, as was the case for Chinese males in the 1940s. Given this tendency, an estimate that one in three international marriages is interracial is probably conservative. When adding these relationships (approximately 396,000 since 1945) to the 700,000 interracial unions noted in the 1986 U.S. Census, there may be at least a million interracial marriages in the United States. While this is not a comparatively large number, considering the population as a whole, the potential influence of these marriages on those around them belies their number.

While we must guess at how many international marriages represent interracial unions, as noted above, we have a better picture of the number and racial composition of interracial marriages already in the United States. We also know something about the number of multiracial households here. As of the 1980 census, there were approximately 2 million children living in multiracial households in the United

States, primarily in California, Texas, New York, Illinois, Washington, and Hawaii. The largest proportion live in Asian-White households, followed by Hispanic-White households (Chew, Eggebeen, & Uhlenberg, 1989). The former households usually involve Asian females, while Hispanic fathers predominate in the latter. For Black-White households, the largest group (38%) is made up of Black women who are single parents. In all cases it remains unclear how many of these children are multiracial themselves or simply live in households with people who differ in race from one another (e.g., White family adopting Black or Asian child). Given increasing rates of interracial and international marriage, the 1990 census figures should indicate a significant increase in the number of multiracial households and children.

Both sets of figures suggest that these relationships are primarily unions between Whites and people of color. Historically, Asian-White combinations have predominated, with far fewer Asian-Hispanic, Asian-Black, and other people of color combinations. Over the last decade, Hispanics (specifically Mexican Americans), Asians, and West Indians have contributed significantly to this phenomenon. Whether there is increased interaction between groups of color is unclear. If many of the international marriages involve a number of military personnel, given the high proportion of soldiers of color in the all-volunteer service of the 1980s and 1990s, many more of the unions will involve two people of color than was true in the past.

The growing numbers of multiracial families and people provide new configurations to family life in America. Many old questions in new bottles will need to be answered. How do these families deal with issues of identity? Toward which communities will individuals from these families feel enmity or closeness? Will they develop new types of identities, interrelated yet different from those of their parent populations? Will they as a matter of course straddle several worlds or create new ones? We are seeing this last trend now among multiracials who argue for a separate status in the U.S. Census.

This trend raises other questions as well. How is this new identity related to the unique style of socialization utilized by many of the parents? How will mothers of one culture raise their children in a foreign land? How will they cope with bringing up offspring of multicultural and multiracial heritage? How do the dynamics of family life differ when the father is the foreign spouse? Bringing up a multiracial child in a country foreign to one's birth must create unique and at times complex issues for both parents and children. We need a better understanding of these issues. Chew et al. (1989) suggest that it is important to know who in the household is of one or another race. First, race and sex intersect to determine the parent's potential earning ability. Whether it is the mother or father who is Black or Asian, for instance, can alter economic prospects. Second, because household members perform different roles in socialization, whether the mother or father is a member of a racial minority will alter the cultural milieu for the child and family (Chew et al., 1989, p. 67).

The most important implication of the present study is the need for more systematic research on international marriages. These relationships, and the recent astronomical increase in their numbers, deserve more attention than they have so far received. Given the potential impact on U.S. society and on our understanding of ethnic identity and socialization of an ever-increasing intermixing of cultural, national, and racial heritages, we need research that examines these marriages by cultural and nationality groups and across the life cycle. As the interracial family form becomes more common, it will become increasingly important that we understand its effects on child and family development. The differential consequences that various international marriage roles have on adult-child interaction patterns and family and child outcomes need to be examined. Particular attention should be given to the husband and wife as a family unit (Cottrell, 1975; Imamura, 1986), the impact of social support networks and children on those relationships, and the effect, if any, of racial and/or cultural differences on the quality of these unions. What we may find will give us another insight into the process of marriage and how people maintain relationships across ostensibly wide social and cultural chasms.

With such limited data available, many things about multiracial families and people are still ambiguous. What is clear, however, is that the presence of these unique families changes the nature of our understanding of race and racial differences. Ultimately, the unusual nature of their existence within the context of this society forces those of multiracial status to straddle several worlds, which enables them to counteract a racist context, to maintain diversity and integrity, and to bring the world within their experience. In so doing, multiracials influence society, creating conflict and hence social change. Change is initially instigated by those who are out of step with prevailing norms, as are those of multiple racial ancestry. Indeed, from this position of marginality comes innovation and new visions of society. Multiracials, by virtue of being in touch with a reality of social facts that most are unable or unwilling to countenance directly, in a sense have right, if not might, on their side.

However, this means they must find their way home, often through uncharted waters. In the process, they may be transformed into something different by the experience. This journey involves shattering convention, mocking tradition, and, in form and grace, transcending old boundaries of life and thought. Part of finding an identity involves carving out a new place in old territory. Out of the ambiguity arises its antithesis, clarity. Each of these families will fight a minirevolution, creating in themselves a new culture and a new society that values diversity and multicultural and multiracial influences. Out of dealing with these tensions, typically characteristic of those who are different, will come the creative social strains that result in a better society for us all.

7

Beauty and the Beast: On Racial Ambiguity

CARLA K. BRADSHAW

"What are you?" the multiracial person is often asked. Though this question is often innocently intended, it reveals an awareness of unfamiliarity due to variances in physical features; underlying this question is the assumption of the multiracial person's foreignness or nonbelonging. Thus the multiracial person experiences an exaggerated emphasis on physical appearance, is often treated as an unfamiliar, one to be correctly racially categorized. This increased attention to physical appearance is expressed in such labels as *exotic, beautiful,* or *fascinating* (the Beauty). Questions regarding the origin of physical features can lead to a devalued sense of self and may increase the individual's external focus for a sense of acceptability. Regardless of physical attractiveness, a person's awareness of his or her racial ambiguity contributes to a sense of vulnerability and a feeling of being an outsider in some situations. Obstacles to claiming racial belonging unambiguously leave the individual constantly vulnerable to rejection and identification as "the Other" (the Beast).

This chapter explores the role that physical appearance plays in the life of the mixed-race person. It also examines the effects of social and institutional racism as they affect the process of racial self-identification in the multiracial individual. I extend the notion that racial categories are essentially politically and economically motivated, imposing artificial social barriers to power and privilege in the lives of multiracial people. Subsequently, some aspects of the phenomenology of racially ambiguous appearance are described. The effects of external pressure for racial accountability on the development of racial self-identity, special considerations regarding the development of healthy self-esteem, and the role of the family in helping the biracial child to integrate these experiences are discussed.

Research on the phenomenology of biraciality has identified several common factors that contribute to problems, issues, and self-perceptions regarding dual race membership. Gaskins (1979) cites consensus around themes of belonging and acceptability ("not fitting into a group"), ambiguity of appearance (not definitely racially identifiable), and the confusion evidenced by other people in spite of personal identity resolution. Kich (1982) found that these themes were repeated in his sample of 15 biracial adults interviewed concerning development of ethnic and racial identity formation. These data indicate that the difficulty encountered by the mixed-race person originates externally to the individual in social structures that idealize racial purity and in which racism is institutionalized. Reconciling the conflict between internal experience of differentness and external attribution of the meaning of this difference is likely a lifelong developmental process, affected by the vicissitudes of both social and personal change. The difficulties and psychopathology that had been ascribed to biracial people in the early literature (Gordon, 1964; Jenkins, 1934; Park, 1928; Stonequist, 1937) failed to acknowledge that "it is the marginal status imposed by society rather than the objective mixed race of biracial individuals which poses a severe stress to positive identity development" (Root, 1990, p. 188). From this perspective, it is clear that any complete understanding of the biracial experience must account for the effects of social and institutionalized racism, false assumptions about racial purity, and intrapersonal and familial factors that affect resolution of self-identity and racial identity.

In our nationalistic world, exclusion is the guiding principle for social order, as evidenced, for example, by rules about citizenship, immigration laws, and apartheid. Social flexibility regarding the rules that govern race relations and perceptions about race would threaten existing social structures by implying that inclusion should replace exclusion as the guiding principle. Symbolically, the biracial individual represents the need for a new social order predicated on inclusiveness and greater fluidity of social boundaries. In her or his ability to interface successfully with different racial communities and ethnicities, the biracial person bridges and titrates the experience of both belonging nowhere and negotiating some belonging everywhere. The multiracial person's very presence is a reminder to those who have achieved false security by denying differences and invoking artificial notions of homogeneity that, existentially, "Fast alle Menschen sind Auslander fast uberall" (Most people are foreigners almost everywhere) (Tautfest, 1990).

The Effects of Social and Institutionalized Racism

The attempt to "pass" as racially pure is sparsely addressed in the literature. When it is addressed, it is almost always used to illustrate an avoidance response to the conflicts of dual racial membership. Mixed race had been considered inherently damaging to identity formation (Stonequist, 1937) because the conflicts of dual racial membership were assumed to undermine the integrity of the individual's self-concept and contribute to moral and general inferiority. Passing, then, is conceptualized as a means of transcending institutional barriers and stigmatization by providing escape from marginality (Burkhardt, 1983, p. 538). However, this explanation is based on false assumptions about racial purity. *Passing* is the word used to describe an attempt to achieve acceptability by claiming membership in some desired group while denying other racial elements in oneself thought to be undesirable. The concept of passing uses the imagery of camouflage, of concealing true identity or group membership and gaining false access. Concealment of "true" identity is considered synonymous with compromised integrity and impostorship.

While passing is an attribution externally made, it is internalized negatively. This denigrating attribution can be made by the majority, dominant group or the minority group. When applied from the majority group perspective, resentment may be based on the individual's attempt to gain false inclusion and status accorded only to majority group members. Attributions about passing made by the minority group may reflect resentment about attempts to gain unfair advantage by renouncing membership in the lower-status group. In cases where an individual attempts inclusion in minority communities by denying majority race heritage, resentment may be based on the individual's lack of racial purity. These examples show that varying perspectives on passing involve value judgments about inherent differences between cultures and races. The concept of passing has validity only in the context of moral judgments, ascribed status, and social barriers associated with marginality. If an ideal world existed, free from the psychology of dominance, where racial differences carried no stigma and racial purity was irrelevant, the concept of racial passing would have no meaning. In fact, passing of any kind loses meaning in the context of true egalitarianism.

To transcend artificial, irrational racial barriers is not an act of deviance; rather, it requires engaging in a process of adaptation. It also requires that one lay legitimate claim to the richness of one's varied heritages and privileges. There is no impostorship unless the individual her- or himself attempts to deny dual racial and social membership. The only people capable of racially passing, and the only people to whom the concept can realistically apply, are multiracial ones. Thus passing, as externally applied, can never be legitimate. The biracial individual must disentangle internalized prohibitions against gaining privileges not accorded to the "other" (lower-status) racial heritage (internalized racism) from legitimate claims to privileges existing in both heritages. The biracial person's difficulty in laying claim to these privileges arises from the knowledge and experience of oppression perpetrated by majority groups against the minority, or of similar interracial oppression among minority groups. Should the dually privileged renounce some of these privileges in service of loyalty to the oppressed? Distorted social mores may imply that integrity demands this; however, this notion is false. Rather, it is rational to challenge the inequitable distribution of privileges that are based merely on race.

Many factors are thought to affect the ability to pass: skin shade, facial features, body size and structure, name, language ability, and level of acculturation and/or assimilation. However, research in the area of race attribution indicates that the position conferred upon the multiracial person by society or community (both White and non-White) is one that will not accept racially impure children or people and one that stigmatizes them, relegating them to having to deny some aspect of their racial heritage. Most biracial individuals, especially children of Black-White interracial marriages, fail to gain acceptance in White society irrespective of the lightness of their skin (Poussaint, 1984; Washington, 1970). Furthermore, research findings indicate that interracial children of Black-White heritage most often identify themselves as Black (Porterfield, 1978; Poussaint, 1984). The researchers have suggested that interracial children assume an absence of choice because of experience or expectations that White communities will reject them. These data suggest that children recognize early in life the realities of social restrictions based on race.

In contrast to the experience of biracial Black-White children, biracial Asian-White children appear to have more access to White communities because of their more ambiguous appearance. However, some data indicate that these children express feeling different regardless of whether they grew up in Asian communities or White ones (Kich, 1982; Morishima, 1980). This indicates that when external attributions of racial identity are incongruous with internal experience and racial self-identification, the possibilities of increased identity conflicts exist. While some biracial individuals may seem successful in either the dominant culture or the minority one, an inner feeling of not belonging may concurrently exist. This is especially likely when both the majority and the minority communities insist on rigid racial classifications based on biases in favor of racial purity.

As long as "outsiders" presume to label and define the experience of biracial individuals, and as long as biracial people fail to speak out and advocate for determining self-identification, externally imposed marginality will continue. Prerequisite to embracing the right to self-determination is an understanding of race as a social and political construct, primarily a tool of dominance (Spickard, 1989).

Self-Identification and Perception

In the racially segregated climate of North America, the racially ambiguous features of the biracial person seem to compel other people to make attributions and to draw conclusions based only on phenotype. These attributions are usually based on racial stereotypes. This external demand for racial accountability often results in special consequences for multiracial identity development. Though stereotyping of any kind is often undesirable, stereotyping of monoracials does not hold the same implications for monoracial identity formation as it does for multiracial identity formation. This is because the monoracial individual's racial self-identification is most likely congruent with her or his phenotype.

In societies that attempt to invoke real or perceived differences to determine allocation of resources, race, like gender, is considered an immutable and fundamental characteristic of identity. Yet the racial self-identity of the biracial person is seldom apparent from physical characteristics alone. Furthermore, the biracial person's racial and social self-perception may be more flexible and not easily accounted for by the familiar racial categories. The assumption by other people that physical features are predictive of race identity is also presumption, because an individual's sense of self is emotionally mediated rather than defined merely by identification with his or her physical attributes (Root, 1990). Hall (1980) found little correlation between physical appearance and self-identification, although she does suggest that there may not have been sufficient variation in her data sample.

The misguided assertion by some that the biracial person is "lucky" to have a choice of which race with which to identify fails to recognize that dual race heritage is not a matter of choice; the act of choosing one racial heritage over another necessarily evokes feelings of disloyalty and incongruity. The critical developmental task for the biracial person is to embrace the right to define and conceptualize his or her own experience, as an "insider" (Hirabayashi, 1985), and to construct a racial identity defined as a whole, rather than by its parts.

THE FEELING OF SPECIALNESS

The development of healthy self-esteem and an integrated sense of self is more complicated for the biracial person than for the monoracial person. The difficulty of natural developmental tasks may be magnified by several factors: the absence of external validation emanating from lack of social acceptance or ambivalent acceptance; the compromised emotional state of the family that may result from social stigmatization, social stress, and difficult family dynamics; the invisibility or absence of biracial role models; and the absence of biracial referents within the family from which to draw a secure sense of identification, belonging, and self-identity. As the object of other people's distorted perceptions or projections, the multiracial individual develops feelings of specialness based on actual or perceived experiences of devaluation or overvaluation. "Specialness," whether experienced as positive or negative, is an issue for all biracial individuals, one that is intimately tied to the experience of self.

Because specialness has a prominent place in the self-concept of the biracial person, it can be misunderstood and misconstrued by monoracial parents, teachers, and clinicians who may not themselves have directly experienced this form of heightened self-awareness or self-consciousness. Generalizing directly from standard developmental theories and personality theories without specific sensitivity to the function this specialness serves in identity formation will tend to pathologize the biracial person. Although the role of childhood omnipotence or feelings of specialness (narcissism) and its resolution is part of any developmental theory and presumed to be a developmental task for all children, these theories are inadequate when applied to the biracial person. This is because the theories, which are usually based on White monocultural experience, fail to incorporate and accommodate the constant questioning to which the minority monocultural and biracial child is subjected regarding identity: What are you? Are you American? Let me guess what you are! Although the monoracial child may find security in the ability to assert unambiguous racial identity, the biracial child does not have access to such a simple response. Monoracial people are also less likely to experience disconfirmation or disbelief of the personal data they do reveal: You're kidding! You don't look it! You look more (other ethnic group). These are examples of ways in which the "self" of the biracial child or person is constantly challenged. Thus patterns of social reinforcement combined with developmental stages of identity formation necessitate that the biracial child clarify feelings associated with self-perception. While racially ambiguous physical characteristics may become a stimulus, like a racial projective test, evoking reactions that reveal the limits of the questioner's racial awareness, such interactions fail to benefit the biracial individual. Though some benefit may arguably be derived from "special" attention, attention that is removed from intrinsic qualities of the individual and is based instead on projected qualities, superficial characteristics, or mere unusualness is at best fickle and at worst demeaning and alienating. This kind of attention, if internalized, comes at the very high cost of the individual's sense of identity.

This *feeling* of specialness is different from the *idea* of uniqueness that is often taught to children in the United States. The intent of such affirmations as "You are unique" by parents, teachers, and society is to instill a sense of individuality within a context of belonging. The desire to establish a position of uniqueness seems to arise out of fears that individuality will be obscured. The proclamation also reinforces the right to individuality and recognition. It is a reassertion of privilege. To the minority and biracial peoples of the United States, the statement is less affirming: The privilege of power and individuality is not self-evident. "Unique" may be experienced as a euphemism for "misfit." For biracial people, the state of belonging out of which a secure sense of individuality can emerge is tenuous. Minority and biracial people are often denied access to greater individual and social recognition. The biracial experience of specialness is another variant of the obscuring of individuality. The experience of tenuous belonging and ambiguous membership to the group requires that the biracial individual psychologically tolerate constant feelings of vulnerability to rejection. At the same time, this vulnerability to rejection must be reconciled with temporary acceptance, whether based on deep or superficial characteristics of the self. It is precisely this dichotomous experience of specialness and vulnerability that can contribute to the biracial individual's experiencing her- or himself as the beauty and the beast.

THE ROLE OF FAMILY

"[Interracial] families' communication about race is really a communication about the resolution and acceptance of differentness" (Kich, 1982, p. 193). The level of the family's ability to resolve interracial issues becomes the basis for a consolidated sense of self. However, the reality for many biracial individuals is that the larger social environment fails to confirm the sense of integration that may have been achieved within the immediate and extended family. Rather, there may exist a large discrepancy between how one is perceived and treated within the family and how one is perceived and treated in larger society. In fact, for some biracial people, awareness about their differentness begins to dawn only in the teenage years, when they first experience a wider social range, beyond the scope of the family. If the family fails to provide an integrated sense of racial consciousness, the denial or devaluation of the child's racial heritages expressed in the family may be repeated in her or his experience in society. In such cases the developmental task of defining an integrated racial self-concept becomes truly difficult. Problems with achieving an integrated racial self-concept may be explained by the absence or inadequacy of racial self-esteem that would otherwise help the individual tolerate and neutralize distorted or hostile input from society or the family.

When the family fails to provide adequate preparation for the racism extant in society and/or fails to provide the developmental experiences necessary for more general emotional health, one possible result is a disordered sense of self-importance or self-denigration. Specific to the biracial person, disorders in self-esteem must to some degree reflect the failure to resolve internalized marginality. However, when this resolution is found, self-esteem provides a buffer against external attempts to define identity and contributes to the enhanced creativity necessary to transcend social barriers.

The feeling of specialness discussed earlier has particular relevance to the ability to cull from the wider environment resources that may be missing in the family. However, for biracial individuals, positive external resources are less available and likely less reliable (i.e., more ambivalent) than for monoracial, especially White, individuals. Therefore, attempts to compensate for parental or family deficits by turning to other social resources are more likely to end either in disappointment or in utilization of positive feedback based only on superficial values or tenuous acceptance. Furthermore, to the extent that cultural and social marginality continues to exist for the interracial relationship in the United States, the parents of biracial children may be more vulnerable to social stress and distressed family dynamics. This in turn may create family conditions particularly conducive to more vulnerable self-esteem for the biracial child.

What are the essential supportive elements families of multiracial children should strive to provide? Descriptive research on ethnic and racial identity formation indicates that open communication about race and racism within the family plays a critical prophylactic role in helping children understand and defend themselves against everyday racism (Jacobs, 1977; Kich, 1982). Additionally, contact with the extended families of both parents tends to provide a congruent interracial experience as well as a diverse array of possible role models (Kich, 1982). Finally, openly communicating information as well as personal experiences about interracial relationships and marriage may help children to prepare for the difficulties they may face in society. All multiracial children, by definition, must deal with the realities of interracial and cross-cultural relationships. By describing how the various normal developmental tasks facing the biracial child and the interracial marriage are amplified by social and environmental attitudes toward race, I hope to have shown that a real understanding of multiraciality requires many levels of analysis.

THE EFFECT OF CULTURE

White American culture tends to deemphasize the roles of family and community opinion in shaping and maintaining the individual's sense of self. This form of interdependence and interrelationship is relegated to an inferior position against a disproportionate emphasis on independence (C. K. Bradshaw, 1990; Doi, 1973). As Doi (1973) points out in a discussion on the Japanese philosophy of dependency and its relation to Western notions of freedom:

> Freedom, in other words, meant an absence of the enforced obedience to another implied in the state of slavery; it is precisely because of this that in the West freedom became tied up with ideas such as the rights and dignity of man, and came to be seen as something good and desirable. Parallel with this, the Western-style of freedom also serves as a basis for asserting the precedence of the individual over the group. (p. 85)

Doi identifies several important assumptions incorporated in the Western notion of freedom: that the precedence of the individual over the group is good and desirable, that this is the only possible definition of freedom, and by implication that this is a superior notion to emotional dependency on the group. This is the American majority view against which the biracial individual is expected to measure personal success. Indeed, given the essential condition of the biracial person, who generally has no singular group with which to identify, and for whom adaptive functioning requires some degree of resolution of feelings of aloneness and individuality, it would appear that the biracial individual could be a personification of the Western ideal of freedom. However, for some racial groups, dependency on the group—whether involving the opinions of elders, family, or community—may be not only the norm, but the requirement for effective functioning. Thus to view the developmental success of an individual only from the perspective of achieving autonomous self-regulation and emotional separation from family and community (i.e., resolution of dependency) is an ethnocentric application of White, Western male cultural standards. The biracial, bicultural individual must bridge both cultural systems, often by making accommodations to the cultural environment. This process of accommodation may be viewed by the culturally unaware observer as the absence of a secure sense of self. The alternative view, however, is that self-definition is derived, in part, in relation to the group and by the accommodation such relationship requires.

Personal and Social Politics

The political climate in the United States appears to be one of degenerating race relations. Even though the political gains won by minority groups over the past few decades have given minority race consciousness more general prominence than had previously been the case, a similar heightened consciousness about multiraciality remains absent. By most accounts the cultural, social, and political climate of North America remains regressive and oppressive toward racially mixed individuals. No attempt has been made to include mixed-race populations by any designation in formal census accounts, and there is no informal nonpejorative language for referring to such individuals. In the Hawaiian Islands, where White racial mixes are now recognized largely without stigma as *hapa haole* (half White) or simply *hapa*, the attitude of acceptance toward racial mixing likely resulted from the eventual proliferation of mixed-race marriages and relationships (D. J. Johnson, in press). In North America, there is no comparable attitude of acceptance, nor is there a similarly accepted semantic acknowledgment of mixed-race peoples.

The polarized racial climate may be particularly difficult for White-minority biracial individuals, for whom issues of race cannot be so easily separated. Racial consciousness and experiences of oppression compel some degree of identification with people of color. However, the political rhetoric of antiracist groups is inapplicable to the biracial person precisely because of the adversarial tone against White society. Though the biracial person may not be individually responsible for perpetrating racial oppression, access to social privileges and power implies identification with the oppressor and may evoke feelings of guilt and betrayal by association. The peculiar social position of the biracial person and the extent of his or her access to White privilege create a powerful opportunity for social action, whether overtly or quietly utilized. However, for the mixed-race individual who prefers not to politicize personal life, the physical appearance of minority group membership or racially ambiguous features may evoke presumptions about minority identification that may not exist. Racially ambiguous features may also evoke racist behavior for assumed minority status or tokenism, all of which may be dystonic to personal experience or personal identity. Regardless of the character of the response, the mixed-race individual seldom fails to evoke some response. This response, whether denigrating or idealized, must be reconciled with personal experience and self-image. The experience of wholeness, so crucial to interracial identity, is a creative act born of the necessity to fill the void.

Conclusion

The purpose of this chapter has been to draw attention specifically to the important role physical appearance plays in the lives of mixed-race individuals. The racially ambiguous look of many, though not all, multiracial individuals has political, social, interpersonal, and intrapersonal implications that have not been adequately addressed in the literature. This is partly because there has been a failure to recognize some of the implicit racism directed at multiracial persons, and largely because, until very recently, multiracial people have been grossly underrepresented in literature, art, and other media. The phenomenology of the multiracial experience in the United States is rich, powerful, painful, and impressive. It is with great hope that this chapter is written—hope that it will urge others to contribute their voices, that they may be heard and counted.

Acknowledgments

I would like to acknowledge George Kitahara Kich for his contribution of ideas and resources, and to thank Valli Kanuha, whose discussions with me about passing were integral in helping me to conceptualize the issues presented in this chapter. Special thanks to Maria P. P. Root for her patient, supportive editing. Above all, thanks to Mitch Marder, who lent his substantial organizing talents, critical feedback, and gentleness toward shaping this chapter that it might more closely meet my expectations.

PART II

Recovering the Multiracial Past

8

Passers and Pluralists: Subverting the Racial Divide

G. REGINALD DANIEL

Multiracial Americans of European and African descent have historically faced unique identity issues because of the respectively dominant and subordinate positions of their two ancestry groups in the social hierarchy of races in the United States. This situation has arisen out of the fact that Anglo-Americans, as part of the strategy for preserving their dominant status, have enforced a "policy of hypodescent" that has designated as Black everyone who is not "pure" White (Harris, 1964), and have maintained both legal and informal barriers restricting the contact as equals between individuals of African descent and Whites in the public as well as the private sectors, particularly in the area of intermarriage. Multiracial individuals for the most part have accepted the racial status quo, and have identified themselves as Black. A significant number of individuals, however, have chosen the path of resistance, such that European American control over the boundaries between White and Black, and between dominant and subordinate, has always been relative rather than absolute.

Individual resistance has taken the form primarily of "passing," a radical form of integration whereby individuals of a more European phenotype and cultural orientation make a clandestine break with the

African American community, temporarily or permanently, in order to enjoy the privileges of the dominant White community. Collective resistance has included the formation of pluralistic elites within the African American community, as seen in the phenomenon of blue-vein societies, or the formation of pluralistic enclaves on the periphery of both the African American and European American communities such as the triracial isolates and the Louisiana Creoles. Membership in these societies has been determined by individuals' phenotypical and cultural approximation to European Americans, creating at least the illusion of having escaped the taint of subordinate group status, if not the actual achievement of equality with Whites.

Going Underground: Passing

The most frequent individual strategy of resistance is commonly called *passing*. As a form of radical integration, passing among individuals of African descent has generally meant shifting one's racial reference group from Black to White. When compared with dramatic frontline battles waged against racial inequality by individuals of African descent, passing thus may appear on the surface to be a form of opportunism, selling out, or a full acceptance of the racial status quo. If viewed as part of a spectrum of tactics, however, it is clear that, while some strategies in the fight against oppression aim to liberate individuals from its chains, passing is an underground tactic, a "conspiracy of silence" (Stonequist, 1937) and a form of racial alchemy that seeks to best oppression at its own game by subverting both the comportment line between dominant and subordinate and the arbitrary line between White and Black.

Sociocultural approximation to European American norms is important in this process. Yet, all else being equal, passing, by its very nature, is necessarily employed by individuals who are already genotypically and phenotypically more White than Black (Day, 1932). Those unable to pass as Anglo-American have often adopted Latin or other non-English names; some have passed as members of other groups of color, such as Asians or Native Americans, that are perceived to have been allotted a more privileged status in the social hierarchy of races (Williamson, 1984).

Considering the clandestine nature of the phenomenon, it is possible neither to pinpoint when passing first occurred nor to do more than conjecture about its quantitative dimensions (Spickard, 1989). Some individuals born from the first contact between Africans and Europeans in the early colonial period may have passed. For the most part, however, these offspring would have been discernibly enough of African descent to have been prevented from passing, even if they had so desired. Quite likely, passing became a greater possibility as the crossings of successive generations of multiracial individuals with each other, as well as with Whites, increased the numbers of individuals having greater phenotypical approximation to European Americans (Day, 1932). It certainly must have become more attractive in proportion to the increase in legally sanctioned discrimination associated with the codification of slavery in the late seventeenth century, the restrictions on Free People of Color in the late eighteenth century, and the implementation of Jim Crow segregation at the turn of the twentieth century (Williamson, 1984).

It would be difficult to say whether passing has actually decreased with the dismantling of segregation and the implementation of civil rights legislation during the second half of the twentieth century. It would be safe to conclude, however, that these changes have cumulatively given Americans of African descent greater access to sectors of society from which they were previously barred, such that the most immediate impetus behind passing has been removed. This is borne out by the fact that during the era of segregation the most common form of passing is believed to have been of the discontinuous type (Spickard, 1989). Whether done for reasons of practicality, out of a spirit of revenge, or for amusement, this generally involved a brief trip across the color line by individuals who presented themselves as White or, more often, simply said nothing about their racial identity, in order to enjoy an evening in a White restaurant or theater, or a more comfortable seat on a train. Some individuals have held day jobs as Whites, but have returned to the African American community at night. Others have passed in various parts of the country, but have returned home periodically to visit family and friends. All have faced the anxiety of operating in two not merely different but antagonistic worlds, while struggling to keep each world and its respective intimacies clearly separate, lest an acquaintance either wittingly or unwittingly unravel their disguise (Spickard, 1989).

Continuous passing, which involves a complete break with the African American community, has been the most sensational sort of crossing over, though it probably has involved fewer people than is generally thought. Considering the need for spatial mobility and anonymity, continuous passing is generally thought to have involved more men than women, and to have occurred more frequently in the urban North than in the rural South (Stonequist, 1937; Williamson, 1984). Like discontinuous passing, it has most often been a means of gaining access to positions of wealth, power, privilege, and prestige normally barred to individuals of African descent. Some people who choose continuous passing may also find it a way of escaping taunts and other forms of social stigmatization from African Americans who have viewed them as being less than bona fide Blacks (Stonequist, 1937). Seldom, however, does an individual of a more European phenotype grow up as African American and then suddenly make an intellectual decision to pass. Rather, continuous passing is a gradual process in which emotional ties to African Americans are severed as ties to European Americans are achieved (Berzon, 1978; Drake & Cayton, 1945). The final break comes when the benefits of becoming White are felt to outweigh the costs of being Black.

However, it should not be assumed that continuous passing exacts no price. One of the most difficult things a person can be faced with is saying farewell to family and friends, or even having to leave without saying anything at all. If some passers have become "White liberals," opening doors that otherwise would be closed to individuals of African descent, others, out of feelings of being impostors and the constant fear of exposure, have adjusted to their new identities by overcompensating, surpassing even the most rabid racists in order to prove their credentials as Whites (Berzon, 1978; Spickard, 1989).

The Light Brigade: Blue-Vein Societies

Passing is necessarily a highly individualistic strategy available to a small percentage of African-descent Americans, and probably only a minority of individuals who could pass actually have done so. Those who were unwilling or unable to pass sought collectively to counter systematic subordination and to compensate for the arbitrary line between White and Black through the formation of pluralistic elites within the African American community where the degree of acceptance was granted in accordance with one's approximation to the dominant "psychosomatic norm image" (Hoetink, 1971). By emphasizing light skin, straight hair, and sharp features, as well as European culture and thought, multiracial individuals were able not only to distance themselves from the image typically held of Blacks, but also to achieve in this way vicarious, if not actual, parity with Whites (Berzon, 1978).

In support of this strategy these pluralistic elites argued that their sociocultural and physical "Whiteness" entitled them to special privileges over the Black masses and made them more deserving of full integration into the mainstream of American life (Bone, 1958/1965). This attitude indicates that they were casualties of the deeper racial oppression embedded in the fabric of American society, and that by having so internalized this oppression, they were themselves in no small part perpetrators of a rather divisive and pernicious colorism among individuals of African descent. Yet, by re-creating the dominant psychosomatic norm image within the subordinate caste, they did bring into sharp focus the "illogical logic" in the rule of hypodescent, which deemed as inferior, and as "Black," individuals who were culturally, and in many cases phenotypically, different from Whites in name only.

The formation of multiracial elites was primarily an urban phenomenon, since rural African American communities generally tended to be too poor for color stratification actually to develop. This is not to say that there was no evidence of rural color consciousness, but rather that color differences were relatively less important because other criteria were absent (Mencke, 1979). In urban areas, however, color combined with sociocultural factors to heighten differences among individuals of African descent. Cities such as Charleston, Washington, Philadelphia, Nashville, Louisville, New Orleans, Boston, New York, and Atlanta, to mention only a few, were well known for their "blue-vein" societies, their "Four Hundred" or "Talented Tenth" (Berzon, 1978; Bone, 1958/1965; Mencke, 1979; Wright, 1985).

Whether it was in the community of a church, college, literary society, or social club, European ancestry (preferably aristocratic), a more European phenotype—specifically, skin coloring that was light enough to make visible the blood running through one's veins—education, industry, thrift, sobriety, fastidiousness in speech habits, manners, and dress, wealth, and, sometimes, close social contact with Whites, in conjunction with professional standing, all combined to qualify one for membership or marriage into a numerically small and select elite (Berzon, 1978; Mencke, 1979; Williamson, 1984). African American colleges such as Howard, Atlanta, Hampton, and Fisk became bastions of the multiracial elite (Bone, 1958/1965; Spickard, 1989). Though it is uncertain whether there actually existed churches with front doors painted a certain shade of light brown to discourage entrance by persons of a darker hue, religious affiliation did frequently follow color, cultural, and class lines. Multiracial individuals gravitated toward Episcopal, Congregational, Presbyterian, and Catholic churches and away from the Baptist or Methodist, though there were numerous congregations, such as that of the Fifth Street Baptist Church in Louisville, that were exceptions to this rule (Berzon, 1978; Wright, 1985).

This multiracial elite, which evolved directly out of the antebellum Free People of Color, was derived from varied sources: those who gained their freedom by enlisting in either the British or American forces during the American Revolution, those who had been emancipated by legislation or court decisions, those who had gained freedom through self-purchase or whose relatives or friends had purchased their freedom for them, those who were born of free parents or of mothers who were free, and those who were runaway slaves (Berlin, 1976; Foner, 1975). More specifically, this elite originated through the preferential emancipation from servitude—both indentureship and slavery—often granted to the offspring of interracial unions, who were "generally freed after a specified term of servitude if the mother was White, or perhaps manumitted by a conscience-stricken White father" (Berlin, 1976, p. 3).

Throughout the antebellum period, the characteristic condition of most individuals of African descent, multiracial as well as Black, was that of slavery. In Anglo-America, there is no evidence to support the notion that multiracial individuals were invariably chosen as house servants or concubines. In the main, they worked in the fields alongside Blacks. Yet, in all regions of the United States, they were, when compared to Blacks, disproportionately represented among the free (Berzon, 1978; Mencke, 1979; Spickard, 1989). European Americans successfully prevented these multiracial individuals from integrating into the mainstream of society as their equals, such that most of them remained illiterate, propertyless, and poor (Berlin, 1976; Foner, 1975). Long before the abolition of slavery, however, many had achieved a certain amount of education and economic security and had established life-styles that not only differentiated them from the slave masses—and by extension the masses of Blacks—but that paralleled, and in many cases mirrored, the social and cultural life of Whites. A natural consequence of these factors was that a more European phenotype and sociocultural orientation among African Americans became visible markers of elite status (Berlin, 1976; Berzon, 1978).

Despite regional variations, European Americans in general had little inclination to recognize distinctions among individuals of African descent. In each census year from 1850 to 1920, except 1880 and 1900, an attempt was made to count African Americans as Black or mulatto; in 1890, the count was further broken down into quadroon and octoroon. The methods, however, were often sloppy and the definitions of *multiracial* varied. The fact that census takers used visual criteria certainly led to an undercount of the numbers of African Americans of partial European descent. In actual practice, the differences between words describing varying degrees of African ancestry were semantic rather than social, and had little or no significance beyond their usage in the creation of a pecking order among individuals of African descent (Mencke, 1979; Williamson, 1984).

The Civil War and Reconstruction brought an end to the previous distinction between slave and free, and the implementation of segregation at the turn of the twentieth century drew an even sharper line between White and Black. The loss of those few privileges that had been associated with color by virtue of freedom during the antebellum period, plus the overwhelming hostility of the larger White world, led to a marked shift of the political consciousness of the multiracial elite in the direction of an alliance with Blacks. In this coalition they provided a not insignificant number of leaders in the early fight for civil rights due to the relatively better opportunities for social, cultural, and intellectual advancement their color had given them in comparison to the masses of Blacks (Berlin, 1976; Mencke, 1979). This diminished somewhat the emphasis that had previously been attached to color. In addition, the cumulative effects of forced endogamy and "internal miscegenation" (Williamson, 1984) between multiracial individuals and Blacks reached such a point by the 1920s that the majority of African Americans were not only well on their way to becoming more or less multiracial, but the census ceased to enumerate multiracial individuals separately from Blacks. Officially and informally, as more Blacks became multiracial, individuals of a more European phenotype gradually came to regard themselves, and were regarded, less as multiracial and more as light-skinned Blacks (Mencke, 1979; Williamson, 1984).

These seismological sociocultural shifts eclipsed the comparatively privileged status that the multiracial elite had maintained for several hundred years. By the end of the first quarter of the twentieth century, individuals of varying degrees of African ancestry were more equally scattered throughout the upper, middle, and lower sectors of the African American social structure; wealth and cultural attributes had became more important than color alone in determining social prestige. Nevertheless, a large or disproportionate number of the elite remained considerably more European in appearance and culture than the masses of individuals of African descent (Mencke, 1979). This was due in part to the fact that these individuals continued to benefit from the advantages vested in them over generations. Also, despite changing political alliances, many sought to resist their loss of status by withdrawing ever more self-consciously into themselves.

Runaways and Refuseniks: Triracial Isolates

Scattered throughout the eastern United States, particularly in the South, there are some 200 or more communities commonly called *triracial isolates.* They are pluralistic in nature, like the blue-vein societies, yet whereas the latter formed an urban elite within the African American community, the former live apart from both Blacks and Whites in communities on the fringes of villages and towns, or in isolated rural enclaves. Many individuals from these groups have migrated to the cities, and some communities can boast of prosperous farmers, professionals, and college graduates, yet vast numbers remain in their rural communities as unskilled laborers or as impoverished tillers of the soil (B. Berry, 1963).

Though these communities have much in common, it would be erroneous to think of them as one identifiable group. While most are small and located in hilly, swampy, or densely wooded areas not accessible to the general public, the Lumbees of Robeson County, North Carolina, for example, have had as many as 30,000 members (B. Berry, 1963). Commonalities among these communities have less to do with actual cultural bonds than with similarities in experience and in living conditions that unite them in their refusal to accept a binary system of racial classification in which individuals suspected of having any African ancestry are necessarily considered to be Black (Wilkins, 1989).

In the American South, any term describing racially blended ancestry generally has included African descent, has been equated with mulatto, and has been translated into Black. Most of these communities thus affirm only two components—Native American and European—if they acknowledge their multiracial ancestry at all (Blu, 1980). In this sense, their quest for identity appears to be more reactionary than revolutionary (Wilkins, 1989). Yet, if they are victims of Anglo-America's binary racial epistemology, these communities are also victors who have created their own third racial identity by manipulating that epistemology to their advantage, and have destabilized binary racial thinking in the process (Wilkins, 1989).

The triracial isolates are known by a wide variety of names. New York is the home of the Van Guilders, the Clappers, the Shinnecock, the Poospatuck, the Montauk, the Mantinecock, and the Jackson Whites. In Pennsylvania, they are called Pools; in Delaware, Nanticokes; in Rhode Island, Narragansetts; in Massachusetts, Gay Heads and Mashpees; in Ohio, Carmelites. Maryland has its Wesorts; West Virginia, its Guineas; and Tennessee, its Melungeons. There are the Ramps, Issues, and Chickahominy in Virginia; the Lumbees, Haliwas, Waccamaws, and Smilings in North Carolina; Chavises, Creels, Brass Ankles, Redbones, Redlegs, Buckheads, and Yellowhammers, all in South Carolina. Louisiana is the home of a host of triracial communities (B. Berry, 1963).

Considering that documentary evidence is scanty, the exact origins of these groups and their names are unknown. This uncertainty is compounded by the fact that at different times in the antebellum period, depending on the determination of the enumerator, the same families in some communities were listed variously as White, mulatto, and Free People of Color (Blu, 1980). To complicate matters further, it was not until the mid-nineteenth century that the last term came to be more or less interchangeable with the categories of Free Mulatto and Free Black. Up to that time, it had actually been a rather illusive term that included Native American reservations; Native American rural communities, multiracial populations of Native American, European, and African descent; multiracial populations of European and African descent; and Free Blacks (Blu, 1980; J. D. Forbes, 1988a). In all probability, the communities evolved from frontier settlements that became magnets for runaway slaves, trappers, homesteaders, adventurers, deserters, outlaws, outcasts, and nonconformists of all racial backgrounds, but "internal miscegenation," fostered by self-imposed isolation, led to a generalized blending over time (B. Berry, 1963).

Appellations such as Chavis and Creel are family names, though many others, such as Brass Ankle and Redbone, are externally imposed, and are clearly meant to be epithets. As such, they are anathema to those who bear them. Names such as Chickahominy and Nanticoke, which suggest Native American derivation, are borne proudly. Some individuals in these communities would in fact readily be taken as Native American. Others are indistinguishable from Whites; a good many clearly show varying degrees of African ancestry in combination with European and/or Native American descent. Enclaves in St. Landry Parish, Louisiana, in Gouldtown, New Jersey, and in Darke County, Ohio, have always acknowledged their African ancestry, though they have somewhat isolated themselves from the mainstream of society and have drawn a line between themselves and other locals of African descent. Most triracial isolates, however, tend to deny African ancestry and hold on to aboriginal descent as a prized possession, despite the fact that they retain little or nothing of Native American culture, have no recollection of their tribal affiliations, and are culturally indistinguishable from local Whites (B. Berry, 1963; Wilkins, 1989).

This positive bias toward aboriginal ancestry is explainable in part by the fact that although both Native Americans and Blacks were enslaved by European Americans, and still experience oppression in one form or another, aboriginal ancestry has never carried the stigma that has been consistently attached to African descent (Crowe, 1975). Not only could the smallest amount of Native American ancestry qualify one for federal assistance, voting rights, and land claims—meager privileges that have not always been available to Blacks—but also, by the twentieth century, the Native American threat to continued Anglo-American territorial expansion had been sufficiently neutralized so as to make possible the romanticization of Native Americans, affording many Whites the luxury of viewing any aboriginal ancestry of their own as a source of pride (Blu, 1980; Crowe, 1975; Snipp, 1986; Spickard, 1989).

Moreover, if racial composition and ancestry have always been dispositive in determining who is Black, there is by contrast no universally accepted definition of Native American (B. Berry, 1963). The U.S. Census Bureau and the Bureau of Indian Affairs have had definitions that have often been at odds with each other, and both have shifted policies over time. The Bureau of Indian Affairs includes on its rolls only those individuals entitled to bureau services. Acceptance by a tribe, however it may be defined, in conjunction with proof of at least one-quarter degree of aboriginal ancestry, is generally required. For census purposes, self-definition has been the prevailing policy for all ethnicities since 1960. In the past, however, enumerators were instructed to record as Native American only those individuals enrolled on reservations or listed in agency rolls, persons of one-fourth or more aboriginal ancestry, or individuals regarded as Native Americans by their communities (B. Berry, 1963). Though these regulations were applied primarily to multiracial individuals of Native American and European descent, or to individuals who were perceived to be completely aboriginal in ancestry, some state codes, and the census in 1930 and 1940, have applied the same criteria to multiracial individuals of Native American and African descent as well as to those of Native American, African, and European descent. For the most part, however, such individuals have been classified as Black (J. D. Forbes, 1990).

Thus prevented by society from affirming all of who they are without also being classified as Black, yet unable to claim residence on a reservation or prove that they meet the ancestry quantum requirements, various triracial communities have, nevertheless, used the flexibility in the definition of Native American to their advantage. By 1980, the Lumbees of North Carolina, the Nanticokes of Delaware, the Houma in western Louisiana, and the Poospatuck of Long Island, New York, after a prolonged struggle, had succeeded in officially changing their earlier classification as mulattoes to nontreaty Native Americans. This status excludes them from government benefits, but it places them squarely on the aboriginal side of the racial divide (B. Berry, 1963; Blu, 1980; R. Thornton, 1987; U.S. Bureau of the Census, 1980). Many, however, have become active in Native American affairs, only to have their claims to aboriginal status meet with reluctance, if not resistance, from treaty or reservation groups such as the Cherokee, the Comanche, and the Choctaw, who do qualify for federal subsidies (B. Berry, 1963; Blu, 1980).

Though African Americans accuse these communities of donning feathers in order to escape the stigma of being Black, various triracial groups have cast their lot with African Americans, and some individuals have committed the "unforgivable sin" of marrying Blacks. Most have long maintained a strong anti-Black prejudice that has in no small part helped bolster support for their own identity by Whites. The clearest example of this was during the era of segregation. Denied entry into White schools, numerous communities not only refused to attend schools and use public facilities for Blacks, but gained support for establishing their own public restrooms and education facilities, as well as separate sections in churches and theaters (B. Berry, 1963).

Groups such as the Jackson Whites and the Issues have succeeded in negotiating alternative identities as "other non-Whites" (B. Berry, 1963; U.S. Bureau of the Census, 1980). Though some individuals have always passed for White, groups such as the Brass Ankles and the Melungeons, who have persistently fought for legal status as White, have met with success in their local communities, if not actually with the government (B. Berry, 1963; Blu, 1980). Other communities enjoy a status just barely below that of Whites; elsewhere their status is hardly distinguishable from that of Blacks. Overall, they seem to have a status intermediate to both. The price for all this, however, has been the denial of African ancestry, sometimes the casting off of darker relatives, and the avoidance of every suspicion of association with Blacks (B. Berry, 1963).

The French Resistance: Louisiana Creoles

The history of multiracial individuals in the state of Louisiana is in many ways a synthesis of other resistance strategies, but with unique features of its own. This stems largely from the fact that the early patterns of settlement in the lower Mississippi Valley, the Gulf Coast, and South Carolina, respectively, differed from those in North Carolina and in the states northward and westward. The Upper South was settled by large numbers of White families and experienced an early balance in the numbers of White males and females. Neither these demographic factors nor the larger ratio of Whites to Blacks prevented miscegenation, yet they quantitatively reduced the amount of racial blending that occurred. In the Lower South, following the Latin American model, White settlers were small in number and primarily single males, who formed liaisons initially with Native American women and, after the introduction of slavery, with women of African descent. As in the rest of the Americas, there were formidable barriers to intermarriage. Informal unions, however, were more or less approved, if not encouraged, by the prevailing moral code and led to miscegenation on a broad scale (Berlin, 1976; Mencke, 1979; Williamson, 1984).

Pervasive miscegenation and the tendency to give multiracial slaves tasks symbolizing greater personal worth and requiring greater skill, in conjunction with the preferential liberation of slave mistresses and their multiracial offspring, made it possible for multiracial individuals early in the colonial Lower South to enter the free classes, where they filled interstitial economic roles, particularly in the artisanal, manual, and skilled trades, for which there were insufficient numbers of Whites. By virtue of this smaller ratio of Whites to Blacks in the Lower South than in the Upper South, the former tended to view Free People of Color as an integral part of the economy. Furthermore, considering that Whites and most Free Coloreds shared bonds of ancestry and culture, the former viewed the latter as natural and valuable allies against the Black slave majority. This often included the suppression of slave uprisings, as well as the catching and returning of fugitive slaves (Berlin, 1976; Mencke, 1979; Williamson, 1984). This comparatively more favorable situation in "Latin North America" was enhanced by the fact that during the colonial period the distant monarchs of Spain, France, and England saw Free Coloreds in the region as a military "balance-wheel against independence-minded Whites" and necessarily provided some protection of their rights (Berlin, 1976). By granting multiracial individuals an intermediate status and privileges superior to those of Blacks but inferior to those of Whites, both the Crown and the colonists in the Lower South won the loyalty of the Free People of Color while maintaining White domination and control (Berlin, 1976; Mencke, 1979; Williamson, 1984).

The large number of Whites in the Upper South not only diminished the need for Free Coloreds to fill interstitial roles in the economy and for their collaboration in protecting the status quo, but this composite of variables precluded the differentiation of multiracial individuals from Blacks. Although Free Coloreds made up a larger percentage of the total population of African descent in the Upper South, there were proportionately more Blacks in their ranks, and the multiracial segment was predominantly rural, of humble White origins, and of modest means. Free Coloreds in the Lower South were smaller in number, but were from comparatively well-to-do White origins, tended to be urban, and were predominantly multiracial. Despite the generally oppressive conditions in both regions, Free

Coloreds in the Lower South thus not only secured a comparatively more favorable status, but also in Charleston and in gulf ports such as Natchez, Mobile, Pensacola, and New Orleans, they formed one vast blue-vein society and enjoyed the most secure position of any Free People of Color in the South (Berlin, 1976; Mencke, 1979).

The largest community of multiracial individuals resided in New Orleans. Overall, however, Louisiana was the home of the most numerically significant and most economically integrated population of Free Coloreds in the South. They worked as carpenters, ironsmiths, tailors, dressmakers, barbers, hairdressers, and the like, and "reached up into business and the professions" (Williamson, 1984, p. 19). The arrival in Louisiana of large numbers of prosperous multiracial individuals fleeing the Haitian revolution in 1804 not only augmented the ranks of Free Coloreds, but certainly enhanced their socioeconomic status and reified the distinction between multiracial and Black (Berlin, 1976; Haskins, 1975; Rankin, 1978).

Many of Louisiana's multiracial citizens were slaveholding planters in parishes such as St. Landry, Iberville, and Plaquemines (Williamson, 1984). Wealth not only made it possible for some to live in luxury and receive an education in Europe, but, most important, it gave them the means "to maintain themselves with poise and dignity in a White-dominated world" (Williamson, 1984, p. 22). One of the most prosperous of these communities was composed of the descendants of an African woman and a Frenchman named Metoyer who inhabited Nachitoches Parish along the Cane River. Initially, the Metoyers often found it necessary to marry among themselves due to the limited numbers of other Free People of Color in the immediate vicinity, the legal restrictions against marriages between Whites and all individuals of African descent, and the taint of slavery that would be attached to marrying Blacks. With successive generations, however, the Cane River colony sought multiracial spouses either from among families newly arrived in the area or from New Orleans, through a process of careful selection in which a more European phenotype and French cultural orientation were highly esteemed. Over time, the multiracial clan expanded in numbers and in wealth, and emerged as a pluralistic enclave much like the triracial isolates in Anglo-North America (Mills, 1977).

All of this changed when the composite Creole population, including Spanish- and French-speaking Whites as well as people of color, in Louisiana and around Mobile and Pensacola came under Anglo-

American control with the annexation of Louisiana (1803) and the Floridas (1810, 1819). Overwhelmed by an English-speaking majority, Creoles of all racial backgrounds remained aloof from the new arrivals, whom they perceived as a threat to their cultural and political survival (Berlin, 1976; Dominguez, 1986). They fought to maintain French civil law, their unique cultural traditions, the teaching of French in public schools, and Creole dominance over local and regional governments. With Americanization, Creoles of color began the long quest to preserve their intermediate status, as they watched Louisiana's ternary system of racial classification polarize into Black and White (Dominguez, 1986).

By the time of the Civil War the tension between Anglo-Americans and Creoles of European descent abated as the former concentrated on securing economic, political, and social dominance by building a united White front against all individuals of African descent. To achieve this they supported ideas of racial purity and devised new criteria of race in which *Creole* was redefined on the premise of having only Spanish and French ancestry (Dominguez, 1986). Abandoned by their White brethren, Creoles of color nevertheless had a vested social and economic interest in the southern way of life (close to one in every three families owned slaves) and thus supported the Confederacy in a desperate attempt to arrest any further erosion of their status (Dominguez, 1986; Haskins, 1975; Rankin, 1978). With the Union capture of New Orleans, most switched their loyalties, hoping that with emancipation, racial prejudice also would fall. However, Union victory not only brought a loss of wealth and property, but dealt another blow to their former status, since all individuals of African descent were now free. Many Creoles of color resisted this decline by denying any similarity or community of interests with the sea of ex-slaves and English-speaking Blacks. Others, benefiting from the social, cultural, and intellectual advantages vested in them over generations, provided a majority of the political leadership of the Black masses, serving as state senators, representatives, and even state officials in the Reconstruction government imposed by a victorious North on a very resistant South (Dominguez, 1986; Haskins, 1975; Rankin, 1978).

The withdrawal of federal troops brought the winds of change to post-Reconstruction Louisiana. A backlash by southern Whites against any ideas of racial democracy thwarted attempts by Creoles of color to hold on to the hard-won franchise and to arrest the segregationist tide. It is no accident that the illogic of Anglo-America's policy of hypodescent played itself out in Louisiana in the 1896 Supreme Court case involving a Creole of one-eighth African descent, *Hommère Plessy v. Ferguson*, which established Jim Crow segregation in public railway transportation and, shortly thereafter, in public facilities and schools (Haskins, 1975; Rankin, 1978).

The full installation of segregation thus dealt Creoles of color the final blow. Some responded by casting their lot with Blacks and became champions in the fight for civil rights. Many left for Mexico and the Caribbean, where racial lines were more fluid, and where color rather than ancestry was the primary criterion used to define race. Others moved to Florida, Kansas, or California, where they crossed the color line or congregated to form Creole residential enclaves. Large numbers went North, where they passed for White. A smaller number passed for White in Louisiana by destroying the birth records in St. Louis Cathedral that were the only legal proof of their ancestry. In a desperate search for solace and seclusion, still others refused to learn English, remained staunchly Catholic, and sought refuge within the narrow confines of their own world in the downtown section of New Orleans north of Canal Street, particularly in the Seventh Ward (Dominguez, 1986; Haskins, 1975; Rankin, 1978).

After more than a century and a half of resistance to Americanization, most Creoles, with the exception of some of the older generation, no longer speak French or the Louisiana variant commonly called *patois*. Though a few French words remain in their vocabularies, they have incorporated a number of "African Americanisms" into their speech and other aspects of their culture. Younger Creoles have felt the "heightened pride and consciousness" (Dominguez, 1986; Haskins, 1975) that have affected all individuals of African descent in the last two decades. Many have begun to realize, like others before them, that it is advantageous to join forces, at least politically, with Blacks in the fight for civil rights, where unity among all individuals of African descent is essential if gains for Creoles as well are to be made. As a consequence of these influences, traditional attitudes toward the color line have softened (Dominguez, 1986; Haskins, 1975). Yet, if Creole identity is changing, it is no less intact. It is a long-established means of fostering a sense of solidarity, belonging, and self-pride that was mobilized in defense against a binary system of racial classification in which one is necessarily either Black or White, and that has relegated to subordinate status individuals who, by virtue of ancestry and culture, were in the past accorded partial rights to the privileges of the dominant Whites.

Conclusion

Anglo-Americans, in order to neutralize the threat to White dominance implicitly posed by multiracial individuals of partial European ancestry, enforced a policy of hypodescent, which relegated these individuals to the subordinate group by designating as Black everyone who was not pure White. The legal and informal restrictions that have historically barred individuals of African descent from access to avenues of contact with Whites as equals has not, however, prevented multiracial individuals from assuming that by virtue of their physical appearance and cultural behavior they should be accorded the privileges of the dominant Whites. Generated by racist pressure that has rewarded Whiteness and punished Blackness, the tactics that multiracial individuals have devised in order to resist the rigid binary racial epistemology and the corresponding dominant-subordinate hierarchy in the United States have themselves tended to be hierarchical and less a reaction to the forced denial of European ancestry than to subordination and the denial of privileges that such ancestry implied. Despite their patent Eurocentrism, these strategies—whether integration through passing or the formation of pluralistic elites and isolated rural enclaves—may be legitimately viewed as diverse tactics of resistance to oppression utilized by individuals of African descent. While some individuals may seek to confront oppression head-on, passers and pluralists seek to turn oppression on its head by subverting the racial divide.

Acknowledgment

I would like to acknowledge Nina Moss for the feedback and moral support she provided in shaping revisions of this chapter.

9

Blood Quantum: Native American Mixed Bloods

TERRY P. WILSON

While marshaling my thoughts about Native American mixed bloods for this writing, I was visited by a former student. She walked into my academic office with an indefinable air of unease. Phenotypically Indian, during her years in the Native American Studies Program at the University of California's Berkeley campus, she had often expressed great pride in her "pure" racial and tribal heritage. Occasionally she had disparaged mixed-blood Native American classmates and faculty as unable to grasp fully the nuances of Indian life because of their adulterated bloodlines. She evinced little initial interest in my analysis of mixed bloods' roles in Native American cultures and disdained enrolling in my course dealing with people of mixed racial descent.

She had eventually conceded that those of us with lesser degrees of Native American blood heritage might occupy a significant place in Indian affairs, but her continued preference for the company of full bloods was marked. Nonetheless, I was glad to see her again, always hopefully curious about our majors' postgraduate experiences. Her obvious discomfort was quickly addressed: "Terry, you know all those talks we used to have about mixed bloods and full bloods? Well, I just found out that one of my grandmothers, who died before I was born, was half White. I'm not a full blood!"

As we discussed this unexpected revelation, I could only contemplate for the thousandth time what a difference a blood quantum can make. Here was a reservation-bred woman, seemingly secure in her identity as a member of our nation's smallest racial minority, suddenly shaken about the very wellspring of her existence because it was found to include a partial non-Indian ancestry. I did not belittle her anxious concern; a lifetime of dealing with mixed-blood Indian status, personally and professionally, had made me only too acutely aware of the complexities behind this woman's struggle to adjust to a new personal reality.

No more knotty issue preoccupies Indian America than that of identity. Before one can address issues such as tribal sovereignty retained by various groups of Native Americans it is necessary to determine membership within Indian groups. This process hinges heavily on blood quantum, or the degree of Indian ancestry expressed in fractions such as one-fourth or three-eighths. Blood quanta are putatively tied to questions of culture and degrees of acculturation and assimilation. Native American social problems, including high rates of suicide and alcoholism as well as lagging educational and economic development, are inevitably deconstructed with special attention to different behavioral patterns ascribed to mixed bloods and full bloods. Few, if any, Native Americans, regardless of upbringing in rural, reservation, or urban setting, ignore their own and other Indians' blood quantum in everyday life. Those whose physical appearances render their Indian identities suspect are subject to suspicious scrutiny until precise cultural explanations, especially blood quantum, are offered or discovered.

Many within and outside the Native American community decry this framework of analysis. They point to the absurdity of attributing cultural manifestations to a person's biological ancestry (Clifton, 1989, 1990). Scholars have noted the ahistorical aspect of linking blood quantum to Indian identity and deplore references to "meaningless" percentages of "blood" in determining membership and inclusion on official tribal rolls. Correctly, they trace these prevalent practices to an imposition of non-Indian racial (and racist) assumptions onto Native American thinking.

In one sense such argumentation, although factually legitimate, begs the question. If blood quantum are widely utilized to fix Indian identities, however wrongly, then biological ancestry possesses a separate reality. An examination of the past, nonetheless, is essential if we are to understand the present perceptions of mixed bloods by Indians, non-Indians, and themselves. What people *believe* to be the truth is as significant as the historical record in this case.

Ethnohistorian Jack D. Forbes has published extensively about early race relations in America, culminating in 1988 with *Black Africans and Native Americans*. Much interbreeding among Americans, Africans, and Europeans occurred, with a resultant population of mixed bloods whose precise designation as *mestizo, pardo, mulato,* or whatever did not reflect racial and class biases until the colonial period. Forbes rails against overly simplistic racial classifications in light of his discovery of earlier than previously known American contacts in Africa and Europe, especially in the ways in which African and Native American heritages go unrecognized as complex cultural and blood mixtures.

Perhaps the most significant aspect of this challenging study is its primary emphasis on African-Indian relations. Social scientific and historical studies as well as popular literature concerned with interracial marriage and/or breeding and the resultant mixed-race children focus on majority White persons mixing with those of one or another colored minority, usually African American. This emphasis—racist in its underlying assumption of the greater importance of White-colored mixtures over colored-colored—has tended to obscure an important social and cultural phenomenon in American history, African-Indian relations.

Not until the 1970s did scholars explore interactions between African Americans and Native Americans in book-length treatments (Halliburton, 1977; Littlefield, 1977, 1978, 1979, 1980; Perdue, 1979). Most of this new scholarship centered on Black slavery among the five southeastern Indian groups known as the Five Civilized Tribes (Cherokees, Chickasaws, Choctaws, Creeks, and Seminoles). Ironically, the "civilized" attribute, acquired from the White man, was the institutionalization of the bondage of Africans. The Cherokee tribespeople had practiced a precontact bondage in which captured children and women who were not adopted into clans and assimilated to tribal life became *atsi nahsa'i*, persons who existed outside the normal living arrangements. These unfortunates were not kept to produce through their labor material wealth, since accumulation of wealth was not a part of the Cherokee system. After contact with Europeans, some

Cherokees became commercial agriculturists and, along with other tribes, engaged in selling war captives to the White colonists as slaves (Perdue, 1979).

Black contacts with the southeastern Indians preceded by generations the institutionalization of Black slavery among the Five Civilized Tribes. Cherokees and other Indians captured slaves in raids on White settlements and resold them, while the colonists utilized Africans in military expeditions against the various tribes. The colonists feared a combination of Indian-Black interests such as those that occurred in South America, where *quilombos,* settlements composed of runaway slaves and Indians, successfully defied colonial authority, often for extended periods of time (J. D. Forbes, 1988a). That these fears were warranted is exemplified in Seminole history, marked by African-inspired and -led opposition to removal from Florida (Littlefield, 1977).

Despite the Indian nations' institutionalization of slavery and passage of state antimiscegenation laws, intermarriage between Africans and southeastern Native Americans was common (Perdue, 1979). Littlefield (1977) suggests that most intermarriages occurred with the Seminoles and Creeks, citing harsh laws forbidding "amalgamation" and the post-Civil War reluctance of the Cherokees, Choctaws, and Chickasaws to adopt the freed slaves as obliged by treaties negotiated in 1866. There was probably considerable "amalgamation," whether or not sanctified by marriage. White slave owners enacted similarly stringent measures against interracial mixing, but abundant proof suggests the codes were largely ignored.

Not only in the Southeast but elsewhere in the colonies and later in the United States, African Americans and Native Americans cohabited to produce a large mixed-race progeny. Studies estimate that from 30% to 70% of the present African American population has partial Indian ancestry (J. D. Forbes, 1988b). Forbes believes many of these African Americans would so identify as mixed Indian and African if past census opposition to mixed-race identification had not discouraged it. Of course, the majority White culture's insistence on classifying as Black anyone with any degree of African ancestry had determined this question of identity for most long before there was a census. Fears of Indians and Africans making common cause against White exploitation influenced European colonists to use Indians as slave catchers and Africans as soldiers against tribes resisting colonization. Eastern state legislatures continually passed laws attempting to discourage if not outright forbid the existence of Black-Indian communities. Generally, pronouncements against these "dangerous" groups expressed outrage that Indian tribes had lost their native identity and were largely "of mixed blood and color, in various degrees and shades" (Katz, 1986, p. 12).

These outrages and alarms quieted with time, but they left a legacy of prejudiced misunderstanding that lingers in the present. As the frontier moved west and nineteenth-century removal policy eliminated the presence of most eastern tribes, attention focused on those Native Americans who fought the last Indian wars and settled on western reservations. Anthropologists and historians virtually ignored these remnants of eastern Indian tribes, largely intermixed with Blacks and Whites, in favor of studying the degree of acculturation and assimilation experienced by western tribes. Since the colonial period, conventional wisdom held that Indians were "vanishing" through depopulation and assimilation. In the eastern states the bipolarity of race relations into White and Black militated against the acceptance of a continuing Indian presence. This was especially true in the southeast, where triracially mixed communities were labeled as groups who "would rather be White, but they can't, so they'll settle for Indian" (Blu, 1980, p. 181).

In 1945, Julian H. Steward flatly stated that "the Indian is virtually extinct in the eastern United States" and in "a matter of years the last survivors will disappear without leaving any important cultural or racial mark on the national population" (quoted in F. W. Porter, 1986, p. 211). Since then a small coterie of researchers have disproved that contention. D'Arcy McNickle, Brewton Berry, William Harlan Gilbert, Walter L. Williams, Gary Mills, Karen I. Blu, Edward P. Dozier, Edward H. Spicer, and, most recently, Frank W. Porter III have demonstrated that reservation and nonreservation, federally recognized and nonrecognized Indian communities continue to maintain viable identities.

Brewton Berry (1963) offers the most comprehensive study of what some social scientists term *triracial isolates.* Wading through local legend and mythology in addition to documentary study and fieldwork, Berry emphasizes the uniqueness of these individual groups, such as the Jackson Whites, Brass Ankles, and Melungeons, according to geographic specificity and their own and their neighbors' attitudes and beliefs about themselves. Unfortunately, Berry's work is marred by the presumption implied by his title, *Almost White.* He regards these groups as peculiarly misplaced in time and space, almost White, but unable to assimilate into the mainstream. Rather than condemn the narrow biraciality that rendered these groups' survival tenuous, Berry concludes that they were the inheritors of misfortune, the inevitable unfortunate by-product of mixing the races.

Two major questions impose upon the issue of mixed-blood Indian communities whether they are located in the eastern or western states: classification as Indian and recognition as such by the federal government. F. W. Porter (1986) summarizes past scholarship and notes that few researchers have considered that miscegenation provided a means of maintaining Indian identity. Generally, scholars have postulated that long-term racial mixing leads to individual and tribal extinction. Porter suggests that loss of communally held land bases to Euro-American expansion left dispossessed Indians with several choices, including assimilation, sexual unions with Whites or Blacks, and migration. Many opted to remain in "marginal environments," clinging to the land and an Indian identity while intermarriage and the acquisition of the majority population's material culture traits often gave them the outward appearance of non-Indians. They became "folk communities": isolated socially and spatially from other groups, appearing physically similar to outsiders, sharing a common identity through family and social structures, and "economically self-sufficient with little class distinction" (p. 21).

Porter (1986) argues that "the most important question to consider is not whether or to what extent these groups are Indian," but "the reconstruction of tribal histories" and "the problems of maintaining tribal identity and achieving federal recognition" (pp. 28-29). The question of federal recognition has remained confused, inextricably linked with the Indian identity issue, itself clouded by popular and scholarly notions of blood quantum, phenotypic appearances, and past treaty relations. In 1972, when the Passamaquoddy Indians of Maine sued for redress of land losses dating to a 1794 treaty with Massachusetts, the initial Interior Department decision was to oppose the suit because it was brought by a nonrecognized group. Federal courts overruled this argument, which led eventually to the creation of the Federal Acknowledgment Project in the Bureau of Indian Affairs in 1978 (F. W. Porter, 1986). This did not end the problem of Indian identification. The prescribed acknowledgment procedure is complicated, expensive, and still concerned, necessarily, with biological descent.

About 10 years ago a representative of an eastern triracial community enrolled at the Berkeley campus where I teach. His major was unrelated to Native American Studies (NAS), but he took several courses in our program and joined the Indian student group, identifying as American Indian—to the consternation of many. Phenotypically he seemed to others to be African American, although obviously of mixed racial background. To my knowledge there were no direct confrontations between him and other Indian students, but several talked to me about the "appropriateness" of his self-identification and membership in their campus community. He had no blood quantum certificate, nor was he the recipient of scholarship money designated for Native Americans. His tribal affiliation was with a group unfamiliar to the others (mostly Indians from western states), but his knowledge of Indian history and customs was apparent. Eventually he was accepted—with varying degrees of reservation—by students and faculty in NAS; however, the attitude of African American students toward him ranged from elaborate indifference through knowing distrust to outright disapproval.

Those African Americans who questioned his motives shared an assumption held by White Americans and many Indians: that an individual of mixed African-Indian ancestry would as a matter of course choose to escape the "obloquy of Blackness" by identifying as Native American. That was certainly the tone of a 1987 documentary film, *Long Lance.* Made through the auspices of the National Film Board of Canada, it traces the bizarre career of Sylvester Long Lance, North Carolina born of parents whose biological heritage included White, Black, and Indian ancestry. The film's narration unequivocally explains this mixed blood's decision to identify as Native American while his family was perceived as Negro to a desire for escape from the disadvantages of being Black in the first quarter of the twentieth century.

This consideration probably influenced his decision; however, Long Lance was intrigued by his reading of books celebrating the "noble savage" image. He entered a federal boarding school in 1907, reporting a one-quarter eastern Cherokee blood quantum. Within a few years he claimed to be "full-blooded" when applying to West Point Military Academy and still later "changed" his identity to western Cherokee when he emigrated to Canada. In the 1920s newspapers called him Chief Buffalo Child Long Lance, the rank self-proclaimed and the additional name an honorary one bestowed when he was adopted by the Canadian Blackfeet. In 1928 he used Blackfeet tribal stories and legends to buttress his "autobiography," a best-seller translated into six languages, and appeared in an "all-Indian" Hollywood film, *The Silent Enemy.* Eventually exposed, his fame receded and he died in Canada amid mysterious circumstances.

I have informally interviewed approximately 100 African Americans encountered on campus and in the community who indicated knowledge of an Indian heritage. Most were diffident about the fact, expressing interest in uncovering more information about the culture and history of their tribal backgrounds and offering no desire to identify as Indian. Some were tracing their genealogies and, when queried about why, invariably replied that they simply wanted to know more about Indians, especially interactions with African Americans. None voiced any motivation other than a personally felt positive attitude about having a biological tie to a culture they admired. Most found a common cause with Indians as another oppressed minority and several alluded to spiritual beliefs combining Native and African American belief systems, much as novelist Alice Walker has celebrated her Indian heritage through writing about intermingled traditions.

While mixed-race African-Indian American history is hampered and difficult to assess because of incomplete documentary records and a prevailing societal standard that identifies as Black those intermixed persons with any African American background, the historical record on the subject of Indian-White mixtures is voluminous. This bias has not prevented the growth of a distorting folklore about "half-breeds," "half-bloods," "breeds," and mixed bloods. Historians generally did not treat the topic at length or as a separate aspect of Indian-White relations until the last 10 or 12 years; no comprehensive study devoted to the subject of mixed bloods in the United States has yet appeared. However, one can expect the recent spate of articles and portions of books discussing mixed bloods to continue, and monographs to follow.

In a survey of 60 Indian historians I made in 1988, a question was posed concerning what areas of scholarship would be most productive to the field of Indian history. Nearly every reply included statements about the need for more research into the roles of mixed bloods in the Native American past. The responses were based partly on current demographics pertaining to Indians and partly on a growing awareness of a glaring weakness in the simplistic historical characterization of mixed bloods, ranging from cultural and assimilative "progressives" to the full-blood "traditionals."

In 1980 the Indian population in the United States, according to the U.S. Census, amounted to 1,366,676, with an additional 42,162 Inuits (Eskimos) and 14,205 Aleutian Islanders, for an overall Native American population of 1,423,043 (R. Thornton, 1987). Indications are that the 1990 census, for which data are not yet available, counted several hundred thousand more Indians than 10 years earlier. Some of the continuing dramatic increase since the population nadir of 1900—demographers estimate the 1890-1900 Indian population at approximately 250,000—can be explained by higher birthrates, lower death rates, and general improvements in health conditions. Indian sociologist and demographer Russell Thornton (1987) explains that a fourth factor contributing to this sharp rise is what he terms " 'biological migration': the migration of non-Indian genes into the American Indian population, that is, the mixing of American Indians with non-Indians, particularly Whites but also Blacks and other groups" (p. 90).

The 1910 census full bloods—150,053 out of 265,683—constituted 56.5% of the American Indian total, with the blood quantum of 8.4% (22,207) not reported. Twenty years later the percentage of full bloods had dropped to 46.3%. This trend was unevenly distributed among the tribes: The Pimas, for example, were reported 98.6% full bloods in 1910 and 97.9% in 1930, while Arapahos in 1910 had 77.5% full bloods and in 1930 only 41.4% full bloods. Intermarriage with non-Indians proved a means of survival for many Indian groups; however, it should be noted that the "biological migration" was not one-way: The 1980 census enumerated about 7 million Americans with some degree of Indian ancestry (R. Thornton, 1987).

To a great extent—alarming and dismaying for many Native Americans—Indian identity, with its mixed-blood / full-blood connotations, stems from attitudes and ideas fostered by the majority White culture and government. Before the White man's coming there was intermarriage and interbreeding across group lines, and no one marked the offspring as mixed blood or kept an accounting of blood quantum to determine tribal membership or degree of culture or acculturation. These notions were introduced by Europeans and Euro-Americans. The European invasion gradually changed that condition, although never completely, as most Indians today still posit their identification tribally and only secondarily as Indian. A 1691 Virginia statute forbade intermarriage of Whites with Indians or Africans to prevent "abominable mixture and spurious issue" (Smits, 1987). This pronouncement reflected a majority sentiment among colonial Virginians, whose first generation in America had contemplated an integrated biracial society until the 1622 Powhatan surprise attack ended an era of relative peace (Smits, 1987).

Racism appears not to have been a factor in the English bias against intermarriage with Indians. Perceived as darker than Europeans, Indians were considered essentially White people whose exposure to the sun and custom of painting the body with ocher and other natural dyes explained their various hues. Colonial Indian haters were abundant, and attacks on Native American sexuality, paganism, cannibalism, indolence, slovenliness, and barbarism were common. Indians were characterized as culturally degraded, as were Africans, but without the negative comments on color and other physical features made about the latter. While Africans were indisputably and immutably "Black," with the disparaging attributions made to that color, Indians' brutishness was judged the result of custom and environment and partially ameliorated by the virtues of physical hardiness, stoicism, and hospitality. Not until the 1750s did Euro-Americans view Indians as a significantly darker race than themselves, and they did not adopt red as the accepted color label for Native Americans until after 1800 (A. T. Vaughan, 1982).

Warfare, alien customs, and the enraging refusal of Indians to accept the White man's "civilization" contributed to a gradual change in English and Anglo-American views of Indians. Eighteenth-century European naturalists, few with any direct contact with Indians, added a "scientific" underpinning to this worsening attitude (see Spickard, Chapter 2, this volume). At first they divided humankind horizontally by observable physical differences. Eventually a hierarchy was established among the subdivisions of humans based on skin color, with lighter hues judged superior (A. T. Vaughan, 1982).

One does not have to agree completely with the foregoing analysis of developing racism to ascribe a virulence to race relations in nineteenth-century America. When a Georgia politician in 1816 echoed Thomas Jefferson's earlier suggestion about amalgamating Indian and White societies through intermarriage, he was soundly reproved by the press: No interbreeding "until it shall please God to *bleach* the Indian's skin" (quoted in Young, 1989, p. 496). Both culture and blood were used by federal judges in determining "Indianness." In *United States v. Rogers* (1846) the court decided that an individual had to meet both requirements to be adjudged Indian. A biological link to the "red" race must be established and those Indians with whom affiliation was claimed had to accept the person as a fellow tribesman. Confusingly, the quantum of Indian blood required was left indefinite, as was the ethnographic evidence necessary to determine Indianness. On one occasion in 1869 a New Mexico Territory court declared that residents of pueblos were not Indians partly because they were peaceable, industrious, and virtuous. Obviously the naturalists' vertical chart of humankind had been accepted (Hagan, 1985).

But what of mixed bloods? Where did they fit into the pattern of race relations between Indian and White? In one sense answers to this question are as numerous and varied as the number of mixed bloods and tribes to which they belonged. And very definitely the answers are complex and worrisome, depending as they do on the questioner's frame of reference. Social scientist James A. Clifton (1989), for example, quite vehemently decries acceptance of a category of mixed blood, explaining that such a distinction is wholly a European concept stemming from "preoccupations with racial classification" (p. 26). He believes that Indian acceptance of this thinking to the extent of defining Indianness by blood quantum "represents a victory of the principles of racial stratification over ethnicity" (p. 27). He sees the problem as a confusion over race and ethnicity, as Indians are viewed and treated variously as a race and as an ethnic group.

Clifton's observations have a historical validity that should not be discounted; however, if Indians and non-Indians subscribe to the notion of blood quantum, and by extension biological determinism, then their beliefs and actions will be guided thus, regardless of historical reality. Such acceptance, however erroneously based, creates a cultural reality within which groups and individuals live. Clifton does offer a useful framework of analysis for examining the lives of culturally mixed historical individuals. He suggests that the practice of attaching a single identity to racially mixed persons is highly inaccurate, and that local social conditions and attitudes within frontier conditions—these he defines not in terms of geography but as a social setting, "a culturally defined place where peoples with different culturally expressed identities meet and deal with each other" (p. 24)—determined the life-style of each individual. Adopting this definition, Clifton includes in his book biographical sketches of "cultural" Indians such as Simon Girty and Sylvester Long Lance.

Interestingly, historians have published a number of biographies of mixed-blood Indians, while anthropologists have tended to research the lives of full bloods. Historians are generally more comfortable with documentary sources, which are usually more extensive and personal for mixed bloods, especially if they obtained leadership status (Edmunds, 1980; Moses & Wilson, 1985). After contact with Europeans and Euro-Americans, many Indian tribes discovered their mixed bloods to be of invaluable help. Generally brought up within the tribal cultures—their White fathers wanted to avoid the prejudicial treatment "half-breed" children would encounter in Anglo-American society—many received formal schooling as well, rendering them bilingual and bicultural. These individuals were uniquely qualified to serve as "cultural brokers" between two societies that were often in conflict.

Precise blood quantum seems to have been a nonfactor in determining how a mixed-blood leader would guide his people. John Ross, only one-eighth Cherokee by blood, utilized his knowledge of the White man's system in the 1820s-1860s to fight against outside encroachment on his tribe's property and forced removal of his people from the Southeast to Indian Territory. Charles Curtis, a Kansa (Kaw) one-eighth mixed blood, lived on his tribe's reservation as a young boy but spent most of his adult life during the early decades of the twentieth century in White society. For him, being an Indian "was less a matter of blood than the fusion of Indian and White into a cultural composite that was committed to private property as the most effective means of fulfilling the assimilationist dream" (Unrau, 1989, p. 5). His advocacy of Indian rights was a mixed bag: He obviously used his Indianness to advantage politically and economically while espousing an assimilationist policy as best for the future of Indian people (Unrau, 1989).

Another one-eighth Indian by blood, John Joseph Mathews, also grew up on his tribe's reservation and left to obtain the White man's education; however, he returned to his people, the Osages of Oklahoma, to live out his life. Mathews served in World War I as an aviator and traveled to England, where he earned a B.A. in 1923 at Oxford. He returned to his home in Osage County (a reservation until 1906) and launched a successful writing career. When the Great Depression depleted the considerable economic reserves of the oil-rich Osages, he became a major political force on the tribal council. He worked hard to preserve the cultural integrity of his tribespeople and to protect their petroleum reserves (T. P. Wilson, 1981).

Full-blood Chief Fred Lookout was confronted by those on the Osage council who complained that Mathews and other younger men, mostly mixed bloods, had seized too much power in tribal politics. As was true in many tribes, animosities between the increasingly more numerous mixed bloods and "unadulterated" full bloods had grown over time around issues of acculturation and resource development. Rather than allow a lower birthrate and intermarriage with non-Indians to widen the numerical gap and erode their power entirely, the Osage full bloods in the 1930s broadened their political base by identifying as "full blood" all tribal members of one-half or more blood quantum (and in some instances even less if the person's physical appearance seemed to warrant the designation) and accepting into their society—and politics—those whose attitudes and conduct coincided with the surviving traditional culture.

Chief Lookout, faced with the necessity of leaning heavily on Mathews and the other mixed bloods' expertise in the White man's world, urged moderation and patience on the full bloods. At the same time he spoke directly to the mixed bloods' responsibility:

> You are young men. You have the thoughts of white men, but you have the interests of your people in your hearts. Do what you think is best. . . . The things which I know are gone. If you let your white man's tongues say what is in your Indian hearts you will do great things for your people. (T. P. Wilson, 1984, p. 52)

Unfortunately for the Osages and other tribes, Chief Lookout's optimistic admonition was frequently ignored by mixed bloods or vastly modified so that they did well for themselves individually while ostensibly representing their people. It should not be overlooked that this scenario was not unknown among full-blood leaders, but normally the biculturalism of mixed bloods offered them more opportunities to capitalize on the economic possibilities of holding leadership positions.

That the U.S. government used the presence of mixed bloods within Indian communities has been demonstrated by several historians. During the last decades of the nineteenth century, when the acculturation-minded government was pressing for individual parceling of tribally held land, the signatures of mixed bloods were sought to satisfy the three-fourths approval of tribal adult males prerequisite to such distribution. On these occasions the government pushed for mixed bloods to be considered full members of the tribe (Hagan,

1985). Contrarily, when strong antiacculturationist or antigovernment stances by tribes have been partially instigated by mixed bloods or when the government has wanted to cut expenditures for Native Americans, U.S. policymakers have tried to categorize as non-Indian those with lesser blood quantum. At such times the Indian Office generally has urged the disassociation from the tribe of those possessing less than a one-half blood quantum.

The question of quantum has sometimes led to confusing and bizarre events. Attempts to implement the 1887 General Allotment Act at the Minnesota White Earth Reservation between 1906 and 1915 illustrate this assertion. As was common elsewhere, the Chippewas on the reservation who were full blood were considered legally incompetent, while mixed bloods were deemed able to handle their own affairs. Physical anthropologists were used as expert witnesses in federal court proceedings in land allotment fraud cases after Congress passed legislation in 1906 and 1907 allowing the sale of mixed-bloods' allotments. Full blood was designated as one-half or greater Indian heritage and the anthropologists were to design a "scientific" means of determining this. That the Chippewas used a cultural standard to define status (those who lived with the tribe were considered Indian and those who lived among Whites were mixed bloods) was largely ignored in favor of physical tests. The anthropologists devised a tedious process in which hair samples were taken (curly hair denoted some White ancestry), feet measured (larger sizes indicated a non-Indian ancestor), and chests scratched (mixed bloods' reactions were "more intense [reddening] as well as lasting") (Beaulieu, 1984, p. 298).

Given this astonishing example, one can readily understand the tendency to take refuge in "simple" blood quantum. Tribes have the last say in deciding membership. As might be expected, there is wide variation in practice, including not only quantum but patrilineality and matrilineality as well. At least one tribe allows those with 1/256 Indian blood heritage to be enrolled while others demand at least a one-half quantum from the *mother's* heritage. The majority follow the U.S. government's dictum of accepting as Indian those who are a "quarter Indian."

In areas such as Oklahoma, where there is much intertribal and interracial marriage, matters can get complicated. I have a friend who describes himself as a "mixed-blood full blood" because his four grandparents are all full bloods but members of different tribes. Record keeping not infrequently stumbles over quantum issues. In one case eight siblings were listed with five different Indian blood percentages, although all shared the same mother and father. A few years ago one of my students related a horror story in which her family's quantum had been reduced to less than one-fourth—on paper. It seems members of a rival family had taken positions at the tribal agency and "lost" the paperwork detailing her family's multitribal blood quantum.

Generally, in the Indian community (if such a term has any meaning for a geographically, tribally, and culturally diverse group) identity is tied to cultural attributes such as a reservation community ties and phenotypicality ("looking Indian") in addition to blood quantum. There is great significance attached to being mixed blood or full blood—or appearing as the latter. In Montana many of my Native American acquaintances were "card-carrying Indians," having miniaturized and laminated their blood quantum certificates, which were drawn from purses or wallets at appropriate or, as it seemed to me, inappropriate times. At one point on the Berkeley campus there was a family of Native Americans enrolled whose physical appearance indicated "full blood or close to it." The brothers and sisters assumed a slightly superior air toward lighter-hued Indian students based on relative darkness of skin until it was discovered they were one-quarter Native American and three-quarters Filipino. (There are many instances of Filipino-Native American mixed bloods, mostly in California, but virtually no scholarly or popular notice. The same is true of other Asian-Native American mixed bloods.)

Most mixed-blood Indians in the United States experience some discomfort stemming from their status and emanating from the Native American and non-Indian communities. Part of this is derived from perceptions of the historical past and the rest, ironically, from the popularity of Indians during the last 20 years. In the nineteenth century, mixed bloods, usually referred to pejoratively as "half-breeds," were often excoriated as social and psychological misfits, caught between two cultures, and frequently betrayers of their Indian heritage by participating in and profiting from the exploitation of their tribes' posterity, especially land and mineral resources. There was the racist assumption that White persons who adopted Indian ways "lost their civilization" living among the savages and produced degenerate, "mongrelized" offspring. At best these mixed-race children were "marginal people of minor significance"; individuals who excelled as leaders were "renegades" or "designing half-breeds" (Calloway, 1986, p. 44).

During the 1960s and 1970s I used to lecture to my classes in NAS that Indians were currently the "in" ethnic group. Our jewelry, our perceived culture, our spiritual ties to nature, our civil rights struggle, our special relation to the U.S. government, and our *identity* are much desired. Recently William Quinn (1990) has written about this phenomenon's fullest flowering in what he calls "the southeast syndrome." He found families and individuals recruiting membership in "pan-Indian" groups, some with wholly bogus ancestry or unprovable native heritage. On an individual level this kind of self-identification, Quinn believes, is harmless, nor does he condemn organizations who meet to discuss Indian history and culture or even act out their version of Indianness. He does believe there is a problem when groups "collectively delude themselves into thinking they are *bona fide* Indian tribes eligible for [recognition and] . . . government-to-government relationships with the United States" (p. 154).

Mixed-blood Indians today are often viewed dubiously by their full-blood brethren, by non-Indians, and quite often by themselves because of past history and present concerns that they are nontraditional, culturally suspect, and possibly fraudulent. Full bloods frequently employ subtle and occasionally pointed references to mixed bloods' minuscule blood quantum, questionable motivations for identifying as Indian, and "lack of culture." Non-Indians express disappointment over physical appearances, and comment about wanting to see some "real Indians." All of this can lead to mixed bloods accepting "second-class Indianness" or "other Indian status." Mathews, the Osage councilman, always carefully differentiated between himself and the Indians (full-blood tribal members), even though he spoke the language, lived among them, and served them politically. Often mixed bloods in response to queries about their ethnicity will reply: "I'm only one-quarter Indian or half Indian," presumably accepting the notion that a lesser blood quantum somehow determines the degree of Indianness.

Most Indian mixed bloods eventually reach a workable solution to identity problems. Some invariably defer to full bloods as "more Indian," others aggressively insist on recognition as native, and still others arrive at a place where they cease worrying about the issue altogether. This does not mean that questions of quantum and Indian identity will disappear, however.

As the pool of full bloods diminishes, the issue may very well attract more heat in the future. Mathew Snipp (1986), a mixed-blood Indian sociologist, has explored the continuing problem of bureaucratic handling of mixed-blood Indians. Like Jack Forbes, he found several categories of "Indian" in census reports. In the 1980 census, race and ethnicity, always elusive concepts, caused much confusion. Snipp organized responses into three distinct populations: a core group he calls "American Indian," who disclose their race and ethnicity as Indian; "mixed bloods," who report their race as Indian but include non-Indian ancestry in their ethnic backgrounds; and "Americans of Indian descent," who give a non-Indian race but cite Indian ancestry as part of their ethnic backgrounds. Of the nearly 7.4 million who reported race and/or ethnicity as Indian, 84% fell into the third category. Snipp concludes that the degree to which mixed bloods are recognized by other Indians, "and the degree to which they are involved in the community life of the Indian population, is hard to assess" (p. 249). He advocates self-identification as the preferable choice among flawed alternatives, including use of blood quanta, genetic tests, and recognition by sight. He recommends buttressing self-identification with supplementary information about involvement in the Indian community.

I cannot imagine that Native Americans will cease their preoccupation with blood quantum and issues of "mixed blood" and "full blood." Not only do social scientists and historians grapple with this phenomenon, but virtually all leading Indian novelists, past and contemporary, have explored the mixed-blood experience (Allen, 1983; Dorris, 1987; Erdrich, 1984; Mathews, 1934/1989; Momaday, 1969; Scheick, 1979; Silko, 1977; Vizenor, 1981, 1984, 1990; Welch, 1974, 1979). This is not surprising, as most of the writers are mixed bloods and utilize mixed-blood protagonists to deconstruct the tensions of modern Indians gingerly negotiating life strongly influenced by the majority culture.

I am convinced that assimilation and "being Indian" are not mutually contradictory (Baird, 1990). There is no fixed list of characteristics that when totaled equals "Indian," nor is there a rational means to certify by blood quantum that one is Native American—"traditional," "acculturated," or whatever. There must be a cultural and self-identifying process operating as well as group recognition. I strongly support the notion of Malcolm McFee (1968) that those who are comfortably half in the Indian world and half in the non-Indian world possess a third positive dimension stemming from biculturality that renders them "150% men." I believe that many Indian mixed bloods approximate that status and that others would fare better if they subscribed to the concept, especially if they can accept the reality that many around them will always disagree.

10

La Raza and the Melting Pot: A Comparative Look at Multiethnicity

CARLOS A. FERNÁNDEZ

The countries of the Western Hemisphere, the so-called New World, share a history of multiethnicity rooted in the expansion of European settlement and domination following the voyages of Columbus. However, the way this shared history has unfolded differs in many significant respects. Perhaps the most telling contrast between the United States and Latin America involves attitudes toward race generally and race mixing specifically. Today, the great majority of Latin Americans are what we in the United States would call "mixed race," predominantly of Native American, European, and African ancestry. The majority of people in the United States are also mixed, but generally of European origins—that is, "White." However, since the African American-led civil rights movement and the realization of many of the legal and political reforms it promoted, the opportunities for interracial personal relationships have been greatly enhanced.[1] Consequently, the numbers of people who are interracial and multicultural—that is, "multiethnic," in the fullest sense—are on the increase.[2] This trend happens to coincide with a rapid increase in the mixed-race Mexican American population as well as a significant upsurge in the numbers of the many distinctive Asian ethnic populations. Together with the African Americans, these groups introduce a new dimension to the American ideal of the "melting pot," one that has been a living reality for centuries in the other America to our south. This cursory, comparative examination of the different experiences of race and racial mixing in the United States and Latin America is an effort to increase understanding and to challenge attitudes that stubbornly persist, even as we enter an increasingly global society.

Latin America: La Raza Cósmica[3]

The year 1992 marks the 500th anniversary of the accidental discovery of the Americas by Columbus under the sponsorship of the Catholic Spanish monarchs Isabella and Fernando. In the United States, we refer to the commemoration of this discovery as Columbus Day. In parts of Latin America, however, they celebrate El Día de la Raza (the Day of the [New Mixed] Race). The different names for the same observance illustrate one of the most fundamental cultural, historical, and even philosophical differences between the United States and Latin America, namely, the way we view race and interracial mixture.[4]

Many Americans are unaware of the "racial" history of Latin America. Evidence for this can be found in the fact that people of Latin American origin or ancestry are included as "Whites" in the U.S. Census, and since about 1980 have come to be referred to as "Hispanic," that is, European (Muñoz, 1989). What is the truth of the matter?

MEXICO AND MEXICANS

By far the largest number of "Hispanics" in the United States today are Mexican American. Historically as well as currently, the majority of Mexican Americans have concentrated in the southwestern part of the United States, the annexed northern territory of Mexico, primarily in California and Texas. Mexican Americans make up the second largest non-White ethnic group in the United States (estimated at 6%, based on survey rates in March 1982 and March 1989; all Hispanics are 9%, African Americans, 12.1%), and are among the fastest growing of all groups (53% all Hispanics). Contrary to popular images, more than 90% of Hispanics are urban; less than 10% are farm workers (U.S. Bureau of the Census, 1990, 1991a).

According to the Mexican American Legal Defense and Education Fund (MALDEF), the majority of Mexican Americans speak English and are U.S. citizens. Los Angeles, America's second-largest city, may have the largest urban concentration of Mexicans after Mexico City, which by now may be the largest city in the world. Upward of 60% of all the children enrolled in the Los Angeles public schools today are Hispanic, primarily Mexican Americans (A. Vargas, MALDEF, personal communication, February 1991).

The racial history of Mexico out of which Mexican Americans have emerged starts with Native Americans. An estimated 25 million Native Americans, the largest concentration in the hemisphere, lived in the region of Mexico and Central America at the time of the Spanish invasion (MacLachlan & Rodríguez O, 1980). The Spanish eventually conquered the Mexica[5] (Aztec) capital city, Tenochtitlán, in 1522, not by superior arms, nor by disease, which took its heavy toll later, but by their ability to muster a huge army of non-Mexica indigenous peoples eager to rid themselves of their reputedly oppressive overlords. The conquest of the Aztec empire was not just a Spanish conquest, but also a Spanish-led indigenous revolt (White, 1971).

Upon the Spanish-Indian alliance's success, the Spanish soldiery and the Native American ruling classes, including what remained of the Mexicas, established mutually agreeable social and political ties, secured in many cases by intermarriage with noble families. The first mestizos born of these relationships were not products of rape; they were acknowledged as "Spanish" or "Creoles" by their Spanish fathers. Of course, the ordinary Native Americans who constituted the masses of the people were not privy to any of these transactions. Indeed, rape and concubinage befell many indigenous commoner women; their children became the first "illegitimate" mestizos. During this early era, the "purely" Spanish constituted approximately 3-5% of the total population, and never grew beyond an estimated 10% throughout the subsequent history of Mexico (MacLachlan & Rodríguez O, 1980; Morner, 1970).

From the beginning of Spanish colonialism, Indian slaves in large numbers were employed in the silver mines. In 1523, the first foreign-origin slaves were introduced to Mexico, mainly as servants. These first slaves were a collection of Spanish Moslems—Arabs, Berbers, Moors (a mixed people of Arab, Berber, and Black African ancestry)—and *ladino* Blacks, that is, Blacks who had been slaves in Spain or one of its colonies prior to arriving in Mexico (MacLachlan & Rodríguez O, 1980). With the opening up of the large coastal plantations, however, the Spanish turned to the principal region in the world where slaves were being offered for sale in significant numbers at the time, the coast of Africa.

The number of African slaves increased dramatically in Mexico between 1530 and 1700. By the middle of the eighteenth century, African and part-African people were the second largest component of the Mexican population. Only the Native Americans had a larger population. Several individuals of acknowledged part-African ancestry played prominent roles in Mexican history; for example, the Independence hero Vicente Guerrero, for whom a state is named (MacLachlan & Rodríguez O, 1980).

Toward the end of the eighteenth century, the mestizo population began to increase more rapidly. By 1800, it overtook the African and part-African groups, who were increasingly absorbed into the mestizo population. By 1900, the mestizos had become the largest ethnic group in Mexico.

Although the 1921 census was the last in which racial classifications were used in Mexico, some estimates are that mestizos (which in practice became a catchall term for all mixtures) today constitute some 85-90% of the Mexican population and Native Americans some 8-10%, with Europeans, mainly Spanish, making up the rest of the total (Morner, 1970). These estimates are highly suspect, however, a fact generally acknowledged by Mexican demographers, because *Indian* has come to mean "someone who speaks an Indian language" or who "lives like an Indian," that is, who is poor. The fact is, many biological Indians have become cultural mestizos who speak Spanish, and hence are regarded as mestizos. There are also many "Indians" and "Spanish" who are actually of mixed ancestry (Morner, 1970). This ambiguity serves to highlight the absurdity and practical irrelevance of racial categories in Mexico today.

BRAZIL AND BRAZILIANS

It amuses me to hear some North Americans in recent years refer to Brazil or Brazilians as "Hispanic." Of course, the largest, most populous country in Latin America is not Hispanic at all. Brazil was founded as a Portuguese colony shortly after the voyages of Columbus, and the majority of its inhabitants these days are of mixed European, African, and Native American ancestry.[6] The culture of Brazil is likewise a mixture, a synthesis of its constituent ethnic groups.

The indigenous people of Brazil first encountered by the Portuguese were by and large nomadic and seminomadic, and, if we are to accept the estimates of the anthropologists, not very numerous. Their numbers were further diminished by the 90% disease mortality rate observed throughout the hemisphere among native peoples (MacLachlan & Rodríguez O, 1980). Miscegenation was common between the Portuguese and Native Americans, and the population of mestizos climbed rapidly. Many indigenous people were enslaved by the Portuguese to work their plantations. However, given the vast size of Brazil and the relative scarcity of indigenous people, the Portuguese quickly turned to Africa for slaves. The demand for slaves grew to such an extent that the African population, including the increasingly numerous *mulatos* (mulattoes, or mixed Black and White), rapidly overtook all other groups and represented more than 60% of the total population of 2.3 million in 1789. The sheer size of the African population often proved unmanageable, and significant numbers of slaves escaped into the countryside and jungle. Some of the escaped slaves formed new tribal communities such as those they had left behind in Africa. Many others joined Native American groups, intermarrying and creating unique islands of Afro-Indian culture, such as the famous settlement of Palmares (see Boxer, 1963; Degler, 1971).

By the time slavery was abolished in 1888, the lines between the races were extremely blurred, as they were throughout much of Latin America. Today, class relationships are increasingly referred to in racial terms, almost irrespective of a person's actual racial ancestry. Thus a *mulato* of means may be called "White" or "bleached," while a *favela mulato*'s Blackness is emphasized.[7] Complicating the picture is the fact that the favored skin tone in Brazil is not white, but light brown (Degler, 1971).

There is insufficient space here to review every one of the Latin American countries with respect to race and race mixture with even the sparse detail given to the examples of Mexico and Brazil above. However, the histories and attitudes are similar throughout the hemisphere in those essential aspects with which comparisons are drawn with the United States.[8]

The United States: The Melting Pot

As early as 1782, it began to be observed that America was a place where people of several ethnic groups were coresident. One newly naturalized Franco-American noted:

> I could point out to you a family whose grandfather was an Englishman, whose wife is Dutch, whose son married a French woman, and whose present four sons have now four wives of different nations. *He* is an American, who leaving behind him all his ancient prejudices and manners, receives new ones from the new mode of life he has embraced. . . . Here individuals of all nations are melted into a new race of men. (de Crevecoeur, 1904, cited in Glazer & Moynihan, 1970)

It would have been as appropriate to notice the "melting" of non-Northwest European peoples, especially Africans, into the American pot, primarily as a result of the concubinage that accompanied slavery. But, because of White racism, and the stigma of illegitimacy, the very idea of including "people of color" in the mix was for the most part ignored, if not regarded as abhorrent.

At the turn of the century, during the period of the greatest immigration into the United States ever, many native-born Americans began experiencing considerable anxiety regarding "foreign influences," by which was usually meant non-WASPs, since most of the immigrants were Catholic or Jewish and from Southern and Eastern Europe. At the same time, the country underwent a period of reform, a period characterized by declarations of high moral purpose and a missionary sense that the more enlightened should help the less fortunate. These two coincident trends translated into a desire to assimilate the immigrants as quickly as possible into American life.

Many reformers adhered strongly to what might be termed an *Anglo-conformity* version of the melting pot. That is, even though the ideal picture of a melting pot seemed to imply some democratic equality of cultures in the process of "melting," the fact was, many believed that the prevailing Anglo-American culture was at once the superior and desirable cultural model to confer. Leading educators believed that the public schools would be the prime instrumentality for producing "Americans" on the basis of Anglo-American culture, thus causing the immigrants to lose their distinctive ethnic identities by becoming virtual Anglo-Americans.

Acculturation of the European immigrant children seems to have occurred, but not entirely in the way envisioned by the reformers. Anglo-American culture itself was permanently changed by the immigrants, in ways too numerous and complex to recount here. Alongside this process of multicultural synthesis, intermarriage occurred among the various European ethnic groups. Today, it is likely that a majority of Americans can claim the ancestry of several European nationalities or ethnic groups (Seller, 1977). Yet it remains a glaring fact of U.S. society that intermarriage between European and non-European Americans has not occurred in nearly the same proportions as it has among Europeans. To the extent that so-called miscegenation has taken place, it has not been recognized or acknowledged as an integral part of the melting-pot ideal.

This disparate treatment of intermarriage is a direct result of racism and racist practices of segregation and discrimination. It also has to do with the fact that the offspring of so-called interracial relationships have not been accorded a distinctive identity, either socially or officially, an identity in which the quality of being mixed is vested, embodied, and otherwise given real meaning. This failure to accommodate what are regarded as interracial relations and people in the United States is, at heart, an unresolved American identity crisis, a dilemma that perpetuates ethnic and "racial" disunion and makes the resolution of the general race problem virtually impossible.

La Raza Cósmica Versus the Melting Pot

The prevailing attitude toward race among the masses throughout Latin America might be summarized as comparative indifference. Of course, this is far from concluding that the region is the exaggerated stereotype of a "racial paradise." Indeed, by observing the disproportion of darker people in the lower classes and of lighter people in the upper classes, one might be led to conclude that race is at least as much of an active principle in Latin America as it is in the United States. But this is not quite true. For example, how is it that the Mexicans could elect a full-blooded Indian, Benito Juárez, as their president around the time of the U.S. Civil War? How is it that Peruvians of today elected an Asian their president? Many Mexican and other Latin American leaders have been and are of mixed blood. Then what explains the apparent tie between race and class in Latin America?

Many sociologists have long noted that in the absence of effective countermeasures, poverty and wealth alike tend to be inherited (Harris, 1971, chap. 18). Thus in Latin America the caste form of racism that was the hallmark of its colonial past has become ensconced, even though legal racial discrimination has long since been done away with. Add to this the blurring of racial lines on a large scale over hundreds of years, such that customary forms of discrimination based on actual ancestry have been rendered impotent. Taken together, these factors are what is usually meant by the observation that the race question in Latin America has by and large been transformed into a socioeconomic issue (Morner, 1970).

It needs to be said, however, that active remnants of attitudinal racism persist. One of these presents itself as "colorism" or even "featurism," neither of which requires proof of actual ancestry to be operative. Professor G. Reginald Daniel of the University of California, Los Angeles, very aptly terms this phenomenon a "recapitulation of racism" (personal communication, February 1991). To what extent this attitude affects whatever social mobility is available to poor people of any phenotype in Latin America remains to be definitively measured. Some evidence for it can be seen in the disproportion of European-looking models and actors in the Latin American media, although another, probably coexistent, explanation for this is that, for socioeconomic reasons, access to the media is easier for the predominantly lighter elite. There is also a conservative tendency to ape the European and U.S. media.

Another remnant of racism can be heard in many derogatory expressions that include the term *indio* (or other, usually vulgar, terms for Black). Though originally directed at *indios*, these epithets have become generalized insults often used even by their supposed objects, the purely racist feeling having been muted or lost (as, for instance, we might use the expression "welshed"). However, in those districts where Native American communities remain relatively intact, such as in the Yucatán, the Andes, and the many isolated mountain settlements throughout Latin America, these expressions still carry their hard edge and reflect a real, present-day situation of unresolved interethnic conflict and outright oppression.

In the United States, it is the biological aspect of race and racial mixture that is essential to racist thinking, quite apart from any other consideration. This attitude finds expression in the failure of our society and its institutions officially to acknowledge racial mixture, potentially the basis for a unifying national identity and a crucial step for breaking down traditional lines of social separation. Such an important omission unnecessarily contributes to the perpetuation of ethnic divisiveness in U.S. society.

Historically Evolved Cultural Factors

Since both the United States and Latin America came into existence from the same expansionary impulse of a Europe reawakening out of medievalism, what might explain the contrasting attitudes regarding race and race mixture?

SEX RATIO DIFFERENCES

An important difference between the Anglo-dominated colonization of North America and the Iberian conquest of Central and South America was that the Spanish and Portuguese came primarily as soldiers and priests, while the British (and Dutch) came as religious rebels and farmers. That is to say, the Iberians had proportionally fewer of their countrywomen with them than did the Anglos. Thus sexual relations occurred more frequently between the Iberians and the indigenous and African slave women, and, consequently, the numbers of "mixed" people began to increase in Latin America relative to Anglo America right from the outset.

Because interracial unions were less common in Anglo America, their rare occurrence was regarded as aberrational and, hence, in a religiously puritanical milieu where anything unusual was cause for alarm, deeply sinful. On the other hand, while the Catholic church was not at all tolerant of any sexual relations outside of marriage, interracial sexual relations within the bounds of marriage were permitted and at times even encouraged. Nevertheless, the vast majority of interracial sexual relations occurred outside of marriage in Latin America, to the extent that the very terms for a mixed person, *mestizo* and *mulato*, became synonyms for *bastard*.[9] In Mexico, use of the term *mestizo* was not really legitimized until the Revolution of 1910. Today it is regarded by most Mexicans as an honorable badge of national identity (if it is given any thought at all) (Páz, 1950/1961).

RACIAL CLASSIFICATIONS

Another striking difference between Anglo and Latin America can be seen in the systems of racial classification. In Anglo America, no mixed category has ever existed officially, except as a means for assigning all people of any discernible African ancestry to the status of "Negro." This principle of classifying Blacks has been referred to as the "one-drop rule." In common parlance, terms such as *mulatto*, *Eurasian*, and *half-breed* (or simply *breed*) have been used, but never adopted as ongoing racial categories.[10] This institutional refusal to make a place for a racially mixed identity is strong evidence for the visceral abhorrence of race mixture in U.S. culture. Further evidence can be seen in that peculiar rule of "check one box only" with which multiethnic children and adults are constantly confronted (which parent and heritage shall be denied today?).

In Latin America, on the other hand, elaborate racial taxonomies gained official recognition from the outset, drawing on Spain's own national experience. Some of these have already been mentioned. In the Spanish colonies, these *casta* designations became distinct identities unto themselves, with legal rights as well as disabilities attaching to each.[11] Most, if not all, of Spain's colonies abolished the *casta* system upon their independence. Classifications based on race persisted in some official documents, but discriminatory application of laws based on race was forbidden, something that did not occur in the United States until the middle of the twentieth century. Today, given the large degree of mixture in the Latin American countries, racial classifications are virtually meaningless and hence, for the most part, are no longer used.

"NORDIC" VERSUS "LATIN" CULTURAL ATTITUDES

The people who came to America from Roman Catholic Iberia and Germano-Protestant England arrived with different historically evolved preconceptions regarding relations with different peoples and other cultures—on the one hand, a distaste for cosmopolitanism; on the other, a relative tolerance. Due primarily to its imperial character, the Roman world of which Spain (Hispania) was an integral part developed over time a multiethnically tolerant culture, a culture virtually devoid of xenophobia. The Romans typically absorbed the cultures as well as the territories of the peoples they conquered. Outstanding among their cultural acquisitions were the Greek tradition and, later, the Judaic tradition. It was the Roman co-optation of Judaic Christianity that the Spanish inherited as Catholicism.

The stamp of Roman cosmopolitanism is unmistakable in the universalism of Catholicism. The spirit of Roman imperialism, with pope substituting for Caesar, is likewise clear in the crusading, missionary aspect of Catholicism. Their descendants (in part), the Spanish Christians, became particularly renowned for their zealousness, reinforced no doubt by their 700-year war against Moslem Spain.[12] This historical inheritance was deeply ingrained in the Spanish soldiery and in the missionaries who followed Columbus into Mexico and Peru (and also in the Portuguese who invaded Brazil).[13] It is not at all inappropriate that their conquered domains became known as Latin America.

On the other hand, the predominantly Germanic peoples of Northwestern Europe emerged into history at the margins of the Roman empire, constantly at war with the legions, not fully conquered or assimilated into Roman life. This condition of perpetual resistance against an alien power and culture must have had a profound and negative effect on the German attitude toward foreigners in general (many ethnic groups were represented in the Roman legions). When Rome finally weakened from within, it was primarily the Germans, the "barbarians," who descended on it—Goths, Franks, Angles, Saxons, Lombards, and so on. The persistence of the German disdain for Romans, non-Germans, and even other Germanic peoples, born of their struggles against the Romans, can also be seen later in history as an important element in the Protestant schism with Rome accomplished by the German Martin Luther. It is no coincidence that Protestantism is primarily a phenomenon of Northwestern Europe while Catholicism is mainly associated with Southern Europe.

THE NATIVE AMERICANS, NORTH AND SOUTH

The difference in the size and nature of the Native American populations in Anglo and Latin America also helps account for the emergence of different attitudes about race. In that part of North America in which the English, Dutch, and others settled, the indigenous peoples were by and large nomadic or seminomadic and not very numerous. Moreover, the socioeconomic and technological distance between the settlers and the indigenous peoples they encountered allowed the settlers from England and other parts of Northwestern Europe to regard surviving Native Americans as savages, mere objects of the wilderness to be moved out of the way. The Anglos, for the most part, felt they had little reason to respect Native Americans (notwithstanding later maudlin stories about the "noble savage"), nor did they feel any need to compromise with them, or to abide by the few compromises that were made.

Entire peoples were segregated, forcibly removed, or exterminated. The occasional exceptions to this history of genocide are few and far between. Although some intermarriage occurred, and some native peoples managed to survive in various desperate, ingenious, and often fortuitous ways, the major outcome was the virtual disappearance of Native Americans as a significant part of North American society (see the contributions in this volume by Daniel, Chapter 8; Wilson, Chapter 9).

In those parts of the Americas to which the Spanish came, particularly Mexico and Peru, the indigenous peoples lived a settled, advanced (even by European standards) agricultural life with large cities and developed class systems. They were also very numerous, despite the estimated disease mortality rate of nearly 90% following the first contacts with Europeans. Eliminating them, even if the idea had occurred to the Spanish, would probably have been impossible. Instead, the Spanish found it advantageous to graft their feudal society onto the semifeudal structures of the Native American civilizations already in place. Spaniards, in the absence of their countrywomen, married into Indian ruling-class families, thereby acquiring key kinship ties to the various peoples composing the Mexican and Incan empires. In short, the Spanish integrated themselves and their culture into communities of civilized (defined as above, in terms of relative technological and socioeconomic development) peoples. Instead of genocide, they opted for a more profitable (and brutally exploitative) *modus vivendi.*

In contrast to the Anglo settlers, many, though not all, of the Spanish came to regard the Native Americans as people rather than savages.[14] The Catholic church itself eventually recognized this and, in theory at least, maintained that an Indian could become the spiritual equal of a Spaniard, if only he or she converted to Christianity. Of course, there was no question about who was superior in secular life, but the very idea of making a place for the Native American in Spanish colonial society demonstrated an attitude far different from the outright genocidal policies carried out further to the north. This difference resulted in a greater permissiveness in the Iberians regarding miscegenation, an attitude that was to some extent generalized to include Africans.

RACE CONSCIOUSNESS AND "SCIENTIFIC" RACISM

A major ideological difference between the United States and Latin America respecting race and race consciousness is a result of the development of "race theory," a pseudoscientific expression of social Darwinism in the nineteenth century. It is this theory and concept of race to which most Americans have become accustomed, particularly in the form of the "three-race theory" (King, 1981; Stepan, 1982). It is also the basis of modern racism.[15]

Whereas the idea that the human species might be divided up into distinct subspecies marked by skin color or other superficial features had occurred before, it was not until the scientific revolution that accompanied the Industrial Revolution in Europe and North America that such divisions were elevated to the status of "science." The first outstanding proponent of the race theory was the Count Gobineau, a petty French noble among whose occupations had been an ambassadorship in Rio de Janeiro from 1868 to 1870. Of that stay, he once wrote, revealingly: "This is not a country to my taste. An entirely Mulatto population, corrupted in body and soul, ugly to a terrifying degree" (quoted in Morner, 1967). His *Essay on the Inequality of the Human Races* became the starting point for a long line of intellectual racists, culminating in the atrocities of the Nazi death camps (Biddess, 1970). Other Europeans and Americans of European ancestry took up the race theory with relish, perhaps noting how conveniently it displaced onto "nature" human responsibility for discriminatory laws and practices, the drawing of territorial borders, the annexation and government of non-Europeans in the interests of overseas commercial empires, and so forth.

Today, most anthropologists reject traditional race theory, though their continued occasional use of its terminology betrays its stubborn influence, and remains a source of ongoing debate. Reputable anthropologists will typically use the alternative term *population* to refer to groupings of humans having various genetic frequencies. But these groups are predefined by the researcher, their boundaries changing depending on what it is that he or she wishes to study. When discussing the very real sociocultural distinctions that exist among human societies, terms such as *tribe, ethnic group, class,* and *religion* are preferred. These labels do not suffer from the disabilities of the term *race* because they are acknowledged to be artifices of humankind, with no pretense or implication of being "natural."

In the nineteenth century, pseudoscientific concepts of race had a decisive influence on the public mind in Europe and the United States, an influence that continues right down to the present. On the other hand, though race theory was disseminated and discussed among the intelligentsia in Latin America, it never caught on among the masses of the people in the same way as it did here. The reasons for this different receptivity have much to do with the various historically evolved cultural factors reviewed above.

DEMOGRAPHIC DIFFERENCES

The outcome of the differing conditions outlined above brings us finally to the most important difference between Latin and Anglo America with regard to race: the fact that people of mixed racial ancestry came to form a much greater proportion of the population in Latin America than in Anglo America. This simple fact meant that, in varying degrees, race was neutralized as a significant social issue (or at least transformed into a class issue) throughout much of Latin America while it remains one of the most salient features of North American life.

MEXICAN AMERICANS IN THE MELTING POT

The United States is poised to integrate the greatest diversity of ethnic groups across all traditional "race" lines that the world has yet seen. As the "browning of America" accelerates through the course of the next few decades, the question of race in all its dimensions will have to be resolved. With their numbers rapidly growing, Mexican Americans, together with their Latino cousins, will undoubtedly exercise an increasing influence on the future development of U.S. culture. Indeed, that influence has already occurred in our folk culture—witness the all-American cowboy, originally the *vaquero*, the Mexican mestizo ranch hand of what is now the American Southwest.

But perhaps the most important contribution is yet to come, that is, in the reshaping of our attitudes about race and especially about race mixture. As the bearers of Latin America's historicocultural experience and familiar with the ways of U.S. society, Mexican Americans are uniquely positioned to upset the traditional Anglo-American taboo against "race mixing" by merely reaffirming their heritage. Concretely, Chicanos and their Latino cousins are also favorably positioned to mediate alliances among the various racial and ethnic groups that make up the U.S. population, something the African American group, for all its accomplishments, could not do, defined as it was (and is still) by the dominant White culture. Latinos, and especially Mexican Americans, have been conditioned by their history, however imperfectly and unevenly, to accept racial ambiguity and mixture as "normal." This attitude might be of enormous benefit to all of us in the United States. First, the race question may be neutralized and energies redirected to other pressing socioeconomic issues. Second, the principle of *mestizaje*, or "multicultural synthesis," as a social norm, a truer expression of the old melting-pot thesis, can free us all from the limits of ethnocentrism by opening us up to a wider repertoire of cultural elements, thereby stimulating our creativity to the fullest. From this, we can reap economic as well as psychological benefits. As a society, we will then be especially well suited to shape the ongoing emergence of a truly global community.

Unfortunately, it must be noted here that the pervasiveness of U.S. culture in Latin America as well as the assimilation of Latin American immigrants into it within this country has had some effect of instilling U.S.-style race consciousness. Thus some Latin Americans will adopt views against intermarriage or repeat what racist Whites say about African and Asian Americans, or even Latin Americans of nationalities different from their own.[16] There are also some who will insist on the purity of their Spanish ancestry and culture, by which they mean White, European ancestry, especially if they are phenotypically light-skinned, even though, for most, such hoped-for purity is extremely dubious.[17] The self-proclaimed "Hispanic" who has definite African or Native American features is particularly absurd and foolish.

Which way will the Latino community go? Nonracial ethnocentrism? Anglo conformity? *Hispanidad*? *Indigenismo*? Afrocentrism? Or *mestizaje*? The decision must be made. In this society, deeply scarred by racism, evading the issue will prove useless. Latinos cannot avoid the reality of their mixed identity without losing themselves. In the process of asserting their mixed identity, Mexican Americans and other Latinos will have little choice but to challenge traditional American race thinking.[18]

Conclusion

Whether we in the United States change our attitudes as a society or not, the numbers of "mixed," "blended," "brown," "cosmic," "melded," or simply *multiethnic* people will grow, in both numbers and complexity. Moreover, our global society is rapidly becoming a union of all cultures, the old cultures not dying, but living on in new forms. It is in the minds of the multiethnic children that the new culture of the future world society is being synthesized. There will be no place for racism or ethnocentrism in this new world, because the multiethnic children cannot hate or disrespect their parents and their heritage without sacrificing their own personal integrity and peace of mind.

What will happen in this future world of race or ethnic irrelevance? As many have speculated, national cultures may indeed disappear as independent entities, to be replaced not by the homogeneous-monotony specter we often hear about (really what narrow cultural nationalism is about—rigid, forced conformity to an ideal, monolithic cultural standard), but by a society that recognizes and respects diversity at the level of the individual.

The fulfillment of the melting-pot and *La Raza Cósmica*—ideals and realities on the continents of the Western Hemisphere—these will form the real New World for all humankind.

Notes

1. Intermarriages of Blacks and Whites, for example, historically among the lowest of all so-called interracial marriage rates, although among the highest in absolute numbers, more than tripled in number between 1970 and 1990, increasing 30% between 1980 and 1990 (see U.S. Bureau of the Census, 1991b, Table 54).

2. Although there is no accurate way of knowing the numbers of "mixed" people, since there is no mixed category on U.S. Census forms, strong evidence for concluding there has been a significant increase can be found in the 1990 census, in which the "other" population, the category chosen by many mixed people, was the third-fastest growing group (45.1% change since 1980) after Asians and Hispanics, and the fourth-largest group in absolute numbers (9,804,847) after Whites, Blacks, and Hispanics (U.S. Bureau of the Census, 1991a, Table 1). Other evidence includes the proliferation of community and campus interracial/multiethnic advocacy and support groups over the last decade, culminating in November 1988 with the founding of the first nationwide organization, the Association of Multiethnic Americans (AMEA).

3. *La Raza Cósmica* is the title of an essay by the Mexican philosopher and educator José Vasconcelos (1925/1979), in which he proclaims and extolls the spiritual virtues that may ensue from the fact that America—in particular, Latin America—has become the site of the first large-scale mixture of "races" in the world. As Minister of Education he took every opportunity to foster a unified Mexican identity. Vasconcelos was responsible for the motto of the National Autonomous University of Mexico (my father's alma mater): "Por mi raza, el espíritu se hablará" (Through my race [the mixed race], the spirit shall speak).

4. Of course, any discussion of race or racial mixing presumes the existence of "race" or, more specifically, the existence of the particular concept of race that holds sway in the popular consciousness. See infra.

5. *Mexica* (pronounced meshEEca), besides being the origin of the name for the country of Mexico, is also the probable origin of *Chicano*, a slang term for Mexican Americans popularized in the 1960s. In colonial times, many in the Spanish upper class did not consider themselves "Mexican," that is, Indian or mestizo. Thus they might refer

to ordinary Mexicans derogatorily as *xicanos*. The usage was carried over into the United States, where Mexican American youths transformed *Chicano* into a term of pride and defiance.

6. There is some debate about this among demographers, some of whom maintain that a majority of Brazilians are "White," but, given the long-cherished tradition of "passing" as well as the different socioeconomically oriented concept of race in Brazil, not to mention the practical difficulties in accurately counting the poor, this assertion is highly doubtful (see Degler, 1971).

7. A Brazilian saying goes, "A rich Negro is a White and a poor White is a Negro" (see van den Berghe, 1967).

8. Cuba, Puerto Rico, and the Dominican Republic are mixed-race countries with the Spanish-African mixture predominant. In Colombia, Venezuela, and Panama, the mixed-race population is the majority, with the Native American, African, and Spanish elements very nearly balanced, biologically and culturally. Bolivia, Paraguay, and Guatemala are countries in which Native Americans are the majority, the mestizos being the next largest group, with Europeans of various nationalities making up the remainder of the population. Argentina and Uruguay are anomalies in Latin America, both having European majorities (predominantly Spanish and Italian), although in Argentina there does exist a significant mestizo minority. Peru, Ecuador, Nicaragua, El Salvador, and Honduras are predominantly mestizo and Indian countries, much like Mexico, with some Asians and people of partial African ancestry. Chile and Costa Rica are mestizo countries having sizable European minorities, mainly Spanish, but in Chile including some English and Germans. (See the Area Handbook Series published by the U.S. Department of State.)

9. The number of terms for the various mixtures of peoples in Latin America far exceeds the two mentioned here. In fact, the race terminology in popular usage and adopted into law by many states in the United States is directly derived from the Spanish: *Negro* (from the Spanish word for *black*), *mulatto* (from the Spanish *mulato*, which means mule, meaning half Black and half White), *quadroon* (from the Spanish *cuarterón*, or one-quarter Black), *octoroon* (from the Spanish *octorón*, or one-eighth Black), *sambo* (from the Spanish *zambo*, or Black and Indian), and *maroon* (from the Spanish *cimarrón*, or runaway Black slave). Many other terms were also used, including *coyote*, *pardo*, *castizo*, *morisco*, *lobo*, and *chino*. Collectively, the mixed groups were called *castas* (castes). See O'Crouley (1774/1972) and Woodbridge (1948).

10. The U.S. Census, for example, included mulatto and quadroon during some censuses, but not consistently, and certainly with no bearing on the legal rights of the people so designated.

11. *Casta* was a term midway in meaning between "estate" and "race." To the extent it meant race it had a spiritual or ethnic sense rather than the genetic sense to which we are accustomed (Castro, 1971).

12. Unlike the German conflict with the Romans, this war was not essentially an ethnic war, since, ethnically, the masses of Christian and Moslem Spaniards were virtually indistinguishable; intermarriage among Arabs, Berbers, Moors, Goths, Jews, Celto-Iberians, Romano-Iberians, and Basques had been common (see Castro, 1971).

13. Both Cortéz and Pizarro grew up near Roman-founded towns and were well versed in Roman legends of conquest.

14. The question of Native American humanity was the subject of a famous debate in Valladolid, Spain, between Bartolomé de las Casas and Juan Ginés de Sepúlveda

during the sixteenth century. Sepúlveda invoked Aristotle's thesis that some people are naturally slaves. Las Casas argued that slavery and generally brutal treatment of Native Americans violated Christian principles. Las Casas won the debate, and the Laws of the Indies resulted. Unfortunately, Las Casas's solution to Native American slavery was African slavery, a view that he later apparently recanted. That any controversy existed at all during this early period says much about Spanish attitudes regarding race compared with those of other Europeans (including their fellow Iberians, the Portuguese) of that or subsequent times. For an excellent examination of this famous debate, see Hanke (1959/1970).

15. I contend that in its most essential sense, racism is a system of thinking, an *ideology*, based on the concept of race.

16. In March 1989, 82% of "Hispanic" men who got married married Hispanic women, while 85% of "Hispanic" women married Hispanic men. The Mexican intermarriage rate was nearly the same as the overall "Hispanic" rate, while it was actually higher (28%) for Puerto Rican men (see U.S. Bureau of the Census, 1990).

17. Even if this is true in any given instance, Spaniards and Spanish culture are a mixture anyway, including the ancestry of Black Africans, Gypsies (from India), and Semites (Jews, Arabs, and Phoenicians), as well as Romans, Celts, Germans, Greeks, Berbers, Basques, and probably more. Today, there are even many mestizo and *mulato* immigrants from Latin America resident in Spain.

18. Interestingly, more than 96% of the 9.8 million people who declined to choose a particular race by checking the "other race" box on the 1990 census forms were "Hispanics" (J. García, demographic analyst, U.S. Bureau of the Census, Ethnic and Hispanic Branch, personal communication, May 1991).

11

From Dust to Gold: The Vietnamese Amerasian Experience

KIEU-LINH CAROLINE VALVERDE

There is a new Southeast Asian immigrant group coming to the United States. Unlike immigrants and refugees of past years, this group is multiracial. Pearl S. Buck coined the term *Amerasians* for them in her novel, *East Wind, West Wind* (1930). In this chapter we use this term to refer to people having Vietnamese mothers and American fathers.

The Vietnam war ended in 1975, leaving approximately 30,000 Amerasian children without legal or social equality; the Amerasians, labeled as worthless half-breeds, endured ostracism from Vietnam's physically homogeneous society. In a culture in which patriarchy is strictly observed, and the father is the symbol of the household, the fatherless Amerasians were not fully accepted by Vietnamese society (Trautfield, 1984).

In the face of rejection from both parent countries, the Amerasian experience may be characterized as that of "marginal man" status (Stonequist, 1937). Amerasians are caught between the politics of two nations, between immigrant and refugee status, between two races, cultures, and philosophies, between subhuman and human status, and between "dust" and "gold." This marginal situation is not one Amerasians accept or want, but without an "Amerasian voice" to empower themselves, they continue to struggle. Their lives consist of enduring hardship in Vietnam and then battling through endless red tape and insensitive immigration laws before coming to the United States and adapting to a new culture. Their hope is to find the "Amerasian voice" and shed the marginal status society has created for them.

Historical and Cultural Characteristics

In Vietnam, the welfare of children from interracial marriages is not a new phenomenon. During Vietnam's long struggle for independence from the domination of its northern neighbor, China, and during French control, many children were born of interracial relationships. At the end of the first Indochina war, France and Vietnam negotiated, among other things, the issue of Vietnamese Eurasians. When discussion started in Geneva in 1954, after the French defeat at Dien Bien Phu, the topics included withdrawal of all the French troops from Vietnam, the release of all French prisoners of war, and the repatriation of all Eurasians (of whom there were estimated to be at that time about 25,000) (A. Bradshaw, 1989). The French government, among other things, offered the Vietnamese Eurasians citizenship at age 18 and provided repatriation travel and, most important, educational opportunities (Trautfield, 1984). The memory of those events remains vivid for a Vietnamese Eurasian living in the United States as she speaks of the period of repatriation for Eurasians to France: "Most of my Eurasians friends went to France to study. They wrote back home to their mothers about their life in France. And some, after getting their French citizenship, brought their Vietnamese mothers to France" (quoted in Valverde, 1988).

In contrast to France's historical arrangement, when the Vietnamese war ended in 1975 the United States lacked policies concerning the Amerasians fathered by U.S. servicemen and civilians. The United States showed no intention of recognizing these children. Domestic issues took priority over the Amerasian situation. In subsequent years, the mass exodus of Southeast Asian refugees captured world attention. The Amerasians, however, were simply forgotten.

Various reasons may account for the apparent lack of concern and interest in Amerasians on the part of the U.S. government. First, with the victory of the Communists in Southeast Asia, the United States severed all diplomatic ties with the respective countries (including Vietnam). Second, Vietnam was the only battlefield in U.S. history from which it did not emerge victorious. The U.S. government, and the American people, simply seemed to want to forget the failure. Finally, the U.S. government directed its attention toward refugee resettlement, servicemen reported missing in action, and prisoners of war (A. Bradshaw, 1989). Amerasians then became victims of international diffidence.

The Amerasian Experience in Vietnam

The Amerasian experience in Vietnam was largely traumatic and dehumanizing. Amerasians abandoned in Vietnam endured Communist persecution because of their mothers' involvement with Americans, prejudice because of their racial makeup in a homogeneous society, and classism because they were fatherless in a patriarchal society (Trautfield, 1984). Cumulatively, these factors sentenced these children to a marginal status in the most negative of senses, and in their eventual departure for the United States placed them between refugee and immigrant status.

After the war, an anti-American campaign encouraged victimization of Amerasians and their family members. It was not uncommon to find mothers of Amerasians singled out for relocation and a difficult life in the harsh "new economic zones." One mother of an Amerasian was assigned to hard labor after the war as criminal punishment for marrying an American (Haselkorn & Lu, 1988). Faced with difficult survival situations, many mothers either abandoned their Amerasian children or sent them to the countryside to stay with grandparents or other relatives. The countryside served as a safe haven from discrimination. Most frequently, Amerasians grew up with unmarried biological mothers or adoptive mothers. It was also common for them to be brought up by aunts, grandmothers, or other close relatives (Felsman, Johnson, Leong, & Felsman, 1989). Even in households with stepfathers, Amerasian children were alienated because of the favoritism bestowed on the monoracial children (J. Dang, Santa Clara certified worker, Amerasian County Project coordinator, personal communication, April 1, 1990).

A Vietnamese saying maintains that "a child without a father is like a house without a roof." In a society in which identity and self-definition are derived through patriarchal lineage, the trauma of an unknown father follows an individual through life (Valverde, 1989b). The fatherlessness of Amerasians thus broadens beyond the issue of abandonment. One Amerasian woman interviewed recalled an incident in which she was humiliated for not having a father. Her teacher had asked the children in her class to write their fathers' names on information cards. When she could not do so because she did not know her father's identity, the teacher made her stand in front of the class to explain why she did not know her father's whereabouts. Then the children teased her and told her to go back to her father's country.

Being physically conspicuous in a homogeneous society worsened the situation for Amerasians. The Vietnamese subjected Amerasians to racial abuse on a daily basis in the form of name-calling: *con lai* (half-breed), *my lai* (American mix), or *my den* (Black American). "I hear them calling me 'my lai' as I pass home from school every day, but I ignore it, keeping in mind that once home, I will be safe," commented an Amerasian woman. She added that this type of teasing hurt her deeply, but she kept her sorrows to herself; not even able to confide in her mother, she endured her pain in solitude (Valverde, 1988).

Black Amerasians encountered the most discrimination because their dark skin made them conspicuous (*Amerasian Update*, January 1991; Felsman et al., 1989). The Vietnamese, much like other Asian groups, look down on dark skin, which they equate with the lower peasant class or *ethnic* minorities. A Black Amerasian woman we spoke with said that she had asked her mother about the likelihood of a marriage between herself and a Vietnamese man. Her mother replied that her only chance of getting married entailed going to Cambodia, a bordering country, and finding a Cambodian husband who would accept her despite her skin color. In another instance, a mother hid her Black Amerasian child in the attic whenever visitors stopped by the house, for fear that he might be harmed; in an interview he told us he remembers occasions, such as New Year's celebrations, when he silently witnessed the festivities through a narrow crack in the attic floor.

Some Amerasians integrated into the homogeneous society because their biracial heritage was less obvious. One Amerasian women commented in an interview that she faced minimal problems in Vietnam and was able to advance in school because she made herself appear "Vietnamese."

Discrimination kept Amerasians from obtaining high levels of education. In the early school years, other children teased them for being multiracial. This often led to low self-esteem, and many opted to quit school altogether. At the high school level, the Vietnamese government purposefully kept Amerasians from advancing (J. Dang, personal communication, April 15, 1989). Blatant discrimination existed as well. One Amerasian boy was told to leave school during the ninth grade because he "gave the school a bad name." Others did not attend school because of lack of funds. In Vietnam, an education is still regarded as a luxury. When Amerasians tried to make a living, they faced the double burden of discrimination in the job market because of their physical appearance and subsequent lack of education.

Vietnamese society defined the Amerasians without looking at their social and cultural circumstances. For instance, Amerasians without supportive families left home and tried to make a living in big cities such as Ho Chi Minh City (formerly Saigon). This contributed to the prejudice, because society saw homeless Amerasians roaming the streets and making money in suspect ways. Consequently, Amerasians came to be referred to as *bui doi* (dust of life), which is equated with homeless or rebellious individuals. The bleak situation of surviving in a society in which they existed as marginal beings left Amerasians with little hope for a better life. Unable to advance because of their multiracial background, their future was to live as dregs of society.

Amerasian Legislation

Although Amerasians have lived in Vietnam since the mid-1950s, only recently has the United States assumed responsibility for Amerasians by offering them the right to immigrate to America. With the passage of the Amerasian Act (Public Law 97-359) in 1982 and the present Homecoming Act, passed in 1988, thousands of Amerasians have immigrated to the United States and thousands continue to arrive. Amerasians, for the first time, feel wanted by the "land of their fathers." Although these breakthrough acts of Congress have benefited Amerasians, they are not flawless. Untimely and insensitive to Amerasian needs, they deserve close scrutiny. Amerasians' two parent countries have forced them to wait for justice, while the United States and Vietnam "negotiated" their lives.

The United States began its involvement in Vietnam as early as 1954, when the first group of military advisers arrived in Saigon. The first combat units arrived in the early 1960s, and the number kept increasing until it reached half a million toward the end of the decade. Many Amerasian children were born during that period. To our knowledge, there are no records or documents demonstrating any awareness of this important issue.

Ignored by the U.S. government, Vietnamese mothers had little knowledge or power with which to assert their rights and those of their Amerasian children. In one incident, a Vietnamese woman attempted to claim American citizenship for her Amerasian son, only to have the father deny his relationship and responsibility by calling her a prostitute (Valverde, 1990).

After the war, the American government continued to ignore the Amerasians and the Vietnamese continued to discriminate against them. The Amerasian plight remained unknown to most of the American people. This changed as journalists and visiting U.S. officials began to go to Vietnam, where they witnessed the Amerasian dilemma. Ten years after the American military presence in Vietnam ended, a *Newsweek* article titled "Where Is My Father?" publicized the living legacy of U.S. involvement in Vietnam (Beck et al., 1985). With the testimonials of those who had returned from Vietnam and wide exposure that followed, the public finally confronted the Amerasian issue. Whether because of purely humanitarian reasons, because of a sense of responsibility, or because Americans once again felt a dire need to save those "less fortunate," the public overwhelmingly sympathized with the Amerasian plight. Stories of Amerasians reuniting with their fathers seemed to be especially attractive, although reunions of fathers and Amerasian children take place in only about 2% of cases (Keegan, 1987). Other "human interest" stories included ones that depicted U.S. citizens as saving their poor half-American children from the terrible conditions in Vietnam. The media stereotyped Amerasians as helpless children searching for their American fathers ("Amerasians Coming 'Home,' " 1988; Cleeland, 1988).

Although the media tended to overdramatize and mislead, they aided in fostering public support for the Amerasian plight. The public proved instrumental in pressuring the government to take action in helping the Amerasians. The little the public knew about Amerasians was enough to convince the U.S. government of its accountability. Subsequent attempts were made to bring the Amerasians to America.

The first piece of Amerasian legislation, the Amerasian Act of 1982 (Public Law 97-359), was authored by Senator Jeremiah Denton (Alabama) and Senator Stewart McKinney (Connecticut). The law offered top-priority U.S. immigration to children in Korea, Vietnam, Laos, Cambodia, or Thailand who were known to have been fathered by U.S. citizens.

Although it represented an important breakthrough, the law was nevertheless flawed. First, it granted admission privileges only to the Amerasians, excluding their mothers and other relatives from the immigration process. Second, mothers of Amerasian minors who immigrated had to sign "irrevocable releases." This requirement revealed cultural ignorance on the part of the U.S. government; in the Vietnamese culture, extended family relationships are highly valued (Trautfield, 1984). Third, this piece of legislation classified Amerasians as immigrants and not as refugees. Amerasians were thus unable to take advantage of refugee resettlement programs and services, which contributed to their difficulty adjusting and adapting to the new society (Mrazek, 1987). Finally, to facilitate paperwork, consular and immigration representatives were required to assist with the legal procedures; since there were no diplomatic relations with Vietnam, this task was almost impossible to pursue. Thus the Amerasian Act only marginally served its purpose.

For the Amerasians, the only way to circumvent the inconvenience of the flawed legislation was to go through the Orderly Departure Program (ODP). The U.S. and Vietnamese governments agreed to the ODP procedure, through the U.N. High Commissioner for Refugees (UNHCR), to "regulate" the flow of the "boat people." In 1982, both governments began processing the Amerasian applicants through ODP as priority cases. Through this program Amerasians gained refugee status and the resettlement benefits that they desperately needed (Mrazek, 1987). The first Amerasians to exit Vietnam via the ODP, in late 1982, were children whose American fathers had filed papers for them and who therefore entered the United States as American citizens.

In September 1984, Secretary of State George Schultz, in statements before the House and Senate Judiciary Committees, announced on President Reagan's behalf that over a three-year period the United States would accept for admission all Amerasians, their qualifying mothers, and their siblings—provided they were released by the

Vietnamese government. At that time the estimates of the number of Amerasians varied from 10,000 to 15,000.

To qualify for admission under the program, Amerasian applicants needed to provide evidence that they had American paternity, but they did not need to prove their fathers' identities. The Amerasians were examined for "American" or Caucasian features. Questions arose, of course, when the father was a person of color. Black Amerasians were usually easily distinguished, but what about half Chicanos, Native Americans, or Asian Americans? This left the Amerasians to prove that their fathers were in fact "Americans" (Valverde, 1989a). Acceptable forms of proof included birth certificates, marriage licenses, or letters from and photos of the father. This was difficult documentation to gather; many of these documents had been burned by the mothers when Vietnam fell to protect themselves and their children from Communist persecution (Haselkorn & Lu, 1988).

Between September 1982 and August 1988, ODP brought approximately 4,500 Amerasian children and 7,000 accompanying relatives to the United States, according to U.S. Department of State statistics (Migration and Refugee Services of the United States Catholic Conference, 1988). However, the flaws of this program enabled it to help only a small portion of the thousands of Amerasian children. One of the flaws was the long application process. It often took years to do the paperwork and to be accepted for the distribution of visas (Cleeland, 1988; Moore, 1990). Some Amerasians lived far from Ho Chi Minh City, and trips there were costly. This was most problematic in rural areas, in which Amerasians had to negotiate with and bribe local and city bureaucrats. The local officials took advantage of the Amerasian predicament; bribery was essential to speed up paperwork (J. Dang, personal communication, January 5, 1991).

Matters worsened when the Vietnamese government stopped the ODP in January 1986 (Mrazek, 1987) because Amerasians were being processed as refugees. The government argued that the term *refugee* implied that the Amerasians were being persecuted by their government and, for that reason, they were seeking safe refuge elsewhere (Mrazek, 1987). Although many Amerasians were persecuted in Vietnam, the Vietnamese government preferred that the term *immigrant* be used to describe the Amerasians. Left stranded at this time were 3,000 Amerasians with exit permits waiting to depart from Vietnam to the United States (Vietnam Veterans of America Foundation, 1989).

In actuality, both the United States and Vietnam contributed to the halt in Amerasian processing. For example, they argued over which airline and flight route Amerasians should take. The United States continued to lump Amerasians together with other refugee quotas, which slowed immigration. Furthermore, the Vietnamese government felt that there should be no intervention by the UNHCR, since Amerasians could be considered as legal immigrants and processed directly by American officials (Goose & Horst, 1988). In short, Amerasians fell victim to international differences. After several bilateral meetings, Vietnam agreed to resume ODP processing in July 1987, but Amerasians were not included in this program.

Just when it seemed hopeless for the Amerasians to leave, Representative Robert Mrazek (New York) and Representative Thomas Ridge (Pennsylvania) successfully passed H.R. 3568 on October 28, 1987. Popularly known as the Amerasian Homecoming Act, it allowed for Amerasians born before January 1, 1977, and after January 1, 1962, to immigrate to the United States. It was a two-year plan that allowed 30,000 Amerasians and their immediate family members to depart from Vietnam by March 21, 1990. The Amerasian Homecoming Act also continued to give immigrant status to Amerasians as well as granting them refugee benefits, such as six months of language and culture orientation.

Although the Homecoming Act was quite an improvement compared with the 1982 Amerasian Act, it was still problematic. For one thing, the bill allotted a two-year period for the immigration of all Amerasians from Vietnam. This was naive, as even the most optimistic official estimates suggested it would be almost impossible to process all the applicants by 1990 (Mrazek, 1987). In a list submitted by the government of Vietnam in March 1989, it was estimated that 8,435 Amerasian would have arrived in the United States by September 1989 (*Amerasian Update*, April 1989), but as of February 1989 there was a backlog of 5,600 approved Amerasians who were still waiting in Vietnam. The backlog, in turn, slowed down further Amerasian departures. Before time ran out on the original deadline, a 1991 extension was added to the bill as a temporary remedy to the backlog situation. When the 1991 deadline too seemed unrealistic, another amendment, the Foreign Operations Bill (Public Law 101513), extended the deadline until all Amerasians who wished to leave Vietnam had that opportunity. This bill was signed by President Bush on November 1, 1990 (*Amerasian Update*, November-December 1990).

Another problem arose because the Homecoming Act allowed for Amerasians to come with their immediate families only. This meant that an Amerasian had to choose between bringing a parent and unmarried siblings or a spouse and children. When the legislation was passed, it did not take into account that Amerasians would have families of their own (*Amerasian Update*, February 1990); Amerasians were still perceived of as children. In reality, the average Amerasian arriving in the United States is now 18.5 years old. To divide a family is inhumane in the Vietnamese extended family culture. Amerasians for the most part picked their parents and half-siblings to come with them, assuming it would be easier for them to sponsor their spouses at a later date. Unfortunately, it has not been such an easy process to sponsor someone for immigration to the United States. However, the Public Law 101513 now allows Amerasians to bring their mothers, siblings, spouses, and their children. The Amerasians already here can apply to have their mothers come over now, but to bring over spouses and children requires more paperwork.

The Homecoming Act authors neglected the need to have a transit center in place when the bill went into effect. With nowhere to house Amerasians while they waited to get information about leaving Vietnam, they often congregated in front of the Ministry Office. After efforts by groups such as the Vietnam Veterans of America, an Amerasian Transit Center opened outside of Ho Chi Minh City in January 1990. The center cost $500,000 to build, and it housed several hundred Amerasians at a time (*Amerasian Update*, December 1989; "Transit Center," 1990). Unfortunately, because the transit center offered a better standard of living than the Amerasians were used to, it fostered unrealistic expectations of what was in store for them in the United States (*Amerasian Update*, October 1989; C. Nakashima, personal communication, August 17, 1990).

Finally, not enough Amerasians were informed of the opportunity to leave Vietnam. Currently, only those in large cities are aware of the Homecoming Act and of their opportunity to come to the United States. The Vietnamese government is not helpful in publicizing the Homecoming Act because of the fear that other Vietnamese could try to pass as Amerasian (C. Nakashima, personal communication, August 17, 1990). Ironically, the "dust of life" (*bui doi*) became valuable commodities to be prized as the "gold children" (*con van*). "Fake parents" turned up who attempted to buy Amerasians in order to get a free ticket to the United States (Moore, 1990).

REMEDIES

Although the Homecoming Act came 15 years after the need for it arose, Amerasians were finally given a chance to construct a new life in the United States. However, making immigration laws to meet everyone's expectations is not an easy task. From the first Amerasian Act to the present-day Homecoming Act, the United States has made strides in aiding the Amerasians. Nevertheless, there is still room for improvement. For example, more timely, practical, and well-written immigration laws would have allowed Amerasians to immigrate to the United States at a younger age, when the problems of adaptation would be easier to overcome. More efficient and more humane acts of Congress could have been passed if there had been greater understanding of and sensitivity to Vietnamese culture and the history of Amerasians. This applies especially to the issue of extended family unity in immigration.

Currently, not enough is known about the Homecoming Act in Vietnam. Though some Vietnamese may abuse the system and pose as Amerasians, it is more important to attempt to reach those Amerasians who might otherwise never know about the chance to immigrate to America. A massive advertising program could be set up by the Vietnamese government and overseen or funded by the United States.

These suggestions are offered here because it is not too late to right the wrongs that have been costly for a people already pained by years of neglect and misunderstanding.

The Road to America

After a long and arduous wait for approval to leave Vietnam, which can take years and can cost a life's savings, Amerasians have not been brought directly to the United States. Instead, their settlement has been further delayed for six months to a year, as they are sent to the Philippine Refugee Processing Center (PRPC) for culture orientation. The PRPC functions as a temporary staging facility as well as a learning center that provides language classes, work, and culture orientation sessions to camp residents. However, instead of being beneficial for Amerasians, this program has added further trauma to the Amerasian experience.

Amerasians' time at the PRPC delays their settlement in the United States, which in some cases means delay in the opportunity to begin their education. Time is running out for Amerasians to receive an education, because many are over 17 years old, disqualifying them for the Preparation for American Secondary Schools (PASS) program (*Amerasian Update*, August 1989; Vietnam Veterans of America Foundation, 1989). Without programs such as PASS, Amerasians' chances for an education become slim. As mentioned earlier, many Amerasians did not receive adequate education in Vietnam; some have not attended school at all. Attendance in the PRPC schools is the first experience in a school environment for many Amerasians; at the PRPC, along with their school lessons, they must learn proper school behavior.

Added to the pressure of learning the school system as well as the lessons is the fact that they are uncertain about their future. They have no idea what part of the United States they will be sent to, or what will be in store for them at these locations. Uncertainty about the life they will have in the United States further exacerbates their insecurities about adjusting.

Crowded conditions in the PRPC expose Amerasians to the kinds of undesirable behavior that can exist in such situations (Vietnam Veterans of America Foundation, 1989), including further trauma. In one incident, a 16-year-old girl became pregnant as a result of being raped in the camp. She was afraid to tell anyone for fear that it would delay her trip to the United States. When she finally arrived in the United States, she was at in advanced stage of her pregnancy and by that time it was too dangerous to terminate it.

REMEDIES

A report published by the Vietnamese Veterans of America Foundation in 1989 recommends that since Amerasians are immigrants, they should not be detained for refugee processing. The solution to this problem is to support a program to bring Amerasians directly to the United States, since the six-month PRPC program does not truly prepare them for the "real" American scene in any case. Many camp residents have reported learning "general" American culture that did not have any relevance for them in their resettlement locations. By bypassing the PRPC program, these new immigrants could start language programs, employment training, and cultural orientation in their resettlement locations. A real community context would be more helpful in giving the proper information about American society.

Although it might be cheaper to have the Amerasians go through the PRPC for orientation and training than to fly them directly to the United States, this step may contribute to adjustments they will need to make it in their new country. The implicit double message is that they are both wanted and not wanted, as they are being kept from reaching their final destinations. The United States has an obligation to protect this already vulnerable group and to place its well-being over economic considerations.

Settlement in the United States

Amerasians have come to the United States with great hope and many expectations, including hopes of finding their fathers and social and racial equality. However, once settled here, they have once again faced a society that labels them and neglects their special needs.

INITIAL ADJUSTMENT AND SETTLEMENT

Amerasians have been settled in approximately 40 different cluster sites across the nation in order to avoid overburdening any one area economically. The U.S. government's Office for Refugee Resettlement (ORR) gave $35,000 to each site to be used in setting up programs for Amerasians; this was an inadequate amount. It takes about a year to set up programs for Amerasians, and administrative costs for such setup alone would be more than $35,000, explained a Santa Clara, California, city worker who has been involved with programs for Amerasians (J. Dang, personal communication, January 5, 1991).

Volunteer agencies (which came to be known as Volags) set up programs for Amerasians funded through the government. Resettlement programs vary from site to site. For the most part, these agencies attempt to understand the needs of Amerasians and to pass this information on to other Volags. There is also the *Amerasian Update*, a monthly newsletter put out by InterAction and Lutheran Immigration and Refugee Service under a cooperative agreement with the Office of Refugee Resettlement. Annual conferences are also held for Amerasians so that they can share ideas on Amerasian resettlement.

As much as the Volags attempted to understand the Amerasians and make their transition to life in the United States an easy one, they still lacked insight into the Amerasian plight. Amerasians themselves could not initially articulate their needs because they were overwhelmed by a new land and adjusting to a new culture and language. They faced the dual problem of being refugees and being multiracial. The Volags generally were not equipped to handle this volatile situation, and they operated by trial and error. They tried to work from set formulas for helping Amerasians that included an uncomfortable focus on Amerasian mental health (J. Dang, personal communication, April 1, 1990), although there were few qualified experts to help Amerasians. The discomfort stemmed from Vietnamese cultural stigmas attached to mental health issues. In any case, very little information is available about Amerasian issues in general, let alone in the area of Amerasian mental health.

Amerasians have the dual burden of the Vietnamese refugee experience and the marginal multiracial experience. Therefore, their needs are different than those of "standard" refugees. Uncomfortable in a new land, still without a voice, they continue to carry these burdens.

Like Vietnamese refugees, Amerasians seem to be experiencing a secondary migration pattern (S. Forbes, 1984). Amerasians, being culturally Vietnamese, tend to congregate in areas with large Vietnamese communities; therefore, they are moving away from their initial settlement sites to areas with large Vietnamese populations. Already the majority of Amerasians settled in the United States live in California, which has the highest Vietnamese population in the United States (Office of Refugee Settlement, 1987). However, the Vietnamese American community, like its counterpart in Vietnam, still harbors various myths and preconceived ideas about Amerasians.

VIETNAMESE AMERICAN ATTITUDES TOWARD AMERASIANS

Members of the Vietnamese community in the United States, despite their rhetoric about accepting Amerasians wholeheartedly as their own people, carry the same stereotypes of Amerasians as those found in Vietnam (Valverde, 1989b). Most commonly, Amerasians are seen as illegitimate, resulting from passing relationships that brought Vietnamese bar girls and American GIs together. The children, consequently, are seen as products of "sleazy" liaisons. This is not always the case, however; the overwhelming majority of the relationships that produced Amerasian children averaged two years in length, and many couples were married under "common law" (Lacey, 1985). The author remembers that when she was a child, a Vietnamese playmate was forbidden to play with her because she came from a "bad family background."

Because the community assumes that Amerasians' mothers were cheap bar girls, they place the same stereotype on Amerasian girls and women. Thus Amerasian women, on top of having to deal with racism and classism, also have to deal with sexism. This attitude can be illustrated by an incident that occurred at the Tet Festival at the Santa Clara County Fairgrounds in California in 1990. An Amerasian support organization, the Vietnamese Amerasian Family, had a fund-raising booth, selling cotton candy. An Amerasian woman was working at the booth when a Vietnamese man approached her and asked her the cost of the cotton candy, and then proceeded to ask her how much she cost. Unable to respond because of cultural modesty and shock, she dealt with her humiliation and pain alone (Valverde, 1991).

Another popular notion among Vietnamese Americans is that all Amerasians are uneducated. With this stereotype prevalent throughout the community, Amerasians feel constant pressure to prove their intelligence. One Amerasian wrote that she was once happy that she could pass as a full Vietnamese because she did not have to deal with the prejudice. However, when the Vietnamese found out that she was an Amerasian and well educated, they were surprised (*Amerasian Update*, September 1990). The author has been told that, because of her education, she is not really like other Amerasians. This implies that she is able to attain intelligence only by rejecting her multiracial identity.

Community prejudice may not be blatant, but subtle words can also hurt. It is common in the community to talk about a multiracial person by using his or her first name and the word meaning "mix" (*lai*) after it; an example would be Tuan Lai. Amerasians do not have a common last name of "lai" or "mix" (Valverde, 1991). Also, when referring to Amerasians, Vietnamese frequently use pronouns such as *no*, which is used to refer to animals or very young children. The author attended a wedding where a beautiful Amerasian bride was dressed elegantly in a white wedding dress—only to have the groom's family and friends refer to her as *no*.

AMERICAN COMMUNITY ATTITUDES TOWARD AMERASIANS

With all the problems attached to the Vietnamese community, some Amerasians opt to fit into the mainstream society. What they find are stereotypes as well as adaptation problems. One Black Amerasian woman attempted to approach Black men after she experienced alienation from Vietnamese men in her community. However, the Black men were not receptive to her either, because she was culturally different and unable to communicate with them. Most Americans know very little about the true plight of Amerasians; all they "know" is what they have seen in the media, which, as mentioned, tend to depict Amerasians as lost children. Also, because of cultural and language barriers, Amerasians find it especially difficult to adjust. One Amerasian boy sat in a Spanish/English class for students learning English as a second language for weeks before he mustered the nerve to tell his teacher that he could not understand Spanish or English. In another incident, an Amerasian gentlemen was pulled over by police for driving above the speed limit. When the officer asked him questions that he could not understand, and thus could not answer, the policeman called him a wise guy and harassed him further.

RECOMMENDATIONS

It is difficult to deal with the problems represented by Amerasians as a group. They are not only immigrants, with obvious culture differences, but they also have their own unique history as a multiracial people. However, as complicated as the situation might be, there are some ways in which aid to Amerasians can be improved. First, the problems of Amerasians are often trivialized, because Amerasians are still perceived by the American public as children. As such, they have not been consulted on their own unique needs. Their problems can include crime, domestic violence, and unwanted pregnancy. Instead of second guessing Amerasian needs, Volags could build programs specifically designed to encourage Amerasians to articulate their own needs, keeping in mind the language and culture barriers that exist for Amerasians.

Vietnamese or Amerasian workers can best assist Amerasians in fostering an "Amerasian voice." Amerasians, as mentioned, have not been able to formulate an identity or a place in society; therefore, programs that encourage self-thought, self-pride, and self-help can be most beneficial. It is important for Amerasians to take leadership positions in the Volags. This would both give Amerasians self-pride and provide Volags with a better understanding of Amerasian needs. Amerasians are in the best position to understand their own people's issues.

At this point, Amerasians have only each other to turn to. But, unlike the Amerasian "third culture" experience discussed by Teresa Williams (Chapter 20, this volume), in which Amerasians growing up in military communities in Japan incorporate the two cultures, languages, and nationality, the experience of Vietnamese Amerasians stems from a very different context. They lived in a country in which they were marginalized and treated as outcasts for being fatherless and physically different. There were no signs of American culture for them to cling to, and they did not have the luxury of being bilingual. In fact, they understand all too well the stereotypes about themselves. For this reason, they often shun each other for fear of being thought of as *bui doi*. The third culture can be an option for these Amerasians only after they have had years to adapt to American culture. They also need time to learn to accept their multiracial heritage and to find self-love.

Conclusion

Amerasians have the double burden of being refugees and multiracial. Unlike multiracial groups in the United States, such as fourth-generation Japanese multiracial people, Amerasians in general do not have family support systems or the understanding of U.S. culture. They are immigrants in a new country.

All their lives, Amerasians have been defined by the society at large. One moment they are told that they are as worthless as dust, and the next they are told that they are precious as gold, with a chance to go to America. However, crossing the Pacific does not mean escaping labels and stereotypes. Voluntary agencies, the Vietnamese American community, and the mainstream community all have preconceived ideas about Amerasians. Through education and self-awareness, these groups can learn to confront their stereotypes about Amerasians. The numbers of Amerasians in the United States will continue to grow, and the Vietnamese American community especially needs to make an effort to shake off stereotypes of Amerasians. It seems that Amerasians will inevitably be an accepted presence in the Vietnamese American community, as there is more intermarriage in the community and many Vietnamese are affected at a personal level, such as by having Amerasian children of their own. Time and awareness for the community and self-acceptance and pride on the part of the Amerasians may facilitate mutual acceptance.

As unique as the Amerasian situation might seem, we have to keep in mind that there are people of part-American descent in Korea, the Philippines, Thailand, Taiwan—the list goes on. Where there is U.S. involvement in Asia, there is a likelihood of Amerasians going through much the same experience as Vietnamese Amerasians. It is hoped that the U.S. government can learn to take on the responsibilities of its involvement in foreign countries and end the painful cycle that causes the suffering of multiracial people; the remedies and recommendations offered in this chapter may help toward that goal.

The Amerasians truly exemplify "marginal status," as they are caught among the numerous facets in our society. However, this is not a permanent state. As their adaptation process continues, their voices will be heard and they can begin to assess their lives and build their identity base. They will brush away the dust to find the golden qualities within themselves.

Vietnamese Amerasians, like any other group of people, have varied personalities and needs; stereotypes and sweeping generalizations must be avoided. Amerasians need to see that they can be important contributing members of the community. They need role models, such as Mary Xinh Nguyen, who was Revlon's Most Unforgettable Woman for 1990; Tuan Le, a Stanford University football star; and others who volunteer their time to help Amerasians, such as Jenny Dang, a county worker and founder of the Amerasian Vietnamese Family organization. This list is growing, and more Amerasians are finding strength to help themselves and each other, as this multiracial group comes of age.

Acknowledgments

Thank you Ba Noi for *everything*! Thank you Cindie Nakashima for your constant support and friendship through it all. Thanks to Jenny Dang for her expertise and heart in aiding this report. And, last but not least, a very special thanks to Thien Do for his patience, love, and wisdom, which make every project enjoyable.

12

An Invisible Monster: The Creation and Denial of Mixed-Race People in America

CYNTHIA L. NAKASHIMA

When I ask a class of undergraduates to define the concept of "race," they usually give answers that sound something like, "A person's race is the group that he or she belongs to, such as European American or African American or Asian American or Latino or Native American." When I ask them then to tell me what factors or characteristics constitute a racial group, they talk about heredity, physical appearance, culture, language, community, and political ideology, in roughly that order. But when, at this point, I ask the class which racial group I fit into, they become very quiet. To some people I seem "White." To other people I seem "Asian." To still others who do not know my last name or my field of research, I seem Latino or Polynesian. To those who are from Hawaii or otherwise familiar with people of mixed Asian-European descent, I seem like a "hapa." But even those cosmopolitan individuals who identify my "race" correctly have a hard time answering my original question: What is race? And further, what race is a person of mixed race?

Interestingly, when I ask the same group of undergraduate students to list their images and stereotypes of people of mixed race, they quite confidently express ideas such as the following: Mixed-race people have a hard time adjusting to their multiple cultures; mixed people feel rejected by both or all of their groups; people who are mixed are always really attractive. But is it not strange, I ask them, that they, as representatives of American society, hold such clearly defined images of and attitudes about people of mixed race, while at the same time they are not able to answer the question of where multiracial people fit into the racial order of U.S. society?

This chapter explores two seemingly conflicting, yet actually mutually reinforcing, strategies that the dominant U.S. culture has adopted in dealing with people of multiple racial heritages. The first strategy has been the creation and definition of multiracial people as a group, through the development of biological, sociocultural, and sociopolitical theories and attitudes; the second strategy has been the denial of the existence of multiracial people, both as individuals and as a group.

Mixed-Race People Making Chaos in an "Ordered" Society

Today, social scientists agree that race is a socially constructed, as opposed to a biologically concrete, concept (Fields, 1982; Omi & Winant, 1986; Spickard, Chapter 2, this volume). This is evident in that race has been and is defined in vastly different ways at different times and in different places. Every society has its own socially constructed definition of *race*—and its own definitions of *ethnicity, culture, community, gender,* and so on.

But what happens when an individual or a group of individuals in a particular society subvert one or more of the accepted definitions by their very existence? And what if they go as far as to demand a restructuring and a reconceptualizing of definitions altogether? Just as people who are transsexual, homosexual, and bisexual have upset and challenged the general understanding of gender, sexuality, and family in mainstream American society,[1] people who are multiracial and multicultural have always upset, and are just now beginning to challenge, the understanding of race, ethnicity, culture, and community in the United States. As Omi and Winant (1986) observe:

> One of the first things we notice about people when we meet them (along with their sex) is their race. We utilize race to provide clues about who a person is. The fact is made painfully obvious when we encounter some-

> one whom we cannot conveniently racially categorize—someone who is, for example, racially "mixed." . . . Such an encounter becomes a source of discomfort and momentarily a crisis of racial meaning. Without a racial identity, one is in danger of having no identity. (p. 60)

People who do not neatly fit into a clearly defined race category threaten the psychological and sociological foundations of the "we" and "they" mentality that determines so much of an individual's social, economic, and political experience in the United States. Mainstream American culture and ideology have been informed by a dominant perception that race is something absolute—that each person is either/or, and that races are mutually exclusive.[2] If a person, by birth, belongs to and identifies with more than one racial and cultural group, the monoracially "hegemonic" American culture is forced either to adjust the system to make room for the person or to adjust the person to fit into the system. At least partially because of, and in order to avoid, this dilemma, the United States has had laws prohibiting interracial sex and marriage for most of its history, from the 1600s to 1967 (Kitano & Kikumura, 1973; Spickard, 1989).

But, regardless of both formal and informal prohibitions against their existence, millions of mixed-race people have been born in the United States over the years, in addition to hundreds of thousands who have been born to American citizens outside of the United States. In order to protect the social order that depends so heavily on clear racial boundaries, it has historically been the people of mixed race who have been shaped and molded by dominant society to uphold and to fit into the American system. An exploration of how this has been done not only supplies significant insight into the history of mixed-race people in the United States, but is also very instructive in the study of the formation of racial ideology in America (Fields, 1982; Omi & Winant, 1986).

The Creation of a Multiracial Mythology

Although it is seldom recognized, people of mixed race, like people of other racial and ethnic groups, have their own socially constructed image in American dominant culture. Legislation, with all of its rhetoric, has been aimed directly at multiracial people and their families; religious ideology has been espoused regarding the morality of the creation of multiracial humans; scientific and academic theories have been proposed regarding the biological, psychological, and sociological aspects of multiraciality; and the venues of popular culture—fiction and nonfiction literature, newspaper and magazine articles, television, film, music, comic books, and pornography—have defined a particular set of stereotypes and images specifically related to people of multiracial heritage. As with all "minority" groups, there has been and continues to be a dialectical relationship between these laws, religious ideology, and scientific and social scientific theories and popular cultural ideology, the outcome being a flexible sort of "folk wisdom" about multiracial people.

Although not every theory or attitude or image regarding people of mixed race has been negative, the majority of the ideology has been troublesome. The attack on intermarriage and multiraciality has traditionally been asserted in two ways: (a) in relation to biological reasoning[3] (that it is "unnatural" to "mix the races"; that multiracial people are physically, morally, and mentally weak; that multiracial people are tormented by their genetically divided selves; and that intermarriage "lowers" the biologically superior White race), and (b) in relation to sociocultural reasoning (that people of mixed race are socially and culturally marginal, doomed to a life of conflicting cultures and the unfulfilled desire to be "one or the other," neither fitting in nor gaining acceptance in any group, thus leading lives of confused loneliness and despair). In the last couple of decades the argument has shifted to a more sociopolitical one: People of color who marry Whites are trying to "raise" themselves economically, socially, and racially; intermarriage and multiracial people represent the loss or the "dilution" of distinct ethnic and racial groups; and mixed-race people and their families have dubious political and social loyalties.

The Biological Argument

HYBRID DEGENERACY THEORY

The once widely accepted theory of "hybrid degeneracy" states that people of multiracial heritage are genetically inferior to both (or all) of their parent races. Multiracial people are described as having no strength in the physical, mental, emotional, or moral senses, leading to early deaths and the inability to reproduce, and thus ultimately to group (and even human) extinction (Castle, 1926; Krauss, 1941; Provine, 1973; W. C. Smith, 1939). The growth of this idea, and of the scientific research done to support it, began around the end of the Civil War, and went on until the mid-1930s, becoming especially well developed with the rediscovery of Mendelism in the early 1900s and the growth of the eugenics movement (Provine, 1973).

The primary function of hybrid degeneracy ideology has been to keep the dominant White race "pure" and in power, separate and superior, both by discouraging White people from marrying and/or having children with people of color and by making sure that all of those people who had already been born racially mixed could not claim any privilege for their European ancestry. As mentioned earlier, antimiscegenation laws were put into effect as early as the colonial days, and they did not disappear from many states until as recently as 1967. The arguments justifying these laws were very often related to the supposedly malign consequences of the creation of multiracial people. For example, in 1896, a judge forbade an interracial marriage based on the following biological reasoning:

> The amalgamation of the races is not only unnatural, but is always productive of deplorable results. Our daily observation shows us, that the offspring of these unnatural connections are generally sickly and effeminate, and that they are inferior in physical development and strength, to the full blood of either race. (Sickels, 1972, p. 48)

That the antimiscegenation laws were aimed at marriages between Whites and non-Whites, not at marriages between two racially different non-Whites, is indicative of the ultimate concern with keeping the White race apart from all others (Spickard, 1989; Weinberger, 1966).

RELIGION AND HYBRID DEGENERACY

Interestingly, hybrid degeneracy theory also played a part in the American "Westward movement." Before, during, and for some time after the Mexican-American War, both the genetic and the theological aspects of the hybrid degeneracy theory were utilized as an "explanation" for the inability of the mestizo Mexicans to run their own country successfully, and thus as a justification for the United States to seize a large part of Mexico for itself (Pettit, 1980). The connection between the scientific and theological aspects of hybrid degeneracy comes from the idea that what is "unnatural" is also against God's wishes. In merging religion and morality with a more "practical" social Darwinism, the impact of the ideology could probably reach a wider audience of "believers."

THE MENTAL AND EMOTIONAL ASPECTS OF HYBRID DEGENERACY

Actually, by the time of the Civil War and the Mexican-American War, the American public had already become familiar with the tormented, pathetic, and often dangerous multiracial Black-White and Indian-White, and to some extent the Mexican-White, all of whom were favorite character types in mainstream fictional literature (Berzon, 1978; Elfenbein, 1989; Pettit, 1980; Scheick, 1979).[4] As stated earlier, one aspect of the hybrid degeneracy theory is that multiracial people exhibit psychological and emotional problems stemming from their "unnatural blend" (Krauss, 1941). They were (and, to some extent, still are) characterized as depressive, moody, discontent, irrational, impulsive, fickle, criminal, chronically confused, emotionally unstable, constantly nervous, and ruled by their passions—all because of an internal disharmony between the genetically determined characters of their two parent races (Berzon, 1978; Bogle, 1989; Elfenbein, 1989; Scheick, 1979; Stedman, 1982).

In Berzon's (1978) study of the mulatto in American fiction, she discusses how the "tragic mulatto" character is often cast as irrational, moody, and completely tormented by his or her "racial disharmony," "clash of blood," and "unstable genetic constitution," typically dying while still young. She quotes a 1950 novel by Elizabeth Coker, *Daughter of Strangers*: "The idea of the mixed river of her blood was whirling in her brain and in her troubled, uneasy frame of mind she had become a stranger to herself" (Berzon, 1978, p. 104). This description of a multiracial African-European is similar to the description of a mixed Japanese-European in the 1921 book *Kimono*: "A butterfly body with this cosmic war shaking it incessantly. Poor child! No wonder she seems always tired" (Paris, 1921, p. 87).

The "scientific" contribution to the idea that multiracial people have emotional and mental problems is evident in the writings of Charles Benedict Davenport, the one-time "leading advocate of eugenics in the United States" (Provine, 1973). In his article titled "The Effects of Race Intermingling," Davenport (1917) elaborates on his scientific beliefs: "One often sees in mulattos an ambition and push combined with intellectual inadequacy which makes the unhappy hybrid dissatisfied with his lot and a nuisance to others" (p. 366).

MORAL AND SEXUAL ASPECTS OF HYBRID DEGENERACY

Perhaps the most common and most constant offshoot of the biological-psychological profile of people of mixed race is the stereotype that they are sexually immoral and out of control. This is especially true of multiracial women—whether they be "half-breed" Indian, Mexican "mestiza," "mulatta," or "Eurasian," they are consistently imaged as extremely passionate and sexually promiscuous (Berzon, 1978; Bogle, 1989; Elfenbein, 1989; Pettit, 1980; Scheick, 1979; Stedman, 1982).

Several factors have played a part in the creation of this stereotype, which is prevalent not only in the United States, but also in many Asian countries.[5] First of all, multiracial people are racial minorities in most countries, and have been labeled as immoral and uncivilized in the same way that racial and ethnic minorities are often characterized by the dominant racial and ethnic group.

Second, in social orders that promote in-group sex and marriage, any person who engages in a relationship with an outsider is considered to be psychologically or socially abnormal. Often they are labeled as immoral, sexually deviant, and/or sexual in an uncontrolled, illicit way (Castle, 1926; Lehrman, 1967). The image of the master and the slave, of a man in a foreign country and an indigenous prostitute, of the rape of a White woman by a man of color, and, most recently, of an "ugly American" and a "mail-order bride" are on one hand horrifying and on the other hand titillating, and are inherited by the multiracial population from their hypothetical parentage. Abolitionists used the "tragic mulatto" stereotype as a prime example of the immorality of slave owners and the institution of slavery (Berzon, 1978; Dearborn, 1986; Elfenbein, 1989). The pathetic "Amerasian" has been utilized by the media as a mechanism to berate American men (most often those in the military) who have engaged in extramarital sex overseas. The mixed-race person is seen as the product of an immoral union between immoral people, and is thus expected to be immoral him- or herself.

A third possible factor in this stereotype is that multiracial people are physical reminders of the biological nature of sex and love. No stories about storks delivering babies can explain how a "Black-looking" baby can have a White or an Asian mommy, or how a Eurasian can look like an Asian person with blond hair and blue eyes. The genetics of reproduction are, as they say, written all over the faces of mixed-race people.

And finally, multiracial females are especially likely targets for sexual objectification because of their real and perceived vulnerability as a group. By this I mean that multiracial women are characterized in academics and in popular culture as vulnerable in the sense that they are mentally, emotionally, morally, and socially weak, powerless, and tormented, and very often the product of sexual and racial domination. At the same time, many multiracial women are, in fact, vulnerable in a social, political, and economic sense. Because of the structure of power and domination in the American gender system (as well as in many other gender systems), weakness and vulnerability can be very exciting and attractive when applied to females. Elfenbein (1989) locates this theme, which she calls the "sexualization of powerlessness" as latent but consistent in the "tragic octoroon" stories that she has studied.

The interplay of the "sexualization of powerlessness" and the real and perceived vulnerability of certain mixed-race groups can create situations where stereotypes of immorality are recreated and reinforced (Gibbs, 1987; Root, 1990). An example of this is the case of many young Amerasian women in both Vietnam and the Vietnamese American community. Amerasians have very few job options, as being racially different and from nonintact families has left many of them uneducated and ineligible for most jobs in both Vietnam and the United States (Felsman, Johnson, Leong, & Felsman, 1989). The Vietnamese consider both Amerasian men and women to be "low class" and "troublemakers," with prostitute mothers and worthless fathers who abandoned them. Thus Amerasian women are often labeled and treated as prostitutes, which functions to encourage many to become prostitutes, often after having been raped or sexually abused in Vietnam or in refugee processing centers (see Valverde & Chuong, Chapter 11, this volume).

HYBRID DEGENERACY AND PHYSICAL APPEARANCE

The discussion of sexual myths about mixed-race people brings up the related issue of physical attractiveness. The idea that multiracial people are beautiful and handsome is one of the most persistent and commonly accepted stereotypes, both historically and contemporarily. This seemingly "positive" image is actually very complex, and needs to be questioned and studied very carefully. For example, is it because multiracial people who are part Caucasian often look like

"Anglicized" versions of people of color that they are considered to be handsome and beautiful? This could help to explain why so many of the "Black" and "Asian" actors and actresses in U.S. media are actually multiracial. On the other hand, for those who are attracted to people with "exotic" looks, multiracial people are often extra exotic looking in that they do not look much like any designated racial and ethnic group. Also, the idea that multiracials are attractive might very well be connected to the stereotype discussed earlier that they are vulnerable and linked to unbridled and illicit sex.

It is really very interesting that people of mixed race have become "known" for having attractive physical appearances, since one of the assertions of the hybrid degeneracy theory was that multiracial people could inherit "disharmonious" physical features from their various parent races. For example, some scientists hypothesized that multiracial people might have circulatory systems too long or big for their bodies, arms and legs that are not compatible in length, and teeth too big or too small for their mouths (Provine, 1973). In Fleming's (1939) scientifically questionable study of mixed-race children in England, he "discovered" that 10% of the biracial African-European persons he examined had a "disharmony of jaws . . . resulting where a well arched jaw was inherited from the negro side and a badly arched one from the white side" (p. 68). Fleming also reports that a significant number of the biracial Asian-European persons he studied had one eye with a "Mongolian fold" and one Caucasian-shaped eye.

THE THEORY OF MEDIOCRITY AND HYBRID VIGOR

Not everyone who has been concerned with the biological consequences of race mixing has believed in the theory of hybrid degeneracy. Many academics and laypersons have claimed that multiracial people, when they are partly Caucasian, are "superior" to their monoracial Black, Indian, and Asian counterparts. This has especially been the case in regard to people of African-European American descent, whom many scholars (and slave owners) have labeled as genetically and culturally superior to Blacks, but as genetically and culturally inferior to Whites (Castle, 1926; Park, 1931; Spickard, Chapter 2, this volume). It is interesting to note that while this was a common sentiment during slavery, when anyone with "one drop of Black blood" was still legal chattel, after abolition Black-White multiracials were overwhelmingly imaged as degenerate and very dangerous (Berzon, 1978).

Some of the more "progressive" academics actually advised that racial minorities be amalgamated with the White group, genetically and socially, so as to raise their position on the hierarchical scale (Gulick, 1914; Provine, 1973). But the more common sentiment was that by allowing Whites to mix biologically with the other races, the superior White race would be "degraded" to the midpoint position that multiracial people occupy (Castle, 1926; Provine, 1973). There were, too, a minority of scientists who considered the possibility of "hybrid vigor"; that is, that multiracial people might inherit the best qualities of their parent groups and actually be healthier, smarter, and better looking than monoracial people (Krauss, 1941). This sentiment is disturbing in its own way, as there is no objective basis for determining what is "best" and what is "worst" about any particular racial or cultural group. Also, the image of the "best of both worlds" is just as "otherworldly" as the hybrid degeneracy "worst of both worlds," leaving people of mixed race as the perpetual "other."

The Sociocultural Argument

THE MIXED-RACE PERSON AS MARGINAL MAN

It seems that around World War II and the horror of the Holocaust, with its Nazi biological determinism, the scholarly argument against multiracial people shifted from a biological one to an argument based on socialization and cultural reasoning (Provine, 1973). Multiracial people were now described as being unable to deal with their biculturality—their conflicting cultures left them torn and confused, and their nonacceptance by either or any racial group meant that they were pathetically marginal and outcast, left to be the target of both of their parent groups' anger and hatred for one another (Fleming, 1930; Park, 1931; W. C. Smith, 1939). Actually, there is very little real difference between the cultural and biological arguments against miscegenation and multiracial people; both connote a hierarchy, with the Caucasian race and European-originated culture on the top and all other races and cultures on the bottom.

Stonequist (1937) names the "racial hybrid" as the "most obvious" type of marginal man. He declares that there are no biological problems with race mixture, only societal problems, which can account for whatever "inferiority" multiracial people might exhibit. He gives several descriptions of the personality characteristics of different populations of multiracial people, assigning them such problems as inferiority complexes, "exaggerated self-consciousness," restlessness, and discontentedness. He says that multiracial people in South Africa and Jamaica function as a buffer zone between the Whites and Blacks, hated and abused by both sides, and that the Eurasians of India and the multiracial African-Europeans of South Africa and Jamaica long to be White and "ape" White ways.

In the media, the multiracial's problems with being both bicultural and socially marginal have consistently made for many fascinating story lines in books, films, and even songs. Stedman (1982) says of his research on American images of Native Americans, "Curiously enough, fiction writers generally saw more difficulties in being part Indian than in being all Indian, primarily because of the consequences of living in two worlds, a situation that writers liked to give full play" (p. 198). Berzon (1978) feels that this is also true of the multiracial Black-White character, who is a longtime fictional favorite, and who is "defined in terms of his marginal position within the culture" (p. 13). It has certainly been the case in the vast majority of the literature that I have looked at in my own research on mixed-race Asian-European characters.

THE DARK SIDE OF THE MARGINAL MAN

But Stedman and others have found that the fictional mixed-blood characters' unique social position could also prove dangerous to White society, as, in the Indian-White case, the "half-breeds" sometimes "made evil use of their status by excelling at betrayal and frontier espionage or by leading the Indians they had cleverly aroused against some settlers or soldiers" (Stedman, 1982, p. 201). The dangerous side of the multiracial's social position was especially perilous if the character could physically "pass" as Caucasian, allowing him or her to move undetected in and out of the White world (Pettit, 1980; Scheick, 1979). As stated by a Japanese villain in Wallace Irwin's "yellow peril" novel *Seed of the Sun* (1921/1979), "Even unto the tenth generation Japanese with blond skins and blue eyes will still be Japanese, quick with the one God-given virtue—loyalty to empire and the Emperor" (p. 233).

Today: The Sociopolitical Argument[6]

BICULTURALISM AND "BRIDGES"

In the last two to three decades, the "concerns" about multiracial people have once again shifted. It seems that the civil rights and Black power movements and the assertion and celebration of cultural and racial differences have been the turning point toward this latest development in the multiracial mythology. It is now more widely recognized that people of color (and some White ethnic groups) in the United States are all somewhat bicultural, and that this can be a very valuable and positive, rather than marginalizing, experience (Blauner, 1972; Steinberg, 1981). Thus contemporary studies of people of multiracial heritage tend to discuss "issues," both positive and negative, rather than focus on "problems" as in the past (Chang, 1974; Dien & Vinacke, 1964; Gibbs, 1987; Johnson & Nagoshi, 1986). There has even been some discussion of mixed-race people as the "children of the future"—the natural "bridges" between the artificial boundaries that divide the humans of the world.

SEPARATISM AND "SELLOUTS"

However, the last few decades have also made it clear to Americans that race is a political as well as a social, cultural, and biological grouping (Omi & Winant, 1986). Racial solidarity is now commonly identified as a means through which group, and thus individual, power can be obtained. In academia, the social science paradigm of "assimilation" has been rejected as both inaccurate and oppressive to non-"Anglos," especially to non-Whites (Blauner, 1972; Omi & Winant, 1986). Popular wisdom recognizes that the idea of America as the "melting pot" is outdated; scholars, administrators, and the media discuss alternative models for a nation of many racial and ethnic groups, such as "multiculturalism," "cultural pluralism," the "salad bowl," and "separatism."

Unfortunately for mixed-race people and their families, many of the new paradigms have made no more room for them and their experiences than have the paradigms of the past. In fact, one of the key factors in the assimilation model is "intermarriage," so the rejection of the model has often been expressed as a rejection of interracial marriage, interracial families, and interracial people. People of color who marry Caucasians are often labeled "sellouts" and "traitors" by other non-Whites. Multiracial people who are part White are seen as inherently "whitewashed"; they are harassed for their light skin or light hair, their loyalty is always in question, and they are not allowed to discuss their multiraciality if they want to be included as legitimate "persons of color" (Furlong, 1968; Murphy-Shigematsu, 1988).

SUMMARY OF THE MULTIRACIAL MYTHOLOGY

In summary, monoracial Americans have crafted a mythological multiracial monster who is genetically, mentally, culturally, socially, and politically distorted. The old cliché, "What about the children?" is still the primary question posed to, or in many cases the primary condemnation aimed at, interracial couples in this country. In this way, multiracial people have been defined completely by others and, in the process, have internalized many of the images of themselves as torn and confused and as fitting in nowhere. This has encouraged them to adhere to the second strategy for dealing with multiracials: the denial of their existence.

The Denial of the Existence of Multiracial People

LEGAL DEFINITIONS AND HYPODESCENT

In the mid-1890s, an "octoroon" (one-eighth Black, seven-eighths White) named Homer Plessy was arrested after he was refused a seat on an all-White car by the conductor of the train on which he was riding. Plessy took the case to court, and, in 1896, the U.S. Supreme Court ruled against Plessy in *Plessy v. Ferguson*, the famous separate-but-equal case (Lofgren, 1987). Although the law was supposedly made to ensure the "equality" of Blacks and Whites, the very fact that a person who was seven-eighths Caucasian and one-eighth Black was automatically considered "Black" ensured racial inequality. Perhaps even more illogical than Plessy's being considered legally Black is the fact that he would have been considered Black in some states and White in others, as different states had different percentage rules (Lofgren, 1987).

As discussed earlier, U.S. society operates under a monoracial hegemonic culture in which race is seen as something solid and immutable. Multiracial people are constantly being shoved into one of the existing monoracial categories. Most of the time, it is the "most" subordinate of the multiracial person's racial groups that he or she is pushed into. This is described as "hypodescent," and it is the manner in which the superordinate racial group is kept clearly defined and in complete political, economic, and social power (Omi & Winant, 1986). The current standard rule that one-sixteenth to one-thirty-second "Black blood" makes a person legally African American, or the fact that anyone with as little as one-sixteenth "Japanese blood" was subject to being put into the U.S. internment camps during World War II, is indicative of hypodescent.

TREASURING RACIAL BOUNDARIES

But I think that it is more than just a desire to keep the White race "pure" and in power that advocates the denial that multiracial people exist in the United States. It seems that in this country, a great deal of people's lives is determined, or at least informed by, what racial group they belong to. Where they live, how they dress, who they vote for, what music they listen to, how they talk, what sports they play, what cigarettes they smoke—all are largely segregated by race. Of course, class, which is very much connected to race, plays a large role in this, but race is salient even outside of class. This is made evident when middle-class third- and fourth-generation Japanese Americans, wealthy immigrants from Taiwan, and welfare-dependent Southeast Asian refugees are grouped together—not only by non-Asian Americans, but by Asian Americans themselves (for instance, in the scholarly field of "Asian American studies" and in periodicals such as *Asian Week*).

In this way, people asserting their multiracial heritage confuse and threaten the boundaries that so comfortably mark people off from each other. It is not only the dominant White group that treasures these boundaries, but all racial and ethnic groups. (Although it seems that with groups that recognize their own multiracial background—for example, Filipinos, Chicanos, and certain Latino groups—the situation is quite a bit different.) The treasuring of clear boundaries is evident in the fact that multiracial African Americans are "allowed" to be full members of the African American community, but only as long as they do not assert multiracial identities; and multiracial Asian Americans, especially when they are part Black, are generally considered "outsiders" and have very limited entrée into Asian American communities, except for those who have become respected or well known for some reason (the "claim-us-if-we're-famous" syndrome).

A very recent example of the denial of multiracial people's existence was the controversy over who should play the role of a Eurasian pimp in a Broadway musical. The musical's producer and directors cast a White actor; the Asian American community felt that the role should be played by an Asian American. Neither side ever mentioned the idea of searching for a person of mixed race to play the role.[7]

THE PRESSURE TO "CHOOSE"

So, in order to have a racial and ethnic group with which to belong, multiracial people have been pressured to "choose," on an individual level, which of their groups to belong to. The direction to "check one box only" extends far beyond the census form to just about every aspect of life (see Hall, Chapter 18, this volume). In many cases the "choice" is made for the person by society, based on his or her physical appearance. However, often a person does not coincide culturally with the monoracial group with which he or she has been placed based on appearance; his or her cultural experience may have been that of a person intimately exposed to multiple racial and ethnic groups and cultures (Williams, Chapter 20, this volume). For those multiracial people whose physical appearance leaves them racially ambiguous, questions about which group they identify with put them under constant pressure, especially when they feel that whoever is asking the question is looking for a particular answer.

Actually, the famous old story of "passing" that has so interested both White and Black writers is really just one version of the phenomenon of choosing (Daniel, Chapter 8, this volume). The ideology implicit in passing is hypodescent—that even if the person is genetically part White and looks physically White, as long as he or she has "one drop of Black blood," he or she is Black. In reality, if the character who passed as White had instead chosen to live in the Black community as a Black person, this would be just another version of passing (Spickard, 1989).

An interesting twist on the phenomenon of "choosing" occurs when a multiracial person chooses to be a different race or ethnicity altogether—for example, an Asian-White person who identifies as Hawaiian, Samoan, Native American, or Latino. And there are those who refuse to identify with any race, who publicly define themselves as "human" or as "Californian," for example. Of course, there are always those multiracial people who do not care to "fit in" with a racial group (or any group at all) and who relish their position as groupless.

PRIVATE VERSUS PUBLIC IDENTITY

Regardless of which group society tells a person he or she belongs to, and regardless of which group a person "chooses" to belong to publicly, a multiracial and multicultural person is essentially who he or she is—multiracial and multicultural. In this way, multiracial people often resist the oppressiveness of having to "choose" one of their groups by maintaining private identities and cultures that reflect their true racial and cultural combinations.

Conclusion

Multiracial people and interracial families are a threat to the "American way of life." The U.S. system has depended on very clear racial categories for its political, social, economic, and psychological organization. In an attempt to keep the categories well defined, two strategies have been employed: the creation of a negative mythology about people of mixed race and their families, using biological, sociocultural, and sociopolitical arguments; and the denial of the existence of people of mixed race and their families. As a result of this environment, which has offered no positive, viable option of being multiracial, it has been difficult for people of mixed race to accept and to assert a multiracial identity. Thus there has been little development of a group consciousness among multiracial people.

But this is changing. In the last decade, a movement has begun among people of multiracial and multiethnic descent, defining and asserting themselves through political and social activism, through scholarship and education, and through self-expression in the arts. In doing this, multiracial people are challenging what this country has traditionally seen as being "race" and "ethnicity," "culture" and "community." By insisting that they exist and that they are what they are, multiracial and multiethnic people have blurred the boundaries between groups. Of course, this upsets a lot of people who depend on group boundaries for privilege or political or economic interest or sense of self, and it worries those who have static, undynamic ways of defining cultural and group pride and preservation. But in the end, less "us versus them" thinking—in this country and in this world—will be good for us all.

Notes

1. These are certainly not the only groups of people who have challenged these definitions. Feminists and feminist theorists have long been challenging definitions of *gender*, *sexuality*, and *family*, as well as *power* and *success*.

2. I am aware that there are distinct regional and ethnic differences within the United States regarding ideas about race. Hawaii does not seem to operate on the monoracial hegemony at all, and certain racial and ethnic groups in the United States, such as Filipinos, Chicanos, and other Latino groups, also seem not to see race as a concrete and immutable concept in the way that mainstream American society does.

3. The biological argument often gets merged with a theological argument in the sense that God and nature are commonly considered to be one and the same.

4. The Asian-White characters that commonly show up in American literature came later, as Asians did not start immigrating to the United States in large numbers until the 1860s. Multiracial characters of non-White mixes, such as Asian-Black, are rarely found in mainstream literature—a fact that is significant in itself.

5. This stereotype might very well be prevalent in other countries and cultures besides the United States and parts of Asia, but this is, as of yet, beyond the scope of my research.

6. The mythology of mixed-race people and their families has mainly been a creation of the dominant culture (i.e., the biological and sociocultural theories). However, in the last few decades people of color have also been active in publicly contributing to this ideology.

7. I have given a very brief and cursory description of the *Miss Saigon* controversy, which is actually very complex. For one thing, there have been accusations that the Eurasian character was originally written as a "full-blooded" Vietnamese but was changed to a Eurasian in order to allow a specific European actor to play the role. If this is the case, it is very disturbing to mixed-race people, as well as to people of color in general.

PART III

What of the Children?

13

Back to the Drawing Board: Methodological Issues in Research on Multiracial People

MARIA P. P. ROOT

The repeal of the last antimiscegenist legislation in the United States in 1967 is an approximate line of demarcation between "old" and "new" bodies of research and analysis. The initial research on racially mixed persons focused on people of combined African and European descent, those groups with the largest difference in social status and privilege in our society. With few exceptions, this research is largely not useful today because of the profound influence of antimiscegenist attitudes on the hypotheses and on the interpretations of findings (Provine, 1973). However, this research does have some utility, to the degree that it reminds us of the influence of sociopolitical history on research methodology.

The old literature was situated in an era marked by linear models of identity, rigid thinking about race and racial boundaries, and overt racism. Consequently, the "in between" social status of some racially mixed persons and the differences between the phenomenology of multiracial and monoracial identity and social belonging cast racially mixed persons as deviant. An irrational, circular logic attributing deviance in multiracial people to the intrinsic consequences of racial mixing was reinforced by the combined forces of pseudoscience and moralistic theology. Subsequently, even more ecologically based theories of the period, such as "marginal man" theories (Park, 1928; Stonequist, 1937), could not be extended beyond a linear analysis.

In contrast, the contemporary literature on multiracial people is characterized by interdisciplinary collaboration and by researcher sensitivity to the uniqueness of the multiracial experience. Research, almost exclusively created by multiracial researchers and scholars and persons intimately knowledgeable about this experience, has increased the quality and meaning of our findings. The foci of this literature have been to recover the country's multiracial history (e.g., J. D. Forbes, 1988a; Spickard, 1989) and to extend our knowledge of multiracial people beyond the bounds of a Black-White duality. More recently, Asian-White (e.g., Duffy, 1978; Johnson & Nagoshi, 1986; Kich, 1982; Murphy-Shigematsu, 1986), Asian-Black (e.g., Hall, 1980; M. C. Thornton, 1983), and Native American-Black (e.g., J. D. Forbes, 1988a, 1990; Katz, 1986; T. P. Wilson, 1991) mixes have been studied.

Attempts to articulate and develop models with which to explain multiracial development have resurrected ecological theories (e.g., Miller, Chapter 3, this volume; C. W. Stephan, 1991, Chapter 5, this volume) and contributed to the expansion and development of multidimensional theories (e.g., Gibbs, 1987; Gibbs & Hines, Chapter 16, this volume) and new ecologically anchored theories (e.g., D. J. Johnson, Chapter 4, this volume; Kich, Chapter 21, this volume). Such ecological theories are useful because they emphasize the interaction of social, familial, and individual variables within a context that interacts with history. They mark a move away from linear models of adjustment and identity development.

To date, almost all studies of multiracial people have utilized relatively small, selectively recruited samples. Few studies have included control groups. Whereas this methodology is conventional and valued in sociology, ethnography, and anthropology, it is inconsistent with conventional methodologies of mainstream psychology (Ponterotto & Casas, 1991). In psychology, the value of a piece of empirical or descriptive research has been correlated positively with the degree to which it meets the ideals of sampling and of control for random variability through research design. Thus researchers who hope to have their results accepted for publication in scholarly journals must include in their studies the standard criteria of large samples, random samples, and control groups. However, meeting these criteria is difficult if not impossible in conducting research with multiracial populations—and sometimes quantitative, controlled studies are too reductionistic for this area of inquiry.

This chapter discusses issues of sampling, research design, and researcher sensitivity to constructs in research with racially mixed populations. It is hoped that this discussion will enable the researcher to consider appropriate flexibility in methodological design in order to harness and combine the strengths of different qualitative and quantitative research designs in order to advance our knowledge of multiracial people and intergroup relations.

Sampling

Obtaining multiracial participants for research studies can be difficult. It is important that researchers consider the issues inherent to sampling this population when designing their studies. Decisions to use qualitative, quantitative, or combined research methodologies will affect the threats to validity that different sampling procedures may pose. For example, sampling or recruiting racially mixed study participants for quantitative research designs is fraught with threats to validity. These threats arise for several reasons: Multiracial people are nonrandomly distributed in the United States; they are a numerical minority in much of the mainland United States, especially among adult age subjects; and identification and recruitment of multiracial subjects is complex. Additionally, a city's or region's history of racial mixing will affect the extent to which the sample is representative of other mixed-race samples.

Recruiting multiracial individuals will almost always yield selective samples. Even the usual selective sampling techniques, such as word-of-mouth or snowballing methods and advertising for multiracial participants, may recruit a very select group of participants. For example, some persons will not respond to advertising because the social environment has rendered multiracial identity as a negative status. Other multiracial persons, such as some African Americans, Filipinos, Latinos, Native Americans, and Hawaiians, may not identify as multiracial; to them, ethnic or cultural identity may be more salient than racial heritage. Advertising specifically for people of color will selectively sample those multiracials who identify as such (e.g., Cauce et al., Chapter 15, this volume) and who may be critically different from those who would not identify as people of color.

Obtaining a multiracial sample is also greatly affected by how the researcher defines and determines race, ethnicity, and culture. Because race is a construct of human design, and its boundaries are mediated by history, legislation, and other aspects of the social order (Root, Chapter 1, this volume; Spickard, Chapter 2, this volume), how it is defined is very important for subsequent comparison of results with other studies. Even "objective" information sources, such as birth certificates or other documents, are not necessarily accurate, because they are subject to the flaws and biases of our racial classification system. For example, Wilson mentions in Chapter 9 of this volume a case in which three sons of the same biological parents were identified as three different races on their birth certificates.

The researcher must also remember that even though the terms *race* and *ethnicity* are frequently used interchangeably, they are not synonymous. Whereas race is an integral part of ethnic identity, the physical appearance of the multiracial person appears to be neither necessary nor sufficient for determining ethnic identity (Hall, Chapter 18, this volume; Stephan, Chapter 5, this volume). Thus *ethnicity* must also be carefully defined in order to avoid confounds (Root, Chapter 1, this volume), facilitate comparisons among studies (Phinney, 1990), and accommodate the normative phenomena of situational (changeable) ethnicity (e.g., Root, 1990; C. W. Stephan, 1991) and simultaneous ethnicity (Duffy, 1978; Hall, 1980) among multiracial persons. Ultimately, forcing a single-choice racial or ethnic identity may yield unreliable and even invalid results.

Seemingly inclusive or progressive attempts to provide a multiracial or multicultural category will also need to be well defined. Indeed, such attempts without prior analyses and/or a well-conceptualized rationale may be premature (Thornton, Chapter 22, this volume). At this point in time, except for special communities such as those described by Williams in her sample of Amerasians raised on U.S. military bases in Japan (Chapter 20, this volume) or in Hawaii, where multiracial persons are the largest proportion of young people and identify as "local" (R. C. Johnson, Chapter 17, this volume), multiracial persons do not have the artifacts associated with ethnicity such as food, history, or music that would lead us to expect similarities in behavior or beliefs (D. J. Johnson, Chapter 4, this volume). Additionally, because we do not know what different effects the various ecological influences have on different racial mixtures such as White-minority versus minority-minority, it may not be appropriate to consolidate mixtures on independent variables such as multiracial status or ethnicity until preliminary analyses are conducted.

The increasing numbers of racially mixed persons are going to pose some serious concerns to methodology, such as Cauce et al. (Chapter 15, this volume) encountered in their study of adolescents. The researchers had not been prepared to find that 20% of their African American and Asian American participants were racially mixed and so identified. Their first impulse, likely to be shared by many researchers, was to exclude the multiracial adolescents from the sample; "monoracial selection criteria" would keep the sample "cleaner" and would give the researchers more confidence in their findings and conclusions. However, they thoughtfully concluded that to do this would reflect an inaccurate picture of the population they were sampling. Researchers will be increasingly faced with first- or second-generation biracial persons in subject samples. I suggest that researchers start anticipating these population changes and take them into account when designing future research, particularly in areas of the country in which multiracial people are clustered.

In summary, the sampling issues surveyed in this chapter demonstrate the need for researchers to be familiar with the communities and the multiracial populations with which they wish to work—and to anticipate increasing numbers of multiracial people in samples. Attempts to obtain "cleaner" monoracial samples may eventually result in misrepresentations of the community at large, or the cultural or ethnic populations being studied.

Research Design Issues

Research paradigms determine what we can learn about a group of people. Basic considerations of research design and methodology include choices regarding the use of case study versus group sample, clinical versus nonclinical samples, and choice of control groups. Ultimately, these aspects of research methodology and design have a profound influence on what is considered "normal" and, subsequently, guide the meaning of differences.

At a time when the folklore regarding racially mixed persons is being examined and corrected (see Nakashima, Chapter 12, this volume), the research is necessarily concerned with understanding what is normative experience for multiracial persons, particularly surrounding the issues of identity and interpersonal relationships. It is important that a significant amount of information about multiracial people come from nonclinical samples. Studying clinical samples before we have a good picture of what is normative may be putting the cart before the horse; clinical samples will yield only more pathological pictures of individuals supporting the negative folklore and stereotypes of multiracial people.

The qualitative methodologies associated with sociology, anthropology, and ethnography rely heavily on observation and description for understanding the phenomenology of the group. These designs and methods lend themselves to small samples, as are usually obtained in working with specific multiracial groups. Ponterotto and Casas (1991) discuss the methodology of "theoretical sampling," in which the number of subjects is not as important as what each participant contributes to understanding. Validity can be established through *triangulation* methods that corroborate data with convergent sources, methods, or multiple interviewers (Fielding & Fielding, 1986; Ponterotto & Casas, 1991).

Qualitative methodologies that lend themselves to studying multiracial people include semistructured interviews, in which general questions and topic areas are explored, and structured interviews, in which specific questions are asked. The research designs include case study and multiple case study. Contemporary utilization of an expanded case study design has provided rich description of the multiracial experience (e.g., Gibbs, 1987; see also, in this volume, Gibbs & Hines, Chapter 16; Jacobs, Chapter 14; Mass, Chapter 19; Williams, Chapter 20) and been integral to determining what normative development is for multiracial persons (e.g., Hall, 1980; D. J. Johnson, in press; Kich, 1982; Murphy-Shigematsu, 1986; M. C. Thornton, 1983).

Unlike quantitative research designs, qualitative research designs are not necessarily guided by hypotheses. This type of research allows the researcher to develop hypotheses for future studies from a contextual understanding of the group and its norms. A particular strength of this methodology is that it is flexible and is more likely to allow for the development and testing of some theories. Unfortunately, qualitative methodologies are sometimes abandoned too quickly for "logical positivism" because of the validity attributed to numbers and statistical analyses (Ponterotto & Casas, 1991).

Quantitative research methods offer researchers the ability to explore cause-and-effect relationships and to have greater confidence in the generalizability of their results. However, because of subtle historical factors in America's racial history, researchers must remain sensitive to the fact that large samples, even with control groups, do not necessarily control for the subtle legacy of history, theoretical limitations, or researcher bias. Relationships and differences that might even be replicable are not necessarily valid. Using multiple methods and multiple measures and combinations of qualitative and quantitative designs can increase researchers' confidence in their findings, particularly when the research question is new. Understanding the context of the research question is particularly important for interpreting unusual results and differences.

With quantitative methodologies, differences will tend to be discussed in terms of the norms with which the researcher is familiar. These norms are implicitly established through the researcher's choice of control groups to which comparisons are made. However, I urge caution in considering whether or not to use a control group in this early phase of research. Cauce et al. (Chapter 15, this volume) provide a clear rationale for their use of adolescents of color as controls for their multiracial adolescents. This group was used to control for the additional stresses related to minority status relevant to multiracial persons and their families. Other researchers have noted the importance of appropriate control groups in helping them to observe patterns unique to multiracial persons (see, in this volume, Jacobs, Chapter 14; D. J. Johnson, Chapter 4; R. C. Johnson, Chapter 17).

Both quantitative and qualitative research methods can be rigorously applied. It is important to note that combining them provides a powerful multiple-method approach to increasing the rigor, depth, and meaning of research results.

MEASURES

The tools that are conventionally used to measure constructs such as identity, self-esteem, and personality may need to be examined for subtle biases that arise out of linear models of development or models that assume a monocultural or monoracial bias. For example, identity measures may be valid if they do not assume the necessity of a single choice or pathologize situational or simultaneous ethnic identities common among multiracially identified persons. Additionally, in their chapters in this volume, Kich (Chapter 21) and Bradshaw (Chapter 7) note that the unique experiences of multiracial persons inform how they perceive themselves and how they perceive themselves in relationship to others. These researchers' analyses of developmental issues suggest that certainly at some developmental stages, some multiracial persons may have personality styles that are different from those of monoracial persons and may be misunderstood.

TERMS

Many commonly used terms, such as *outmarriage, passing,* and *exotic,* should be reexamined for their connotations and bias against multiracial persons and *assignment* of ethnic identity. For example, discussions regarding biracial persons' tendencies to outmarry reflect the difficulty communities of color have in accommodating the reality of a multiracial and multiethnic experience and the internalization of dichotomous rules regarding group belonging. From some perspectives, almost all marriages for multiracial people will be outmarriages in some sense. The term *passing* is derived from rigid racial boundaries and rules of hypodescent (see, in this volume, Bradshaw, Chapter 7; Daniel, Chapter 8). *Exotic,* a word used to described multiracial women more frequently than multiracial men, often has a sexually oppressive connotation stemming from the folklore associated with multiraciality (Nakashima, Chapter 12, this volume; Root, in press-b).

WHO DOES THE RESEARCH?

At this point in the research much of the goal is to establish what the experiences and developmental patterns of racially mixed persons are. Thus it is important what research questions are asked and how they are asked. I suggest that it is also important that much of this initial research be done by multiracial persons and/or persons who are intimately informed of the experience by living a multicultural existence and in a multiracial environment. This relationship to the sample allows the researcher to ask questions from a position of knowing. His or her subsequent interpretations of results are then more likely to be placed in a social ecology relevant to the multiracial experience and less likely to be bound by implicit or explicit linear theories. Admittedly, a possible drawback may be a tendency on the researcher's part to interpret findings in a positive light and with less objectivity because they may have personal implications for him or her. However, triangulation methods, mentioned above, can control bias.

Conclusions

The contemporary research on multiracial persons has successfully utilized different methodologies and designs that are providing a foundation for determining what normative experience is. The sensitivity with which the majority of this research has been conducted has increased the quality and meaning of the research.

The sociopolitical context of multiraciality must be taken into consideration in designing a study, recruiting subjects, selecting and training researchers, and interpreting results. Further, any theory or discussion of results must take into account the relevant *interaction* of variables such as history (national, community, familial), immigration, politics (e.g., legislation around miscegenation and blood quantum to designate "legal" racial or ethnic identification), socioeconomic status, heritage (race, ethnicity, and culture), gender, generation of multiracial heritage (immediate or distal, generation in this country), community (ethnic, cultural, racial, class, income representation), geography (e.g., West Coast versus Midwest), and media depictions of multiracial persons (e.g., the current desirability of "exoticness," unstable personalities).

Yes, such research will be complicated; the challenge it presents requires creative approaches. Ultimately, the paradigms we choose guide our hypotheses and determine the types of information we are able to obtain. The rigor of qualitative research designs might best be directed toward understanding definitions, establishing norms, developing theory, and generating hypotheses. The rigors of quantitative designs might be best utilized to explore group differences and to determine the contributions of different variables to constructs such as identity—once norms have been established through qualitative methods. These methods are compatible; neither is intrinsically better than the other, but they are best suited for different purposes.

Acknowledgment

I wish to thank Ana Mari Cauce, Ph.D., for helpful feedback on the development of this manuscript.

14

Identity Development in Biracial Children

JAMES H. JACOBS

This chapter explores the development of racial and personal identity in young, biracial, Black-White children. It began as a dissertation study 15 years ago. The original research was an in-depth study of 10 children, 3 to 8 years of age, and their families. Parents were interviewed by a Black-White biracial couple. Each child was extensively interviewed and tested. The most important research instrument was a doll-play task designed to sample several dimensions of identity in young children. It was conceived as a methodological advance over previous materials and procedures used to assess racial identification and attitude. The results of this research led to a theory of cognitive-developmental stages in the emergence of racial identity and to a reinterpretation of the meaning of racial ambivalence found in earlier research with Black children. Since the original study the doll-play instrument has been used clinically with more than 100 biracial children.

In this chapter the background studies and research leading to the development of the new doll-play instrument are summarized and critiqued. Then the instrument itself is described and the developmental findings are reported. Biracial children are seen to go through three stages of racial identity development. It is suggested that increasing cognitive maturity leads to a biracial self-concept. However, societal prejudice colors that self-concept with negative racial evaluations. Exploring and coping with these negative evaluations or ambivalence is seen as a necessary task on the road to a positive biracial identity. Finally, suggestions for biracial child rearing are made.

Background

Although no one had specifically looked at racial identity formation in biracial Black-White children before the development of this instrument, the period from 1940 to the mid-1970s produced an abundance of studies on racial identity formation in Black children and in White children. Horowitz (1939) was the first person to measure racial self-identification using test materials. She used line drawings of a Black boy and a White boy and had Black and White children point to the one that looked most like themselves.

Horowitz found that Black children often chose the White drawing. She interpreted this misidentification as "wishful activity." Although Kenneth and Mamie Clark (1939) confirmed Horowitz's findings, they were not convinced that "wishful activity" was a necessary and sufficient explanation for the identification of the Black children with the drawings of the White child. In a follow-up study using the same method, they grouped their children by skin color—light, medium, and dark—and found that choosing the drawing of the White child increased from the dark group (40.5%) to the medium group (41.7%) to the lighter group (56.5%) (Clark & Clark, 1940). After looking at the combined effects of color and age of the 3-, 4-, and 5-year-olds tested, they concluded that the children were choosing the drawing of the White child on the basis of an actual match with their skin color rather than in terms of socially defined group differences. They assert that selection based on social definitions of racial group membership occurs at a later developmental stage, beyond the age of 5, when light-skinned children would have to "make identifications contrary to the objective cue of their own skin color." With regard to "wishful activity," Clark and Clark continue: "It is only when more concrete factors, i.e., dark skin color, would tend to militate against a given choice that one would be justified in utilizing intangible concepts for an interpretation of the results" (p. 166). They maintained this position in subsequent studies using a similar method but changing from line drawings to dolls: one Black and one White, blond, and blue-eyed (Clark & Clark, 1947).[1]

The 1940 study by Clark and Clark was important in pointing out that children may respond to their objective skin color (perceptual matching) earlier than they respond to socially defined racial categories. However, by 7 years of age, seven light-skinned children identified themselves with the Black child (Clark & Clark, 1947). Clark and Clark's assertion that the child's choice may represent either a perceptual matching or social identification is a conceptual advance over Horowitz's assumption that all choices are social. But this conceptual advance was accompanied by only a minor methodological advance: the grouping of their children by skin color. A further methodological advance would have been to increase the differentiation of the stimulus materials by skin color as well as grading the children by skin color.

J. Porter (1971) attempted to resolve the question that Clark and Clark (1940) raised: Are children choosing a doll on the basis of an actual match to their own skin color or in response to understanding their social classification based on race? She assumed that self-identification can be interpreted as self-acceptance or -rejection on racial grounds if racial awareness is controlled. That is, if children can point to the "Negro," White, and colored dolls, they are aware of racial categories and their self-identified dolls can be regarded as choices based on the social definition of race and not necessarily as matching their own skin color. Measuring awareness of racial categories would seem to describe the child's development of the racial concept that Clark and Clark's suggestion requires, but Porter's index of awareness of racial terms is probably not sufficient to demonstrate that the child understands racial categories. Two of the three terms (White and colored) are color words as well as racial words, so only one of the three words relates specifically to a racial category.

Porter also argues that controlling for attitude can help clarify the meaning of self-identification. Attitude is measured by doll choices in response to questions such as "Which doll is nice?" "Which doll is bad?" "Which doll would you invite home to play?" Most children of both races express preference for White dolls on the attitude measures. Porter hypothesizes that combining the two measures (self-identification and attitude) further clarifies the meaning of self-identification. High own-group preference and correct self-identification would suggest positive group identity. This is the typical response of White children. High own-group preference and incorrect self-identification would suggest confusion about racial identity; this was found by Porter among White children who presumably were confused by the White doll's hair color (i.e., the doll had blond hair and many of the White children who misidentified were brunette). Other-group preference combined with misidentification is mainly found with Black children and is inferred to mean self-rejection on racial grounds and a wish to be White. The final possibility, other-race preference and correct self-identification, is not discussed, but presumably it represents an acceptance of devalued racial status by Black children.

Porter's work represents the most refined attempt to relate doll choice measures to each other—for example, awareness of racial terms and attitudes toward self-identification. Whereas Porter's use of the method is more subtle and complex than that of Clark and Clark (1940, 1947), it still has the same deficiencies. Choices are made between only two dolls, and only the choices themselves enter the analysis. Inferences are made based on the investigator's preconceptions, with the child's own rich associations left out.

A major perspective that has been overlooked in exploring the development of racial identity is the child's use of conceptual tools in dealing with the complex affective and sociocultural forces and conflicts that he or she experiences. Piaget's (1954, 1973) description of the preoperational child's thinking suggests a difference in the task of developing a racial identity for a biracial child as opposed to a Black child or a White child. In the preoperational period the child is capable of simple classification and has the basic cognitive structures needed to realize that she or he is either Black or White and can begin sorting the world along such lines. The description of the preoperational child's thinking immediately suggests a challenge in the task of developing a racial identity for a biracial child as opposed to a monoracial Black or White child. Does a biracial child accede to a simpler definition of her- or himself as being just Black in the same way that society and the child's peers usually define him or her? If the child is very light-skinned, does she or he define her- or himself as just White? Might he or she go from one to the other of these positions (temporally and/or role defined) in a preoperational attempt to integrate who he or she is? Or, on the other hand, does the complexity and importance of the situation promote cognitive growth, so that the child can deal earlier with that complexity? Experience and affect could potentially facilitate an earlier cognitive organization, permitting assimilation of the idea of being both Black and White and something else (tan or mixed or biracial, or whatever). Biracial children may possibly have increased urgency concerning this task, derived from other children's questions and epithets, in some ways similar to monoracial children of color. For example, Goodman (1964) found that Black children tend to develop higher levels of racial awareness earlier than White children. Other studies demonstrate that the issue is more complex (e.g., J. Porter, 1971), but the single best interpretation is that experience and affect promote earlier racial awareness.

Extending Piaget's notion that children's development is an active, constructive process, Kohlberg (1966a, 1966b) examined the consistency of children's belief in constancy by correlating conservation of physical objects (mass and length) with the more social and emotionally charged constancies of species (Could a cat become a dog if it wanted?) and of gender. He found them to be highly correlated, implying an underlying "structure of thought," with species constancy attained first, followed by gender constancy, and finally conservation of mass and length.

Kohlberg suggests that a number of identities are being constructed in the 3- to 4-year-old child, with size and gender being the most important and universal. Kohlberg does not discuss racial identity, but the racial doll-choice literature just reviewed would indicate that racial identity is of equal importance and may be similar to gender identity in its developmental course. By combining Kohlberg's work on size and gender identity and the findings in the racial doll-choice literature, the probable sequence of development would be size, then gender, and finally race, with the course of each overlapping the other two. These are also the only significant identities that are readily representable in visual form—that is, as opposed to religious, social class, or surname identities.

The incorporation of stimulus materials on which all three of these identity dimensions (size, gender, and race) could vary would correct for the distortions of oversimplification produced by examining only one identity. The inclusion of these three identity dimensions would allow the investigation of the patterning of and cognitive imbalances among these identities, as well as provide a more inclusive view of the particular identity under investigation.

Of the three identity dimensions under discussion, only gender is dichotomous. Size and color are continuous. The two "races" represent a continuum of skin colors and skin and hair color combinations. A doll-play instrument that offers dolls differing systematically in skin color and hair color combinations would allow the child to choose a doll that closely matches his or her actual skin color and hair color. The extent to which choices deviate from an actual match of her or his skin and hair color could be calculated by the interviewer by rating the child on the same scale of dolls from which the child chooses. Such a scaled series of dolls would provide a more sensitive and subtle indicator of racial preferences and awareness as well as of identifications, especially for biracial children.

A more exhaustive exploration of race would also include a group outside of the Black-White dimension. The possibility of considering another race, such as Asian, would allow the unconfounding of skin color and racial group membership because the defining characteristics of Asian racial group membership are based primarily on facial features and not skin color. The availability of an Asian doll then offers a further opportunity for the biracial child to signify that she or he has achieved the concept of racial self-awareness that transcends color alone. An Asian doll could be added to the series of dolls varying along the Black-White dimension by placing the appropriate facial features on a doll with light skin and black hair.

Size, unlike gender or skin color, continuously and predictably changes throughout childhood and adolescence. Since size is not a fixed attribute in childhood, it does not lead to the formation of the same constancy concept that is developed for gender and skin color. Rather, size or age identity leads to a complementary or parallel constancy conservation concept in which predictable inconsistency (maturational transformation) must be assimilated, including remembering and anticipating the corollary changes in roles and competence.

Color, gender, and size are the three identity dimensions that vary within a family. Utilizing all three in stimulus materials for an identity instrument makes such an instrument particularly suited for studying the dynamics of identity development within the family.

The Study

DOLL-PLAY INSTRUMENT

The doll-play instrument consists of 36 hand-painted, wooden, freestanding dolls specifically made for this interview (see Figure 14.1). They include six skin and hair color combinations (dark brown with black hair, medium brown with black hair, light brown with medium-brown hair, white with black hair and Asian features, white with brown hair, and white with blond hair). The 4 intermediate dolls can be viewed as steps between the traditional Black doll and blond-haired White doll in typical doll-preference studies. Asian features were used on the white doll with black hair to give participants the opportunity to demonstrate concepts in classifying people outside of the Black-White spectrum and to reveal attitudes about another important racial group. Each of the six color combinations is represented in three sizes: adult (3.2 inches), child (2.4 inches), and baby (2 inches). Both sexes are represented in each size and color combination. Painted-on clothes are standardized across the six colors for each age and sex doll. The dolls are transported and then displayed to the child in a case with a removable front panel (22½ inches by 18 inches by 4 inches). The dolls were grouped by color to facilitate the children's making direct comparisons.

TASKS

The doll interview consisted of nine separate tasks; these are described in turn below.

(1) Story. The first task consisted of a 5- to 10-minute period of free play with a group of dolls the child selected, followed by the child telling a story from the free-play situation.

(2) Matching. In this task the child was asked to match a stimulus doll with one of three choice dolls, each differing from the stimulus on one dimension (color, size, or gender). In each of the following six trials the child was given a doll (stimulus) and three other dolls (choices) were placed in front of him or her. The child was asked, "Which doll looks most like this one?" "Why?" The task was scored for how many times the child ignored each of the three identity dimensions.

Figure 14.1. The Doll-Play Instrument

(3) Self-identification. The child was instructed, "Pick the doll that looks most like you." The child was then asked, "Why does the doll look like you?" "Why else?"

(4) Family identification. The child was instructed, "Take some more dolls to make a family like your own." Questions and probes were used to establish the identity of each doll. If anyone in the family was omitted, the child was asked, "What about your [brother]?" and was encouraged to pick a doll to represent that person. The choices for self- and family identification were compared with the interviewer's skin color ratings of the family.

(5) Preference, sibling. The child was asked, "Is there a doll you would like to be your brother or sister?" "Which one[s]?" "Why?" If the child did not want a brother or sister, she or he was asked, "Let's pretend you did want a brother or sister, which one would it be?" "Why?" "Which doll wouldn't you want for a brother or sister?"

(6) Preference, play. The child was asked, "Which doll would you like to invite to your house to play?" "Why?" "Is there a doll that you would not want to invite to your house to play?" "Which one?" "Why?" If the child said she or he wanted to invite all of the dolls, she or he was asked, "What if you could invite all of the dolls but one?" "Then which one would you not invite?" "Why?"

(7) Preference, like/dislike. The child was asked, "Which doll[s] do you like best?" "Why?" "Which dolls don't you like?" "Why?" If the child said he or she liked all of the dolls, he or she was asked, "Which doll[s] do you least like?" or "Which dolls do you like a little less than the rest?"

(8) Sibling of the light-brown boy doll. In this task the child was handed the light-brown boy doll and asked, "Which doll is the brother of this one?" "Why?" And then, "Which doll is its sister?" "Why?" This doll represents the most typical biracial doll. Our purpose was to see how closely a child would match the color of this doll in choosing a sibling. It was expected that biracial children, who experience a good deal of color variation in the family, would show some latitude in selecting a sibling for this light-brown doll. The choice and reasons for the selection might provide additional information about the child's racial identity in the context of the family.

(9) Constancy of racial identity. The child was presented with the six same-sexed adult dolls and asked which one he or she would look most like when he or she grows up. After inquiring about the selection, the child was handed the doll that was two steps darker than his or her self-identified adult doll and asked, "Could you grow up to be

like this one?" "What if you really wanted to?" "Why?" "Why not?" The procedure was repeated with the doll two steps lighter than the self-identified one. If the child chose the lightest or darkest doll in the beginning, the corresponding part of the task was omitted. If the child chose a doll one step from the lightest or darkest, he or she was presented with a doll one step lighter or darker, that is, the lightest or darkest. If the child maintained that change was possible in either condition, he or she was classified as pre-color constancy. If the child stated under both conditions that change was impossible and resisted countersuggestions, he or she was said to have attained color constancy. If the child was not sure and vacillated in one or both conditions or changed a correct response when faced with a countersuggestion, she or he was said to be transitional to achieving color constancy.

Two further measures were used to cumulate verbalizations across the entire doll-play interview. The first, salience, was simply the total number of spontaneous comments about each of the three identity dimensions (color, gender, and size). The other measure consisted of totals of all the racial comments referring to Black, biracial, White, and Asian people. These comments were further divided by attitude into positive, neutral, and negative. The patterning of evaluations across races is considered an index of racial attitude, and the total number of racial responses is seen as an index of the child's willingness to verbalize about race.

Throughout the doll-play interview the interview questions served as starting points in exploring the child's thoughts and feelings on the subject at hand. All terms and concepts dealing with race and gender were initially introduced by the child, then used by the interviewer. This was especially important in probing the potentially sensitive area of race. Adapting each interview to the individual child in this way facilitated his or her verbalizations while minimizing the reactivity of the interview. In addition, pursuing the child's own line of thought made the conversation one of discovery for the interviewer, suggesting new lines of inquiry and stimulating new formulations on the child's racial concept, identity, and attitude formation.

Stages in the Development of Biracial Identity

Despite the variability in racial conceptions, attitudes, and identifications, it is possible to describe a developmental course for the formation of racial identity in biracial children based on experience in the initial research and subsequent clinical use of the doll-play instrument. Color is used in different ways by different biracial children, as well as by the same child at different times.

Four factors emerged that were crucial in understanding the identity development of biracial children: (a) constancy of color, (b) internalization of an interracial or biracial label, (c) racial ambivalence, and (d) perceptual distortions in self- and family identifications. Our method of rating the attainment of color constancy and perceptual distortions in self- and family identifications has also been described. A child was considered to have internalized a biracial self-concept if at any point in the interview the child said she or he was brown, tan, mixed, interracial, part White and part Black, and so on, and contrasted such a label with a statement about having a White parent and a Black parent. Typically, biracial self-concept statements were made during the self- and family-identification interviews and in the color constancy task. A rating of the intensity of racial ambivalence was made and the racial group(s) toward which it was directed was specified. The rating was based on the doll choices in the preference sections of the doll-play interview and on comments made throughout the interview.

Research and clinical experience with the doll-play instrument suggest that preadolescent biracial children go through three qualitatively different stages of identity development. Each of these stages is described below.

STAGE I, PRE-COLOR CONSTANCY: PLAY AND EXPERIMENTATION WITH COLOR

In this preconstancy period the child engages in liberal play with color, as demonstrated by flexibility in the choices of dolls for family members. His or her use of color is generally nonevaluative. Color constancy has not been attained, so color can be explored with no firm classification into social groups by race. The typical child in this stage accurately identifies his or her own color and playfully experiments with color in family identifications and doll preference. Some children do not show the playful, exploratory behaviors that are characteristic of the freedom from conceptual boundaries in Stage I. Low self-esteem and/or painful personal experience of racial prejudice can lead to avoidance of exploratory play with color or to precocious rageful evaluations by color in the young child who has not yet achieved color constancy.

STAGE II, POST-COLOR CONSTANCY: BIRACIAL LABEL AND RACIAL AMBIVALENCE

The child usually attains this stage at about 4½ years of age. In this stage the child continues to experiment with roles and identifications, but, given the fuller understanding of color meanings (especially prejudice against Blacks) and the knowledge that his or her own color will not change, the child becomes ambivalent about his or her racial status. White preference and rejection of Blackness is the most common first phase. Sequential ambivalence, first toward Blacks and later toward Whites, is common. Displacement of ambivalence from the Black-White dimension to the Asian dimension is another common pattern, with some children idealizing Asians and others scapegoating them. Ambivalence was demonstrated by doll preferences (e.g., "Which dolls don't you like?" "Why?") and spontaneous racial comments during the doll interview (e.g., "The Black ones are mean."). This stage of ambivalence is necessary and as significant as free play with color in the preconstancy period. If the child can maintain ambivalence, his or her development of racial awareness moves forward to the level where discordant elements can be reconciled in a unified identity.

The Stage II child's racial self-concept rests not only on the knowledge that his or her color will not change (color constancy), but also on the coemergence of a biracial label that the child has internalized and begins to use as a cognitive base to construct his or her racial identity. Whereas color constancy seems to be spontaneously constructed by the child, a biracial self-concept may require the parents' presentation of a biracial label to the child. Typically a child is labeled in response to a question about his or her race or color. The parent will usually say something like, "You're part Black and part White; you're both [or tan or brown or interracial]." In all but one of the child interviews in which we had knowledge that a biracial label was provided by the parents, the child described him- or herself as biracial, usually using the same words that the parents related to us. Subsequent clinical cases have suggested that a child may construct a biracial identity without being presented a biracial label, as his or her own attempt to make sense out of having parents of two different races. In some cases children have expressed biracial identity even when their parent(s) have instructed them to consider themselves simply Black, as they will be defined by society.

Once the child has assimilated a biracial label, he or she constructs his or her family in ways that define membership in a biracial group that has one parent who belongs to a Black group and one parent who belongs to a White group. Frequently a child who has detailed the colors of the dolls (e.g., into white, light brown, medium brown, and black) will choose a doll "most like him- or herself," that is, one or two steps darker than our rating of his or her skin color. In the original study five of the seven children in Stage II chose darker dolls for themselves in order to make their color more clearly brown or biracial, while none of the three children in Stage I saw themselves darker. Half of the siblings of Stage II children were seen darker, and all of the Stage II children described their siblings with the same biracial label they used for themselves. For example, one child chose dolls darker than our ratings for both herself and her sister, but made her sister darker than herself, reflecting a slight difference in their actual skin color. However, verbally she puts herself and her sister in the same biracial class, saying, "We're both brown; Mommy's White and Daddy's Black." Another way in which the Stage II child frequently extends a biracial label into a self-concept is to rate his or her Black parent darker to make the distinction greater between "I'm brown and Daddy's black."

It should be emphasized that these color distortions in the self- and family identification tasks do not reflect any valuing or ambivalence. These choices should be seen as simply in the service of the children's defining themselves in the class of biracial people and separating that class from the class of Black people and the class of White people.

Perceptual distortion is also developed by the child's active attempts to understand racial class membership. The Piagetian notion of physical conservation is that intelligence overcomes perception. For example, in conservation of mass a pancake may look bigger than a ball, but the child who has mastered conservation knows that the increased width of the pancake is compensated for by its decreased height. The biracial child in Stage II uses intelligence to overcome perception in a different way. The child distorts self and or family member's color so that it more nearly matches the typical color of the racial class to which he or she is socially assigned. These children's racial intelligence (knowledge of Black, White, and biracial) forces the perceptual mistake. Cognitively, these "darker" choices represent a more mature stage than accurate choices that do not imply class membership, that is, choices based on a perceptual match alone.

STAGE III, BIRACIAL IDENTITY

This stage was observed by extending the doll-play methodology to 8- to 12-year-old biracial children. In Stage II the child's concept of social grouping by race is still confounded with skin color, as evidenced by the perceptual color distortions. In Stage III the child discovers that racial group membership is correlated with but not determined by skin color. Rather, racial group membership is determined by parentage. The child is not interracial because his or her father is black in color and his or her mother is white in color, but because the child's father belongs to the social class of Black people and his or her mother belongs to the social class of White people. In Stage III the child's discovery that his or her parents' racial group membership and not color per se defines the child as biracial allows him or her to separate skin color and racial group membership and rate him- or herself and family members' skin color accurately.

Clinical use of the doll-play instrument has supported the finding that ambivalence toward Blacks and then toward Whites is often sequentially explored and that racial ambivalence generally diminishes across Stage II. For example, one boy's parents reported that at age 5 he wanted his hair to be straighter, but by age 7 he complained that he could not grow a "real" natural. Children who are the exception to this pattern often have had painful racial experiences and may show symptoms of psychopathology. As the child enters Stage III, the trend of ambivalence decreasing with age observed in Stage II may continue to a point where discordant elements of racial identity are fully reconciled in a unified ego-identity. Another possibility is that the restructuring of sexual identity in adolescence may bring renewed racial ambivalence that must be maintained, expressed, and worked through, as was the case for the ambivalence of Stage II.

Implications for Biracial Child Rearing

Understanding the stages of identity development in biracial children suggests several factors as supportive of psychological health and positive biracial self-concept formation: fostering ego strength, biracial labeling, supporting the child's racial feelings (including ambivalence), and a multiracial environment. These factors are discussed below, as is the suggestion that greater social recognition of a biracial identity would be supportive of self-esteem in biracial people.

FOSTERING EGO STRENGTH

The development of a positive biracial identity in the face of racism depends on early ego-enhancing treatment of the child in the family. This includes the building of secure attachments, the support of individuation, the fostering of social and physical competencies, and encouragement of self-assertion. A strong self-identity is seen as a prerequisite of the timely advance from the free play with color in Stage I to the emergence of a biracial self-concept and the attainment of racial ambivalence in Stage II. Self-identity is also seen as a basis for exploring and mastering the racial ambivalence that is a major task of Stage II.

BIRACIAL LABELING

The development of a biracial identity is assisted by the presentation of a biracial label to the child by the parents. A biracial child, being neither Black nor White but both, is different from either parent and must assimilate a racial and ethnic label that is more complex and less readily available outside of his or her family than the labels of Black, White, Asian, Chicano, and so on. A Stage II child successfully articulates a label consisting of two parts: (a) a statement that he or she is part of both parents and both races, such as "I'm both Black and White" or "I'm part Black and part White," and (b) a statement that he or she is something different from either race or parent, such as "I'm brown," "I'm tan," or "I'm mixed."

Parents usually provide a label for their child in response to a racial question or problem that the child raises. A single instance of labeling is frequently sufficient for the child to internalize and cognitively explore the meaning of his or her biracial identity. However, parents should feel free to repeat the label whenever the child is not clear about his or her racial classification or identity. Although the parents' provision of a label may not always be needed for the child's cognitive accomplishment of attaining a biracial self-concept, it is a means by which parents can support the child's emerging positive racial self-identity.

AMBIVALENCE AND RACIAL MATERIAL

It is important for parents of biracial children to realize that their children's racial ambivalence is a developmental attainment that allows the continued exploration of racial identity. Children need help from their parents to verbalize racial thoughts and feelings. Supportive interest rather than alarm at the child's ambivalence will facilitate identity development. If the child's racial ambivalence is suppressed, he or she will likely stop actively exploring his or her racial identity and will feel that there is something inherently wrong with or degrading about his or her racial status. Although biracial children may be quite variable in the intensity, duration, and direction of the racial ambivalence they experience, some common patterns of ambivalence can be discerned. Ambivalence usually increases for about a year after entering Stage II (at around 4½) and then gradually decreases until about 8 years of age. Ambivalence is generally first directed toward Blacks. After a period of expressing ambivalence toward Blacks, many children explore ambivalent feelings toward Whites. The working through of ambivalence seems primarily influenced by the parents' supportive interest in the child's racial feelings and secondarily by a racially supportive environment outside of the family.

MULTIRACIAL ENVIRONMENT FOR PARENTS AND CHILDREN

A multiethnic community and social environment was basic to the life-styles and philosophies of the research families and to most of the clinical families observed. Whereas a multiracial environment may not be as necessary for the racial identity development of a Black child or a White child, such an environment is supportive of the development of a positive biracial identity in children.

Summary

The research presented in this chapter suggests that preadolescent biracial children go through three qualitatively different stages of identity development. Stage I children experiment freely with color, as they have not yet classified people into socially defined racial categories and do not yet understand that skin color is invariant. Children in the second stage have attained the concept of color constancy and have internalized a biracial label. Both the attainment of color constancy and the internalization of a biracial label appear to form the foundation of racial ambivalence. Experiencing and working through racial ambivalence is seen as a necessary task for people of color, including biracial children, as a consequence of racial prejudice in society. The internalization of a biracial label also leads to a perceptual distortion of self and family members' skin color. This distortion does not imply any racial evaluation or preference; rather, it is in the service of more clearly classifying self and family into socially ascribed racial categories—Black, White, and biracial. In Stage III, ambivalence is greatly diminished or absent and perceptual distortions are no longer necessary because of the child's understanding that racial group membership is determined by parentage, not skin color.

The biracial self-concept observed in the children in this sample is a tribute to the strength of their families and to the capacity of children to acknowledge and explore both positive and negative evaluations and stereotypes present in their socially defined racial identity. The significance of this accomplishment is apparent not only because Blackness is still largely devalued in our society, but also because there is no social recognition of biracial people in the United States. In the biracial families observed, parents were generally concerned that both races be offered as equal components in the child's heritage and identity. The social, legal, and institutional acknowledgment of children's biracial group membership would facilitate the difficult task of constructing a positive biracial identity.

Note

1. Although questions are being raised about the doll-choice paradigm, it should be pointed out that the seeming clarity of its results has been important in changing social policy. The 1954 *Brown* decision of the U.S. Supreme Court (integrating schools) is a case in point. Clark and Clark's work was specifically cited in the decision, illustrating that "separate but equal" cannot possibly be equal because of the "personality damage" (self-negation) done to Blacks by segregation.

15

Between a Rock and a Hard Place: Social Adjustment of Biracial Youth

ANA MARI CAUCE
YUMI HIRAGA
CRAIG MASON
TANYA AGUILAR
NYDIA ORDONEZ
NANCY GONZALES

Approximately two years ago, the first author of this chapter set out to conduct a study focusing on how the social environment affects the psychological adjustment and well-being of African American and Asian American early adolescents in greater Seattle. She felt strongly about the importance of recruiting a multiracial and multiethnic team to collaborate on the research, and viewed the project as an opportunity both to contribute to the study of ethnic minority adolescents and to demonstrate that a predominantly ethnic minority research group could do high-quality work without falling prey to many of the biases so often present in research with ethnic minority participants.

In the initial phases of the project, careful attention was paid to the recruitment of adolescents who would represent the full diversity of their populations. We sought research participants who were poor, middle-class, and wealthy, those raised in single-parent households as well as those with two parents, those in private and public schools, and children in functional and less functional families.

We planned to limit our Asian sample to Chinese Americans, but upon further reflection opened participation to all Asian Americans, and our sample now includes Japanese, Korean, Filipino, and Vietnamese Americans. We did this because it became clear in our recruiting efforts that some of the sharp divisions between Asian communities that characterize other locales are more blurred in Seattle. There is no "Chinatown," but rather an "International District" that is pan-Asian in its character, and we did not want to impose demarcations between ethnic groups that would be ecologically artificial within the community.

As is typically the case, our criterion for ethnicity was self-definition. Our recruitment materials clearly stated that we wanted to interview early adolescents who were Black/African American or Asian American. But, because it was our goal to have at least one of our interviewers be of the same ethnicity as the youth, rather than waiting to have each participant check a box to indicate ethnicity, we asked about it over the phone when setting up interviews. Feeling self-congratulatory about the high degree of racial/ethnic sensitivity we possessed, we began our first interviews. And then a curious thing happened.

When setting up an interview with an adolescent, we inquired about ethnicity, and the reply was, "Well, my mother's Japanese, but my father's White." In another case, the adolescent told us she was Black, but when we arrived for the interview one African American and one White parent were waiting to be interviewed. With all our talk of diversity, these were not scenarios we had anticipated. Like most other researchers, we had neglected to consider the biracial child.

We discussed what to do about these adolescents. In the name of methodological purity, we considered excluding them, but this did not seem appropriate. Exclusion would go against our self-defined goal of obtaining a diverse sample. And, after all (we thought at the time), there would surely be just a few biracial families.

We have yet to conclude recruitment for the larger study, but at the time of this writing, 96 African American and 26 Asian American youth have been interviewed. The number of youths who proved to be biracial, in most cases with one White parent, were far from just a few. A total of 17 of the African American youths and 5 of the Asian American youths were biracial, accounting for about 20% of the total sample. The present study is our attempt to reckon with the existence of this overlooked and ever-increasing population of youth.

Methodological Underpinnings of the Present Study

Much of the early research on biracial persons utilized the case study method. A case study involves the intensive description of one or just a few individuals. Due to the lack of methodological rigor inherent in this technique, the case study has not been the research method of choice in almost any area of scientific investigation. In general, this approach has been used to study rare phenomena, in cases where it would be difficult to obtain large enough samples to allow for statistical comparisons (Kazdin, 1980). Since biracial individuals are so often viewed as "unusual," it is not surprising that, although they are far from rare, the bulk of the research in this area has utilized the case study method until recently.

Many case studies of biracial persons have left us with the impression that they are troubled by their status and confused about their identities, and that they experience more difficulties with families and peers than do others. These studies have also led us to believe that biracial persons are poorly adjusted (e.g., Gibbs, Huang, & Associates, 1989). However, because case studies are not necessarily representative, it is crucial to move beyond them in order to view biracial persons in proper perspective.

Biracial persons, like all humans, undoubtedly experience difficulties and challenges throughout life. Yet, to ascertain whether they experience more stress or distress than others, we must compare them to persons similar to themselves in ways other than their biracial status. This entails designing research studies that include a comparison or "control" group. It is also important that studies of biracial persons be developmentally sensitive. Issues surrounding biraciality vary by developmental stage; 3-year-old biracial children may not yet be aware of their status, the 13-year-old may be in the midst of dealing with it, and the 30-year-old may be fully comfortable with it.

In our review of the empirical literature on biracial persons, we encountered a dearth of studies that met the criteria just outlined. Indeed, we could identify only three studies that included control groups at all (e.g., Dien & Vinacke, 1964; Johnson & Nagoshi, 1986; Kinloch, 1983) and only one that utilized a matched control group (Dien & Vinacke, 1964).

In the present study, the 22 biracial adolescents previously mentioned served as our sample of biracial persons; of these, 17 (10 females) were African American-White and 5 (4 females) were Asian-White. All were in either seventh or eighth grade, representing an age range from 11 to 13. The control group was drawn from the larger population of youth in our sample and was closely matched with the biracial youth on age, year in school, and gender. We also matched for family income and family composition (e.g., one- or two-parent home), since these two factors systematically vary by ethnicity and race in our society. Finally, biracial adolescents were matched with others who had parents of the same ethnicity as the biracial youths' parents of color; that is, biracial youths with a White parent and an African American parent were matched with similar youths with two African American parents.

Due to the nature of biraciality, we could choose between two types of control groups. Our control group could consist of monoracial White adolescents or of monoracial adolescents of the same ethnicity and race as the parent of color. Our decision to do the latter was based, in part, on convenience. There were also compelling theoretical rationales for this decision. Individuals who are not 100% White are generally viewed as non-White and are treated as such in their communities. This has historically been the case for African Americans. In many sections of the South, persons with as little as one-sixteenth African ancestry have been considered Black on birth certificates and within society. Indeed, on a biological basis it is unlikely that there is much racial difference between the biracial White-African Americans in our sample and "monoracial" African American youths, who likely possess significant amounts of White ancestry. Estimates of the amount of African American genes accounted for from Caucasian ancestry range up to 50% in samples typically considered "monoracial" (Anderson, 1989; Reed, 1969). Thus biracial and "monoracial" groups are probably quite similar, except that one is considered biracial by virtue of the parents' racial composition.

In addition, all of the biracial youths in our study to some extent self-identified as Asian or African American by responding to our recruiting materials. Finally, by choosing a control group made up of people of color, we are, in part, also controlling for the effects of racial discrimination related to growing up as people of color in this society. That is, any differences obtained between the biracial and control groups are more likely due to the unique circumstances associated with biraciality than to the more pervasive difficulties that face all people of color.

Data from the 44 adolescents (22 biracial, 22 comparison) who constituted the final sample were obtained during one- to two-hour face-to-face interviews either in their homes or at the Department of Psychology at the researchers' university. Their mothers also participated in separate face-to-face interviews. A total of 17 of the "biracial" mothers were White, 3 were African American, and 2 were Asian. Interviews were conducted by a multiracial team of graduate students or advanced undergraduates and included the administration of a series of standardized questionnaires.

The subsequent sections present an overview of issues of concern to biracial adolescents, followed by results of our comparisons. Comparisons were conducted using matched *t* tests. Because of the large number of tests that were run, the Bonferroni correction method, which controls for experimentwide error, was applied to final results to minimize the likelihood of capitalizing on chance findings. The results presented here reflect that correction.

Coming of Age Biracially

Early adolescence is a time of accelerated development. After infancy, these years are characterized by the highest amount of biological, cognitive, and social growth (Lipsitz, 1977). As such, it is not surprising that normative studies have found that life stress peaks dramatically from the ages of 12 to 14 (Coddington, 1972a, 1972b).

No longer children, and still far from adulthood, early adolescents are typically just beginning to date, attend dances, and form friendship cliques. They participate in after-school and evening social activities that are increasingly more unstructured and less supervised by adults. They are expected to expand their responsibilities, such as deciding upon "electives" in school and taking on part-time jobs. Many are also faced with decisions about whether or not to drink alcohol, smoke marijuana or "crack," participate in street gangs, or engage in sexual activity. Given this combination of rapid change, life stress, and added responsibility, compared with children at other developmental stages, early adolescents typically feel *most* insecure about their looks, competencies, and, in general, who they are.

These normative stressors may be heightened for biracial adolescents, who must also deal with difficulties unique to their biraciality (Gibbs, 1985, 1987; Gordon, 1964; Ladner, 1977, pp. 102-125). These added difficulties may include incorporating two different heritages into one identity, experiencing racism from two ethnic groups, and dealing with and integrating two distinct parenting styles and beliefs. Because of these potential obstacles, some have suggested that biracial adolescents face greater risk of depression, conduct problems, low self-esteem, and peer conflicts (Gibbs, 1987; McRoy & Freeman, 1986). However, others have suggested that the unique problems that biracial adolescents face instill in them a sense of resilience and strength, which may serve to steel them against such difficulties (Adams, 1973; Hall, 1980; Johnson & Nagoshi, 1986; Poussaint, 1984).

This study examines differences between biracial adolescents and a matched comparison group of adolescents of color in those areas that have been noted to be potentially troublesome for them. More specifically, we examine their family and peer relations, life stress, self-esteem, and psychological adjustment.

FAMILY RELATIONS

The family plays a large role in the development of all children. This is no less the case for biracial children, as it is within the family that the child first begins to learn about racial differences and how others respond to them. The family environment is crucial to biracial children's understanding of their heritage, background, and identity. Supportive families can help the child integrate the two identifications of the parents and develop a strong self-concept (Jacobs, 1977; Miller & Miller, 1990).

The parents of biracial children must come to terms with their own interracial differences and the reactions of society. In many, if not most, areas of this country interracial couples are not readily accepted. If the parents are unable to deal with this stress, their attitudes will be transmitted to their children. The nature of the parents' attitudes toward racial difference may even affect the way they treat their children.

Vital to the development of biracial children are their individual relationships with their mothers and fathers. Biracial children must learn to cope with the different parenting styles each parent brings to the relationship. Parents incorporate the values they grew up with in their distinct cultures. This can affect the child if the parents disagree on such matters as dating, family rules and regulations, and career aspirations. For example, Posadas (1989) states that Filipino fathers often believe in strict hours and close supervision for their children, as is the custom in the Philippines. This may be quite at odds with the somewhat more authoritative, and at times laissez-faire, style that might have been present in the home of a middle-class White mother. Such differences might lead to conflict, not only between the parents, but between the parent and the child.

Potential difficulties go well beyond conflicting parenting styles. Each parent may wish the child to identify more with his or her own race (Piskacek & Golub, 1973). If, for example, the child begins to identify with his or her African American father, the child's mother may feel rejected, and the relationship between mother and child may suffer. Some studies have reported that children often do identify more with one race than the other. Poussaint (1984) found that many of the biracial African American students in his sample identified as African American and were embarrassed about their White parent, who made them feel less "authentically Black." Such feelings can, in turn, cause the child to feel disloyal and guilty (Sebring, 1985).

During the adolescent years, all these potential difficulties may be complicated by the age-appropriate search for identity that is just commencing. Parents of early teens must typically learn to allow their children to engage in age-appropriate exploration, but parents of biracial adolescents may have extra worries about allowing their children freedom, as they try to protect their children from discrimination and persons who hold racist beliefs, and prevent their internalization of oppressive attitudes. This parental protection may result in the adolescent becoming either too dependent upon the parents or too rebellious (Gibbs et al., 1989).

In sum, interracial and cultural differences, and the stresses they create between parents and between parents and their children, may lead to more difficulties within the family environment and to more conflict and less warmth between parent and child. This hypothesis was addressed by examining differences between the biracial and comparison groups on the following indices:

(1) *Family Environment Scale* (FES; Moos & Moos, 1981): completed by mothers, a widely used scale that yields scores on measures such as Family Control, Religious Orientation, Organization, and Cohesion[1]

(2) *Inventory of Parent and Peer Attachment* (IPPA; Armsden & Greenberg, 1987): completed by the adolescents, yields measures of Trust, Communication, and Alienation with respect to mothers and fathers separately

(3) *Child-Rearing Practices Report* (CRPR; Bloch, 1965, as adapted by Rickel & Biasetti, 1982): completed by the mother, assesses two overall dimensions of parenting—Nurturance and Restrictiveness

(4) *Family Support Scale of the Social Support Rating Scale—Revised* (SSRS-R; Cauce, Ptacek, Smith, & Mason, 1991): completed by adolescents

All measures in this study possess adequate psychometric properties. They were chosen because they were appropriate for use with adolescents and, in general, had been used previously with persons of color.

Table 15.1 reports the means and standard deviations for both the biracial participants and the comparison group. In terms of family relations, comparisons yielded a significant difference only on parental restrictiveness, with the mothers of biracial adolescents reporting less restrictiveness. This finding is consistent with previous theory and research suggesting that both African and Asian Americans exercise more restrictive or controlling parenting styles than do White parents (Dornbusch, Ritter, Leiderman, Roberts, & Fraleigh, 1987; Henggeler & Tavormina, 1980; Lui, Cauce, Kwak, & Mason, 1990). The less restrictive styles reported by mothers of biracial children may indicate their own White parenting style, since 17 of the 22 mothers were White.

No differences between the two groups on any of the other family measures were indicated. This suggests that the two groups are essentially similar in the other domains of family functioning and parent-child relationships that were assessed.

PEER RELATIONS

For all children, having friends is the utmost social achievement and an indication of social competence (Hartup, 1978). Interaction

TABLE 15.1 Family Relations

	N	*Biracial* Mean	*Biracial* S.D.	*Matched* Mean	*Matched* S.D.
Parent Information					
Child-Rearing Practices Report					
Restrictiveness	22	47.40	9.22	57.13	10.76*
Nurturance	22	78.68	6.80	76.74	5.32
Family Environment Scale					
Cohesion	21	12.73	2.39	12.83	1.60
Organization	21	10.19	2.56	11.71	2.19
Religion	21	11.29	3.65	12.11	3.32
Conflict	21	9.97	2.24	8.59	2.04
Child Information					
IPPA-Mother					
Trust	22	42.05	5.89	39.99	6.87
Communicate	21	31.26	6.61	34.05	6.18
Alienation	22	14.33	4.50	15.49	4.62
IPPA-Father					
Trust	19	37.58	9.92	37.54	9.72
Communicate	19	26.79	7.38	29.63	10.62
Alienation	19	16.26	5.23	15.63	5.08
Social Support Rating Scale					
Family	19	45.31	9.69	43.03	9.67
Formal	13	18.73	5.77	19.62	6.76

*$p < .05$, after correction

among peers was initially assumed to represent complex extensions of early relationships with parents, but more recent research suggests that peer relations uniquely influence children's social and intellectual competencies (Hartup, 1978). Successful peer relations help children assimilate and adapt to their environment, master their aggressive impulses, and learn to be better role takers and more socially effective (Gottman, Gonso, & Rasmussen, 1975; Hartup, 1970, 1979). On the other hand, children who are rejected by their peers are more likely to drop out of school, have higher rates of delinquency, and are at higher risk for developing mental illness (Coie & Dodge, 1983; Coie, Dodge, & Coppotelli, 1982; Hartup, 1979).

Adolescence is an especially crucial period in the development of peer relations. At this age children are spending growing amounts of time with friends (as opposed to adults), their friendships are becoming deeper and more intimate, and they are increasingly turning to friends for companionship and support (Berndt & Perry, 1986; Czikszentmihalyi, Larson, & Prescott, 1977; Furman & Buhrmester, 1985; Hunter & Youniss, 1982).

Skin color or race does seem to influence peer acceptance, but the small amount of research so far conducted on biracial children's friendships has yielded mixed results. A study reported by Sebring (1985) on biracial White-African American children found that they are more popular with White peers than are African American children, and more popular with African American children than are White children. This suggests that biracial children may have access to a wider circle of children from whom to draw friends, which may provide them with richer and more diverse experiences, as suggested by Hall (1980).

Conversely, Gordon (1964) has suggested that children of "mixed" marriages may lack a strong peer social network. Vander-Zanden (1963) similarly suggests that biracial children may develop more uncertain feelings about both sociocultural groups from which they stem. Finally, biracial children run the risk of being rejected by members of both races, as illustrated in the case of Mary (Lyles, Yancey, Grace, & Carter, 1985). Mary states:

> My skin is light, but I don't like it the way that it is. Everybody kids me and calls me "mixed zebra," "red-faced dog" and "black eyed pea." I laugh, but it hurts. Black and White kids pick on me. It's rough being mixed. . . . It does not mean I should not have friends.

In this study, the peer relations of adolescents were assessed using the Peer Trust, Communication, and Alienation subscales of the IPPA and the Peer Support and Peer Conflict subscales of the SSRS-R. In addition, adolescents' reports of the values held by their peer groups were measured by the Peer Values scale developed for the larger study. Means and standard deviations are presented in Table 15.2. No significant differences between the biracial adolescents and the comparison group were noted in terms of peer relations, as measured by trust, communication, alienation, support, or conflict in friendships. Biracial adolescents did report that their friends held more positive values than those in the comparison group. More specifically, the Peer Values scale measures attitudes toward behaviors such as skipping

TABLE 15.2 Peer Relations

		Biracial		*Matched*	
	N	*Mean*	*S.D.*	*Mean*	*S.D.*
IPPA-Child					
Trust	21	42.24	6.31	39.25	8.78
Communicate	21	30.67	6.80	28.19	7.15
Alienate	21	15.48	5.19	16.27	4.69
Peer Values Scale					
Negative Peer Values	22	33.28	4.10	36.49	4.32*
Social Support Rating Scale					
Friends	20	30.87	5.06	28.83	7.14

*$p < .05$, after correction

school, fighting, cheating, and stealing, and biracial children indicated that their friends viewed these behavior more negatively than those in the comparison group.

SELF-ESTEEM, LIFE STRESS, AND PSYCHOLOGICAL ADJUSTMENT

The comparisons between the two groups of adolescents on self-esteem, life stress, and psychological adjustment are at the heart of this study. As the sections on family and peer relations have already suggested, biracial adolescents may find themselves to be "socially marginal" and isolated, without a clear cultural group to identify with. This sense of difference may be highlighted as they search for identity, often considered the central task of adolescence. They alone know how it feels to be biracial. Neither their parents nor many of their friends are apt to understand their struggle fully. Such difficulties may make biracial teens more prone to depression, anxiety, and lower self-esteem (Gibbs, 1987; Root, in press-b).

Yet, as previously mentioned, these same difficulties may "steel" adolescents and increase their resilience. They must work harder to overcome stresses, which may strengthen their self-esteem. Indeed, some studies have suggested that biracial adolescents may have as high or higher self-esteem than monoracial adolescents (Chang, 1974; Duffy, 1978; Gibbs, 1989; Jacobs, 1977). However, methodological problems and the lack of carefully matched control groups weaken our ability to draw conclusions based on such findings.

In the present study, the Junior High School Life Events Scale (JHLES; Swearingen & Cohen, 1985) was used to measure life stress. This scale yields separate scores for Positive Events and Negative Events. The former are those life changes that adolescents indicated were "good" (e.g., making new friends); the latter are those that were viewed as "bad" (e.g., parents fighting more than usual). The State-Trait Anxiety Inventory—State Version (STAI; Spielberg, 1973), the Child Depression Inventory (CDI; Kovacs & Beck, 1977), and the Child Behavior Checklist (CBCL; Achenbach & Edelbrock, 1982) served as the primary measures of psychological distress and adjustment. The first two scales were based on self-reports by adolescents. The CBCL was completed by parents and yields scores on two primary dimensions, Internalizing and Externalizing. Higher scores on Internalizing are associated with social withdrawal and depression; higher scores on Externalizing indicate more "acting out" behaviors, such as aggressive or antisocial activities. The Self-Perception Scale for Adolescents (SPS; Harter, 1982), which is completed by adolescents, was used as an indicator of perceived self-competence in various realms, including School Competence, Social Competence, Romantic Competence, and General Self-Worth.

Means and standard deviations for both groups of adolescents are reported in Table 15.3. Results of comparisons did not suggest significant differences on any of the measures examined. This failure to find any area of difference is particularly noteworthy, given that more than 13 comparisons were conducted. Thus the key analyses in these studies suggest that biracial adolescents were indistinguishable from adolescents of color who were similar to themselves.

Conclusions: Where's the Rock and What's the Hard Place?

The results of our comparisons indicate that, in relation to the comparison group, biracial children reported that their peers held more positive attitudes and that their mothers had less restrictive parenting styles. These two findings may not be unrelated. It is possible that the mothers of biracial adolescents may be less restrictive as a result of their children's more favorable peer environment. However, this less restrictive parenting could instead reflect the fact that

TABLE 15.3 Psychological Adjustment Scores and Self-Esteem

		Biracial		*Matched*		*Norms*	
	N	*Mean*	*S.D.*	*Mean*	*S.D.*	*Mean*	*S.D.*
Child Information							
State-Trait Anxiety Inventory—State Version							
Anxiety	22	33.91	5.22	35.17	7.30	40.49	10.35
Child Depression Inventory							
Depression	22	34.01	5.61	34.54	7.02	10.78	7.63
Junior High School Life Events							
Bad change	22	2.73	1.91	2.95	3.39		
Good change	22	3.95	1.86	5.27	2.55		
Total change	22	6.68	3.12	8.23	4.54		
Self-Perception Scale for Adolescents							
School	16	15.00	2.78	14.47	3.54		
Athletic	16	13.13	4.32	12.63	3.76		
Social	15	15.73	2.79	15.47	3.54		
Physical	16	11.25	3.82	12.94	4.22		
Behavioral	16	14.83	3.40	14.97	2.51		
Friendship	16	16.56	2.42	14.75	4.11		
Romantic	12	11.25	3.19	11.21	3.64		
Global self	16	15.63	2.55	14.81	3.02		
Parent Information							
Child Behavior Checklist							
Internalizing	22	54.36	8.86	51.73	13.34		
Externalizing	22	53.77	9.60	52.05	13.84		

many of biracial children's mothers are White, and less restrictive parenting is more typical of White parents when compared with either African or Asian Americans. Even for those mothers of biracial adolescents who are themselves women of color, the parenting style of the White father may influence them to be less restrictive.

In any case, none of our results suggests greater difficulties among biracial adolescents. Indeed, based on adolescents' self-reports, biracial adolescents did not differ from the comparison group on any qualitative aspects of family and peer relations (e.g., support, trust, alienation), and maternal reports did not indicate any difference other than on restrictiveness. Perhaps most important, neither self-reports nor maternal reports suggested any differences between the groups in terms of life stress, behavior problems, psychological distress, competence, or self-worth. Biracial adolescents did not report greater distress or poorer competence and self-worth. Thus the key finding of this study is the relative lack of significant differences between the groups. Biracial early adolescents appear to be remarkably similar to other children of color matched on basic demographic variables.

This does not mean that the adolescents were not experiencing difficulties, either as individuals or as a group. It does imply that to the degree that such difficulties were experienced, they were no greater in our sample of biracial adolescents than they were in similar adolescents of color. An inspection of the means for both groups also suggests that scores on all indices of psychological adjustment and distress are well within the "normal" range. In sum, no rock or hard place was found, and our results clearly suggest that biracial adolescents can be reasonably healthy and happy.

LIMITATIONS OF THE PRESENT STUDY AND FUTURE DIRECTIONS

In generalizing beyond this study, it should be noted that our sample size was small and lacking in geographic diversity. The larger social environment is expected to have a major impact on the adaptation of biracial adolescents, and the greater Seattle area may be a more benign environment for them than many other parts of this country or even Washington State. Environments characterized by less racial tolerance would be expected to place greater strains upon biracial persons.

It should also be noted that biracial adolescents in our study responded to recruitment materials geared toward adolescents of color. As such, this study's findings should not be generalized to those biracial adolescents who view themselves as White or who may be ashamed of their Asian or African American heritage. It is unlikely that such adolescents would have responded to our recruitment efforts and it may be just those adolescents who would experience the greatest degree of problems (L. Fields, personal communication, January 25, 1991).

In addition, it is important to keep in mind that these were early adolescents. Although many of our adolescents had begun to date, and a few had "steady" boyfriends or girlfriends, in general the dating was casual, and even the steady relationships could not be characterized as truly serious. Indeed, the adolescents in this study were somewhat younger than the age at which other researchers have suggested that problems come into full bloom (Hall, 1980; Miller & Miller, 1990; Root, 1990).

On the other hand, this study included several methodological strengths, most notably the inclusion of a comparison group matched on key demographic variables. This allowed us to place the reports of biracial adolescents in appropriate perspective. Another strength of this study was its assessment of both adolescents and their mothers across a broad array of contexts, including family and peer relations, social competence, and intrapersonal distress.

Nonetheless, much important work in this area is still to be conducted. In particular, we believe that there is a need for studies that help us better understand why some biracial persons adapt well to their biraciality, whereas others experience great difficulties, either during a particular life stage or throughout their lifetimes. Longitudinal studies would be especially useful in this respect.

What types of environments, both within and outside of the family, lead to healthy adjustment among biracial persons? What coping skills do well-adjusted biracial persons find most useful? How do biracial persons acquire a sense of positive racial identity, and how does this identity develop and change across the life span? Are specific biracial "mixes" (e.g., African American-White, Latino-White, Asian American-White, Latino-African American) differentially vulnerable or resilient? Is any specific age group or gender associated with greater difficulties? What environmental factors lead to optimal adjustment in biracial youth? These are all questions begging to be answered, and more empirical work is sorely needed.

Our study suggests that biracial adolescents can be healthy, competent, and well adjusted. This is a good thing, since such youngsters may presage the future of our increasingly multiracial society.

Note

1. The Family Environment Scale yields scores on other subscales, such as Family Conflict, however, various subscales did not meet criteria for adequate internal reliability (alpha > .60) and they were not used in our analyses.

Acknowledgments

This study was funded by a grant from the National Institute of Child Health and Human Development (HD 24056) to the first author. This study would not have been possible without the help of many dedicated undergraduate research assistants; key among these were Emmaly Williams, Marco Sanchez, Dale Helt, and Linda Jones.

16

Negotiating Ethnic Identity: Issues for Black-White Biracial Adolescents

JEWELLE TAYLOR GIBBS

ALICE M. HINES

Since the end of World War II, American society has undergone several radical social changes, one of which has been the increase in interracial marriages. By 1988 there were 218,000 Black-White married couples in the United States, more than three times the number (65,000) in 1970 (U.S. Bureau of the Census, 1991b). As a result of these interracial relationships, a new generation of biracial youth has emerged in our society, particularly in urban areas of the Northeast, the Midwest, and the West Coast.

There are an estimated one million biracial children and adolescents in this country, but no separate reliable estimates of Black-White youth are available (Collins, 1984). Since Black-White marriages currently constitute 22.8% of all interracial marriages, it is reasonable to assume that these unions produce nearly one-fourth of the biracial children. Reliable estimates of these youth are further confounded by the issues of validity and reliability of racial designations on marriage and birth certificates, variations in state laws requiring vital statistics by race, and variations in reporting the child's race in out-of-wedlock births to mothers of a different race. Despite these methodological difficulties, the growth of this biracial group can be clearly documented from articles in the mass media, observations of educators, and the growth of interracial family support groups (Collins, 1984; Muse, 1986; Njeri, 1988b; Poussaint, 1984).

One of the major issues frequently reported by biracial adolescents is the problem of labeling themselves with a racial or ethnic identity. As the offspring of interracial unions, these youth have legitimate claims to two racial heritages, yet they often experience social pressures to choose a Black identity even though they may prefer to identify as White or "mixed." Historically in the United States, due to the legacy of slavery, any person with a known Black ancestor was considered Black, which resulted in stigmatization and discrimination (Frazier, 1949). This practice has persisted, so that children of Black-White unions are usually labeled Black and assume Black social identities. As the numbers of biracial Black-White people have grown and their consciousness has developed, they have begun to challenge the practice of labeling themselves as Black rather than as mixed, biracial, or some other nonracial designation (Muse, 1986; Njeri, 1988b). The search for a more inclusive label to reflect a dual racial heritage could perhaps be interpreted as an underlying ambivalence toward a Black identity in a predominantly White society, or as a positive affirmation of racial duality in an expanding multicultural world.

The purpose of this chapter is to examine this issue using results from a study of biracial adolescents and their families conducted by the authors in a San Francisco Bay Area community from 1987 through 1989. From earlier clinical investigations of biracial adolescents in mental health settings, the senior author had developed a model of identity conflicts and coping strategies exhibited by these youth in treatment situations (Gibbs, 1987, 1989). This model, based on Erik Erikson's (1959) psychosocial framework of adolescent development, identifies conflicts in five major areas of identity development for these biracial adolescents: conflicts about dual racial heritage, conflicts about social marginality, conflicts about sexuality and impulse management, conflicts about autonomy from parents, and conflicts about educational and career aspirations. Among adolescents referred for treatment, these conflicts were manifested in the school settings by academic underachievement or failure, behavior problems, truancy, substance use, conflicts with peers and teachers, social isolation, and depression (Gibbs & Moskowitz-Sweet, in press).

In community settings these conflicts appeared in the forms of delinquency, sexual acting out, and self-destructive activities such as substance abuse and suicidal behavior. However, it is important to note that monoracial adolescents also experience these conflicts and often demonstrate inflexible defenses, although their symptoms and behaviors may be different in source and intensity (Adelson & Doehrman, 1980; Offer, 1969).

In the course of clinical assessment and treatment, it was noted that these biracial adolescents developed fairly consistent patterns of defense mechanisms and coping strategies that enabled them to defend against the anxiety generated by these identity conflicts (Gibbs, 1987). Their defense mechanisms tended to vary between extreme polarities and included denial or rejection of their Black or White heritage, overidealization of their White or Black heritage, identification with the aggressor in social situations, repression or sublimation of sexual and aggressive feelings, lack of individuation or premature separation from parents, and overcompensation or self derogation in educational or work situations. Defensive strategies of these biracial youth, compared with other monoracial youth, seemed to be more extreme, less flexible, and dynamically related to issues of race and ethnicity. Coping strategies that were the behavioral correlates of these defense mechanisms were also characterized by extreme responses. These strategies ranged from overt rejection of the White or Black parent to "switching" between White and Black peer groups, choosing to identify socially with only one racial group, excessive inhibition or acting out of sexual and aggressive feelings, immature dependence on or pseudomature autonomy from parents, and conscious overachievement or deliberate underachievement in school and work settings (Gibbs, 1987, 1989).

This model of identity conflicts and coping strategies was generally supported by findings from previous clinical studies of biracial youth, most of which were conducted on small samples. These studies found that biracial children frequently exhibited confusion over their racial identity, feelings of low self-esteem, divided family loyalties or parental rejection, and psychological or behavioral problems (Faulkner & Kich, 1983; Gordon, 1964; Jacobs, 1977; Ladner, 1977; Payne, 1977; Piskacek & Golub, 1973; Teicher, 1968; Washington, 1970). However, other models of ethnic identity development have been proposed by authors who view this process as a gradual acceptance and integration of majority and minority cultures, through a series of stages of ego identity development (Atkinson, Morten, & Sue, 1979; Cross, 1987; Phinney, Lochner, & Murphy, 1990). These models, based on findings from developmental and cross-cultural studies, illustrate the complexity of ethnic identity development and predict a variety of outcomes, including ultimate resolution and achievement of a positive identity.

Some studies of racially mixed youth in school settings have described them as having academic and behavioral problems as well as identity conflicts (Gibbs & Moskowitz-Sweet, in press; McRoy & Freeman, 1986). Identity conflicts were also found among some biracial adolescents who were adopted in early childhood by White parents, but the majority seem to be well adjusted (McRoy, Zurcher, Lauderdale, & Anderson, 1984; Silverman & Feigelman, 1981; Simon & Alstein, 1977).

Empirical studies of biracial children indicate that their racial attitudes and self-concepts may develop differently from those of either Black or White children (Gunthrope, 1977/1978; Payne, 1977). Gunthrope's finding that accurate racial identification decreased as skin color darkened suggests that darker mixed children have more negative self-concepts. Conversely, a few studies have found that biracial children had levels of self-esteem equal to or higher than those of their monoracial peers (Chang, 1974; Duffy, 1978; Jacobs, 1977).

More recent reports of biracial youth in nonclinical settings such as universities and integrated neighborhoods have portrayed them more positively, as self-confident, creative, and well adjusted (Gay, 1987; Njeri, 1988b; Poussaint, 1984). Positive outcomes are associated in these cases with supportive families, cohesive social networks, and integrated schools and neighborhoods.

Contradictory findings about the psychosocial adjustment of these youth can probably be attributed to differences in research designs and sampling. Most of the studies assume that these biracial youth face special challenges in negotiating their ethnic and racial identity, but this assumption is largely based on findings from clinical and empirical studies, which limits their generalizability. Thus the current study was designed to evaluate the psychosocial adjustment of a nonclinical sample of biracial Black-White adolescents, with a particular focus on the process of negotiating an ethnic and racial identity in the broader context of resolving a series of developmental tasks to form a stable personal identity, which Erikson (1968) has described as "a sense of personal sameness and historical continuity."

Description of the Study

In 1987 a two-year study of biracial adolescents and their families was initiated in order to investigate the psychosocial adjustment of the adolescents, the process by which they negotiated racial and personal identities, and parents' perception of their adjustment to being reared in an interracial family. The study was conducted in the San Francisco Bay Area communities of Berkeley and Oakland, California, from 1987 to 1989.

A "snowball" method of sampling was utilized. Interracial families were identified through an organization called I-Pride, a support group for interracial-intercultural families in the Bay Area. Families were contacted first by letters, then by follow-up telephone calls, and asked to participate in the research project if they had one or more adolescents in the 12-18 age range. Families that met the criteria were then asked to identify other such families in the area; this method eventually yielded 10 families with 12 adolescents. Parents and adolescents were asked to complete consent forms to participate in the study and were assured of confidentiality at each stage of the research.

The following measures were used in the study: a Biracial Adolescent Psychosocial Interview, the Achenbach Youth Self-Report, and the Rosenberg Self-Esteem Scale for Adolescents. In addition, parents were asked to complete a Parents' Questionnaire.

The Biracial Adolescent Psychosocial Interview covered 12 major areas of adolescent attitudes, behaviors, and experiences with a series of questions dealing with the subject's racial self-concept, racial identity, and attitudes about being reared in an interracial family. This interview, modeled after a questionnaire developed by the senior author for a previous study of adolescent females (Gibbs, 1985), encompasses questions about self-esteem, health behaviors, school attitudes and achievement, peer relations, parental relations, sexual attitudes and behaviors, illicit substance use, delinquent behaviors, work experiences, community activities, and educational and occupational aspirations.

The Achenbach Youth Self-Report (Achenbach & Edelbrock, 1987), designed for 11- to 18-year-olds, consists of 20 standardized items that reflect youths' views of their own competencies and problems. Test items are grouped into Competence Scales, which form two subscales (Activities and Social Competence), and Behavior Problem Scales, which form seven subscales (Depression, Somatic Complaints, Unpopular, Thought Disorder, Aggressive Delinquent, and Self-Destructive/Identity Problems). These Behavior Problem Scales are further grouped into Internalizing Scales, Externalizing Scales, and Mixed Scales. Data on the validity and reliability of this measure are reported in the *Manual for the Youth Self-Report and Profile* by Achenbach and Edelbrock (1987), who note that Blacks and Whites have been included in the recent normative samples.

The Rosenberg Self-Esteem Scale is a 10-item self-administered scale to measure the adolescent's level of self-esteem. Widely used in research on Black and White adolescents, its validity and reliability are described in Rosenberg's *Society and the Adolescent Self-Image* (1965).

The Parents' Questionnaire covered areas related to the teen's developmental and health history, school and social experiences, community support groups, family activities, and parents' perceptions of the adolescent's attitudes about being biracial and being reared in an interracial family. Both parents in intact families were asked to participate, but only one parent was usually available.

The entire battery of measures for the adolescent and his or her parents took approximately three hours to complete. Two female interviewers, one Black and one White, conducted the interviews in the homes of the subjects. Parents and adolescents were interviewed separately to maximize privacy and confidentiality.

Due to the small sample size, the data were analyzed with a combination of descriptive statistics and qualitative analysis, which provided an in-depth perspective on these subjects, their attitudes, behaviors, and conflicts. This chapter focuses primarily on the results of the interviews with the adolescent subjects.

Discussion of Findings

DESCRIPTION OF THE SAMPLE

The sample included 12 adolescent participants, 6 female and 6 male, ranging in age from 13 to 18 years old; their average age was 15. Of the 12, 4 (33.3%) were born in the Bay Area, 6 (50.0%) in other parts of California or the United States, and 2 (16.7%) were foreign-born; 8 (66.7%) of the respondents attended public schools.

A total of nine parents participated in the study: seven mothers and two fathers. Of the mothers, five were White and two were Black; both fathers were Black. The parents' ages ranged from 45 to 56, with a mean age of 48 years. Only two of the parents had been born in the Bay Area.

Two of the parents had two adolescents in the study, and one parent participated even though her child refused. Two of the adolescent participants were first-year college students whose parents were not able to be interviewed.

Marital statuses of the parents were as follows: two married, one separated, five (55.5%) divorced, and one never married. Family sizes ranged from one to five children, with an average of three children per family. Only three (33.3%) parents reported particular religious affiliations, either Catholic or Protestant.

Five (55.5%) of the parents had grown up in predominantly Anglo-American communities, three (33.3%) had grown up in predominantly Black communities, and one in a racially mixed community. The parents were well educated—40% had finished college and 40% had completed two or more years of graduate school. Family income ranged from $20,000 to more than $50,000 per year, with an average annual income of $30,000-$39,000.

ANALYSIS OF FINDINGS

Results of this study are analyzed according to the framework of identity conflicts proposed by Gibbs (1987), whose previous work was based on clinical samples of biracial and bicultural adolescents (Gibbs, 1987, 1989; Gibbs & Moskowitz-Sweet, in press). The purpose of this analysis is to explore the salience of the conflicts and the framework proposed by Gibbs when applied to a nonclinical "normative" population.

Conflicts about racial/ethnic identity. This conflict involves the basic question, "Who am I?" Gibbs found that problems arose due to a partial or complete failure to integrate the racial and ethnic backgrounds of both parents into a cohesive identity. In several cases, the teen either identified with the White parent and rejected his or her minority heritage or overidentified with the minority parent and adopted stereotyped minority behaviors and a negative identity. Some teens expressed ambivalent feelings toward the racial and/or ethnic backgrounds of both parents, alternately accepting and rejecting characteristics of both groups, feeling pressured to identify with one group or the other. Other biracial adolescents expressed "divided loyalties," switching from one culture to the other depending on situational demands and/or the environmental context.

In response to the question "How do you think about yourself racially?" six (50%) adolescents identified themselves as mixed race, two (16.7%) as Black, and one (8.3%) as Afro-American; two (16.7%) were unsure how to respond. According to parent reports, six (60%) said they taught their children that they were Black, six (60%) identified their children as Black when filling out forms, and three (30%) labeled their children "mixed." When adolescents were asked how they generally labeled themselves, the majority of eight (66.7%) replied "mixed."

When asked what they liked about their racial identity, responses included their appearance (16.7%), being different and unique (16.7%), and the ability to fit in with all groups of teens (33.3%). They did not like name-calling (25.0%), their minority status (16.7%), and being conspicuous (25.0%). Seven subjects (58.3%) reported having had difficult experiences growing up as biracial children, nine (75.0%) had been targets of racial slurs, and ten (83.3%) had been questioned about their appearance, their parents, and whether they were Black or White.

Regarding experiences within the family, seven subjects (58.3%) reported having had exposure to both races, which was initiated by the mother in the majority of the cases. While seven (58.3%) said that their families discussed racial and ethnic differences, the same number expressed the desire to talk more frequently about racial and identity issues at home. Seven (70%) parents stated that they sometimes discussed race and related issues with their teenagers, and five (50%) said these discussions took place regularly. Parents reported discussing topics such as racial slurs, identity issues, and reactions from their teenagers' peers and classmates.

When asked which race they would prefer for a marital partner, the majority (58.3%) said it did not matter; three (25.0%) responded Black and two (16.7%) biracial. Regarding the race of their children, all but one said it would not matter; the other respondent said he preferred his child to be White. Responding to whether or not they wished to belong to a different race, ten (83.3%) subjects replied that they were satisfied being biracial, one (8.3%) replied Black, and one (8.3%) White.

Conflicts about social marginality. The basic question in this area, "Where do I fit?" is one that besets all adolescents, but it may be especially problematic for biracial teens. Problems in the social arena may emerge as these youth enter high school and become involved in a larger social context. Since conformity is highly valued during adolescence, biracial teens are often rejected by both majority and minority groups because they do not "fit in" easily with either group.

Subjects reported that their schools were mixed racially, with high percentages of Black, White, Asian, and Hispanic students in most of their schools. While all of the students reported having White teachers, 10 (83.3%) had Black teachers, 4 (33.3%) had Asian teachers, and 5 (41.7%) had Hispanic teachers. None had been exposed to teachers who identified themselves as mixed or biracial.

Regarding peer relationships and social activities at school, all subjects reported having good relationships with their classmates; eight (66.7%) subjects stated they got along well with others, and five (41.7%) said they enjoyed school. When asked about what they disliked at school, only two (16.7%) subjects reported that teachers treated them unfairly, or were "prejudiced." Nine subjects (75%) participated in school activities such as sports, music, clubs, and art. Nine of the teenagers also held part-time jobs—babysitting, working at a recreation center, delivering newspapers, or working in a fast-food restaurant.

When asked about which ethnic or racial groups they associated with most frequently, the most common response was Black (eight, or 66.7%); second was White (seven, or 58.3%) and third was Asian (four, or 33.3%), followed by mixed race (four, or 33.3%) and Hispanic (three, or 25.0%); least common was Native American (one, or 8.3%). Five (50%) parents reported that their children's closest friends were Black. While most stated that the race of their children's friends made no difference, two (20%) wanted them to have more Black friends.

When asked if they had racially mixed friends, all but two subjects (83.3%) responded affirmatively. As for problems with other ethnic groups at school or in the neighborhood, five (41.7%) subjects stated they occasionally had arguments with other groups, and three (25.0%) had been in trouble with school authorities; none reported getting into trouble with the police.

Nearly half of the subjects reported occasional conflicts with other ethnic groups, but this may reflect the ethnic tensions in their multiracial schools. These teens might have used extracurricular activities as a vehicle to find a compatible group of peers, since three-fourths of them were active in sports, music, art, or clubs. Thus they could establish "alternative" identities as "jocks," "rockers," or "hippies," group identities that cross racial and ethnic lines.

In summary, the majority of this group appeared to be comfortable with their social identity as biracial persons and had established positive relations with Black, White, and other mixed-race and minority peers. Those few who were insecure in their social identity were more likely to avoid socializing with Blacks and more likely to be ambivalent about labeling themselves as Black, and their parents were more likely to express a desire for them to have Black friends. It is interesting to note that the racial labels preferred by these teenagers for themselves were somewhat discrepant from those attributed to them by their parents. The behaviors of this subgroup are associated with social marginality, suggesting that this phenomenon occurs in the process of identity formation for a segment of biracial adolescents in the community.

Conflicts about sexuality. Conflict stemming from the question "What is my social role?" can be expressed in issues of sexual orientation, gender identity, patterns of sexual activity, and general impulse management. Gender roles and sexual orientation are linked to positive identification with each parent and may be conflictual for biracial teens who have ambivalent or negative feelings toward the parent of the same or opposite sex due to racial and/or ethnic membership.

Choice of sexual partners and patterns of dating and/or sexual activity can also be problematic and complicated for biracial teens. According to Gibbs (1987), patterns of dating and sexual activity are sometimes expressed as an "all or none" situation, with some biracial teens becoming sexually promiscuous and others becoming celibate to avoid the risks of intimate relationships.

In this sample, all but one of the adolescents (91.7%) said they dated, with an average age of 12.5 years at the first date. All of them went out on "group dates" that included shopping, parties, music, and movies, and eight (66.7%) went on dates alone. Only four (33.3%) female subjects reported having had sexual relations as unwilling participants. None reported having ever been pregnant or having had an abortion.

When asked about which ethnic and/or racial group they preferred to date, all 12 subjects said they would date Black, biracial, or Hispanic individuals; 11 (91.7%) would date Whites; 10 (83.3%) would go out with Asians; and 9 (75.0%) would date Native Americans. When asked to specify their preferences, 5 (41.7%) subjects had no preference, 4 (33.3%) preferred Blacks, and 2 (16.7%) preferred Whites.

Findings in the area of sexuality conflict indicate that this group represented a range of behaviors. While all but one teenager had dated heterosexually, only one-third reported having had sexual relations. This rate of sexual activity is consistent with recent estimates of teen sexual activity for this age group (Dryfoos, 1990). Three-fourths of the subjects either preferred to date Blacks or had no racial preference, but two preferred White partners. Interview responses did not indicate any serious conflicts about sexual behavior or gender identity, nor did these subjects have obvious problems with managing their impulses. However, some subjects seemed socially immature, had dated primarily in groups, and were uncomfortable discussing sexual issues. Biracial females were somewhat more likely than males to have concerns about dating, sexual activity, and availability of appropriate male partners. These concerns are consistent with reports from previous studies (Gibbs, 1987; Logan, Freeman, & McRoy, 1987).

Conflicts over autonomy and independence. The basic question in this area is "Who is in charge of my life?" Negotiating separation and individuation from parents is a difficult developmental task for most adolescents and may be particularly complicated for biracial youth. Parents responding to their own negative experiences as an interracial couple may attempt to shield the adolescent from similar experiences. Some of these youth may become overly dependent on parents, displaying compliant and conforming behavior and the failure to mature socially and physically. Others may become rebellious and seek premature independence, behaving in an assertive, confrontational, and risk-oriented manner. They may engage in delinquent activities and experience more conflict with parents, siblings, and peers.

Parents of biracial teens may also be physically or psychologically removed from the adolescent due to conflict within the marriage, separation and divorce, or the burdens of being a single parent. Adolescents growing up in such problematic family situations may also have a difficult time separating, as there is no stable foundation from which to separate gradually. These teens may also be forced into premature separation or may cling to childhood for security.

In this study, all but one (91.7%) of the subjects reported getting along at least moderately well with their mothers, and seven (58.3%) got along moderately well with their fathers; only one person reported not getting along well with either parent. These responses were corroborated by parental reports, with five of the parents describing their relationships with their teens as very open, two moderately open, and two as shifting between open and closed.

Four (33.3%) subjects reported problems with their current family functioning, including family tension, parental conflict, and issues of separation and divorce: Two (16.6%) complained that parents interfered and pressured them excessively, and six (50%) reported other related problems. However, seven (58%) subjects stated that they would like their own future families to be like their current ones. Four (33.3%) subjects said they would not like to be divorced, and two (16.6%) expressed a preference for their own families to be more open, less conservative, and closer emotionally.

Findings in the area of autonomy and independence indicate that the subjects seemed to experience normative tensions due to separating from their parents. Nearly all of these teens reported getting along well with their mothers, while just over half felt as positive about their paternal relationships. This could reflect the reality that half of the subjects did not live with their fathers and did not interact with them frequently. While nearly one-third reported tension or conflicts in their current families, two-thirds complained of excessive parental pressures and other related concerns. The fact that nearly half of the subjects wished their future families to be different from their families of origin reflects their dissatisfaction with their current family functioning. Responses indicated that some teens felt their parents were emotionally distant, while others felt they were overprotective and too intrusive. Although there was no clear relationship between these subjects' perceptions of their parents and their own adjustment, the younger and more immature teens tended to be concerned about parental expression of affection and the older and more independent teens reported concerns about overprotective and intrusive behaviors. As previous studies have suggested, parents of biracial children often struggle with the balance of maintaining a protective haven to insulate them against racial prejudice and encouraging their freedom to separate and cope with the real world (Logan et al., 1987).

Conflicts over educational and career aspirations. The basic question in this area is "Where am I going?" and conflict arises from ambivalence about achievement and upward mobility. For biracial teens who identify with White middle-class culture, academic achievement may be a way to gain acceptance and demonstrate values that they share with White peers. However, awareness of prejudice and fear of failure in the academic realm may lead some of these adolescents to impose limitations on their academic achievement and ambitions. For those identifying with the minority culture, academic aspirations and studious behavior may invite ostracism or provoke ridicule. Due to fear of rejection by their peers, these teens may become involved in truancy, deliberately fail their courses, or engage in other self-defeating behaviors.

In this sample, all adolescent subjects reported doing good to average work in elementary school, junior high school, and high school. At the time of the study, nine (75%) subjects reported that their grades were in the A-B range. When asked about future educational plans, three (25.0%) subjects reported planning to complete college and nine (75%) wanted to go to graduate school. Regarding future plans, five (41.7%) subjects stated they wanted to work to save money, travel, have a family, and pursue a career. Seven (58%) subjects said that their parents were the major influences in determining their career and occupational choices.

In this area of educational and career aspirations, three-fourths of the subjects were performing above average academically, with the same proportion planning to go to graduate school. However, fewer than half had made specific plans about careers or future life-styles. Their educational aspirations appeared to be influenced primarily by their parents, whose average educational and occupational level was high, rather than by specific occupational goals. Thus their biracial identity did not seem to have had a negative impact on their future aspirations by foreclosing any options or repressing their ambitions, which seemed realistic and congruent with their academic performance.

General psychosocial adjustment. Evaluating subjects' health and mental health is an important measure of psychosocial adjustment. All subjects reported being in good or average physical health. Seven (58.3%) described themselves as usually happy and only one (8.3%) as usually sad or depressed. Six (50%) of the subjects had been to a mental health agency, with four (33.3%) referrals due to personal reasons and family conflict.

Self-reported rates of substance use among subjects in this sample were low compared with their age peers. None of the subjects smoked cigarettes. Seven (58%) reported occasionally drinking alcohol, including beer, wine, and champagne; eight (66.7%) said their friends occasionally drank alcohol. Three (25.0%) subjects reported occasional use of drugs, specifically marijuana, and six (50.0%) said they had friends who sometimes used drugs.

These subjects' infrequent use of alcohol and drugs suggests that they are somewhat more inhibited, or ascetic, than their peers, who they reported are more likely to use these substances. Their low rates of substance use could also be interpreted as a fear of losing control or a fear of confirming a negative social identity as a "Black drug user."

This group of biracial adolescents has higher-than-average self-esteem compared with the norm group. Seven (58.3%) of the teenagers felt fairly positive, and only one (8.3%) felt fairly negative, in regard to self-esteem and feelings of self-worth. The mean score for the total sample on the Rosenberg Self-Esteem Scale was 2.00, indicating moderately high self-esteem. Four (33%) subjects reported their worst characteristics to be temper and mood swings, two (16.7%) said they were too introspective, two (16.6%) said they were stubborn and that they tended to show off, and one (8.3%) reported being lazy. Seven (58.3%) subjects felt that their mothers would describe them positively, but only five (41.7%) felt that their fathers would do so.

On the Youth Self-Report Inventory the means of the subjects' standardized scores on the four scales were as follows: 50.66 for females, 52.16 for males on the Competency Scale; 57.80 for females, 53.16 for males on the Internalizing Scale; 53.60 for females, 44.16 for males on the Externalizing Scale; and 58.20 for females, 46.66 for males on the Total Problem Scale. Scores of both male and female subjects on all scales were well within the normative range of scores for non-clinic-referred adolescents. Female subjects reported more problems and scored slightly higher than males on both the Internalizing and Externalizing Problem Scales, although there was a greater tendency for them to internalize.

Summary

The findings of this study of a nonclinical sample of 12 biracial adolescents from the San Francisco Bay Area present a somewhat differentiated perspective on the psychosocial adjustment of adolescents from interracial families. While the sample is admittedly small and not randomly selected, the comprehensive multidimensional research design provides an in-depth description and appraisal of these youth. Since all but two of the subjects were interviewed in their homes, the researchers were generally able to observe the home environment, the family dynamics, and the neighborhood environment for additional insights.

In summary, nine (75%) of these subjects appeared to feel positive about themselves and comfortable with their biracial identity. In contrast to subjects in previous clinical studies, they have learned to negotiate an ethnic identity that incorporates positive aspects of their Black and White racial backgrounds, to establish satisfactory peer and social relationships, to manage their sexual and aggressive impulses adequately, to achieve a relatively healthy separation from their parents, and to set appropriate educational and career goals.

However, three (25%) subjects did show evidence of more problematic psychosocial adjustment. In comparison to the other subjects, an analysis of their responses on the two psychological instruments as well as their interview responses revealed lower self-esteem scores, greater ambivalence over labeling themselves as Black, higher levels of social and sexual immaturity, and less certainty about future goals. Age alone did not account for these differences, since these three subjects ranged in age from 14 to 17. Thus their poorer levels of adjustment could conceivably be attributed to their ambivalence over being biracial and their inability to develop cohesive ethnic and personal identities.

Factors that were associated with positive psychosocial adjustment in this group were intact families, higher socioeconomic status, attending integrated schools, living in integrated neighborhoods, having a multicultural social life, and having open, warm relationships with parents. In families where both parents and adolescents confronted the issues of biracial identity, teens appeared to be better adjusted. These families actively promoted and participated in a multicultural life-style, encouraging their children to explore both sides of their racial heritage and exposing them to a range of ethnic activities, institutions, and role models.

Conversely, subjects who were less well adjusted were more likely to live in single-parent families, to have less contact with the noncustodial parent's family and friends, and to avoid talking about racial issues. These results are consistent with findings from other studies that found important effects of family environment, school and neighborhood environment, social support groups, and open family communication on the positive identity formation of biracial children and adolescents.

Results of this study generally support recent models of ethnic identity development, in that these subjects can be viewed along a continuum of stages in the integration of their dual racial identities and in the resolution of their conflicts about ethnicity. However, these findings are limited in their generalizability to the total population of biracial adolescents for several reasons: The sample is small and nonrandom, participants represent a self-selected middle-class group, the community is unusually liberal and tolerant of diverse life-styles, and subjects may have volunteered as a way of asserting or dramatizing their special status.

Despite these limitations, the in-depth assessment measures provide some valuable insights into the process of identity development and the resolution of ethnic identity in these biracial adolescents. Collateral information from their parents adds an important dimension to the study and provides an additional perspective on their attitudes and experiences growing up in interracial families. Moreover, this study has implications for parents, teachers, and health, mental health, and social service professionals who interact with these families. In order to facilitate the optimal growth and development of biracial youth, parents should support the integration of their dual racial heritage, teachers should provide multicultural learning opportunities, and mental health and social service professionals should develop programs of prevention and early intervention to minimize the potential social problems and identity conflicts sometimes experienced by these youth. As the incidence of interracial marriages continues to rise, the expansion of this population of children and youth will pose a major challenge to researchers, educators, and clinicians to provide more information about their social and psychological needs, as well as to determine the most effective child-rearing strategies to assure their healthy development and positive identity formation.

17

Offspring of Cross-Race and Cross-Ethnic Marriages in Hawaii

RONALD C. JOHNSON

A large number of prior writers on the topic of biracial individuals have taken the position that offspring of cross-racial, cross-ethnic, or even cross-religious group marriages are at risk for becoming psychologically maladjusted (e.g., see the citations in the review of the literature in Johnson & Nagoshi, 1986). This greater risk has been attributed to (a) a negative response to intergroup marriage and to the offspring of such marriages on the part of significant others and of the general community, (b) marginality and confused cultural identity of offspring of intergroup marriages, and (c) psychological deviance or self-rejection on the part of persons entering into intergroup marriages that influences offspring adjustment adversely, both as a consequence of marital disharmony and through direct influences on offspring.

Authors claiming that offspring of intergroup marriages will be maladjusted typically have limited their support for their views to anecdotes or case histories. Even in Hawaii, where, as will be shown below, intermarriage was and is frequent, it is argued (without data) that persons entering into intergroup marriages have personality problems and are self-rejecting (Char, 1977) and that the offspring of such marriages are at risk (Mann & Waldron, 1977). When data are brought to bear on these beliefs, they are shown to be incorrect, at least in Hawaii.

Before going further, let me describe the limitations of the data to be presented. First, available data have to do chiefly with members of Hawaii's five major racial and/or ethnic groups—persons of Caucasian,[1] Chinese, Filipino, Hawaiian or part Hawaiian,[2] and Japanese ancestries—and with offspring of within or across group matings of members of these groups. For example, a good deal is known about patterns of within- and across-group marriages in these five groups (e.g., see Ho & Johnson, 1990; R. C. Johnson, 1984) but not with regard to other groups, such as persons of Korean (the next largest ethnic group after the five listed above), Samoan, Tongan, African American, and other ancestries. Second, those data that were generated from the Hawaii Family Study of Cognition (HFSC) were obtained from a large sample (1,816 families) of paid participants. Even though paid for participation, families making up the sample were of higher educational and occupational levels than the population at large. Finally, the reader will note, perhaps, that a sizable proportion of the research papers cited are papers of which I am author or coauthor. This cannot be helped; despite much interest in the topic of intergroup marriage and the offspring of such marriages, interest rarely has progressed beyond the level of expressing opinions and gone on to actual data acquisition and publication.

Intergroup Marriage in Hawaii

To help the reader understand intergroup marriage in Hawaii, and the effects of being an offspring of such a marriage, I will begin with a history of intergroup marriage in Hawaii. I then will move to the present, and discuss variables influencing who marries whom and the current rate of intergroup marriage in Hawaii. I will then present data having to do with personality, cognitive, and behavioral attributes of offspring of intergroup marriages in Hawaii. Data are not available regarding all possible intergroup combinations, so I must limit my report to those combinations for which data are available.

The first two persons not of Hawaiian ancestry to reside in Hawaii, more than 200 years ago, were Isaac Davis, a seaman who was the sole survivor of a Hawaiian attack on the ship *Fair American*, and John Young, boatswain on the *Eleanora*, kidnapped by the Hawaiians.

Davis and Young were in charge of King Kamehameha's artillery—much of it taken from the *Fair American* before she was stripped and burned—as he moved up the island chain conquering and uniting the islands (except for Kauai, which remained independent for several more decades). Both married high ali'i chieftainesses, and one of Young's descendants became queen (for histories of Hawaii, see Daws, 1968; Lind, 1980). The haoles (*haole* means, literally, "stranger" or, more exactly, "one who cannot speak," and the first group of strangers to arrive were Caucasians) and Hawaiians met on a basis of equality, with each group having resources that the other group wanted. The Hawaiians had resources, such as sandalwood for trade and food for revictualing ships, as well as land, women, and political power under a great king who had united the islands under his rule. The haoles had the guns and technical skills that resulted in Kamehameha's success, as well as other manufactured goods. The first Chinese to arrive, more than 200 years ago, were ship's carpenters, employed by Captain George Vancouver in Canton, who, once arriving in Hawaii, decided to stay. By 1808, one of these Chinese had established a plantation growing sugar and rice on the island of Kauai. The Russians and their Aleut crewmen-sea otter hunters arrived shortly afterward. Then came the whalers (and almost a third of whaling crews were African American, along with Native American, Fijian, and other non-White crewmen).

The ethnic mix had well begun before the beginning of importation of plantation labor in the 1840s, but the present ethnic mix largely results from the importation of contract laborers willing to work on sugar plantations. The first plantation laborers were Chinese. Labor agents then began to import laborers from almost every part of the world desperate enough from want to sign on. Portuguese, most of them from the Azores, more Chinese, Japanese, Koreans, Puerto Ricans, and, finally, Filipinos were the largest groups imported. Fijians, Gilbert Islanders, Norwegians, Germans, Spaniards, and Russians also were imported, but in most cases only one shipload each—usually because they were not sufficiently subservient. (The Russians held a strike on the dock as soon as they disembarked.) Along with the plantation laborers, Mexican (Paniolo) cowboys were imported as ranch hands; two migrations of Samoans took place, the first group sponsored by the Mormons and the second consisting for the most part of the *Fita-fita*—the Samoan "national guard" during World War II—and their families; a second wave of Filipinos (usually well educated and not plantation labor) arrived; and, largest of all, a recent (post-World War II) influx of "mainland haoles" (Caucasians from the U.S. mainland) took place.

Many regions have had as much immigration, but few as rapidly as Hawaii, and none as heterogeneously as Hawaii. Except for the Portuguese and the Japanese, who frequently migrated as family groups, migrants to Hawaii who came as plantation laborers were young men. If they were to marry, they had to marry outside their own groups. The 200 "Year 1" men (men who came to Hawaii in 1868, the year of the overthrow of the Shogun and the restoration of the Meiji emperor in Japan) arrived and their offspring vanished within the gene pool before the next Japanese arrived, about 20 years later, and the same thing happened to other small groups of early migrants. It was only after substantial numbers of people arrived from any area that they came to have a feeling of ethnic identity and (especially if women formed part of the migrant group) came to regard within-group marriages as in some way better than across-group marriages.

C. E. Glick (1970) has shown the same pattern of changes in intermarriage rates with years in Hawaii for a number of different racial and/or ethnic groups. He proposes three stages:

(1) Nearly all incoming persons are male, and they intermarry.
(2) More females arrive (as with the haole immigrants and their kin in the 1820s and 1830s, the Chinese in the 1870s and 1880s) and intermixture is discouraged.
(3) Americanization, loss of parental influence on offspring marital choice, and increased intercultural marriage take place.

All groups in Hawaii are now in the third stage.

The number of residents of the state of Hawaii (excluding short-term resident military and military dependents) is 919,366. Of these, 201,884 are of part-Hawaiian ancestry and 102,985 or more are of mixed but not Hawaiian ancestry, for a total of 304,869. Almost exactly a third of the residents are of mixed ancestry; this is the largest group of residents. (The largest groups of unmixed ethnicity are the 234,194 persons of Japanese ancestry and the 183,460 persons of Caucasian ancestry; State of Hawaii, Department of Planning and Economic Development, 1989.) Persons of part-Hawaiian ancestry generally view themselves and are regarded by others in the community as being Hawaiian. Persons of half-Asian (Chinese, Japanese, or Korean, less often Filipino) and half-Caucasian ancestry usually are regarded by others and by themselves as *hapa haole* (half Caucasian) and persons of thoroughly mixed ancestry, usually Polynesian, Asian, and European, often use the term *cosmopolitan* or *local* as a self-description. With persons of mixed ancestry already the largest group in the population, and with a present intergroup marriage rate of 45% (resident marriages only, but with military and military dependents counted as residents; State of Hawaii, Department of Health, 1988), it is clear that a person of unmixed racial and or ethnic background, except for immigrants, will be a rare specimen in a few generations.

All of the material presented above does not mean that Hawaii is devoid of xenophobia or of prejudice. Compared with the proportion of Chinese persons in the population, persons of Chinese ancestry have the highest ratio of within-group to across-group marriages, despite the fact that the Chinese percentage of outmarriage is the highest of the five (Caucasian, Chinese, Filipino, Hawaiian or part Hawaiian, Japanese) major ancestral groups of persons residing in Hawaii. Haole or Japanese American young people will meet between a quarter and a third of their prospective mates who are of the same group as their own; for persons of Chinese ancestry, 19 of 20 persons who might be considered as prospective mates are of a different group from their own. Personal and family preferences cut the odds to less than 1 in 2 from the expected frequency of about 1 in 20 for Chinese within-group marriage (Ho & Johnson, 1990; R. C. Johnson, 1984). The same is true, to lesser degrees, for other major racial and/or ethnic groups. Personal and family preferences for within-group marriages are present, but are overwhelmed by the influence of sheer numbers of prospective mates from other groups as well as by other variables such as educational and occupational attainment and personal attributes only marginally related to race and/or ethnicity.

Preference for one's own group exists in Hawaii. So, too, do racial and ethnic stereotypes. Vinacke (1949) and Narikiyo (1987) obtained data concerning Hawaii's different racial and ethnic groups. They obtained both stereotype (what others think of a given group) and self-stereotype (how group members describe the group) data. Stereotypes and self-stereotypes are highly similar, and they have not changed much across the nearly 40 years between these two studies. They include quite negative attributes, and both researchers found that people tend to view the faults of other groups as more offensive than their own.

Here we have a multiethnic society, with no group forming a numerical majority, and the largest segment of the population of mixed ancestry, and each group has a set of stereotypes about each of the other groups and a set of self-stereotypes in almost total agreement with the stereotypes held by others and accepts these stereotyped and/or self-stereotyped attributes, whether positive or negative. Yet, personal and family preferences for within-group marriages, stereotypes concerning other groups, and all to the contrary, Hawaii will have an almost totally mixed population in a few generations. I think that the reason is clear. As population geneticists such as Lewontin (1972) have demonstrated, the vast majority of variance in any trait is within race and within group, rather than across group (e.g., Japanese versus Chinese). Race and ethnicity are trivial unless we go out of our way to make them important. Personal attributes, once separated from race and ethnicity, are important. Through a combination of good luck, goodwill (for which the native Hawaiians deserve much credit), and opportunities to meet and know persons from other groups, we in Hawaii have been fortunate to live in a place where race and ethnicity have had little influence and personal qualities a great deal of influence on intergroup marriage and on treatment of offspring of such marriages.

Supposed Basis of Maladjustment of Intergroup Marriages

After this long preamble—longer than what follows it—what about the supposed negative influences on the adjustment of offspring of cross-racial or cross-ethnic marriages in Hawaii? One variable supposedly leading to maladjustment is a negative value placed on intergroup marriage and on offspring of such marriages. As noted above, pressures exist in favor of intragroup marriages. This can be discerned in the far-greater-than-chance rates of within-group marriages among members of Hawaii's major groups (Ho & Johnson, 1990) and also in the fact that second or later marriages are more often across-group marriages (Jedlicka, 1975) (probably because the opinions of parents and others are less influential by this time in the participants' lives; Johnson & Nagoshi, 1990). Even so, with a population in which the plurality of persons are of mixed ancestry, and about half of current marriages are across racial and/or ethnic lines, family or community opposition has not been prohibitive.

A second argument that cross-group offspring are more at risk is that they are marginal persons—not fully accepted by or accepting of either ancestral group. Here, in Hawaii, while many persons of mixed ancestry refer to themselves as part Hawaiians or cosmopolitan, they almost all will say that they are "local"—that is, not mainland American, but "local"—people with their own set of values, and quite indifferent to whether or not they are "marginal" to either or both of their ancestral groups. Whether or not one is local is vastly more important, in social relations, than one's ancestry. Being a local implies that one is family centered, concerned with consensus more than accomplishment, and so on (see Oesterly, Conrad, Darvill, Johnson, & Higa, 1989). Race and ethnicity are trivial compared with the distinction between local and nonlocal. Consequently, offspring of intergroup marriages are not marginal persons in Hawaii.

Duffy (1978) is the first person to have obtained data regarding marginality of offspring of intergroup marriages in Hawaii. Studying offspring of Caucasian parents, Japanese parents, and couples with one parent from each group, she concluded that there were no differences in self-esteem among the groups, that they did not differ in types of interaction with parents, and that offspring of intercultural marriages maintained a simultaneously dynamic ethnic identity. C. W. Stephan (in press) contrasted Asian American, Caucasian American, and mixed Asian-Caucasian subjects from Hawaii on a number of measures (e.g., self-esteem, anomie, dogmatism, xenophobia, intergroup anxiety) that might be expected to relate to marginality. Differences among the three groups were relatively slight though often statistically significant, with the hapa haole subjects nearly always being intermediate in scores between the two other groups. Stephan's data do not support the belief that offspring of intergroup marriages are marginal or maladjusted.

Psychological deviance or self-rejection of persons entering into intergroup marriage is said to have negative influence on offspring both as (a) a result of marital disharmony and (b) a direct influence of parental pathology on offspring risk for maladjustment. With regard to marital disharmony, it is only since 1985 that resident and nonresident marriages have been separable in the published statistics of the State of Hawaii Department of Health. Data do not support the belief that cross-ethnic marriages are less harmonious than are within-group marriages, and, in consequence, result in maladjustment among offspring. The ratio of divorces to resident marriages for 1985 through 1988 is *lower* for across- than for within-group marriages (Ho & Johnson, 1990). Prior claims that across-group marriages are more likely to be disharmonious (e.g., end in divorce) result from the fact that almost all nonresident marriages are within-group marriages and, if they result in divorce, result in divorce somewhere other than Hawaii.

The last argument that offspring of intergroup marriages are at risk has to do with the belief that persons who marry across groups are psychologically deviant and/or self-rejecting. This argument has been put forward, without supporting data except personal opinion, even in Hawaii, where a large proportion of marriages are across racial or ethnic lines. No data are available regarding supposed self-rejection, but data are available regarding personality attributes of persons who marry within and across groups. As part of the Hawaii Family Study of Cognition, involving the testing of 6,581 persons (parents plus adolescent or older offspring) from 1,816 families, a sizable number of persons were administered personality tests. Among the parents, these included 543 spouse pairs who had married within their own racial and/or ethnic groups and 83 interethnic sets of parents. The results (Ahern, Cole, Johnson, & Wong, 1981) showed that women who married across groups generally were less subservient and more independent than women who married within their own groups and that men who married within versus across groups differed very little from one another. Further, the Ahern et al. data showed that the lower the proportion of persons in a given group marrying cross-ethnically, the more they differed from those marrying within group. This is not surprising; only unusual persons do unusual things. The couples who were assessed in the Ahern et al. study were, on the average, married in the late 1940s or early 1950s, when intergroup marriage was less common than it is at present, particularly among the large Japanese American group. At present, with intergroup marriage much more frequent than it was 40-50 years ago, the amount of within- versus across-group dating among dating couples is not at all related to personality attributes of individuals (Johnson & Ogasawara, 1988) and couples marrying within versus across groups do not differ in personality (Nagoshi, Johnson, & Honbo, 1990). These reports show no evidence of psychological disturbances on the part of persons dating or marrying across racial and/or ethnic groups.

Attributes of Offspring of Intergroup Marriages in Hawaii

Reasons given for the belief that offspring of intergroup marriages should be expected to be at risk for being psychologically damaged are without any empirical support in Hawaii. Now, finally, what are the offspring of intergroup marriages like here in Hawaii? The data provided below are sparse, and often are limited to information concerning the largest racial or ethnic groups in Hawaii, in the areas of psychological adjustment, cognitive abilities, and "other" (attitudes toward, responses to, and use of alcohol) characteristics.

PSYCHOLOGICAL ADJUSTMENT

As noted above, Duffy (1978) found that the offspring of Japanese-Caucasian marriages were not "marginal" but, instead, maintained a "simultaneously dynamic ethnic identity." Johnson and Nagoshi (1986) reported on personality test data obtained from 1,024 offspring of within-group and 180 offspring of across-group marriages. We found no differences between the groups on personality dimensions that seemed closely associated with adjustment (ego strength, neuroticism), and found significant differences on only 3 of 14 dimensions, with the "good-adjusted" end of the dimension being problematical on each of the three obtained significant differences (e.g., is it "better" or "worse" to be more extroverted than a comparison group). C. W. Stephan's (in press) data include measures of adjustment, and indicate that offspring of intergroup marriages are not maladjusted. The only empirical data available support the position that whether one is the offspring of a within- or across-racial mating does not significantly influence one's personal adjustment.

COGNITIVE ABILITY

The second topic is that of cognitive ability. It is well demonstrated (e.g., see Daniels, Plomin, McClearn, & Johnson, 1982) that offspring of consanguineous marriages (usually cousin marriages) score lower on ability and/or IQ tests than persons whose parents are not related, presumably because the majority of deleterious genes are recessive, relatives are more likely to have similar recessive genes, and their offspring are more likely to be double recessive on these genes so that they manifest themselves. The probability of two unrelated persons of the same ethnic group (e.g., two Swedes, two Japanese) carrying the same relatively rare deleterious recessive genes is small, but the odds of persons of different racial groups carrying the same recessive genes is smaller still. It follows, then, that to the degree that genes influence performance in ability tests, offspring of cross-ethnic matings should perform better than offspring of within-group matings.

We were able to test this out, contrasting offspring of within- versus across-group marriages who were tested as part of the Hawaii Family Study of Cognition. Offspring of cross-ethnic matings did perform significantly better on the first principal component (the equivalent of *g* or general ability) of the test battery, and, further, the degree of superior performance of offspring of cross-group marriages on the 15 tests that made up the test battery was significantly correlated with the degree to which each test was a measure of general ability (Nagoshi & Johnson, 1986). While trivial in a real-world sense, the superiority of the cross-ethnic offspring is of some interest, since it conforms to expectations from genetic data having to do with the effects of inbreeding. Offspring of cross-ethnic matings are at a slight advantage in terms of cognitive test scores.

ALCOHOL

The only other major area for which data are available has to do with alcohol. Wolff (1972) was the first to investigate the flushing response (in which the face and sometimes the rest of the body turns pink or red following the ingestion of even a small amount of alcohol). Many persons of Asian ancestry flush after drinking a small amount of alcohol, while most Caucasians do not. (A fair proportion of Caucasians flush, too, but it takes a very heavy dosage of alcohol to produce the flushing.) Wolff (1973) showed that hapa haole and even one-fourth Asian and three-fourths Caucasian subjects flushed like Asians, suggesting that the flushing response is inherited as an autosomal dominant gene. Wilson, McClearn, and Johnson (1978) found that hapa haoles flushed like Asians but drank like haoles. While it is true that Asian Americans drink less and flush more than Caucasian Americans, when one contrasts flushers and nonflushers within groups (e.g., Japanese American males), reported consumption is only slightly related to whether or not the person flushes (Schwitters, Johnson, McClearn, & Wilson, 1982). There is less there than it seems. The genetic biological interpretation of group differences in alcohol use now is dominant, but, on examination, is difficult to defend. Group differences in Hawaii and elsewhere appear to result from social learning, not from genes. (See Johnson & Nagoshi, 1989, for a review of the literature on this matter.)

Summary

Supposedly negative influences (e.g., community opprobrium, deviance of persons entering into such marriages) on cross-group marriages do not exist in Hawaii, at least for the five major ethnic groups residing in these islands (the only groups assessed in this study). Offspring of cross-group marriages show no signs of psychological disturbances and are not alienated or marginal persons. They perform significantly better than offspring of within-group marriages on tests of cognitive ability and are not more at risk for problem drinking. The results reported herein may be true only for Hawaii and places like Hawaii (the Cayman Islands and Brazil come to mind), where personal attributes are regarded as more important than race in mate selection. It is heartening to be able to report results such as those presented herein. Hawaii provides a model that may come to be followed elsewhere.

Notes

1. The reader might ask why all Caucasians are lumped together, while persons of Asian ancestry are categorized in terms of nation of origin. The answer is that this reflects social reality: All Caucasians are considered to form a single category. This has its advantages; for instance, Hawaii was and is spared from anti-Semitism, largely because local people do not differentiate, and, if they think of the matter at all, consider Jews and Christians to be roughly comparable to followers of two differing Buddhist sects.

2. Persons of part-Hawaiian ancestry are regarded as being of Hawaiian ancestry by state and federal agencies and nearly always will regard themselves as being Hawaiian.

18

Please Choose One: Ethnic Identity Choices for Biracial Individuals

CHRISTINE C. IIJIMA HALL

During the late 1970s, 30 half Black and half Japanese individuals were extensively interviewed on their experiences of and attitudes about being racially mixed. This exploratory research project was initiated to uncover the ethnic identity choices made by these individuals, the factors affecting their choices, and life experiences/attitudes of these mixed individuals. In the past, most research (Teicher, 1968) had been conducted on mixed children in psychiatric hospitals or clinics. Consequently, research on this population yielded data that indicated maladjustment. Very few published works could be found, at the time of the present study, on a nonclinical sample of biracial individuals. Therefore, I endeavored to interview a nonclinical sample of individuals with Black fathers and Japanese mothers.

Park (1928) coined the phrase "marginal man" to represent a person who lives in two cultural worlds. Stonequist (1937), Park's student, popularized the term but took a different perspective on the marginal person. Stonequist viewed the position as a negative one, with the marginal person being one

> who is poised in psychological uncertainty between two or more social worlds; reflecting in his soul the discords and harmonies, repulsions and

> attractions of these worlds, one of which is often "dominant" over the other; within which membership is implicitly based on birth or ancestry (race or nationality); and where exclusion removes the individual from a system of group relations. (p. 8)

Stonequist's view of marginality was challenged by other sociologists and psychologists (Antonovsky, 1956; Gist, 1967; Goldberg, 1941; Green, 1947; Kerckhoff & McCormick, 1955; Wright & Wright, 1972). The most prominent complaint was that Stonequist made no distinctions among marginal person, marginal status, and marginal personality (Kerckhoff & McCormick, 1955). A marginal person is biologically or culturally from two or more races or cultures. Marginal status exists when an individual occupies a position somewhere between cultures but does not wholly belong to any. This person is tied to groups culturally, socially, and/or psychologically. The individual has a marginal personality when he or she has trouble dealing with the marginal status position, is torn between cultures, and develops psychological problems. With these distinctions, Goldberg (1941) made the important determination that the mere fact of being a marginal person does not lead to a marginal personality. In fact, there was growing belief that marginal people may be multicultural, with the ability to identify with more than one culture and acquire a wide range of competencies and sensitivities (Ramirez, Castaneda, & Cox, 1977).

> The fate which condemns him [the marginal person] to live, the same time, in two worlds is the same which compels him to assume, in relation to the world in which he lives, the role of a cosmopolitan and a stranger. Inevitably he becomes, relative to his cultural milieu, the individual with a wider horizon, the keener intelligence, the more detached and rational viewpoint. The marginal person is always relatively the more civilized human being. (Park, 1937, p. xvii)

One group of individuals living in the United States who must live in two worlds is people of color who are living in White America. This group has at least three identity choices: to identify with their ethnic group, to identify with the White group, or to meld the two into a third (sometimes "hyphenated") identity, such as Japanese American (or Japanese-American).

Americans of mixed racial/ethnic heritage must also live in two worlds. Mixed individuals who have minority and majority (ethnic and White) heritages have similar choices to those mentioned above. The choices are multiplied when the individual is a dual-minority combination (e.g., Black-Japanese). Ethnic identity for all racially mixed groups is exacerbated by the fact that they are racially mixed in a nonmixed society. They are a numerical minority, have few role models, and are usually not totally accepted by either ethnic group with which they share heritage.

The present study looked at a group of "marginal people" gathered from a nonclinical population to investigate ethnic identity choices, factors that influenced these choices, and attitudes and experiences regarding their bicultural and biracial existence.

Method

RESPONDENTS

A total of 30 (15 women and 15 men) Black-Japanese respondents were recruited through word of mouth and newspaper articles in the *Los Angeles Times* and the *Rafu Shimpo* (the primary Japanese American newspaper in the Los Angeles area) describing the proposed research.

Respondents, ages 18-32, were from the greater Los Angeles area. The requirement that they be over the age of 18 was included in an attempt to eliminate adolescent "identity crisis" (Erikson, 1968) as a factor in their responses. Additionally, only individuals with Black fathers and Japanese mothers were interviewed. (If other combinations had been included, the number of participants would have had to increase exponentially due the cell sizes needed to obtain statistical power.)

QUESTIONNAIRE

Respondents were interviewed using a researcher-designed questionnaire (the Hall Ethnic Identity Questionnaire) that consists of a self-administered section and an interviewer-administered section. The self-administered section contains established measures of self-esteem (Dien & Vinacke, 1964; Rosenberg, 1965) with some adaption for the Black-Japanese sample population. In Dien and Vinacke's (1964) Ideal Self measure of self-esteem, a list of adjectives are presented to respondents, who rate themselves on a 6-point Likert-type scale (strongly agree to strongly disagree). Two adjectives added to the scale for this research study were *Black* and *Japanese*. The 10-question Rosenberg Self-Esteem Measure was used without adaptation.

The interviewer-administered section was of my own design; it solicited information on the areas described below.

Ethnic identity choice. For this study, *ethnic identity* was operationally defined as the category chosen by the respondent on a multiple-choice question commonly used for affirmative action purposes at many institutions. It is a questionnaire that instructs a person, "Please choose one" of the ethnic categories. Then listed are the usual federal delineations of ethnicities (Black, Hispanic, Asian, American Indian/Alaskan Native, White, and so on). An option of "Other: Please specify" was also included.

Demographics. Respondents were asked questions on their sex, age, and generation of mother (immigrant to the United States, first generation born in the United States, and so on).

Ethnic composition of neighborhoods and friends. Respondents were asked to give ethnic breakdowns of their past and present neighborhoods and friends.

Subjective measure of cultural knowledge. Respondents were asked how much they knew about the Black and Japanese cultures (answering items using a scale of 1 to 6).

Objective measure of cultural knowledge. This section was composed of questions adapted from the Chitling Test (Aiken, 1971) and comparable Japanese culture questions. Sample questions were "How do you say rice in Japanese?" and "What is a blood?" This section is now endearingly titled the Sukiyaki-Chitling Test.

Racial resemblance to a particular ethnic group. Respondents were asked to self-assess their resemblance to various ethnic groups (Japanese, Black, Filipino, Polynesian, White) on a 4-point scale ranging from "very much" to "not at all."

Involvement in political movements. Respondents were asked questions about their participation in Asian, Black, and other movements.

Acceptance of and by particular ethnic groups. The Bogardus (1925) Social Distance Scale was adapted for this measure. Bogardus discusses individuals' acceptance of particular groups as being a criterion for identification or inclusion with the group. For this particular research, acceptance by particular groups may have been additionally important for ethnic identity choice.

Ethnic identity decision process. Respondents were asked whether they had experienced periods when they had to decide to be Black, Japanese, or any ethnic identification.

Results and Discussion

Of the 30 Black-Japanese interviewed in this study, 18 (60%) chose the category "Black" on the "Please choose one" question, 10 chose the "Other" category (7 of whom specifically identified themselves as Black-Japanese), 1 identified as Japanese, and 1 chose not to place himself into a racial or ethnic category. The 10 people who chose "Other" commented that they did not wish to be categorized simply as Black or Japanese, which would deny one of their cultures. They found that checking "Other" on a list that instructed "Please choose one" was a viable choice. Statements such as the following illustrate the frustrations and discovery: "It made me so mad to have to choose one." "It took me a long time before I realized that there was a place to check 'Other.' "

The one person who identified as Japanese did so because she had lived in Japan most of her life. The respondent who did not wish to categorize himself from a checklist was not much different from the rest of the respondents in his reactions to the interview and the questions. He simply did not believe in racial categorization.

In order to perform statistical analyses on the ethnic identity (dependent) variable, the ethnic choices were divided into two categories, Black ($n = 18$) and Other Than Black ($n = 12$). Dichotomizing this dependent variable was necessary to conduct the primary statistical analyses for this study—regression with the aforementioned factors hypothesized to influence ethnic identity as the independent variables (demographics, ethnic composition of neighborhoods, and so on).

ETHNIC IDENTITY CHOICE REGRESSION

To determine the relative influence of each of the variables on ethnic identity, a regression was computed (see Table 18.1). The ethnic identity choice regression, with Black as the dependent variable, yielded four significant variables accounting for 56% of the variance ($F = 8.3$, $p < .01$). It showed that those Black-Japanese who were young, had

TABLE 18.1 Ethnic Identity Choice Regressed on Black Identity

Analysis of Variance	*df*	*SS*	*MS*	*F*	R^2	*Adjusted* R^2
Regression	4	4.05	1.01	8.03*	.56	.49
Residual	25	3.15	.13			

Variables	*Beta*	*Standard Error*	R^2
Age	–.29	.02	.06
Percentage of times the respondent reported having Black friends	.42	.002	.24
Subjective knowledge of Black culture	.38	.19	.14
Perceived acceptance by Japanese American peers	–.36	.12	.12

*$p < .01$.

knowledge of the Black culture, had predominantly Black friends, and perceived nonacceptance by Japanese American peers tended to identify as Black. When these variables were regressed on the Other Than Black dependent variable, the regression showed that those Black-Japanese with the opposite attributes—who were older, had less knowledge of Black culture, reported fewer Black friends, and were accepted by Japanese Americans—had a greater likelihood of choosing a category other than Black. Because these "Other" respondents did not possess the attributes needed to predict Black identity, their category choice should not be seen as a fallback choice. If this were a fallback choice, it most likely would have influenced self-esteem. As reported earlier, this was not the case. There was no significant correlation between ethnic identity choice and self-esteem. Thus the choice of a category other than Black was not seen as choosing a "marginal" or "outcast" category, but as choosing a viable racial category that respondents felt comfortable with and proud to report.

Demographics. The mean age of respondents was 24 years. Age was correlated, although not significantly, with ethnic choice ($r = -.29$). (However, age made a significant contribution to ethnic identity choice in the regression analysis.) It appears that younger respondents had a greater tendency to identify as Black than did other respondents. Cheek (1972) has reported similar findings with his Black respondents. His explanation for this age difference is that with youth comes race militancy and a stronger race ideology. This militancy stage is also discussed by Cross (1978) as a necessary stage in the process of "Nigrescence." Kitano (1974) and Piskacek and Golub (1973) also theorize a stage where a minority individual may choose to reject one culture. The young Black-Japanese interviewed in this study may, therefore, have been experiencing this stage of strong identification with and/or rejection of one culture.

Another explanation can be found in Goodman's (1964) book on race awareness. Goodman observes that young children see race as a unidimensional trait; it may be that the younger Black-Japanese individuals in this study view race as an "either/or" category. The older Black-Japanese may have reached a point in their lives where they can conceive of race as being multidimensional, and thus are able to identify as both Black and Japanese. These respondents concluded that a biracial category was a viable alternative; they actualized that a multiracial and multicultural existence was possible. This awareness may occur through maturation, experience, and self-evaluation (Cooley, 1902). For example, one respondent reflected, "When I was younger, I thought I had to choose between the Blacks or the Japanese. Now I realize that I can be both and who cares what other people think I should be."

No sex differences in ethnic identity choice were indicated in the analysis. Contrary to past research (reviewed in Brand, Ruiz, & Padilla, 1974), females in this study did not differ from males in their ethnic identity choice. Same-sex identification was not substantiated. An interesting possible explanation for this lack of sex difference is that sex roles may be less important than race/ethnic roles for minority males and females.

A total of 24 of the respondents' mothers were first-generation immigrants from Japan (*Issei*); 6 were second-generation Japanese Americans (*Nisei*). It was surprising that no generational effects developed, given that past research has shown generation to be a salient factor in ethnic identity among minorities in the United States (Clark, Kaufman, & Pierce, 1976; Matsumoto, Meredith, & Masuda, 1970). Perhaps this lack of influence was due to the respondents' belief that they were a new people or new race (Hall, 1980). Generation of mother would have no significant influence on their ethnic identification if they considered themselves the first generation of Black-Japanese.

Ethnicity of neighbors and friends. Respondents reported that, averaged over their lifetimes, approximately 46% of their neighbors had been White, 31% had been Black, and 14.5% had been Japanese. Percentage of times they reported having White, Black, and Japanese friends were 42%, 67%, and 26.4%, respectively. There was a greater tendency toward Black identification when the respondents reported a predominance of Black neighbors ($r = .39, p < .05$) and friends ($r = .49, p < .01$). These results are in accordance with past research findings (Cheek, 1972; Criswell, 1939). It should be noted, however, that a strong correlation does not explain the direction or timing of the choice. That is, a person could have had a predominance of Black friends and thus chose a Black identity *or* he or she could have had a Black identity and thus chose to have more Black friends.

Knowledge of culture and language. Ethnic identification choice and the objective and subjective measures of culture were significantly correlated ($r = .48, p < .01$). The more a respondent knew about Black culture, the more likely he or she was to choose a Black identity. Though not significant, strong correlations similarly indicated that the more knowledge a respondent had about Japanese culture, the more he or she tended to choose a category other than Black. Again, correlations do not give information about causality. Knowledge of culture may also have been the consequence of ethnic identity choice. If an individual identifies with a particular group, he or she is more likely to practice the customs and rituals of that group more often than an individual who does not identify with the group. Conversely, knowledge of culture could be the antecedent in this case, since many of the respondents reported practicing Black and Japanese customs at home (before the social influence of friends could come into play). As they grew older, they may have realized that these customs were group specific and may therefore have sought others who would maintain and accept these customs. This process may have led to an identification with a specific group.

There were 16 respondents who felt they could speak Japanese well, somewhat, or a little, and 19 who felt they could speak Black English well, somewhat, or a little. There was no significant correlation between language proficiency and ethnic identity choice. This was surprising, given that language proficiency has been shown to be a powerful influence in ethnic identity (Sotomayor, 1977; Taylor, Bassilli, & Aboud, 1973; Taylor, Sinard, & Aboud, 1972; Uyeki, 1960). In fact, of all the cultural knowledge measures, it had the lowest correlation with ethnic identity.

The lack of influence of Japanese language proficiency may have been due to the Black-Japanese respondents' referent group for Japanese identity. That is, the respondents tended to see Japanese Americans, close to their ages, as their Japanese peers. Since most Japanese Americans around the age of 24 tend not to speak Japanese very well (Clark et al., 1976), it was not surprising that the Black-Japanese respondents' criteria for Japaneseness did not include language proficiency.

The lack of influence of Black English proficiency is, however, confusing, because many respondents commented that being able to participate in street talk was necessary for relating to the Black experience. The ability to speak Black English may be important for interaction with Blacks but may not necessarily be a criterion for Blackness or Black identity. For example, many Black leaders (e.g., Martin Luther King, Jr., Jesse Jackson, Ralph Bunche) do not speak Black English in their public addresses and yet still have strong Black identities.

Political involvement. The only significant variable in this area was that of involvement in other ethnic movements ($r = .38, p < .05$). This variable seemed to predict that those involved in other ethnic movements (e.g., United Farm Workers and MECHA) tended to put themselves in a category other than Black more often than those not so involved. This could mean that those who chose this category saw themselves as more multicultural and were able to become involved with other ethnic movements besides those of their Black or Japanese heritage.

The lack of influence of participation in Black and Asian movements was surprising, however. Perhaps involvement was viewed as a forced choice—as having to choose Asian over Black or Black over Asian. In the 1970s, Blacks and Asians were pitted against one another. Involvement with human rights and other ethnic issues was more diverse and cut across racial lines.

Perceived acceptance by and of various groups. Perceived acceptance *by* Black peers and lack of acceptance *by* Japanese American peers showed moderate but nonsignificant correlations with ethnic identity ($r = .32$ and $-.23$, respectively). However, lack of acceptance by Japanese Americans did emerge as a significant predictor in the ethnic identity choice regression that will be discussed later.

The perceived acceptance by groups may have been an antecedent or a consequence of ethnic identity choice. The perceived acceptance by Blacks as an antecedent to Black identity is logical. That is, if one is accepted by a particular group (of which one is at least partially a member), the probability of one's identifying with that group in-

TABLE 18.2 Perceived Racial Resemblance (in percentages)

Race	*Very*	*Somewhat*	*A Little*	*Not at All*	*N*
Black	57	37	6	0	30
Japanese	0	23	54	23	30
Latino	10	24	35	31	29
Polynesian	34	23	37	6	30
Filipino	28	24	20	28	29
Malaysian	17	21	38	24	29

creases, because membership is readily accessible. This may have occurred in this study, as comments similar to the following were made repeatedly: "They accepted me while others didn't" and "Blacks have accepted me for a long time." As a consequence of ethnic identity, perceived acceptance by Blacks could have been high because the respondents had already identified with the group.

The perceived lack of acceptance by Japanese American peers was not unexpected. Much has been written about the lack of acceptance among Japanese of other groups, especially Blacks (Strong, 1978; Wagatsuma, 1967, 1976), and this was supported by comments made by many respondents. Since many of the Black-Japanese were aware of this lack of acceptance by Japanese Americans, they may have decided to identify with their other ethnic group, Blacks. As some respondents stated, "They [Japanese] did not accept me, but the Blacks did."

The results of acceptance *of* various groups by the respondents was also interesting. Both acceptance of Blacks and acceptance of Japanese correlated with Black identity, although the acceptance of Blacks was significant ($r = .46$, $p < .01$) while acceptance of Japanese was not ($r = .34$; n.s.). Here again the direction of influence is unknown. Respondents may have accepted Blacks and therefore chose to identify with them. Conversely, they could have chosen to identify with the Blacks and then began to accept them. Logic seems to predict the former explanation of acceptance and then identity, while cognitive dissonance theory (Festinger, 1957) could suggest the latter.

Racial resemblance. The self-reported racial resemblance to different groups varied among the Black-Japanese interviewed (see Table 18.2). Most, however, felt they looked more Black than they did any other race. Only one respondent, however, in my opinion, looked completely Black; he made the same judgment about himself. There was only one respondent who looked all Japanese (to me), but that respondent did not report that she resembled Japanese to a great extent. Most respondents did not believe they resembled Japanese very much. The other races they did feel they resembled were Polynesian, Filipino, and Malaysian.

Most reported they felt that Black-Japanese are very attractive people; *exotic* was the word many used for personal descriptions. Skin color varied from dark brown to very light; hair texture ranged from very coarse to fine and from curly to straight. The most prominent Japanese feature to emerge was usually the eyes; but, again, this varied from very Japanese looking (one respondent said that his eyes were more Japanese than most full Japanese he knew) to slightly Japanese.

Some respondents were asked if they could recognize another Black-Japanese, and most said yes. Thus it seems that just as most Blacks can recognize another Black (even those who are fair-skinned enough to look White), so it seems many Black-Japanese have the ability to determine whether another person is Black-Japanese. It is difficult to explain to a "nonmember" what the salient characteristics are in determining another member, but it appears that many mixed individuals experience the same phenomenon. It seems that Whites concentrate primarily on skin color, while people of color (who vary tremendously in skin color and ancestry) attend to other features, such as eyes, hair, nose, body build, and stature.

None of the racial resemblance variables emerged as significant in correlations with ethnic identity choice. This was surprising, given that Cooley (1902) and Clark and Clark (1939) found that an individual's physical image has much to do with the manner in which society (and the individual) reacts to him or her. It was believed that the more one resembled a particular ethnic group, the more likely one would be to identify with that ethnic group. This lack of correlation could perhaps have been due to the lack of variability in the self-ratings of racial resemblance. That is, almost everyone in this sample felt she or he looked very Black, and few felt they looked Japanese. With little variance, it is difficult to obtain significant correlations.

Resemblance to Blacks and Japanese did not emerge in the ethnic identity decision regression. This was unexpected, since, as one respondent said, "I looked Black, lived with Blacks, and was accepted as Black; there was no decision to make." Two other respondents made similar comments.

The only variable that did produce a strong, but nonsignificant, correlation to the ethnic identity decision process was that of resemblance to Polynesians. The respondents who felt they resembled Polynesians were more likely to experience ethnic identity decision processes than those who did not resemble Polynesians. This may be because resembling Polynesians represents perhaps the epitome of Black-Japanese "physical marginality." That is, Polynesian characteristics seem to be a combination of Black and Japanese features. Thus, if individuals look Polynesian, they are perhaps able to have a larger choice in their ethnic identification because they are physically able to enter many groups.

Self-esteem. There was no significant correlation between self-esteem scores and the ethnic identities chosen by the respondents. It seems that regardless of whether the respondents chose Black or other than Black identities, their self-esteem was unaffected. This shows that the choice of a category other than Black can be called neither "marginal" nor "maladjusted."

ETHNIC IDENTITY DECISION PROCESS

The majority ($n = 18$, 60%) of respondents experienced a period in their lives when they had to decide on an ethnic identity. Of these 18 respondents, 10 identified as Black and 8 identified as other than Black. The identity decision process reportedly began around the age of 14 or 15 and lasted approximately three to four years. Experiencing this process seemed to have no influence on whether the respondents chose the Black or other than Black category. Thus it seems that the process was a normal one, experienced by many but not correlated with the respondent's ethnic identity choice.

It was interesting that there was no significant correlation between experiencing an ethnic identity decision process and ethnic identity choice. It could be that respondents actually experienced decision processes without being unaware that those processes had occurred. Erikson (1968) believes that all individuals (multicultural or otherwise) must experience a decision process for adequate adjustment. Indecision may result in a marginal personality. That the respondents seemed to be adjusted (as shown by self-esteem scores) suggests that all must have encountered conscious or unconscious ethnic identity decision processes. For example, many respondents who lived with Blacks, looked Black, and were accepted as Black said that they had

TABLE 18.3 Degrees of Blackness and Japaneseness

	Strongly Agree	*Moderately Agree*	*Slightly Agree*	*Slightly Disagree*	*Moderately Disagree*	*Strongly Disagree*
Black	10	13	5	1	0	1
Japanese	8	8	10	2	1	1

not experienced a decision process. However, they may have made a decision (unconsciously) to be Black. That is, there are Blacks who live in Black communities, look Black, and so on, who decide not to identify as Black (Hare, 1965).

INTERRELATIONSHIPS BETWEEN BLACK AND JAPANESE CULTURES

A multiple-choice, forced-choice question is designed to measure dominance of one variable over another. Thus the ethnic identity question of "Please choose one" was used to assess which racial identity was dominant over the other. To assess choice in a more liberal manner, the adjectives *Black* and *Japanese* were included in the Likert-type Ideal Self Measure. The respondents rated their "Blackness" and "Japaneseness" on a scale of 1 to 6; 28 (93%) of the respondents rated themselves as high on Blackness and 26 (87%) rated themselves high on Japaneseness (see Table 18.3). The correlation between the respondents' Blackness and Japaneseness was also very strong (.74). This can be seen as a measure of multiculturality using an analogy to Bem's (1974) theory of androgyny. Bem found that when people were forced to choose between identifying as masculine or feminine, they usually chose the sex-appropriate category (i.e., men chose masculine and women chose feminine). When asked how feminine they were, however, separately from how masculine they were, data showed that many people were both feminine and masculine simultaneously. In a similar manner, when having to make a forced choice between Black and other categories, the majority of respondents in this study chose Black. However, when asked about their Blackness and Japaneseness on two separate continua, 26 reported that they were high on both; they were biracial and bicultural—their version of androgyny.

Since many believe that society forces one to make a specific racial choice, the majority of racially mixed people probably choose one race over another. When allowed, however, to express the many facets of themselves, the respondents in this study tended to identify highly with both of their racial and cultural backgrounds.

EXPERIENCES AND ATTITUDES OF BLACK-JAPANESE

When asked about the negative and positive points of being racially mixed, the respondents made positive comments twice as often as they made negative comments. Their negative experiences occurred primarily during the early years of the respondents' lives. Some negative experiences were still sometimes encountered, but most respondents commented that being mixed was more difficult for them when they were children. Problems consisted of people calling the respondent derogatory names, not being understood or not having anyone to relate to, being the focus of jealousy from others, having conflict between cultures, and developing self-hatred.

As Stonequist (1937) hypothesized, some of the respondents reported that one of the negative points of being biracial is not being totally accepted by either group. This difficulty was reported by 9 of the respondents; 3 others said they were not totally accepted by Blacks, and 3 reported a lack of acceptance by Asians. Thus a total of 15 (50%) of the respondents reported a marginal status position.

The choice of identifying with both cultures was positive for some in the respect that it helped the individuals realize they did not have to try to fit into a single racial mold. The negative aspect of this, however, was that with so few Black-Japanese, they become a minority within a minority. Role models, reinforcement agents, and support groups were scarce for this group and alternate "others" had to be sought by individuals in this group.

Other problems stemmed from the dating situation. In fact, racial identity decision processes seemed to begin around dating age—15 years old. Two respondents could not decide whom to date. Six other respondents reported that dating Blacks was difficult because many potential dates did not accept the respondents as all Black and refused to date them.

Again, positive comments far outnumbered the negative. The most frequently mentioned positive comments concerned the benefits of being from two cultures and heritages and obtaining the best qualities of both, and the ability to accept, empathize with, and understand people of other cultures and races. The next most popular responses were that being biracial made one novel, and gave one the "best physical features of both races." Many commented that Black-Japanese were very beautiful people. Having good parents and a strong family unit was also mentioned by many. Several respondents said that being multiracial and multicultural had made them strong people with diverse and positive perspectives on life.

This Black-Japanese group could be seen as at risk for developing marginal personalities. As Garmezy (1978) has shown, however, these "at-risk survivors" emerge stronger than the average individual. Thus, in spite of (or because of) all the detours and adjustments, the Black-Japanese in this study were well adjusted in their heterogeneous heritage. In fact, most found their biracialism and biculturalism to be assets, as reflected in the following comments: "I feel like a richer, more diverse person"; "I've got the best of both worlds"; "It makes me more sensitive and understanding to other minorities." These Black-Japanese are, indeed, the "cosmopolitan people" discussed by Park (1937) and the "multicultural people" considered by Ramirez et al. (1977).

19

Interracial Japanese Americans: The Best of Both Worlds or the End of the Japanese American Community?

AMY IWASAKI MASS

One of the major social changes currently seen in the Asian American population is the marked increase in the rate of interracial marriages. An examination of rates of outmarriages among Chinese, Japanese, Koreans, and Vietnamese in the last two decades shows that this phenomenon has been especially notable in the Japanese American community. In Los Angeles County the highest rates of outmarriages in the Asian American community occurred in 1977: Japanese, 60%; Chinese, 49.7%; and Korean, 34.1% (Kitano & Daniels, 1988). In contrast to outmarriage data on Asians in Hawaii, Japanese in Los Angeles County outmarried at a higher rate than Chinese and Koreans through the 1970s and the 1980s (Kitano, Yeung, Chai, & Hatanaka, 1984). This marked increase in the growth of intermarriage among Japanese Americans is confirmed by studies in others parts of California and the continental United States (Endo & Hirokawa, 1983; Tinker, 1973).

AUTHOR'S NOTE: This study was supported in part by the National Research Center on Asian American Mental Health (NIMH #R01 MH44331).

Two major concerns have been expressed about this trend. First, some Japanese Americans are afraid that this movement will mean the end of the Japanese American community. They fear that Japanese Americans will become completely assimilated into mainstream America and lose their sense of community and ethnic identity (Kodani, 1989; Yoshimura, 1986). This concern is echoed by scholars who view the presence of multiple identity among mixed-heritage Americans as an indication that ethnic boundaries may be eroding through intermarriage (Stephan & Stephan, 1989). A second concern is one that has been at issue since the early days of the Japanese immigrant in America: If Japanese intermarry with other races, what will happen to the children? Implicit in this question is the assumption that interracial marriages have an adverse effect on the offspring. Since society in general was not accepting of interracial marriage, it was believed that children of such unions would not be accepted by either of their parents' racial groups, and the children would be the primary victims of such unions.

Most past writings about interracial Americans have been based on observations by clinicians, clergy, historians, and social scientists of Black-White mixes. Through the 1980s most of these writings support negative concerns about children of intermarriage (Park, 1931; Piskacek & Golub, 1973; Teicher, 1968; Wagatsuma, 1973). In the 1980s there was an emergence of a number of studies in which interracial Japanese Americans spoke for themselves about their interracial experience (Hall, 1980; Kich, 1982; Murphy-Shigematsu, 1986; Nakashima, 1988; M. C. Thornton, 1983). These studies suggest that interracial Japanese Americans do not necessarily lose their sense of ethnic identity; in fact, they may be more aware of their Japanese heritage because they have to struggle to affirm and come to terms with their dual racial background. The studies also indicate that not all offspring of interracial marriages show social and psychological damage from their experience of being interracial.

The Study

Based on the hypotheses generated by these exploratory studies, I conducted a study on psychological adjustment and ethnic identity development in interracial Japanese Americans. The two major research questions were as follows: What is the psychological adjustment and self-concept of interracial Japanese Americans? How do interracial Japanese Americans fare in terms of ethnic identity and acculturation?

SAMPLE

A sample of 53 college-age White-Japanese respondents were compared with 52 monoracial Japanese American college students. The monoracial Japanese American respondents were mostly Sansei and Yonsei (third-generation and fourth-generation Japanese Americans, respectively). Most of the respondents were attending the University of California, Los Angeles. Their ages ranged from 18 to 42; the mean age was 23. Of the interracial respondents, 39 had mothers of Japanese ancestry and 14 had fathers whose backgrounds were Japanese.

PROCEDURE

Each respondent completed a series of five questionnaires, and 33 of the respondents were also seen for follow-up interviews. The questionnaires were as follows:

(1) *Japanese American Ethnic Experience Questionnaire:* provides demographic data and background information on the ethnic composition of the neighborhood in which the respondent was raised, ethnicity of closest friends, physical appearance, racial experiences, support networks, and role of the family
(2) *Tennessee Self-Concept Scale:* provides a multidimensional description of self-concept, including identity, self-satisfaction, behavior, physical self, moral-ethical self, personal self, family self, and social self
(3) *Omnibus Personality Inventory:* measures psychological adjustment
(4) *Suinn-Lew Acculturation Scale:* examines behaviors such as food, language, and entertainment preferences and associations in the community
(5) *Ethnic Identity Questionnaire:* examines self-identification and identification with Japanese and American groups

Results

There were no significant differences in the psychological adjustment and self-esteem of the two groups as measured by the Omnibus Personality Inventory. According to the Tennessee Self-Concept Scale, total self-concept scores were also similar. However, interracial Japanese Americans showed less identification with being Japanese than their Japanese American counterparts on the Ethnic Identity Questionnaire, and interracial respondents were more acculturated than the Japanese American sample on the Suinn-Lew Scale. Although the overall scores of monoracial Japanese Americans showed a somewhat higher level of identification as Japanese than those of the interracial respondents, interviews with interracial Japanese Americans revealed that many of them are strongly identified with their Japanese heritage and consider it an important part of who they are. Thus there was considerable variability on these indices. This first level of statistical analysis did not show the complex intertwining of many factors that explain why some Japanese American feel fully assimilated into mainstream America while some interracial Japanese Americans have a very strong sense of Japanese identity.

The interviews also revealed a broad range of individual experiences related to psychological pain and social rejection because of race. For example, Ellen M (all respondent names used here are pseudonyms) was placed in a Mexican American foster home for two years when her parents divorced. There she was subjected to ugly racist comments on a daily basis. Her brother remained with their Japanese mother, and Ellen felt she was rejected by her mother because she looked more Caucasian than her brother. Her mother remarried a Japanese man, and Ellen always felt she stuck out because she did not look like her brother or her half siblings. On the other hand, her brother has envied Ellen, because she looks White and was accepted more easily in mainstream American society than he was. Ellen still occasionally feels it would be easier to be all Japanese or all White; she fantasizes that someday she will find the right group of people for her.

By contrast, Glenn I had a very different experience regarding his biracial identity. His mother died when he was 4 years old, and his father left him with relatives in Japan for two years. Even in Japan (where many respondents reported strong disapproval of interracial children), Glenn said his relatives gave him the message that he was different in a special way. Because he was more than just Japanese, they felt he could be better than the average person. His father remarried a Japanese woman, and they raised him to feel he had the best of both worlds. His parents encouraged him to be tough and to associate with people of different races in the rough New York neighborhood where he went to elementary school. Because he could speak both languages he was able to interact comfortably with both Japanese and Americans, and he felt it helped him to be open-minded.

As the two cases discussed above illustrate, some respondents experience much anguish and conflict because of their racial backgrounds, while others have mostly positive experiences related to being interracial.

LOCATION

One of the most prominent variables affecting respondents' self-concepts was the geographic region in which they were raised. Japanese Americans who grew up in Hawaii and in communities such as Gardena and Montebello (in California), where there were large numbers of Japanese Americans, experienced few or no problems related to race. They noticed differences in people's attitudes toward them when they moved to communities where Anglo-Americans were the predominant racial group. For example, Nancy N, a Yonsei, said she never experienced racism in Hawaii and was surprised to find it when she came to California for graduate school. Yonsei, Linda Y transferred from the University of California, Santa Barbara, to UCLA because UCSB lacked diversity. Until she got to college, she did not realize she was different. She was always proud of her Japanese cultural heritage and in Gardena and Torrance, California, where she grew up, she was never excluded because of her Japanese ancestry. It was a shock for her to find out that at Santa Barbara one is not considered attractive unless one is "blond, blue-eyed, and tan."

Reiko K, a Sansei, was raised in Minnesota in a community that was "99.9% Caucasian." From kindergarten on, she felt very different from other children in the neighborhood. She remembers that in elementary school she was surrounded by the big boys and taunted at least once a week. Because people (including adults in the community) saw her as different, she did not have to conform. In retrospect, she realizes this helped her to become an individualist. When she moved to California she again felt different; this time she realized she was different from the Japanese Americans in her Central California community. She found she was more direct than other Japanese Americans, and not as polite.

Sansei Alan Y also grew up in a mostly White neighborhood, but his home was in a suburb of Los Angeles. Although there were very few people of color in Alan's schools, Southern California is a diverse enough community that Alan was not treated as strange or unusual. His mother was well accepted in the neighborhood, and she was a leader in the PTA and other organizations related to school and sports activities for her children. Alan and his brothers participated in sports throughout elementary, junior, and senior high school. His close friends were the Caucasian teammates he played with and went to school with. When he went to college he continued playing the same sports and pledged the same fraternity that his teammates did. Alan noted that the only area in which he feels different from his Caucasian friends is that he does not feel comfortable dating Caucasian girls. He found it curious that Asian women in the Greek houses regularly date Caucasian men, but most of the Asian men do not date Caucasian women as much.

Interracial Japanese Americans also found that location played a significant role in how they were accepted. Most of the interracial respondents who spent their childhoods in Japan had been called *gaijin* (foreigner) and felt outcast by the Japanese. Some recalled painful experiences of being taunted, chased, and beaten up by Japanese classmates in elementary school. Being stared at on trains and at public gatherings was also a common experience. Those who lived on military bases in Japan felt that the base was a community where they could feel more at home because there were other interracial people and other Americans. These respondents also felt out of place in the small midwestern or southern towns their fathers came from. They were acutely aware of how different their Japanese mothers were and felt a combination of protectiveness and embarrassment toward and about their mothers. In the United States they found themselves uncomfortable about their Japanese heritage when townspeople referred to Pearl Harbor and the war atrocities the Japanese committed. In Japan they had been blamed for the U.S. bombing of Hiroshima and Nagasaki.

A few of the interracial respondents who were raised in Japan said that they felt special and unique because of their biracial and bicultural heritage. In these cases, the respondents had a strong sense of support from their fathers, grandparents, and other Japanese relatives who buffered them from racist remarks or actions of other people. Sometimes these families felt that the Americans and Japanese were superior to all other nationalities, and they assumed the biracial children would be accomplished and successful in whatever they did.

Interracial Japanese Americans growing up in the United States also found location an important factor that affected their sense of self-esteem as it related to acceptance and a sense of belonging. Susan P spent her first nine years in a Los Angeles neighborhood where all types of ethnic groups were represented. She did not experience any discomfort about her father being Caucasian and her mother being Japanese American until her family moved to Glendale, at that time an all-White suburb of Los Angeles. There she realized she was different when the school principal asked her mother if Susan and her two sisters spoke English when they were enrolling at their new school. The strong feeling of being different followed her all through junior and senior high school. She noticed that her mother became more and more isolated and secluded after the family's move to Glendale. Where formerly she had been active in the PTA and other functions at Susan's school in Los Angeles, in Glendale her mother rarely left home and she made no new friends.

By contrast, Sheila C grew up in a stable neighborhood in South Pasadena, California. Before she and her brother were born, her parents checked neighborhoods such as Glendale and San Marino (an exclusively White neighborhood in the early 1970s), but they chose a home in South Pasadena because the city had a mixture of Asian, Caucasian, and other ethnic groups. Sheila is still close friends with an Asian and a Caucasian she has known since she was 5 years old. Sheila could not recollect having any negative racial experiences while growing up. She feels that being biracial has definitely enhanced her life, and she takes pride in her mother's Japanese heritage as well in her father's German, French, and English background.

Cheryl B remembers being teased and called names when she went to a private, predominantly White school for 5 years. In high school she attended the local public school in Montebello, where she lived. The community of Montebello was made up of a mixture of Asians, Hispanics, and Whites. The people in the community thought it was special, in a positive way, to be "half and half." Cheryl felt very accepted and good about herself in the Montebello public school setting.

COMPARISON OF JAPANESE AMERICANS AND INTERRACIAL RESPONDENTS

A comparison of the experiences of interracial respondents and their Japanese American counterparts reveals a number of similarities. Racial name-calling in elementary school was a common experience for both Japanese Americans and the interracial respondents.

The universality of this experience in the United States and Japan speaks to the characteristic of latency-age children to focus on any aspect of people that makes them different from the majority group. Thus Japanese American children in a school setting where they are not part of the majority will encounter such experiences as much as interracial children who are identifiable because they look different from the rest of the population or are known to have a parent of a "different" race. Hawaii was the one area identified by both Japanese Americans and interracial respondents as a place where they felt accepted and where racial background was not an issue.

Another area dealt with by both sets of respondents was the sense of living in dual worlds. A number of respondents spoke of different phases of ethnic awareness in which they would identity more strongly with one group than the other. When they were objects of rejection or disparagement because of their racial ancestry, they would want to be more American (or more Japanese, for interracial respondents who lived in Japan). At other times they felt they were not accepted by Japanese American cliques that rejected people who were not exclusively identified with Japanese Americans. They suffered when they felt they had to choose one over the other. These observations suggest that the social environment complicates identity resolution. Most respondents who were interviewed were able to identify a process of ethnic identity development confirming the view of a number of social scientists that ethnic identity is not a given, but rather a dynamic product that evolves throughout one's lifetime (Phinney, 1990; see also, in this volume, Hall, Chapter 18; Kich, Chapter 21; Stephan, Chapter 5).

Scott K, a Sansei, said he had no contact with the Japanese American community during the first eight years of his life. Because his parents were quiet people who were not assertive and who did not express feelings openly, he often wished he could be more like the open, expressive people in his predominantly Caucasian social group. In the fourth grade he started to attend a Japanese American church, and he felt at home when he was there. By the time he was in high school he had become more assertive and outgoing, and he was elected student body president. One of his inner conflicts was that when he identified strongly with one group, he felt he was "selling out" in respect to the other group.

Scott's experience shows that Japanese Americans also experience a sense of conflict and marginality about their ethnic identity. Suffering because of a dual heritage is not restricted to children of interracial marriage. This is a common experience for many Americans of color as they struggle to come to terms with their ethnic identity in a society where race plays a significant part in whether or not one will be accepted and affirmed (Cauce et al., Chapter 15, this volume).

Of the 33 respondents who were interviewed, 31 had arrived at a point in their lives where they felt better about their ethnic heritage than they had in the past. In retrospect, they felt that being bicultural enhanced their sense of self-worth. The fact that these respondents were a self-selected group who volunteered to be interviewed probably accounts for the large percentage of the sample currently feeling good about their ethnic background. People who want to work on these issues and have spent some time on them are more likely to participate in such a study than people who are unconcerned or wish to avoid looking at identity issues.

Although a few respondents still struggled with negative racist experiences, most reported they no longer suffered because of their racial backgrounds. Many respondents credited psychotherapy and Asian American studies courses as ways of resolving their conflicts, raising consciousness about their heritage, and understanding their personal experiences in terms of broader issues for Asian Americans. Interracial respondents who had felt excluded by some Japanese American communities and social groups were pleased with the acceptance and understanding they experienced in Asian American studies programs.

Physical appearance was the area in which differences between the interracial and monoracial Japanese Americans were most evident. Interracial respondents who did not look Japanese sometimes found themselves in an awkward position if people they were with made disparaging remarks about the Japanese. They struggled with whether they should speak up and draw attention to their Japanese heritage or avoid an uncomfortable social situation by letting the comments pass. Some respondents said they made a point of explaining their dual heritage whenever they were introduced to new people in order to avoid misconceptions and potentially embarrassing situations. These respondents felt it was important to assert their self-identity so that others would not impose incorrect assumptions on them and treat them accordingly.

The problem of not being recognized and accurately identified by others also creates significant problems at a personal level. Even when interracial Japanese Americans explained their racial backgrounds, they found that many people placed them in either one category or the other (see Hall, Chapter 18, this volume). Some people even argued that they could not be part Japanese (or part Caucasian) because they did not look that way. Especially when they were children, they heard teasing, hurtful comments such as "You must be adopted" or "Your mother must have been fooling around."

The lack of external confirmation of one's self-image can be disturbing and confusing at a psychological level (Kich, Chapter 21, this volume). This happened to Betty N, a Sansei, who felt out of place a number of times as she was growing up. Although both of her parents were Japanese American, she looked Hispanic or like an interracial Japanese American. She found that this discrepancy between her looks and her biological heritage and last name created a number of unpleasant social experiences for her. At Nisei Week events and at Asian American dances people stared at her or questioned her racial background. What hurt her the most was that her friends always reminded her that she did not look Japanese. When she was disturbed about prejudice against Japanese, one of her friends said, "What do you care? You don't look Japanese anyway." She did not like to eat fish, and her friends would say it was because she was not "really" Japanese. Although she knew these comments were intended only to tease her, they were made often enough that it was a trial for Betty.

Although social scientists and parents of young people who contemplate interracial marriage have expressed concern about the experience of marginality and psychological distress children of interracial marriages will have, this study shows that such experiences are not limited to interracial children. Monoracial Japanese Americans who live in a bicultural world can also experience conflict and confusion in relation to their ethnic identities and self-concepts.

PARENTAL INFLUENCE

Parental attitudes and behavior in regard to racial issues were another important factor in how respondents felt about their racial heritage. Both Donna J and Kim R are interracial Japanese Americans who grew up in Southern California suburbs that were predominantly White. However, their personal experiences and self-concepts differ significantly. Donna experienced a great deal of psychological pain and turmoil about being biracial, but Kim did not. Donna's mother considered Japanese culture to be superior to American ways, and expressed many disparaging views about Americans. Mrs. J had had a number of experiences in which Americans had treated her badly when she first came to the United States. She remained angry and bitter toward Americans. Whenever Donna was messy or lazy her mother said it was because of Donna's American side.

Donna regretted that she felt ashamed of her mother and her Japanese ways, but being called a "messy American" was very painful for her. Because she found her father was more accepting of her, Donna identified more positively with her Caucasian background as she was growing up. Most of her friends were Caucasian, and when she came to UCLA she realized she was not like many of the other Asians on campus.

By contrast, Kim said that although her mother was "very Japanese," she was very supportive of her children's fitting into American ways. Kim's mother studied English, tried to understand American ways, and supported Kim's activities with her friends and at school. Although Kim was aware that her mother was different from her friends' mothers, this was not a problem for Kim. She thought of the Japanese as neat, clean, honorable people, and she was proud of who her mother was. Although Kim eats Japanese food and can identify with Japanese people, she has not spent time in Japan and does not know much about Japanese culture. She thinks of herself as an American with a Japanese mother.

John T grew up feeling that being half Japanese was positive and unique. His parents made him feel good about his biracial heritage. His father was a French Canadian who grew up in New York. His mother was proud of being Japanese but did not think that being Japanese meant being superior to other races. John's father was a very open-minded man who actively crusaded against racism; he taught his children to judge others on the basis of individual behavior rather than by societal preconceptions based on race. He had parties at their home where he would make a point of having guests who were from different racial and socioeconomic backgrounds.

John remembers being worried one day when the MPs patrolling the military base in Japan where his father was stationed questioned his Japanese friends who were visiting him after school and started writing down their names. Just then his father came home and told the MPs that the boys were his guests. John felt his father always stood by him and supported him. He realized that he was different from the

Japanese children in Japan and the White children in the United States, but he did not find this a problem. John liked being unique and standing out in a crowd. He felt his parents' attitudes and his experience in a variety of military locations helped him to be open-minded and to feel at ease in any ethnic group. He found this to be an asset when he attended different schools, and he now finds it equally advantageous in the business world.

Although Cheryl B's parents divorced when she was 7 years old and she lived with her Caucasian mother and stepfather, Cheryl's mother encouraged her to maintain regular contact with her Japanese American father and his family. Cheryl has remained very close to her Japanese American grandparents and regularly attends their Buddhist church, Nisei Week events, and other Japanese American social and community activities. She is strongly identified with the Japanese American community and feels fortunate that she was raised biculturally. She feels equally at home with both her Caucasian sorority sisters and her Japanese American friends; she states, "I've been able to have the best of both worlds."

These examples illustrate the important of parental acceptance and support in developing a positive sense of ethnic identity and self-esteem in interracial children. For children to feel good about their biracial backgrounds, they need parents and other relatives to affirm both sides of their racial heritage and to provide concrete help and support when they face difficulties related to race.

Implications of the Study

For many years, parents, religious leaders, novelists (Hagedorn, 1990; Silko, 1977), scholars, and clinicians (Lyles, Yancey, Grace, & Carter, 1985; Park, 1931; Stonequist, 1937; Wagatsuma, 1973) have asserted that offspring of interracial marriages will suffer social rejection, have unstable personalities, and be unable to attain coherent identities because of their dual or multiple biological heritages. The evidence from recent studies indicates that such dire results are not inevitable in contemporary times (Chang, 1974; Johnson & Nagoshi, 1986; Nakashima, 1988). As seen in this study and others (e.g., Cauce et al., Chapter 15, this volume; Hall, 1980), the experiences of interracial Japanese Americans vary, from strongly positive to quite painful. The sense of ethnic identity also varies for this group. Some are strongly identified with one race, some feel torn between the two, and others clearly affirm both of their heritages. Throughout the process of ethnic identity development, one person can experience any or all of these feelings. The current study also shows that one cannot assume that psychological suffering related to race and conflicts about ethnic identity are solely the experience of the offspring of interracial marriage; monoracial Japanese Americans experience a number of the same problems.

Rather than ask, What will happen to the children? a more appropriate question today is, What is the best way to facilitate a positive growing-up experience for interracial children? Primary factors affecting children who suffer conflict because of their racial heritage include the geographic location in which they grow up, the degree and quality of parental understanding and help in dealing with racial issues, and the sense of support and acceptance from social networks such as grandparents, other relatives, friends, and members of the wider community. Parents are the key agent in making decisions and marshaling resources to aid children in the development of self-esteem. Contributing to the development of a positive racial self-concept in their children includes trying to choose a home community where the sense of being different or unacceptable is minimized. Children need help to deal with issues related to growing up in a society where there is a hierarchical preference for certain races over others. Children need both parts of their racial heritage accepted and affirmed; maintaining positive connections with people from both cultures is a concrete way parents can provide such experiences for their interracial children. The latter is especially important where children may lose contact with one set of relatives because of divorce.

The question of ethnic identity and the concern that the increase in the number of interracial Japanese Americans will hasten assimilation into mainstream culture and result in the end of the Japanese American community raises a number of complex questions. Perhaps the most difficult of these is how ethnic identity is defined and assigned. Sociologists, anthropologists, and psychologists have used a number of indices to measure ethnic identity, including biological heritage, cultural membership, behavior (such as languages spoken, foods eaten, ethnicity of friends), attitudes, and values. Ethnic identity is a dynamic concept. People's ethnic behaviors and the way they identity themselves may change over a period of time (Miller, Chapter 3, this volume; Root, 1990). Even within the same period of time, people may switch their ethnic identification depending on which ethnic group they are with (Root, 1990; T. P. Wilson, 1991). Such changes in behavior may be accompanied by psychological conflict, as Scott described above, or they can be a comfortable, harmonious, adaptive mechanism, such as Cheryl's sense of belonging and feeling at ease with both her Caucasian sorority sisters and her friends at the Japanese American Buddhist church.

Although they acknowledged that their biological heritage was Japanese, some of the Japanese American respondents felt far removed from Japanese language, culture, and the Japanese American community. They felt they were much more American than they were Japanese. Most of their close friends were Caucasian, and their food habits, recreational activities, and life-styles were those of mainstream America. Self-definition of ethnic identity is personal and subjective. How people feel about their ethnicity and how they identify themselves may differ considerably from how others identify them. A stranger might be likely to categorize a Japanese American on the basis of physical appearance, but the self-identification of that person might be quite different.

A number of interracial respondents in this study said that people treated them differently from the way they saw themselves. If Japanese Americans fear that their community may disappear because interracial Japanese Americans will not look "pure" Japanese, their concerns about the end of the Japanese American community may be valid. However, such a definition of ethnic community, based solely on race or racial appearance, reflects the same kind of racist conceptualizations that characterized antimiscegenation laws and Japanese exclusion policies in the early 1900s. Such a definition of community excludes people who are not purely of a favored race. Most scientists currently agree that the concept of race is not a biological category but a social construct that serves to separate people (Spickard, Chapter 2, this volume). Racist policies such as restrictive land covenants throughout the United States and separate-but-equal school policies in the South historically excluded people of color in certain communities, but these policies have been both outlawed and widely defined as socially unacceptable since the early 1960s.

If, on the other hand, the Japanese American community were to adopt an inclusive view of community, as the Hawaiians have, the community can continue to grow and be enriched by its interracial members. Anyone who is part Hawaiian is accepted and identified as part of the larger Hawaiian community; hapas (Japanese-Whites in Hawaii) are accepted as Hawaiian Japanese. Many interracial Japanese Americans affirm both sides of their heritage; they are very acculturated into American society and identify strongly with their Japanese heritage.

Ethnicity needs to be affirmed by the external world if it is to be sustained. If the Japanese American community welcomes and accepts interracial Japanese Americans as part of the community, not only will it be unnecessary to worry about the end of the Japanese American community, but interracial Japanese Americans will be affirmed and strengthened in their Japanese American identity and in their ability to experience the best of both worlds.

20

Prism Lives: Identity of Binational Amerasians

TERESA KAY WILLIAMS

The literature on Amerasians raised across national, cultural, linguistic, and racial borders is virtually nonexistent. Most studies on Amerasian identity look primarily at those who have been raised in the United States (Hall, 1980; Kich, 1982; Murphy-Shigematsu, 1986; M. C. Thornton, 1983). The literature on those raised in Asia usually refers to the fatherless Amerasians living as obscure marginals (Burkhardt, 1983; Felsman & Johnson, 1989; "Japan's Rejected," 1967; Kaneko, 1951; Kosakai, 1982; Shade, 1981; "Tragedy of Korea's Mixed-Race War Babies," 1975). Research on Amerasians up to this point has not considered the Amerasian populations, especially in Asia, that are growing up in biracial, bicultural, bilingual homes with their families. Amerasians have therefore been viewed as either abandoned in Asia, longing to return to their fathers' country, or raised as Americans in the United States with their immigrant Asian mothers and American fathers.

This study's goals are simply to show yet another dimension of the Amerasian existence; to identify the varying issues and challenges brought about by the different cultural and racial backgrounds of Afroasians and Eurasians; to illustrate their common Amerasian culture, upbringing, and identity; and to document the valuable experiences of bicultural *haafus*, who live and operate in many worlds, as they create their own blended culture, speech forms, and practices. The focus of this exploratory, interdisciplinary, descriptive study is on various identity issues of Japanese and Euro-American and Japanese and African American individuals, raised in Japan or near U.S. military bases.

The study is based on lengthy interviews with 43 Amerasians—29 Eurasians, 16 females and 13 males; and 14 Afroasians, 10 females and 4 males. In order to examine the lives of mixed-race, cross-national, and bilingual Amerasians, I sought those between the ages of 16 and 35 who had lived in Japan (with U.S. military affiliation) for at least six years of their adolescence. Most of them resided on or near Yokohama and Yokosuka bases.

Theoretical Frameworks: Colonialism and Marginality Versus Third Culture and Multiculturalism

Colonialist and marginality theories explained meetings of dominant and subordinate peoples through war, conquest, and migration, which resulted in the emergence of new populations (Gist & Wright, 1973; Park, 1928; Stonequist, 1937). Most of the research on racially blended peoples and their families reflects Eurocentric bias, painting interraciality as problematic (Gist & Dworkin, 1972; Park, 1928; Stonequist, 1937). However, recent scholarship on multiracial populations has begun to question the old theoretical frameworks—especially the broad term "marginal man," since it does not distinguish the differences among marginal statuses, marginal personalities, and marginal life experiences (Hall, 1980; M. C. Thornton, 1983). The negative dimension of marginality has been overemphasized, denoting the neither/nor status, cultural maladjustment, limited social assimilation, incomplete biological amalgamation, and pathological personalities due to the extricable relationship between marginality and colonialism. Marginal peoples were viewed and treated as byproducts of exploitative sexual unions between colonialists and members of indigenous or colonized groups, resulting from social, psychological, and physical domination of the former over the latter (Rex, 1971/1983). The positive side of marginality, on the other hand, has broadened the understanding of the marginal person, describing him or her as possessing insight and knowledge of two or more distinct and often antagonistic worlds, which enables him or her to lead the parent societies into transcending their differences (Thornton, Chapter 22, this volume). Moreover, recent studies have painted a portrait of interracial peoples as possessing a broader worldview because of their multicultural understanding of the world (Hall, 1980; Kich, 1982; Murphy-Shigematsu, 1986; M. C. Thornton, 1983; Washington, 1970); they have also established the importance, for interracial peoples, of identifying with all of their heritages in order to develop healthy and holistic self-identities (Arnold, 1984; Jacobs, 1977).

New paradigms that describe multicultural and multiracial realities are now replacing old ones. The "third culture" is one such model, defined as "the behavior patterns, created, shared, and learned by men of different societies or sections thereof, to each other" (Useem, Useem, & Donoghue, 1963, p. 169). The third culture concept was initially applied to Westerners raised in non-Western societies, who learned behavioral and cultural patterns through intercultural interaction. For Amerasians raised primarily in Japan on U.S. bases, the first culture would be their mothers' Japanese culture. The second would be their fathers' American culture. Finally, the "third culture" would be the intercultural meeting of the first and second cultures or the creation of a new culture through the synthesis of the two parent cultures. However, the significance of the Amerasian experience is not merely cultural, but also the physical embodiment of a binational third culture.

Michael Thornton (1983) has put forth the multicultural person as "one who is struggling with the dialectic among these various cultures" (p. 196). Being multicultural is not merely about being racially mixed, and it is not simply about appreciating different cultures; being truly multicultural means possessing an affinity for and loyalty to two or more social and cultural institutions (Adler, 1974; M. C. Thornton, 1983).

The Amerasians and their families discussed in this chapter can be viewed as having developed a third culture, as well as having experienced life as multiculturalists. On one hand, they have constructed a new culture by synthesizing contradictions and meshing dichotomies, as they relate back to the original cultures. On the other hand, their experiences have reflected the struggles of resolving simultaneous loyalty to more than one culture. Raised and socialized in bilingual homes and in multicultural settings, they have come to embrace Eastern and Western values, beliefs, and behaviors in all aspects of their lives. They have learned to develop new and different ways of psychologically processing their identities and have created what they can call "their own" cultural reality (M. C. Thornton, 1983). For example, the romanized word *haafu* (from the English word *half*, connoting a glamorous blend), created by the Japanese media to refer primarily to Eurasians, was used in interviews by both Eurasians and Afroasians as a term of identification. Many of the interviewees extended the term to refer to internationally and interracially mixed persons who were products of other than Asian and American unions.

Although the Eurasians had a tendency to see only Asian and Euro-American mixtures as *haafu*, when asked if they thought of Afroasians as members of their in-group, all of them answered yes without hesitation. However, most Eurasians expressed reluctance to include Black-White biracial people as *haafu*. Afroasians, on the other hand, tended to include all biracial peoples as *haafu*, with a disclaimer that although biracial Black-White people were "mixed" like Amerasians, they were "full American," as opposed to being "half American." One Afroasian man explained, "Half White-half Black *no hito tachi* [people] are *haafus* of another kind; they're like the all-American *haafus*. They speak all English and act all American, *desho* [right]? Their only difference is *shiro to kuro* [White and Black], not different countries like our parents."

Both old and new paradigms permit researchers to test, label, systematize, and make sense of the truly dynamic and complex world of multiracial peoples by applying them empirically, interactively, and complementarily to their "subjects." These paradigms are essential in the examination of people who transcend the traditional boundaries of race and culture. The old ones provide an understanding of how multiracial peoples have suffered in-between status, social misidentification, and psychological confusion, while the new ones highlight the complex realities of these people, who possess multiple sensibilities from both insiders' and outsiders' perspectives and the capabilities of adapting to various environments, different cultural settings, and paradoxical situations.

The Military Environment: A Sense of Community

Most U.S. military installations in Japan are self-sustaining communities. They are equipped with facilities that provide services and support for military personnel and their families, such as recreation centers, Department of Defense schools (K-12), correspondence and night college programs, hospitals, dental clinics, community centers, chapels, dining clubs for the various military ranks, banks, and so on. Much like Japanese society, they are structured hierarchically, with the family defined by the rank of the active-duty member. Rank, authority, orders, and regulations form the pillars of the military family and the larger community. The military bases, with their accelerated forms of patriotism reinforced institutionally by every sector of the community, has come to symbolize the "American" aspects of the Amerasians' lives (Tomkins, 1981). English is the official language on the bases, although the Japanese language is heavily used—after all, the host country is Japan and the bases employ thousands of Japanese workers. Though Americans need not speak or understand the host country's language to function on the base, the atmosphere is strongly bilingual.

Ann Cottrell (1978) found that biracial individuals residing in military communities suffered less from conflicts and confusion because being military dependents became their primary and overriding identity. Her study also suggests that the atmosphere of military bases is more racially tolerant, as different people interact and come together on the basis of their common background as military dependents. Indeed, because of their U.S. military or civilian dependent status, these Amerasians did not have to interact with dominant Japanese society on its terms and directly suffer institutionalized Japanese racism. Since Amerasian families often constitute a significant portion of the dependent population on many of the U.S. bases in Asia, they enjoy the company of families like their own (Lykins, 1989; Shade, 1981). Unlike Cottrell's findings, however, the Amerasian respondents stated that being multicultural and multiracial was often more important than being a military dependent or that both the multicultural and military aspects of their identities held similar significance.

Relationships

Primary and secondary relationships played a critical role in the identity development of the Amerasians in this study; these relationships often affected the Amerasians' experiences and interests, influenced their perceptions of the outside world, and affected the decisions they made in their lives, and often determined whether Amerasians developed low or high self- and group esteem.

RELATIONSHIPS WITH MOTHERS

Most respondents described their generational and cultural conflicts with their mothers as necessary steps in exploring their passage into adulthood. At times, however, the intercultural characteristics of their families did exacerbate their differences. For example, a 28-year-old Eurasian man reflected:

> When my mom caught me smoking, she started crying. She thought she had failed as a parent and all that jazz. She said, "Daddy *ni sumanai wa.*" She didn't know how to apologize to my dad. She started going off on what she would have to explain to her family and all that. She thought she would lose face with my Japanese relatives. She kept telling me I was a big American *haji* [embarrassment] for her. I was just a teenager experimenting.

Cultural barriers were sometimes used as excuses for why the parents and children experienced difficulties, but overall the sources of their conflicts were typically generational: the children's fashion statements in hair and clothes, school grades, dating, wearing makeup, staying out late, smoking cigarettes, and not cleaning their rooms.

Most Amerasians reported cultural barriers with their mothers rather than with their fathers, probably because their social references were primarily dominant American and they spent more time with their mothers. Most of the Amerasians perceived their mothers' strictness and competitiveness as "being Japanese." According to many respondents, their mothers placed emphasis on "what other people think," "getting better grades than others," and "going to college to show Japanese people you're smart." One Afroasian man related:

> My mom made me go to *juku* [supplementary classes] to learn *soroban* [abacus] and stuff. I remember having *kateikyooshi* [tutor] after *kateikyooshi*, especially over summers. She pushed me to do sports and other extracurricular activities like speech club, national honor society, math club, and all. It was tough being a kid of a Japanese mother. *Demo* [but] what got me is that to the other Japanese ladies or American mothers, my mom would say that she was "hands-off" with my schoolwork and I was the one who motivated myself. I wanted to tell my mom, "I wish you were hands-off!" All my friends' moms were like that too. They secretly forced us to achieve. Everyone knew, but that's the Japanese way. We [Amerasians] were all *kage de* [in the shadows] competing.

Many complained about their "Japanese" mothers' high expectations, strictness, and competitiveness, but also expressed a special quality about them. As one person stated, "They *tsukusu* [sacrifice/serve] about twenty times more [than American mothers]." Many of them attributed their ability to accomplish goals in their lives to the cultural values instilled in them by their mothers, such as *gaman* (perseverance) and *doryoku* (hard work).

RELATIONSHIPS WITH FATHERS

The respondents' relationships with their fathers were often constricted by the fathers' military obligations. For example, when a father had sea duty or TDY, he could be gone for six to nine months out of the year. The mothers rationalized the fathers' prolonged absences as doing their military duty, protecting Japan and the United States. Not having been able to share their early childhood and adolescent years with their fathers on some level seemed to affect the ethnic identity development of both Eurasians and Afroasians, but especially Afroasians. Because of the lack of a viable African American community on and off the base, Afroasian children's only tie to their African American heritage was through their fathers and through what little African American history was offered in the Department of Defense schools. Thus their fathers' absence meant the absence of their African American heritage. An Afroasian man reflected on his father's role in the family and its effect on his identity:

> As a little boy, I guess I was happy to see him, but now I see my father as [having been] a nonparticipant member of our family. Maybe that's one reason I saw myself as half Japanese/half American rather than half Black-American. He left no impression on me. My mom was the only parent in our home. She was the one who came to my baseball games, my honor society induction, my graduation, and all that. When I was applying to college even though she knew practically nothing about the stateside schools, she was the one who gave me advice and encouragement. *Haha wa tsuyoshi da yo* [Mothers are strong].

When distance existed between the fathers and their children, most of them said, it was caused by their fathers' military duties, not by pronounced cultural differences.

THE FAMILY

Many of the Amerasians spoke of the importance of the immediate family's nurturance during times of trial and tribulation. Parents often provided a positive foundation of acceptance and affirmation for their children by articulating their blended heritage to them and encouraging them to embrace the other parent's background. One Eurasian stated, "When I hated Japan and wanted to erase my Japanese side and go back stateside, my father, he says, 'Be proud of your Japanese mother. You're part her and that's why you're so *kirei* [beautiful].' *Kan'geki shichatta* [I was emotionally overtaken]." Another interviewee explained how his father humorously handled the sometimes painful amalgamation of the Afroasian's three worlds:

> Japanese kids told me "*Hiroshima wa omae no sei da zo*" [Hiroshima is your fault] and American kids told me to remember Pearl Harbor. Then, White people didn't like my dad. . . . My mother would cry and tell us we'll all go live alone together in an island in the middle of the Pacific Ocean where Japanese and Black and American will melt under the hot sun and live happily ever after. Then, my dad says, "Michi, what are you talking about? The boys are a happy melt *Chotto* cheeseburger special *mitai desho?*" [We're a little like cheeseburger specials, aren't we?]

The immediate families often provided a foundation for a positive (or negative) ethnic identity development. They also gave social and emotional support, especially in combating prejudices foisted upon them by Japanese society, White Americans, and Americans of color. A Eurasian woman summarized, "*Yappari*, our family has to be close because if we aren't, when Americans and Japanese discriminate against us, it'd be hard. We'll really need each other."

PARENTAL DEATH, DIVORCE, AND COMING OF AGE

Amerasians whose parents divorced or whose fathers passed away reported some difficulty dealing with their international situation. (No mothers were deceased.) Many Amerasians found their parents' divorces and fathers' deaths psychologically draining and legally exhausting. When divorce took place, the mothers lost their U.S. military privileges. If the mothers had become naturalized U.S. citizens, they had to find sponsorship to stay in Japan. Their Amerasian children, who qualified as their fathers' dependents, thus became their mothers' link to the base facilities. The Amerasians, most of whom were U.S. citizens, also faced similar problems of staying in Japan after their fathers' U.S. Status of Forces sponsorship expired or was severed because of divorce, death, or transfer. After 18 years of age, all dependents must have proof of full-time enrollment in college to maintain their dependent status. They are no longer entitled to military dependent status after age 22.

The breakup of Amerasian families due to divorce or death took on an "American versus Japanese" dimension, especially for the divorce cases. And, sooner or later, Amerasians had to make a choice between staying in Japan and returning to the United States—which necessitated dealing with legal questions of citizenship, sponsorship, and residency.

EXTENDED FAMILY

The majority of the Amerasians stated that their Japanese relatives found it initially difficult to accept their mothers' decisions to marry Americans, though they reported close or fairly close relationships with them today. Only 2 Afroasians of the 43 respondents stated they had no contact with their Japanese grandparents. They, however, enjoyed fruitful relationships with their mothers' sisters, which helped heal the pain of rejection. Some of the Amerasians expressed resentment toward their Japanese relatives, usually male, for treating them differently from their "pure" Japanese cousins.

On the other hand, many Amerasians revealed that they felt socially and psychologically distanced from their American relatives because they had spent most of their lives in Japan. One Eurasian woman said, "I don't feel any *chi no tsunagari* [blood ties] to my American relatives. . . . Sometimes they send us money for Christmas and graduation *toka* [etc.]." Typical responses given by both Afroasians and Eurasians about their American relatives were that they knew them only from photographs or visited them when they were young. In general, both Eurasians and Afroasians seemed to enjoy positive and close relationships with their Japanese relatives and distant but affirmative ones with their American relatives.

FRIENDS, DATES, MARRIAGE PARTNERS

While the older Amerasians (25-35 years) said they had no preference in the selection of friends, they still seemed to associate "naturally" with other Amerasians. Those between the ages of 16 and 24 clearly stated that they "preferred" other Amerasians as friends and dates. When asked to identify the ethnic makeup of their close friends, most of them reported (a) half Japanese or *haafu*, (b) Euro-Americans, (c) Japanese, (d) Americans of color.

More than half of the Amerasian respondents (26 of the 43) were dating or married to other Amerasians with a similar upbringing. Bilingual communication, cultural familiarity, and physical attractiveness were the top three reasons Amerasians gave for preferring "their own kind" as dating and marriage partners. One Eurasian man who was dating an Afroasian woman reflected:

> That's *atarimae* [natural]. We're both half Japanese and half American. Her father just happens to a Black person. We still speak the same languages and do the same kind of cultural stuff—take off shoes in the house *toka* [like], eat *gohan* [cooked rice] *toka*. I feel so comfortable with *haafus*—no matter what race their fathers are, as long as their mothers are Japanese, *raku da ne* [it's comfortable].

Intimacy and comfort, according to many of the respondents, were easily and "naturally" established with people of "their own kind."

Among this sampling, the awareness of Amerasians and/or racially mixed individuals like themselves as possible and even desirable mates existed. A sense of being an ethnic group of their own or having something in common with other Amerasians and racially mixed American persons thus had been imprinted in their consciousness by the time many of them reached ages to select their friends, dates, and marriage partners.

Amerasian Lives

COLOR AWARENESS IN EARLY CHILDHOOD

Both Afroasians and Eurasians seemed to learn awareness of racial differences at young ages. Racial differences often became the source of pain, fear, shame, and exclusion. As young children, some said they associated their parents' races with the colors of their crayons. Although most respondents expressed that "race" was not an important factor in their lives, it was often brought to their attention by others from early on.

One Eurasian man said that when his mother came to pick him up from the last day of kindergarten, a Euro-American boy exclaimed, "Ooh, your mother is yellow!" He always thought his mother was "pink like *sakuran'bo* [cherries]," so he recalled feeling "very sad" about his mother's "yellow color." He said he repeatedly asked his father what his mother's "real" color was. His father replied that his mother was the same color as himself so he need not worry. He concluded, "*Dakara* [so] when I drew pictures of my family, I always used pink for my mother and my father and me." One Afroasian interviewee said his father taught him to associate brown and black colors with strength and bravery in order to counter the Japanese and Euro-Americans who ridiculed his dark complexion.

The concept of "race" did not seem to be of much concern for most of the interviewees, but particularly for Eurasians; it was something that was brought to their attention by others. While they had their own ideas about "race" and biases against certain groups, they placed more emphasis on culture and language. Most of the Amerasians employed cultural categorizations and labels (e.g., half Japanese, half American, Japanese customs, American things) over racial ones (e.g., White, *hakujin*, Black, and *kokujin*). Many of the Amerasians stated that although they were not constantly bombarded with issues of "race" in Japan, they often became "spectacles" when they were among the Japanese. The bases, where many groups interacted with and tolerated one another, freed them from constant identification, as one Afroasian jokingly called it, "*irochigai*" or "color differences" (Cottrell, 1978).

PHYSICAL APPEARANCE

For Amerasians raised in Asia, physical appearance has visually and identifiably separated them from the dominant monoracial Asian groups (Shade, 1981; Wagatsuma, 1973). The phenotypes of the Amerasian respondents varied tremendously. Depending upon who viewed them, they were perceived, defined, and treated quite differently. While Americans may have treated the "Amerasian look" as exotic or novel in the United States, most interviewees stated that both Black and White Americans usually did not make an issue of their physical differences. The Japanese, on the other hand, noticed the Amerasians' slightest physical deviation from them, such as dark skin; green eyes; chiseled, bigger, deeper, or *hori ga fukai* features; fine, wavy, "kinky," or light-colored hair; and large frame or *oogara*. The interviewees all described how Japanese people in general were "envious" (*urayamashigaru*) of or "disgusted" (*kimochiwarugaru*) by their physical characteristics. Most Amerasians were not bothered by Japanese society's focus on their biological makeup, because they could retreat back to the U.S. military bases, where they were not constantly reminded of their physical differences. However, other Amerasians mentioned that it became tiresome to be identified constantly. One Afroasian man said that when he was stopped in the streets outside of the base and treated as a *bakemono* (monster), he pointed right back and did the same to his "admirers," as he expressed his ill feelings in fluent Japanese.

In many cases, Amerasians liked standing out and enjoyed receiving special attention. Some even stated that if Japanese people did not notice them as racially and culturally mixed, they would make a point of being recognized as *haafus* by certain behavior, dress, or speech, differentiating themselves from their parent groups.

Many Amerasians said they did not realize people viewed them as other than American, Japanese, or *haafu*. During their visits to the United States, many found they were commonly mistaken for Latino, Russian, Ethiopian, Egyptian, Polynesian, and Arab, to their surprise.

Physical appearance, as a variable, seems to play an important role in the ethnic identity development of racially mixed peoples (Hall, 1980; Spickard, 1989; M. C. Thornton, 1983). How so is still quite unpredictable, because of individual variations. Darker-skinned Afroasians did not automatically relate to African Americans, nor did lighter-skinned Afroasians necessarily identify with their Japanese parentage. Eurasians who appeared more Caucasian did not always blend in naturally with Euro-Americans; those who looked relatively more Asian did not always accept their Japanese background willingly and readily. One Eurasian woman, who resembled only her Euro-American ancestry, but who spoke and understood limited English, identified herself as a *haafu* who was *motto* (more on the Japanese side). Her outwardly Anglo appearance overshadowed her Japanese mannerisms and speech, but her social and psychological makeup was far more Japanese in orientation.

Whether or not dominant American or Japanese society and the various ethnic American communities accepted an Amerasian was not always the decisive factor in why he or she would choose a certain reference group. Whether or not an Amerasian looked relatively more

Japanese, more Afro-American, more Euro-American, or possessed various degrees of "physical in-betweenness" (which depended upon the social context) did not always explain why he or she selected a particular identity. Indeed, most interviewees were aware of their physical appearance and how it coincided (or did not) with their own feelings about self and others. Respondents indicated that the social effects of their physical appearances on their ethnic identity choices were important, but not definitive.

LANGUAGE: THE WORLD OF HALF-AND-HALF *HONNE*

"A man who has a language consequently possesses the world expressed and implied by that language," wrote Franz Fanon (1967, p. 18) in *Black Skin, White Masks*. Studies have indeed found positive correlations between language proficiency and ethnic identity (Omedo, Martinez, & Martinez, 1978; Uyeki, 1960). Language is an integral part of cultural knowledge and participation (Hall, 1980). It plays a major role in the transmission of culture and information and serves as a vehicle through which individuals understand, process, relate to, and function in their social worlds.

Bilingualism had a major impact on the interviewees' mannerisms, behaviors, thoughts, and identities (Taylor, Bassilli, & Aboud, 1973). Being bilingual, many said, "forced" them to see the world through both Japanese and American eyes, which gave them little or no choice but to embrace both cultural heritages. As a result, many reported having been interpreters "all their lives" for both their Japanese mothers and American fathers. One Eurasian woman said, "Since I could talk, I was translating for my parents. It's natural, no big deal *yo*."

When asked in which language the interviewees felt the most comfortable communicating their feelings and thoughts, most of them reported that they spoke English to their fathers and to Americans and spoke Japanese to their mothers and to Japanese people, in general. Some also noted that they often spoke "half-and-half" to both parents and to members of their parent groups who had some knowledge of both languages. There were 4 respondents who stated that speaking English was the most comfortable form of communication, but they had no problems conversing in either language, while 2 said Japanese was more comfortable. However, an overwhelming 37 out of the 43 respondents stated that code switching or, in their own words, *chan'pon* (chop suey), half-and-half, Japlish, and *Eihon'go* (Englinese) were the most comfortable forms of communication. When conveying intimacy or expressing their innermost thoughts or their *honne*, the majority of them said they used this mixed version of Japanese and English. One Eurasian woman noted, "I notice that when I speak English it's so *chan to shita toki* [a formal situation]. When I'm comfortable, I speak half-and-half. I have to be close to someone [when] speaking Japanese. Half-and-half means we're really really close." Thus alternating between languages enabled Amerasians to draw from the strengths of their two languages, use their entire speech repertoire, and express a broad range of meanings (Valdes, 1988).

As already mentioned, many interviewees indicated that language also played an important role in the selection of dating and marriage partners. Several interviewees stated they "could never date anyone who couldn't speak Japanese and English" because they would not be able to explain their *honne* (true feelings) to their mates if they spoke only Japanese or English. Thus, for many, language was a key factor in mate selection.

Whenever they teased and joked in informal situations, many said they were far more comfortable speaking conversational Japanese or a "mixed" version of Japanese and English. Many said they understood Japanese humor much better than American humor; one Eurasian woman reflected:

> When American TV came to [the] base, we were all excited. We made popcorn and stayed up watching shows. There was a show called *Soap*. All the full-American people were laughing and laughing. The *haafus* just sat there. We were *akke i torareteta no* [dumbfounded]. I think the *haafus* were disappointed because American jokes seemed stupid to us.

The respondents stated that when engaging in serious discussions or conversing in formal situations, they tended to fall into English. Formal Japanese, on the other hand, was used only on rare occasions (e.g., weddings, funerals, job interviews, talking to strangers or elders). Many reported that if a certain kind of formality was required, they usually spoke in English. Even in many formal Japanese situations, many Amerasians said they often spoke in English because they were usually being entertained as the "American" guests and were spoken to and treated as such.

Most parents emphasized speaking both languages in the home, which helped many of the respondents develop native fluency and positive feelings toward both heritages, although some of their

American teachers and school administrators disagreed. Less than one-third of the respondents had taken classes in English as a second language sometime during their secondary school years. Some had limited vocabularies and poor grammatical understanding of both English and Japanese, but they all possessed the ability to pronounce English like native speakers—unlike many of their mothers, who had difficulty pronouncing the letters *r* and *v*. Four Amerasians of Euro-American background spoke Japanese with a slight accent, while the remaining respondents spoke and pronounced Japanese with native proficiency. For simplicity and succinctness, many of their fathers "lowered" their level of speech in the home and used limited vocabularies so their Japanese wives could understand. Thus the level of English spoken in their homes was not always equivalent, in some cases, to that in "all-American" homes. As "Americans," many said they had to work at reaching the levels of native English speakers, while most did not worry about not matching up to the Japanese because they were *gaijins* (foreigners) anyway.

All 43 Amerasians stated that their bilingual ability influenced their self-perception and group identity. Being bilingual, along with being biracial, meant having to deal with a multitude of issues. Knowing, understanding, speaking, and thinking in two and three languages (including ethnic English and various Japanese dialects) meant living and operating within those worlds as in-group members. However, due to their physical distinction, social distance, and ability to speak the *other* language, the Japanese, Euro-Americans, and African Americans often categorized Amerasians as outsiders or "stagehands," even though they were insiders with a front row seat to the main stage of their parents' worlds. As one Eurasian stated, "[I'm] not quite an insider."

Although many felt they gained much from knowing two languages, they also talked about the pain, anger, and exclusion brought about by it. Japanese people did not always acknowledge the interviewees' Japanese fluency. One bitter Eurasian interviewee was filled with rage and sarcasm as she explained:

> I hate the Japanese. I HATE them. Every time they see me, they see American written all over my face. All they want from me is free English lessons or a tour of the base. First, it was neat, the attention, but now on purpose I speak only Japanese to them. Sometimes our conversation is a battle. They speak broken English to me as if I can't speak Japanese so I keep speaking Japanese and they keep speaking broken English. It

> sounds so silly. I just wanna say, "Look, you *Nihonjin* [Japanese person]. I've mastered your language. Admit it!" Whoever finally breaks down and speaks the language the other person is speaking is the [loser]. Of course, I defeat them because my Japanese is ten zillion times better than their English. I'm tired of Japanese people not accepting my Japanese. It's dumb because on the phone, no one can tell I'm a *gaijin*. But of course, no non-Japanese could ever master their language!

One Afroasian man, who did not speak "Black English," described the humiliating experience of being denied *arubaito* (a part-time job) as an English tutor for Japanese students. When the mother of his prospective students learned of his African American parentage, she said she did not want her children learning "substandard" English.

Code switching, which was initially a matter of family communication, became the unofficial language of the Amerasian—an inseparable part of his or her psyche. Many also learned when to keep quiet about their knowledge of the *other* language and when to disclose it. Sometimes Amerasians pretended they could not speak either language, to get special attention or for mere convenience. Depending upon the circumstances, Amerasians spoke English, Japanese, or employed code switching to adapt to their social contexts (Hall, 1980; Omedo et al., 1978; Sotomayor, 1977). As Fanon (1967) put forth, "To speak a language is to take on a world, a culture" (p. 38). Amerasians took on many worlds: the Japanese-speaking world of their mothers, the English-speaking world of their fathers, and the marriage of the two (or more) languages in which they created their "half-and-half" world. As a system of symbols with socially governed guidelines, bilingual code switching allowed Amerasians to relate to their parent groups, to express their sense of self, and to formulate a group solidarity and belongingness to their very own multiethnic group. Through their languages, they thought, spoke, and lived in multiple consciousness.

AMERICA: THE HOME AWAY FROM HOME

For these respondents, the United States symbolized a somewhat scary and challenging place to which Amerasians must one day "return." Some respondents had never lived in the United States; three had never even visited. Whether they actually did nor not, most of the interviewees held the notion of having to "return" to the United States sooner or later. For many Amerasians, the only America they knew was the U.S. military way of life, so they were surprised by the civilian way of life in most of the United States when they had visited as adults. For example, several interviewees explained that in base movie theaters, before the feature films began, everyone had to stand up and listen to the national anthem; they thought this was done in all American theaters. Others had high expectations of the United States because they were "half of that great country," which, many believed, gave birth to and put into practice such concepts as democracy, individualism, freedom, justice, and equality; many said they were anxious to return "home" and get a taste of those ideals.

While no one expressed strong resentment or hatred toward the United States as some had for Japan, some of the respondents' childhood memories and experiences in America were not all positive. An Afroasian man who lived in North Carolina for three years described his experience:

> It was awful. We were "niggers." Then, we were "Japs." Then, we were "Chinks." I finally got so mad that I went, "Make up your minds." So they settled with "nigger." I really didn't know much what that meant, but I knew it was bad. I thought the southern Whites were bad. 'Til this day I don't care for them. Our whole family wanted to go back to Japan.

Afroasians in Japan, personally affected by the Black-White racial schism in the United States, saw the Japanese versus American cultural paradoxes as affecting their lives more. However, a few of the Afroasians who left Japan as adults to live in the United States discovered that what they had been told about segregated neighborhoods and the plight of their fathers' people was indeed still a reality. One Afroasian man said:

> I never thought that discrimination against Blacks still existed. My father would complain that because he's Black, he was treated bad or because he's Black, he didn't get promoted and I thought, "C'mon Dad, you're talking ancient history here." But I saw with my eyes and felt it when I finally went to live in the States when I was 19 years old.

An Afroasian woman described her initial encounter with American racism:

> We moved to Maine. People in my *atarashii gakkoo* [new school] were really nice to me and thought I was really special. Everyone asked me

> how to say their names in Japanese or how to write different kinda things in Japanese writing. One day my father came to pick me up from school and everyone said, "Is that your father?" Since then, everyone treated me like a Black person. Then, I found out that being Black was not a great thing in the States.

For Afroasians, going to the United States gave them a chance to interact with African Americans, whose presence in Japan was usually minimal or negative. All 14 Afroasians talked about how once they went to the United States and interacted with African Americans, they found they did not relate to them as well as they did to other Amerasians, Japanese people, and even Euro-Americans. Furthermore, going to and living in the United States "forced" Afroasians to deal with their African ancestry, which was sometimes self-aggrandizing and distressing. However, many Afroasians said going to the United States allowed them to embrace their African American heritage, which was a process of positive awakening. Prior to going to the United States for college, one Afroasian man, who was raised in Japan for 18 years, stated:

> I used to say I was half Japanese-half American, because that's who I thought I was. After going to the States for college, living there, and working in the mainstream, I realized that I was also part Black American. I never grew up with the culture and I don't like the militant kind of attitude of some of them but you know, I realized that I am part Black and I am really proud of that heritage and its contribution to the U.S. Now, I tell people I'm half Japanese and half Black.

Both Afroasians and Eurasians described their interactions with Asian Americans as the most uncomfortable, because they had never really known Asians who "spoke and acted full-American." One Eurasian woman explained, "How weird! *Nihonjin no kao shite, Eigo ga pera pera* [They have Japanese faces and speak English fluently]. *Chotta* [a little], I couldn't accept it. My face is more American, but I'm *zen zen* [by far more] Japanese than them." Most Eurasians, even those who had never been to the United States, felt that the United States was more racially tolerant, as one Eurasian said, "*Nihon to chigatte motto chigau jin'shu ya kuni no hito ga iru kara* [unlike Japan, because there are people of different races and from different countries]." Overall, both Eurasians and Afroasians reported positive dealings with American society. One Eurasian man stated, "When I lived in the

States, I was home. No one teased me as a *gaijin* and everyone just saw me as an American, kind of like just a generic person. I like that a lot."

Many respondents stated that the United States was foreign, and yet not foreign, to them; when they had finally gone to the United States, they said a part of them felt at home, yet another apart felt like wide-eyed tourists taking mental notes on America's many peoples and life-styles. Some Amerasians were initially shocked, disappointed, or overjoyed once they went to visit or live in the United States. Many adjusted smoothly to American ways. Others needed time to settle down and get acculturated. There were also those who did not want to leave Japan, even for a visit. Nevertheless, most of them agreed that "part of them" could relate to the United States.

JAPAN'S LITTLE AMERICA

The U.S. military bases served as protection and escape from the often unaccepting Japanese. In many cases, being "on base" meant one had to live, act, and speak as an American, while being "off base" meant operating and functioning in a more Japanese mode. To many of the respondents, physical and mental boundaries existed between Japanese society and the American military community that reflected their own psychological and cultural understanding of how they should behave. They themselves often drew a line of Japanese versus American territorial and mental demarcation. One respondent explained:

> When I go off base, I think I become more Japanese automatically cuz I have to speak Japanese and treat people—like older people—with respect to get by. Even though I'm comfortable [in] either place, as soon as I pass the guards at the main gate, it's a different world. [It is] kinda like I have to switch gears.

Some of them employed different national, cultural, and linguistic modes of behavior, depending on the situation or location, or simply "*muudo ni yotte* [depending on my mood]," as one Eurasian said.

The Amerasians born in the late 1950s reported the most hardships in Japan; they discussed the painful experiences they had to endure. They reported being stared at, called names, and physically touched by Japanese people once they left the bases. Many expressed bitter anger and strong resentment about the stares, name-calling, and harassment. On the other hand, many of the Amerasians enjoyed the special attention they received by the Japanese. One Eurasian man said, "When the Japanese treat me like everyone else it makes me mad. I'm *haafu da yo!*" An Afroasian man also stated, "If they treat me like I'm Japanese, I hate it. I let them know I'm part Black and I'm cool!"

Having the bases as an escape also allowed Amerasians to discard unwanted and infeasible aspects of both American and Japanese ways of life. From the respondents' varied replies, it was apparent that each person interacted with the American and Japanese environments differently, sometimes in calculated ways and other times more spontaneously. Amerasians assessed their own situations and interacted with different people accordingly. Thus the American military and Japanese cultures in juxtaposition set the stage for a multicultural identity and development of a third culture for Amerasians and their families.

A *Haafu* Sense of Identity

Although larger social and political forces affected the lives of the respondents with structural limitations and barriers, individual experiences were so diverse that each Amerasian person responded differently to these forces and environments during different periods of their lives. Some interviewees related more to their Japanese heritage and others more to their American. Most stated that they would switch depending upon the immediate situation, sometimes knowingly and other times unknowingly.

The majority of the Amerasians considered themselves "a kind of an American" or, in one respondent's words, "a half-Japanese American," even though some referenced themselves within the larger Japanese society with a *haafu* label. Social subordination and constant reminders of being an *Amerikajin* (American) and *gaijin* (foreigner) in Japan and their "patriotic" American military socialization and Department of Defense education assisted in shaping their prevailing American or "kind of American" identity.

AFROASIANS

The Japanese and Euro-Americans' negative and condescending views of Africa and Black America have not allowed the evolution of a fully positive Afroasian image to take place in Japan or the United

States ("Blacks Blast Japanese Racism," 1988; Jordan, 1974; "Old Black Stereotypes," 1988; Strong, 1978; "Takeshita Apologizes," 1988; Wagatsuma, 1973). In many cases, Japanese and American societies tried to confine them to the "one-drop rule" in keeping with the Black-White dual system of race relations in the United States (Degler, 1971). Some members of the African American community also viewed Afroasians' multiracial and multicultural background as hindering the development of a positive African American heritage. These views affected how Afroasians were treated by the three communities with which they had to interface. One Afroasian woman explained, "*Moo yada,* I hate when White people and *Nihonjin* think I can only dance and sing or if my dad is a *jyanguru no dojin* [native of the jungle]."

Most Afroasians were aware of the racial differences between their Black fathers and the Eurasians' White fathers. They were also aware of Japanese and American societies' comparative views of the two American parent groups. They experienced differential treatment by Euro-Americans and the Japanese, depending on the situation. As for race relations in the United States, Afroasians had an awareness of the Black versus White and majority versus minority dichotomies through their fathers' experiences. Therefore, in the United States, Afroasians tended to identify readily as being "American minority" members, but in Japan, they reluctantly accepted a *gaijin* label. They preferred being acknowledged by Americans and the Japanese as *haafu*. Although some stated that Eurasians were "snotty" or "stuck up" because they thought they were "more special," the Afroasian respondents all reported various degrees of "we-ness" with Eurasians. Even with the added issues and complications of having to deal with "race" at a much deeper level, Afroasians did not identify much differently from Eurasians.

EURASIANS

Eurasian respondents said they believed that little or no difference existed between themselves and Afroasians. Most Eurasians asserted a kind of "color-blind" synopsis of the two Amerasian experiences: "We are all the same, half Japanese." Eurasians tended to overlook the Afroasians' fathers' racial background until it was brought to their attention. Some Eurasians frowned upon unions between Japanese females and African American males; one woman revealed, "I don't understand why some of those Japanese women like *kokujin no* [Black] sailors, and some of 'em are really pretty too."

The "almost color-blind" Eurasian worldview seemed to result from their relative freedom from the chains of "race" and skin color in both Japanese and American societies. They often viewed the *haafu* experience from their own Japanese and Euro-American lenses and translated all Amerasian experiences in which "race" was not a pressing concern. In many ways, this Eurasian blindness parallels that of Euro-Americans, who consciously and unconsciously lay claim to the "American experience" or promote the "universality of the human experience." If Afroasians pointed out their African American heritage as having suffered from White or Eurasian prejudices, many Eurasians usually dismissed that as "*monku*" or "complaining." They could, however, accept and even relate to the prejudicial attitudes and discriminatory actions of the Japanese toward all Amerasians, regardless of racial ancestry. Many of them said they would not accept a "minority" label in the United States, including eligibility for affirmative action scholarships, but would resign themselves to a *gaijin* status in Japan, although they too—like Afroasians—opted for the *haafu* label. Finally, Eurasians subtly and overtly expressed how they often benefited from the gridlock of mutual respect the Japanese and Euro-Americans have for each other, resurfacing the old perception of the Eurasian as possessing a "hybrid vigor" or as the combination of the "master races" of the East and the West. As one woman said, "*Yappari*, being White and Japanese makes the best looking and most smartest *yo, ne*?" (Nagaoka, 1988; Spickard, 1983).

Many of the experiential and perceptual differences between Eurasians and Afroasians were largely based on the dominant societies' views and treatments of them. In this way, they were largely affected by the streams of external influences. However, both Afroasians and Eurasians were able to dodge many of the North American Black-White racial divisions and ignore many of the negative Japanese notions about their mixed racial heritage as they were growing up, because of their relatively privileged and protected "nonracial" military-dependent life and environment.

The perceptions of Amerasians as "war babies" and products of the postwar Occupation still linger, and the negative images of unions between American servicemen and Asian women still lurk in both Japanese and American minds. As a result, some respondents continued to experience condescending treatment by Japanese people, nonmilitary-related Americans, and American families on the bases, particularly by the Euro-American officers' families. Both Eurasians and Afroasians said that they would tell people their fathers were businessmen or U.S. embassy employees. This accorded them a genuinely *kokusaiteki* (international) status, free from the images of World War II, General MacArthur, Madame Butterfly, and the orphaned *kon'ketsuji* (mixed-blood children).

Conclusion

In order to exist, one must be named (Freire, 1970). Having a name and label such as *haafu* or *half Japanese* meant this group of Amerasians existed; it meant the Japanese, the Americans, and they themselves acknowledged their existence as a category of people, and it meant they had successfully negotiated and manufactured an identity where none existed initially (M. C. Thornton, 1983). Although elements of rejection and marginality were not altogether absent, these Amerasians were neither invisible individuals trying to be seen and heard nor social rejects falling through the cracks of their parent societies (Condrill, 1990; Lykins, 1989). Moreover, in the U.S. military environment, they did not suffer from mistaken identities by constantly being labeled something they were not. They were ever present in the eyes of their parent societies and their own peers. Neither the Americans nor the Japanese, for example, could ever take away their bicultural mind-set and bilingual skills; these qualities belonged to them by birth and upbringing. The very nature of their life-styles served as bridges or interpreters between their two or more worlds.

The process of identity development is fascinating and dynamic, yet personal and complex. Although the respondents shared a common bicultural orientation, each individual had his or her own beliefs, values, and idiosyncrasies that were uniquely his or her own. Amerasians, like most human beings, suffered pain and rejoiced in their happiness, accepted life and rebelled against it, experienced failures and sulked in their letdowns, boasted their accomplishments and gloated over their successes, acted as victimizers and suffered as victims. Whether Eurasian or Afroasian, each Amerasian will make his or her own choices of reference and identity within his or her own social context. Each one will taste what the larger society has to offer and will spit out what does not suit him or her. Each one will influence and be influenced by the many social, psychological, economic, and political forces that surround him or her. Ultimately, each person will formulate his or her own human identity, which includes an ethnic and racial dimension, as did the 43 Amerasians who unselfishly shared their experiences and illuminated our understanding of their prism lives.

Acknowledgments

From Japan, my motherland: First and foremost, I would like to thank my family—my life force: my dearest parents, Nobue Suzuki and Tracy James Elwood Williams, whose guidance is forthright, *omoiyari* selfless, and love unconditional; my brother, best friend, and most cherished gift from Santa for my sixth Christmas, Tracy Jay, whose *kyoodai omoi* succors my often weakened spirit; my brother, Jerry Dean, and sister, Nancy June, who departed from this world before we could know and love them; Pinky and Brandy, whose *kawaii shigusa* melt our hearts. My deepest *kansha* to *Obaachama* Hatsuko Suzuki, whose *bi, magokoro,* and *aijoo* I miss; *Ojiichama* Kakugoro Suzuki, Harue Suzuki, Chieko Shimura, the Suzuki-*ke* from the heart of Edo; Jay's *Osananajimi,* Mariko Albritton, Yoneko Morino, and the 43 *haafus* who shared their valuable life stories and made this study possible.

From the United States of America, my fatherland: My appreciation goes to Grandpa Lonnie and Grandma Tellie Williams, Myrtle Ross, Ruby Furrow, Fred Williams, Billie Hatcher, Margie Tyree, and the Miller-Williamses from the roaring hills of "almost heaven" West Virginia. To a proud descendant of the Spanish and the Cakchiquel Indian people, Luis Alfredo Xicay Santos, whose unyielding courage and enduring love gave me strength, *gracias con mucho cariño.* To Velina Hasu Houston, whose Amerasian spirit of bamboo—bending, but never breaking—and dazzling creativity continue to inspire me, *itsumo arigatoo.* Special thanks to Reggie Daniel, Nancy and Roosevelt Brown, Steve and Celeta Cheney-Rice, Michael Thornton, Leland Saito, Kane Nakamura, Torey Vaughn, Maria Root, Walter Allen, David Lopez, Melvin Oliver, Marlies Dietrich, Sucheng Chan, Salley Foxen, Arleen de Vera, Christine Hall, Glenn Omatsu, Don Nakanishi, UCLA Asian American Studies Center, the Amerasian League, Multi-Racial Americans of Southern California, and the JACL.

From Hawai'i Nei: Aloha kakou and warm *mahalos* to the three people who believed in me: a very dear friend and fellow *hapa haole,* Thomas Reid, and my mentors and parents in academia, Haunani-Kay Trask and David Stannard. Thanks to Paul Spickard, Franklin Odo, and the beautiful people of the islands who touched my life.

Kokoro kara, I thank you all and the countless others for guiding me through the journey of my many worlds. *Aratamete, orei o mooshi agemasu.*

21

The Developmental Process of Asserting a Biracial, Bicultural Identity

GEORGE KITAHARA KICH

Although biracial heritage may be determined easily by the fact that one parent is of one race and the other parent is of another race, it is less clear how biracial people cope with this heritage, given the generally negative social, legal, and cultural history of race, ethnicity, and intermarriage in this century (see the following contributions by other authors to this volume: Daniel, Chapter 6; Fernández, Chapter 10; Miller, Chapter 3; Nakashima, Chapter 12; Spickard, Chapter 2; Wilson, Chapter 9). In this chapter, I want to present an expanded picture of who biracial people are by examining the developmental roots of healthy self-acceptance as biracial.

For a person who is biracial, a positive expression of that reality is the integration and assertion of a biracial identity. The self develops in interaction with others (parents, peers, family, community), through experiences of recognition, acceptance, and belonging. The ethnic group reinforces the development of an ethnic identity through mutual expressions of relatedness and belonging, which in turn enhances and strengthens the ethnic group (Shibutani & Kwan, 1965). This process of mutual recognition and acceptance continues and extends the development of the ethnic group, which consolidates and gives credibility to the person's ethnicity. For biracial people, positive identification of themselves as being of dual or multiple racial and ethnic heritages has not been accepted or recognized in any consistent manner over the last several centuries (Gist & Dworkin, 1972; Henriques, 1974a; Jacobs, 1977). My research on biracial and bicultural Asians (Kich, 1982), my involvement with multiracial community groups, and my clinical experience with people of many different racial and ethnic heritages serve as the basis for examining the developmental roots of healthy self-acceptance. By focusing on the experiences of biracial, bicultural people, I will present a heuristic developmental model of biracial identity that may have applicability to all people of multiracial heritage.

Stages of Biracial, Bicultural Identity Development

My original research sample, 15 biracial adults of White and Japanese heritage, ages 17 to 60, provided personal information and history during extensive semistructured interviews. Analysis of the content of those interviews, of the themes that emerged, and of each subject's sense of self over his or her life span resulted in an understanding of the stages of biracial identity development. The developmental stages describe not only the subjects' growth through childhood, adolescence, and into adulthood, but also their transitions and passages throughout life. They all progressed through three major stages in the development and continuing resolution of their biracial identity:

(1) an initial awareness of differentness and dissonance between self-perceptions and others' perceptions of them (initially, 3 through 10 years of age)
(2) a struggle for acceptance from others (initially, age 8 through late adolescence and young adulthood)
(3) acceptance of themselves as people with a biracial and bicultural identity (late adolescence throughout adulthood) (Kich, 1982)

These three stages describe a biracial person's transitions from a questionable, sometimes devalued sense of self to one where an interracial self-conception is highly valued and secure. The major developmental task for biracial people is to differentiate critically among others' interpretations of them, various pejorative and grandiose labels and mislabels, and their own experiences and conceptions of themselves. Differentiation involves both an ability to discriminate among the images others have of one's identity and an ability to evaluate the differences between self-perception and others' perceptions. Differentiation and subsequent self-acceptance necessitate a resolution of the experiences of dissonance and of the initially indiscriminate wish to belong somewhere. Subsequent integration and continuing expression of a biracial identity involve a complex interplay among the dynamics of the family, the community, and oneself. Cyclic reenactment of these stages emerges during later development, often with greater intensity and awareness. The validity of these stages has been confirmed through both clinical and anecdotal experience.

STAGE 1: AWARENESS OF DIFFERENTNESS AND DISSONANCE

Differentness can be seen as neutral, based on an objective comparison process (Pinderhughes, 1989). Dissonance, however, often an uncomfortable and negative experience of conflict, implies a negative judgment about the difference, where the comparison process results in an experience of devaluation and discrepancy. Biracial people describe being seen as "different" as generally involving an experience of dissonance. It is significant that all biracial people, of whatever racial background, have had similar early and ongoing experiences of differentness and dissonance. The initial awareness of being biracial, of being both yet neither, brings with it the additional awareness of being different and a rudimentary interracial self-concept.

Biracial people either are seen as different or feel themselves to be different from every other group. The experiences result from personal comparisons with others or from being noticed as different by others. Appearance, name, birthplace, and parents' races are factors in the comparison process. The single most commonly asked question of biracial people—What are you?—continually underscores the experience of differentness. Varieties of the initial experience of differentness are repeated many times throughout their lives, in both strange and familiar settings, within ethnic communities and outside of them.

Jacobs (1977) discovered that biracial children (ages 3 to 8 in his sample) spontaneously referred to themselves as racially different from each of their parents. The children made exploratory identifications with each parent's race, examining themselves in comparison. Emotional and cognitive advances provided the bases for the child's abilities to construct meaning out of his or her perceptions (e.g., the fact that skin color would not wash away, the recognition of skin color and facial feature differences from their parents) and to use and later internalize an interracial label to describe him- or herself. Within a family context of safety and security, the experience and labeling of differentness as biracial can be positively valued. However, when being different is devalued or is the source of rejection, the experience of dissonance becomes an additional hurdle for the biracial person.

The first memory of an experience of differentness and dissonance for many biracial people is usually during the earliest phases of their transition into peer and reference group contexts outside of the family (school, church, or community events). In general, they remember it as occurring between the ages of 3 and 10, when they experienced themselves as not fully belonging to any of the comparison groups. For example, one adult who uses the label "Eurasian" had traveled and lived in various parts of the world by the time she was 6 years old. Her initial experience of differentness as devaluation occurred when a neighbor yelled a racial epithet at her in the United States. For biracial Asians growing up in the United States during the postwar period, differentness and dissonance were experienced in relation to most groups: to European American, Asian, and Asian American reference groups. In general, biracial and bicultural people are seen as different and "other" by most groups and therefore ambiguous in terms of group identity, a constant reminder of the discrepancy between their developing self-perceptions and others' perceptions of them.

The devaluation of differentness complicates and confirms the experience of not belonging. Looking different, with a name perhaps discrepant from appearance, and having parents or a birthplace that is noticed as "weird" or as "gaijin" (foreigner) increases the ways in which biracial people experience "not belonging." Devaluation of self results from a self-negation fostered by the internalization of experiences of discrepancy, ambiguity, and rejection—what has come to be called "internalization of racism" (Pinderhughes, 1989) and "internalized oppression" (Root, 1990). The self-negation occurs in the context of negative social and community definitions of the biracial experience, an experience that often is not understandable to others and therefore becomes a reason for exclusion.

Parents, by providing their children the structure and the words that help them make sense of their experiences as they develop their self-concept and self-esteem, play a crucial role in the lives of biracial children during this early stage. Providing open communication about race and an interracial label validates and fosters the child's rudimentary interracial self-concept (Jacobs, 1977). Expressed through support, communication, and comfortableness in discussing feelings and racial/cultural facts and experiences, parents of biracial children plant an early seed for subsequent identity resolutions. The valued communication about racial and ethnic experiences by the parent can provide an understanding of the social devaluation of differentness as well. In valuing each of the child's racial and ethnic heritages, parents structure emotional safety and confidence through a positive interracial label and through modeling an ability to discuss racial and ethnic differences openly. For many biracial people, although actual discussion may be limited, the family's openness to cultural and interracial differences (foods, languages, extended family, multiethnic friends, and so on) conveys a similar message of acceptance and positive valuation of being biracial.

Biracial people often become aware much later of the difficulties their parents may have experienced in being an interracial couple. During their own experiences of dissonance, they are not able to have compassion for their parents' struggles. It is important to emphasize that the parents were most likely under immense strain, struggling to deal with the personal and social aspects of their interracial marriage, usually without community acceptance themselves. In wanting differences to wash away, the parents attempted to convert their own uniqueness into the American ideals and stereotypes of success and happiness. Inadvertently, some parents also tried protectively to push away their children's uniqueness and the struggles that would come from it. Without parental structuring, biracial people's experiences of dissonance are intensified. Rather than engendering a curiosity about parental heritages and a self-exploration of differentness, biracial people experience an increased self-consciousness and a sense of isolation and aloneness about their racial experiences. For many biracial people, one consequence was that they saw their parents as negatively valued in comparison to other children's parents. The painfulness of this observation was often made more complicated by the need to keep silent their fears, questions, and curiosity. The biracial person's need for communication could be thwarted by the family system's need to be enshrouded in silence about its own differentness and unresolved past (Chabran & Hirabayashi, 1987).

Although all the parents were remembered as generally loving and accepting of their biracial children, the subjects in my original research sample described their fathers and mothers as generally not providing clear and coherent modeling of racial conflict resolution or of open communication about race and ethnicity. These biracial people realized that they had to find their own validation and resolution, which engendered a fragile self-reliance, pushing them prematurely to experiment with their own rudimentary interracial concepts, especially for those growing up during the civil rights movements of the 1950s through the 1970s. Denial or avoidance as a defense against their feelings of isolation and pain was not a solution for them, since other people were constantly reminding them of their differentness. In the biracial person's quest for personal understanding and mastery, they began to seek their own explanations for the dissonance, and they initiated a struggle to belong and to find acceptance by others, which moved them into the next phase.

STAGE 2: STRUGGLE FOR ACCEPTANCE

The struggle for acceptance often occurs in the context of school or community settings. In reaching out of the parental and extended family orbit, children become more aware of how others see them and their families. Friendships characterize the beginnings of this stage. Experiences of differentness are heightened and intensified by school attendance. For instance, being the "only one" who is interracial, the biracial Asian person often initially responds to the "What are you?" question by making reference to being "Asian." It is the mark of differentness, either confirmed or made discrepant by the person's own name and appearance. Many biracial people sense that the answer seems required by the questioner, as if the answer becomes a passport into understanding:

> There's always this whole routine, ever since I was a little kid. They'd ask my name and, after I'd tell them, they would say, "What kind of name

> is that?" and I'd say, "It's Japanese," and they'd say, "You don't look Japanese" and I'd explain, "Well, I'm half Japanese" and then they'd want more explanation, about my mother and my father.... I'd say, "My mommy's Japanese and my father's American." (quoted in Kich, 1982, p. 137)

Although some gradually begin using an interracial label because their parents give it to them, most refer to being interracial by listing their parents' heritages. They want to be known yet often are ashamed and outraged at being so persistently judged in their differentness. Biracial people want acceptance, hoping no one will ask about their different names or appearances. Yet, after they answer the questions and feel some acceptance by others, there is often only a bittersweet sense of triumph in this recognition.

Parental comfort or discomfort plays a major role in biracial persons' degree of isolation and embarrassment about themselves and their families' interracial differentness. The tension between loyalty toward parents and a wish to be accepted by school friends often heightens the need to feel separation between home and school. Although the family can be seen as a refuge from the possibility of peer group rejection, it is also the source of the differentness itself. Experiences of dissonance are very difficult to resolve during this period. Often, biracial people attempt to separate off aspects of themselves as a response to conflicting loyalty and acceptance needs. For some biracial people in the sample, for instance, eating ethnic foods was something to be done at home—they would never bring such foods for lunch at school. However, as the physical embodiment of dual racial origins, they are constantly reminded of their interracial situation. Maintaining a separation between family and social life can be used only temporarily as a defense against fears of rejection. Being reminded of their interracial life continually provides biracial people with the need to resolve their fears of exposure as not belonging to any group and their gradual self-recognition as unchangeably interracial.

An underlying difficult struggle can be the question of identification with one parent or the other, often showing up as a question of loyalty. Although both parents were important to the biracial people of the research sample, the Japanese or Japanese American parent embodied the differentness they themselves experienced, since the families often were minorities in a European American society. This experience was somewhat different for those growing up in Japan.

For many during this stage, an ambivalent relationship is formed with the parent who most personifies the person's experience of differentness and an overidentification occurs with the other parent. However, fostered by parental reluctance or inability to share racial concerns themselves, the biracial person often suppresses the feelings of embarrassment, disappointment, or self-doubt underlying the conflict. Frustration and anger, longing, and fear of inferiority manifest in questions of loyalty toward one parent or the other. Exacerbated by the normal adolescent conflicts of this society, the biracial person's struggle for acceptance perpetuates attempts at isolating home from social life. At times the home can become a private, secret place, away from the daily questions and doubts engendered by peers and other social groups. Maintaining the parents as separate from the external world would preclude having to choose between them. However, as a partial resolution, most of the biracial people I have interviewed often took on with varying degrees of success the tasks of mediating and acting as a bridge between their parents and their friendship and community groups. Through this process, biracial people attempt to master the need to integrate divergent aspects of themselves and their heritages.

Divorce between the parents only superficially and painfully solves the question of loyalty. The excluded parent becomes a significant though absent force (see Williams, Chapter 20, this volume). A reconnection with the absent parent, during the high school or college period, appears to be a necessary step toward the later development of biracial people's self-acceptance.

Rapid fluctuations in self-perception are evident during the high school period, structured by changes in reference groups, extended family contacts, and personal psychosocial capacities. By the end of this period not only do biracial people learn and use specific interracial labels for themselves, but they become aware of their parents' heritages as valuable aspects of themselves and of their roots. By becoming more involved with their extended families, biracial individuals find that a cross-generational self-awareness can increase their sense of confidence in their developing interracial identities. For those who benefit from early and ongoing connection with extended family from both sides of their heritages, their interracial self-concept is further strengthened.

Increased experimentation and exploration, heightened by limit testing and peer group involvement, marks this important stage.

Although this process confronts biracial people with emotionally charged acceptance and rejection experiences, they can develop a heightened ability to negotiate this racial and ethnic mine field. Biracial people change their involvement in and alliance with different reference groups, sometimes bypassing the racial dimension altogether by focusing on nationality or ability (e.g., "I'm American" or "I'm a tennis player"). Many who experience themselves as different from everyone and feel the need to fit in take on an exaggerated form of role playing, mimicking others, usually people having a higher social or peer status. This chameleon ability (changing self-expression in order to fit in and become acceptable) allows them a temporary sense of freedom and relief from the restrictions and ambiguities of being "both" and "neither." However, to mimic the other means that the self-as-interracial, as different, is devalued temporarily in favor of an assured though momentary acceptance. These attempts at "passing" as an acceptable person in the eyes of the group are developed as a means of escaping a socially devalued dimension of themselves that they do not completely understand. At the same time, for those who are able to make the transition through this stage, their ability to take on or accept roles becomes a powerful means of empathically understanding others, of exposing for themselves the mechanisms of acceptance and rejection interactions, and of clarifying some of the complexities of race and ethnicity. In the process, they are searching actively for a peer group that can mirror their own struggles and identity questions. These experiences add to their repertoire of roles and defenses, but they also increase their need to resolve loyalty and acceptance questions, within both their families and their peer groups. Where do they belong? Involvement with various reference groups is another way biracial people can attempt to escape the "White American" or "Japanese" loyalty dilemma often posed by their parents, by community groups, or by institutions (e.g., on forms including racial designation). Like all other adolescents, biracial youth struggle with finding an accepting place outside the home. But, unlike others, biracial and bicultural people do not find an easy or comfortable recognition, acceptance, and membership with others like themselves.

Continually reminded of being interracial (via appearances, names, and experiences), biracial people also more openly experiment with and explore the heritages that make up their various "sides." For instance, the biracial people in my study traveled to Japan, learned the Japanese language, met and spoke with extended family members of whichever heritage had previously been silent or distant, and began meeting other biracial people. Travel to other parts of the United States confronted them with extended family that had previously been rejecting or rejected. If they had previously sought acceptance only with European Americans, they reactively explored the Japanese or Japanese American community. Some rejected their Japanese American relatives and explored relationships with people of other racial and ethnic backgrounds, a reaction not unlike the experimentation of other ethnic and racial minority groups (Atkinson, Morten, & Sue, 1989; Fanon, 1967; Shibutani & Kwan, 1965).

During this difficult period, biracial people at times further intensify their struggles by more actively and consciously choosing sides. No longer simply exploratory, the choice often is based on their own convictions and an emerging interracial identity assertion. They have become more clearly differentiated from their parents and more aware of their parents' unresolved issues. They begin to see their parents as separate people who had to struggle with their own difficult identity and racial issues. By beginning to recognize and accept themselves as interracial people, they are beginning also to see themselves as more firmly belonging to a different ethnic/racial category than either parent.

> When you're with another Eurasian there's a lot of things it seems like you don't have to explain, that you might have to explain to other people . . . that's not explainable anyway. It's just an understanding that you have. (quoted in Kich, 1982, p. 181)

Self-exploration takes on an independent character, separate from struggles to please parents. Biracial people realize that their parents generally have not understood them and gradually recognize that being interracial is different from being in an interracial relationship. In their newfound hunger for self-knowledge, they actively learn about their own personal and family histories, sometimes exposing painful secrets long dormant. Many also learn about other interracial people and their histories in the United States and in other parts of the world. Identifying themselves as interracial, biracial, international citizen, hapa, Amerasian, or whatever, is often amplified by a mutual process of identification and connection with others who are also biracial. Along with a realization of themselves as a unique category, biracial people at the end of the search-for-acceptance stage recognize the limitations of standard racial categories in general. However, despite their own developing clarity in their self-recognition as biracial, other people continue to confront them with mislabels, questions, and rejection.

Although biracial people know about and have experienced the racism of other racial groups, they often do not recognize their own interracial stereotypes until later. Initial self-acceptance sometimes includes the step of wholehearted and overinflated identification with the stereotypes of intelligence, beauty, and exoticness. At the same time, the person may be easily affronted by other people's misperceptions based on the same stereotypes. Many become more politically aware and identify with Third World and global politics, beginning to see the implications of the social and structural bases of their experiences of dissonance and of not belonging. They begin to understand that their experience of not belonging results partially from their socially undefined position within the categories of race, ethnicity, and sometimes nationality. They slowly understand their personal feelings within the context of political, social, and community structures. Often, this larger framework helps free them from a sense of isolation and personal devaluation during especially difficult periods, since they can begin to see that being biracial is not necessarily a personal problem or a stigma. However, a renewal of the experience of dissonance and devaluation, either a mislabel or a racial epithet, even about another race, might forcefully bring back the old uneasy and conflicting feelings. Although they can more effectively handle their feelings of dissonance and not-belonging, no amount of personal self-understanding or political awareness can prevent the social or community situations from continuing to recur. The work of an ongoing and stable self-acceptance continues into the next stage.

STAGE 3: SELF-ACCEPTANCE AND ASSERTION OF AN INTERRACIAL IDENTITY

Self-acceptance, substantially different from, yet influenced by, the quest for other-acceptance, may never be fully achieved by anyone. However, the biracial person's ability to create congruent self-definitions rather than be determined by others' definitions and stereotypes may be said to be the major achievement of a biracial and bicultural identity. This ability to define him- or herself positively is an important reversal of the social construction of a previous identity as devalued, unacceptable, and anomalous.

The stable self-acceptance of a biracial and bicultural self-identity begins to occur generally after high school, and more finally during and after the college or occupational transitions. Responses to parents appear to come more from compassion and an understanding of their struggles as an interracial couple who themselves had no models or community support, having instead experienced discrimination and prejudice. Communication in the family becomes more of an attempt to develop a two-way dialogue, with efforts to understand each other. The biracial person's achievements may have exposed the parents to the possibility of a more assertive revaluation of themselves as well. Extended family contact, the result of adult choice, is often developed or maintained by biracial persons as a necessary and conscious link to aspects of themselves. Ethnic heritage, history, ritual, and culture are valued and sought out, yet tempered by an awareness of the self as also being American.

In addition to the use of an interracial label in answer to questions or mislabels, the generally more self-confident biracial people are able to assess the other's capacity for understanding and to be self-expressive and educative as well as self-protective. The response to others' mislabels or prejudicial statements becomes a differentiated and multiple answer, often with more consideration for the other person's dilemma. Biracial persons in this stage begin to understand that not all questioners are racist or intent on defining them negatively. This indicates an increased stability of differentiation concerning their identity as biracial. Rather than a reactive response, a need to please or provoke the other, they are able to measure their answers to their personal needs as well as to the needs of the situation. They more clearly understand the confusion of the other person, essentially the confusion of the rest of society about race and ethnicity. They are less dependent on the other person's recognition or confirmation and rely more on their own integration of a self based on a clearer and heightened awareness of their heritages, their extended family, interracial history, and mutual acceptance with others like themselves.

With self-acceptance, the biracial person can be self-expressive rather than defensive and reactive. Knowing when to fit in and when to expose or confront distortions about differences becomes a more conscious self-protective task for the biracial person. Self-acceptance opens up skills learned in prior stages, especially those associated with "passing." From a negative point of view, passing is equated with not having self-acceptance and needing the acceptance of others to compensate for this lack. In the prior stage, passing could be understood as an acceptance by others without question, without a "passport" or identity papers of some kind, but as a defense against rejection, coming from a place of unconscious self-hatred. From a positive point of view, the skills associated with passing (an ability to move safely within difference, a knowledge of different groups' languages and secrets, the ability to have an even larger field in which to expand self-acceptance) allow practice of the personal and social interactions necessary for mutual and interdependent survival. Passing becomes a temporary process to handle social confusion and limitations about race and identity (Bradshaw, Chapter 7, this volume; Daniel, Chapter 8, this volume). The interpersonal skills associated with passing in this framework become ways of negotiating within rigid and limiting expectations. Because of these prior attempts at acceptance within many different groups, biracial people often can recognize the parameters of group roles, rules, and characteristics. As a result, their ability to gain some acceptance by many different groups potentially is expanded. However, experiences of dissonance and of being labeled as too different for acceptance still continue, since others generally do not understand the biracial person. Many actively seek out the involvement of other biracial and bicultural people, as well as those of other ethnic and racial groups. They want contact that is not inhibited and that does not require a "full explanation" of their heritages. During the stage of self-acceptance, biracial people generally have come to value their identity as something constructed out of the relationship between personal experience and social meanings of ethnicity, race, and group membership. The simple assertion of being who they are, of being biracial, is the developmental achievement of this ongoing and unfinished process.

Summary

The development of a biracial, bicultural identity occurs over three stages. Feeling different and discrepant is a painful aspect of the first stage. As part of a second stage, biracial people search for acceptance and understanding from others as a way of understanding themselves. Self-acceptance and the assertion of a biracial identity are the third and continuing processes of a lifelong task, which seems to repeat at different levels of complexity during major crises or transitions throughout the life span. The unavoidability of the self as biracial, known in a rudimentary though real way in early childhood and recapitulated and asserted throughout development, requires ongoing social and personal understanding and acceptance, since personality development continues to occur throughout life. A person may cycle through attributes of the stages more quickly at later points in life, allowing other, perhaps subtle, resolutions to occur.

The assertion of the self as biracial requires both the personal organizing structure of a biracial self-label and the interpersonal and social recognition of the individual as biracial. The assertion creates and fosters a coherent, whole sense of self.

A biracial identity does not necessarily mean an equal apportionment or valuation of each parent's ethnic and racial heritage. Parents are crucial facilitators of the biracial person's self-acceptance. If parents can be comfortable talking about race and ethnicity with their biracial and bicultural children and model the resolution of conflicts, especially those involving racial and ethnic issues, they can actively cultivate the family as an important medium through which a biracial sense of self develops.

Even without social or parental structuring or guidance, the biracial and bicultural person strives for a totalness, a sense of wholeness that is more than the sum of the parts of a person's heritages. The preservation of the sense of a biracial and bicultural identity, of being "both" and "neither," throughout life results from the creative interplay between a gradually developing social acceptance and the self's ability to actively reverse the dissociating effects of discrepant experiences. Rather than a process of dissociating and separating off aspects of the self, the development of a biracial person who achieves a biracial and bicultural identity is marked by an ongoing integration of different and sometimes contradictory heritages, histories, and parental, social, and community messages.

PART IV

Challenging the Census

22

Is Multiracial Status Unique? The Personal and Social Experience

MICHAEL C. THORNTON

Most of us use the term *race* with little difficulty. We can even describe the various races, usually by referring to physical and other overt qualities. Nevertheless, the apparent consensus over the meaning and use of the term remains so only on the surface, for when asked for details beyond physical differences, we are at a loss for words, often citing cultural artifacts to explain racial differences. Ultimately, there is no real consensus on the meaning of the term. This puzzlement is due to a misunderstanding of what race is, how it is commonly perceived by society, and how racial minorities experience it. This confusion about race is most visible in how we view multiracial people.

Race and racial differences seem somehow self-evident and distinct. However, what we perceive as race is often intertwined with culture and biology. Physical qualities, the belief goes, reflect biological influences, which seem tied to attitudinal, life-style, and socioeconomic factors (in toto, culture). Biological factors still underpin explanations of racial differences observed in our society.

But what is race, and what does it explain about group differences? Biologists and geneticists talk of races possessing dissimilar gene pools, revealed as obvious physical disparity. Furthermore, these gene pools are not distinct and in fact overlap. Because there are no such things as pure races, technically we are all interracial. Therefore, the significant distinctions among racial groups are socially constructed artifacts. Racial differences explain how society parcels out resources and privileges and have little to do with biological deviations of any note. Race is important because we say it is.

Thus societies have developed subjective social measures to identify racial groups. In the United States, these groups are said to be distinct and well-defined entities. For example, one is considered "Black" (i.e., has a Black identity) if one has an African heritage or "Black" blood. Nevertheless, there are significant cases that deviate from this rule. By the above definition, Hispanics and Native Americans should be but are not considered Black. Further, we are all regarded as members of only one racial group. You are, for example, Black *or* Asian *or* White. For a number of people such a designation is problematic. Multiracial people present a quandary for the either/or, dichotomous racial classifications used in this society. This is reflected in a lack of labels for those of multiple racial heritage and in our ambiguous treatment of non-Black-White combinations. If you are Asian and White are you White or Asian?

The subjective nature of racial labels is emphasized by a debate that appeared in a recent *Los Angeles Times* article titled "Call for Census Category Creates Interracial Debate" (Njeri, 1991). In it, a self-proclaimed multiracial female (Asian, Black, and Native American heritage) argued that multiracial people deserve to have their distinctive status legitimated by the creation of a unique census category. In opposition, a Black male (who, while not defining himself as multiracial, also has Native American ancestry) suggested that the present categories are sufficient. A new grouping would negatively affect Black representation.

Often racial labels become a political tool to measure strength of identity. This tendency can be seen in an allegation that the woman described above desires a separate category in part to deny her African heritage. It is acceptable to make statements about one's multiple ancestry (I am part Asian, Polish, or whatever), but not about identity; a private but not public affirmation of multiple heritage is acceptable. As Jack Forbes (1990) has noted, in embracing White notions of racial cataloging, some Blacks are trapped by a system that blocks self-identification and serves to reinforce what racists have long advocated. Nevertheless, it is understandable why they take this stance. The campaign by the United States to subordinate and oppress people of color has forced them to forge a united front to generate pride in what Whites have declared to be inferior. In this environment many multiracial people pass or take pride in their mixed heritage for the wrong reasons, exalting in their White (or higher-status) ancestry and denying their ethnic origins. An authentic identity cannot be developed while an individual is in a state of intellectual and emotional subservience to racism. Still worse is to accept only one's majority and not one's minority ancestry. To lean toward the former is to undermine the struggle for self-determination, while aligning with the latter at least maintains an alliance with the oppressed.

The man in the debate described above assumes, with little evidence, that his opponent reveals latent racism. While he ostensibly attempts to support the idea of Black unity, for the woman to do as he suggests would be subversive to self-identification, an antithesis to the primary thrust of the Black power movement—self-determination. In this regard, pressure is from both Black and White society, and in the same direction—for both seem to accept White definitions of Whiteness and of race—the presence of African ancestry is the sole determinant of racial status.

These underlying assumptions can be seen in the categories selected for the U.S. Census. Interestingly, although in the census racial and national labels are supposedly measures of self-identity, it is clear that the universe of self-designations is limited to socially decreed categories. Racial labels are not objective configurations, but are political in nature. African heritage equals being Black because we as a society say it is so, although Blacks are realistically a number of diverse people—Jamaican, Ethiopian, Nigerian, and so on.

The process of labeling of course oversimplifies how race is experienced. There is no intrinsic personality related to race; what develops is a complex interaction between individual and social definitions. Individuals are expected to locate themselves "accurately" within established racial structures (such as current census categories), finding where society places them and reconciling this placement with what they want to be. Ideally, individual choice and social designations are psychologically satisfying for the individual and socially approved. The woman in the debate described above has not found that ideal, for society denies the validity of her perceptions and experience. For her, a census category would legitimate an otherwise socially ambiguous status.

Thus individual experience often differs from social expectations of that experience. The secular existence of multiracial people overlaps but differs from other racial minorities. Socially they are often treated like their monoracial compatriots, but psychologically they encounter life in unique ways. The contrast is between, as Jack Forbes describes it, fruits and apples; fruits are the general class, apples are the specific. Fruits are not the same as apples, yet the two overlap. In the present context, an Asian American's experience and a Black-Asian American's experience, for example, will overlay one another, yet they are not the same. If self-identification were the goal, then a mixed racial category would be part of the census and would serve to legitimate this status.

Such a new category would suggest that there is an experience that ties all multiracial people together; any label utilized implies important continuity in experience. If all multiracial people have some basic background in common, what is it and how does it bind them more closely to one another than to their parental racial groups? What is the unifying theme? There is little evidence indicating other than some superficial basis for commonality between groups of different racial mixture. The two protagonists in the *L.A. Times* piece show the complexity in combining people of all racial mixtures into one group. Both are of mixed racial heritage, but one identifies as mixed and the other does not. It is predictable that many people would exclude themselves from this category, a trend perhaps more pronounced among those of particular combinations, Black-other than, say, Asian-White, because of the virulent nature of racism against Blacks. What would the new designation mean if one were allowed to choose among a number of possibilities?

Further, the other groups that have designated census categories have more clear-cut bases on which to expect similar experiences, both because society identifies and treats them as separate groups and because they have common heritages (i.e., cultures). None of these categories exists simply because of common experience. Do multiracials have a core (cultural) heritage, or are they viewed as alike by others in society? Are multiracials seen as a different (racial/ethnic) group from, say, Blacks? In fact, what seems to bind multiracial people is not race or culture, but living with an ambiguous status, an experience similar to that of all people of color. Facing a different set of dilemmas does not make one an ethnic or racial group, or signify a culture. As a group, multiracials are too diverse to categorize. This group is more biologically diverse than others, and has no common ancestry and little community. These are things one cannot say about the other census groupings.

In comparing people of so-called multiracial status to monoracials, it is clear that the former have a different flavor to their lives. Society defines race as distinctive and homogeneous; multiracial people experience it as multidimensional. That background should and must be appreciated in and of itself. But that experience is irrelevant in a social sense. Race is a social and political tool not meant to reflect the range of experience or the diversity found within any group to any great extent. By definition, racial labels are tools used to categorize and to separate and/or exclude. There remains insufficient social justification to exclude multiracials from other groups. While there is experiential rationale for identifying a unique experience, that alone is not reason enough, and does not provide a consistent basis, to describe multiracials as one sort of people.

23

Coloring Outside the Lines

CHRISTINE C. IIJIMA HALL

The buzzword around the nation is *diversity*. By the year 2000, more than one-third of the U.S. population will be composed of people of color. In many states, that proportion exists now. With the increase in people of color (immigrants and nationals), there will undoubtedly also be an increase in interracial marriages and interracial children.

The number of multiracial individuals has already become visible in America. Numerous organizations have been established to aid individuals in developing and understanding the multiethnic identity. I believe that a "critical mass" of multiracial people is forming now. This is evident in the numerous recent media appearances in which multiethnic individuals have been highlighted. For example, *Essence* magazine interviewed Quincy Jones about his marriages to White women. He talked about his biracial children and how the issue of identity was important in child rearing. NBC's *A Different World* featured a Black-Japanese woman as a love interest of one of the main characters. Her ethnicity, ability to speak Japanese, and knowledge of Japanese customs were highlighted throughout her tenure on the show.

We are everywhere, and the United States will have to adjust to our presence in many ways. For years, I have believed that the U.S. Census Bureau and other institutions need to expand their ethnic categories in order to obtain more precise data on the U.S. population. Racially mixed individuals will be counted incorrectly if this readjustment does not occur. A Census Bureau employee once told me that if I checked "Other" on the census form and specified "Black-Japanese," I would be counted as Black because that was the first race I mentioned. I disagreed adamantly, but he spouted that the system could not accommodate such esoteric identities. I have also asked smaller, private guilds and organizations to change their ethnic identification forms. Most have said also that it is too much trouble to go through for such a small group of individuals. I have disagreed with this, pointing out that computers can be programmed to receive more than one category. That is, programs can be written that would allow individuals to check two ethnicities and/or two races. I hope these agencies will eventually see the need to expand their understanding of diversity.

The racial and ethnic nomenclature for mixed individuals will also change at some point. This is not necessarily good or bad; it is just inevitable. People in the United States tend to need labels, and if a group does not take the lead in labeling itself, another (outside) group will take on the task. The labeling issue has caused heated discussions at several multicultural conferences and meetings. Some people believe that labeling will lead us into stereotypes and categories that we have all fought against, while others believe that it will solidify our identity.

As many of the chapters included in this book have shown, the antecedent to the labeling issue is American society's overwhelming obsession with putting people into racial categories that are restrictive and evaluative. Should we conform to these practices and construct additional categories? In general, I have no problem with categories. We categorize animals, plants, and minerals. The problem develops when we attach value judgments to these categories. An avocado is no "better" than a banana. The cost of an avocado may be greater, because it is rarer or requires more cultivating, but that does not make it the better fruit. In the "salad bowl" theory of diversity, each ingredient is appreciated for its unique contribution to a colorful and tasty dish. This is quite different from the old melting-pot image. Thus, rather than blending people all as one generic group or color, we now have the opportunity to enjoy people as individuals who are members of particular groups without the judgments that have been attached historically.

I believe that multiracial individuals are beginning to feel more comfortable with and to value their unique ethnic heritages. This is probably due to their having more visible role models and a nation's understanding that biracial individuals other than Black-White do exist. This validation of their existence, combined with their not being viewed as "deviant," is very important to young children and adults who are formulating their identity. I recently met a 17-year-old Black-White woman who recognized me as being racially mixed. She was excited to meet an adult who could share in her identity understanding, be a role model, and help her work through some issues. There are many mixed individuals in her school, so she does not feel like a "freak," but she was very excited to meet someone of mixed race who is both professionally successful and very happy with her personal existence.

As a multiracial researcher, I am excited to see how research and publications on issues of multiraciality have increased over the last 11 years. It was difficult being one of the first to approach the subject in an educational milieu. People tried to dissuade me from my choice of topic; they did not understand the need for research in such an "esoteric" area. As a young researcher, I held steadfast and pursued my lifelong dream of publicizing the issue of mixed-race identity. I am moved to see how far we have come in our understanding of ourselves and in conveying this information to others.

The research needs to continue. The different racial mixtures need to be investigated. There are many questions to be pursued. For instance, how is a person who is part White and part Asian different from someone who is part Hispanic and part Asian or part Black? Is being a dual minority mixture different from being part majority mixture? What will our children identify as? The United States may physically and genetically become the melting pot that has been predicted by some. Politically and sociologically, however, I do not think the melting-pot theory will come to fruition. The majority of the respondents in my original study believed that being mixed did not mean a person blended with an existing race; on the contrary, it made the person a member of a different race.

This *new race* may be a valuable one. Most of the mixed people I know are able to interact with many ethnic groups. They, like me, despise the fighting among the different ethnic minority groups in America. They are able to act as bridges among groups, fostering communication and cooperation. The future role of mixed people may be that of negotiators. Since they belong to many groups, they will be seen as insiders, with vested interests in making plans work for all sides.

Diversity is indeed the buzzword of the 1990s. Multiracial and multicultural individuals will play a major role in this decade, because they are extremely diverse in thought, culture, and being.

24

Multicultural Identity and the Death of Stereotypes

PHILIP TAJITSU NASH

Each of us pays the price of racial and cultural stereotypes every day of our lives. We either buy into them and live with their insidious effects or stand up to them and risk the wrath of those who benefit from them. Multicultural people have a special role to play in combating stereotypes. When we are around, athletic ability cannot be deduced by kinkiness of hair. Math aptitude cannot be gleaned from the shape of eyes. Language ability cannot be identified by color of skin.

Those of us with parents of two distinct "racial" backgrounds are a visible reminder that *everyone* is multicultural and deserves to be treated as a multifaceted individual. We are all shaped by language, local custom, "race" (a pseudoscientific term that we all need to reexamine), religion, education, social class, gender, and sexual orientation through socialization that attaches meaning to these differences. No two children are ever born into the same family. Each of us grows up in unique circumstances.

Because we are not a monolithic bunch, however, multicultural people will play different roles in the struggle against stereotypes at different times in our lives. For example, some individuals will choose to identify almost exclusively with the part of themselves that society devalues before ultimately feeling comfortable with all aspects of self. Others will identify with the dominant society and be unaware of the internal struggles that other devalued minorities will be going through. As a person who has self-identified as "just like everyone else American," Japanese American, Asian American, Asian/Pacific American, Third World person, and person of color, I can testify to the ongoing difficulty of the task.

Unfortunately, the struggle against stereotypes is made more difficult by the fact that both societal and personal barriers prevent us from acknowledging the multicultural heritage of every person. These barriers arise from unequal power relationships that have become rooted in both everyday language and stereotypical media images. For example, no one usually questions why we follow Greenwich Standard Time, which makes London the center of the world at high noon as the new day breaks in the Pacific. Movies and television shows almost uniformly revolve around a European-derived male who saves the day for the woman and infantilized people of color.

If these images and subliminal messages lead us to accept uncritically the myth of the monolithic European-derived male and his values and culture as the norm, how can we who desire to live in a stereotype-free, multicultural world change things? First, we must stop thinking in simplistic categories. Reality is complex, varied, nonlinear, noncategorical. Human beings define the categories that are useful to them in social interaction. We must make the effort to see ourselves and others in nonstereotypical ways, and take a stand whenever others are victimized by stereotypes. This is happening in our lifetime through the efforts of individuals such as Bill Cosby, whose weekly television show presents positive African American images, and organizations such as the Council on Interracial Books for Children, which presents educators and textbook publishers with models of nonsexist and nonracist publications. Second, we must change the system that has led to some people being valued more than others. Why should we aspire to individual success as defined by a morally flawed system? This means speaking out every day for the rights of people of color, women, and other "minorities" devalued in contemporary U.S. society. Finally, we must begin to define human beings in ways that do not buy into hierarchies based on wealth and social status. Rather than seeing myself as an Asian American or a European American, why can't I find strength and wisdom in each and both? If my ancestors included both farmers and legislators, why must I feel prouder of one than the other?

I have no illusions that all stereotypes can be identified, challenged, and overcome in my lifetime. Nevertheless, not to participate in this process is to accept a world where each of us must be a little less than our whole self, and where none of us can be treated as an individual.

Stereotypes must die so that our whole selves can live.

25

Beyond Black and White: The New Multiracial Consciousness

G. REGINALD DANIEL

The New Epistemology: From Either/Or to Both/And

The dismantling of Jim Crow segregation, particularly the removal of the last antimiscegenation laws in June 1967, and the implementation of civil rights legislation over the last 20 years have dissolved the formal mechanism barring individuals of African descent from having avenues of contact with Whites as equals. Not only has the number of interracial marriages increased dramatically (Gibbs, 1989; Njeri, 1988b; Tucker & Mitchell-Kernan, 1990), but many of these couples, seeking to bring both Black and White heritages to the identity of their offspring (Wardle, 1987; Gibbs, 1989; Spickard, 1989), have called into question the justification for institutional policies and informal social attitudes that maintain the rule of hypodescent (Njeri, 1988b; Snipp, 1986).

Indeed, today's comparatively more fluid intergroup relations and more iconoclastic attitudes toward racial identity, fruits of the civil rights movement, seem themselves to be reflective of even more fundamental epistemological shifts that are seeking to move our society away from the "either/or" paradigm of binary thinking, which clearly delineates things into mutually exclusive categories, to one that incorporates concepts of "partly," "mostly," or "both/and" (Salk, 1973; Teitelbaum, 1990). As the epitome of this absurd, yet almost sacred "Law of the Excluded Middle" (Teitelbaum, 1990)—cornerstone of Western logic and of Anglo-American thinking in particular—the old epistemology studies things in isolation and in parts, and acknowledges no shades of gray (Ramirez, 1983; Teitelbaum,

1990; Tofler, 1980). The new epistemology, perhaps best expressed in the principle of new mathematical theory called "fuzzy logic" (Teitelbaum, 1990), argues that many things cannot be categorized by binary thinking and emphasizes instead contexts, relationships, and wholes (Tofler, 1980; Ramirez, 1983). This thinking has made itself felt not only in new models of multiracial identity, but in a variety of disparate, yet ultimately related, phenomena such as the environmental, feminist, and holistic health movements, interdisciplinary thinking in universities, and Gestalt therapy in the field of psychoanalysis, to mention only a few examples of what in vernacular culture is called the New Age (Capra, 1982; Ferguson, 1980; Tofler, 1980).

A Road Less Traveled: The New Multiracial Consciousness

As an expression of this epistemological shift, these new models of multiracial identity challenge Anglo-America's dichotomous system of racial classification as have other resistance strategies, yet they differ radically from those tactics. Previous strategies—whether integration through "passing" or the formation of pluralistic urban elites or rural enclaves—were generated by the legal system of segregation, which sought to control the potential threat to White dominance posed by individuals of African descent. Those strategies were not only tactically hierarchical and Eurocentric, but were less a reaction to the forced denial of one's European ancestry than to being subordinated and to being denied the privileges that ancestry has implied.

The carriers of the new multiracial consciousness—benefiting as have other individuals of African descent from the comparatively more fluid intergroup relations and from socioeconomic gains resulting from the first steps toward civil rights, particularly as evidenced in affirmative action programs—are not, therefore, seeking special privileges that would be precluded by identifying as Black. Whether they call themselves "mixed," "biracial," "interracial," or "multiracial" (Radcliffe, 1988; Wardle, 1987), these individuals represent, rather, the next logical step in the progression of civil rights, the expansion of our notion of affirmative action to include strategies not only for achieving socioeconomic equity, but also for affirming a nonhierarchical identity that embraces a "holocentric" racial self (Daniel, 1988).

Although most individual experiences of the past are unknown and unreported, there have been cases of notoriety, such as that of interracial couple George and Josephine Schuyler, who in the 1940s encouraged their daughter Philippa to follow the path of this "road less traveled." Several groups—the Manasseh Clubs (named after the biblical Joseph's half-Egyptian son) in Milwaukee and Chicago between 1892 and 1932, the Penguin Club in New York during the 1930s, the Miscegenation Club in Los Angeles, and groups in Washington, D.C., and Detroit during the 1940s—also sought, with the support they provided interracial couples, to help multiracial individuals affirm both their heritages—in this case, Black and White (Spickard, 1989).

More than 30 similar organizations, with names such as Interracial/Intercultural Pride in Berkeley, Multiracial Americans of Southern California in Los Angeles, the Biracial Family Network in Chicago, and a national umbrella organization called AMEA (Association of Multiethnic Americans), have come into existence over the past decade (Grosz, 1989). Composed primarily of Black and White interracial couples and their multiracial children, the membership in some cases includes other interracial couple combinations and their offspring, plus a smaller proportion of individuals who have ancestries that have been multiracial for several generations and who have been classified by the general society as Black. These individuals differ from African Americans (who for the most part are multiracial in ancestry but monoracial in identity) in that they seek to resist the "one-dimensional images" of their identities and replace them with more "multidimensional portraits" (Forbes, 1988a, p. 271).

The Controversy: Color, Culture, Class, and the New Racial Divide

Many opponents fear that the new multiracial consciousness, despite its egalitarian rhetoric, will actually sharpen stratification among individuals of African descent by perpetuating and widening the divide between the less privileged Black masses and the privileged few, who have tended to be disproportionately of more "visible" European descent and comparatively less Afrocentric in consciousness and cultural orientation.

This occurrence of intragroup stratification, often referred to as *colorism,* has varied regionally and historically in intensity. It retreated somewhat under the influence of the Black consciousness movement of the 1960s and 1970s, but persists into the present due to the enduring Eurocentric bias in the larger American society (B. B. Berry, 1988; Hughes & Hertel, 1990; Njeri, 1988a). Overall, however, the impact of colorism on the integrity and solidarity of intragroup relations among individuals of African descent has always been attenuated by the long history of stratification and segregation in intergroup relations of that same larger society, where the rule of hypodescent (the "one-drop rule") has ascribed all individuals of African descent, regardless of color (phenotype), culture, and class, to a social status subordinate to the dominant Whites and to a reference group identity more exclusively operational within the Black community.

The greater fluidity in intergroup relations facilitated by the removal of institutionalized barriers to racial equality has not only increased the affluence of the privileged few, but has also augmented their numbers by opening these ranks to the Black masses through expanded opportunities for educational attainment. More significant, however, is the greater social mobility that has made it possible for this sector of individuals to operate more fully, and often completely, outside the parameters of the Black community, and to participate alongside Whites within the "general middle class" of the larger society (Spickard, 1989).

The economic affluence and social acceptance achieved by the privileged few have led some experts to conclude that culture and class have become more salient variables than race in determining discrimination and social stratification (W. J. Wilson, 1980) and the formation of interpersonal relations and intergroup alliances (Spickard, 1989). Yet, according to critics, these changes ushered in by the erosion of the legal base of inequality have meant neither a diminution of racism nor an end to racial discrimination (Clark, 1980; Omi & Winant, 1986). They mean simply that "the attitudinal and behavioral bases" have gone underground (Mitchell-Kernan, 1985), such that racial discrimination has become more refined and more difficult to discern (Pettigrew, 1981).

Critics would agree that expanded opportunities for educational attainment increasingly have made it possible for the less privileged Black masses (B. B. Berry, 1988) to enter the ranks of the privileged few, and that the achievement of increased affluence and social mobility has liberated the privileged few from the constraints that heretofore were rigidly ascribed by the rule of hypodescent. For the most part, however, they maintain that changes in the relationship between race and opportunity, combined with the persistent Eurocentric bias in the larger society and the disproportionately higher percentage of individuals of more "visible" European descent in the affluent classes, actually have afforded these individuals even greater access to wealth, power, privilege, and prestige when compared with the Black masses (B. B. Berry, 1988; Hughes & Hertel, 1990; Njeri, 1988a).

The disintegration of de jure racial inequality has not therefore led to a decline in the significance of race per se or an increase in the importance of culture and class, but rather to a shift away from race defined solely by the one-drop rule to a more situational definition that places increased emphasis on color, working in combination with culture and class. By loosening, if not completely severing, those traditional ties of oppression that formerly have bound the privileged few of more visible European ancestry and less Afrocentric consciousness and cultural orientation, this modification in the social articulation of race in the superstructure of American society has, nevertheless, created the illusion of racial equality. As a consequence, many European Americans have come to view the enforcement of any further remedial action on the racial front as at least no longer necessary, if not a form of "reverse discrimination." The successes of the privileged few have thus not only diverted attention away from the racial inequality that continues to affect the lives of the less privileged Black masses, but have equally disguised the fact that the ultimate fate of all individuals of African descent, regardless of color, culture, or class, is inextricably tied to the infrastructure, which remains de facto racist to the core (Omi & Winant, 1986; Pettigrew, 1981; Ringer & Lawless, 1989).

Assimilation and Apartheid: The Common Denominator

Given these insidious toxins in the racial ecology, it is feared that the recognition of multiracial identity will simply replace the binary model of race relations in the United States with the ternary, but equally problematic, models of race relations characteristic of Brazil or South Africa (Douglas, 1988; Njeri, 1988b; Radcliffe, 1988).

Opponents do acknowledge the fact that the comparatively greater fluidity of race relations and the more generalized blending of the overall population in Brazil have made the line between Black and White imprecise at best. They contend, however, that this is not in and of itself indicative of the absence of racism. Black and White are relative, representing, nevertheless, the negative and positive extremes, respectively, on a continuum of intermediate grays, where physical appearance, in conjunction with socioeconomic and cultural factors rather than ancestry, has come to determine one's race and place in the hierarchy (Daniel, 1989). In this process, Whites have maintained a policy of inegalitarian integration, that is, assimilation—an open door of individual vertical mobility termed the "mulatto escape hatch" (Degler, 1971). This social device has not only granted individuals of multiracial descent collectively speaking a somewhat more favorable lot than Blacks, but, most important, has made it possible for these individuals to be awarded the rank of provisional Whites, and with it the privileges of dominant group status, in accordance with their approximation to European phenotypical and cultural traits and with their economic standing.

Prior to the emergence of the Black consciousness movement in Brazil during the 1970s and 1980s, pervasive miscegenation and the "mulatto escape hatch," combined with the fact that Brazil has never known anything comparable to Jim Crow segregation, had helped to perpetuate the myth of racial democracy. This national schizophrenia and amnesia had, generally speaking, deflected attention away from racism, and had impeded the political mobilization of individuals of African descent, since inequality and, by extension, prejudice and discrimination were said to be based primarily on culture and class (Daniel, 1989).

More strident voices point to the worst-case scenario of South Africa. Like the United States, South Africa uses ancestry as the primary criterion in determining race. Its official policy of separate and equal development is actually a form of pluralism even more extreme in its inegalitarianism than Jim Crow segregation (Marger, 1985). The difference is that apartheid has circumscribed multiracial individuals—the Coloureds—to a structurally intermediate identity separate from and significantly subordinate to the dominant Whites, but separate also from and only somewhat superior to Blacks. In South Africa, as in Brazil, the growth of the Black consciousness movement over the last two decades has narrowed somewhat the divide between multiracial individuals and Blacks. Historically, however, the South African government has sought, and continues to seek, ways of fragmenting any alliance between these two oppressed groups that might topple White supremacy (Lewis, 1987).

Based on the dynamics of Brazilian and South African race relations, opponents believe that the recognition of multiracial identity in the United States will operate in a similar "divide and rule" fashion, undermining the integrity and solidarity of individuals of African descent. They contend, furthermore, that this would have a potentially even more detrimental impact in the United States. That is to say, by decreasing the number of individuals who, under the present system, would be counted as Black, it would reduce prized slots in the already beleaguered programs aimed at tracking historical patterns of discrimination and arriving at target goals for achieving social and economic equity (Daniel, 1989; Douglas, 1988; Radcliffe, 1988).

The Twilight Zone: Finding Common Ground

Various studies indicate that many individuals—whether they view themselves as possessors of an integrative identity, with both the Black and the White communities as reference groups, of a pluralistic and intermediate identity that blends aspects of both Black and White but is neither, or of an identity that operates more or less from both of these trends (Root, 1990)—are successfully navigating the challenging and uncharted waters of the new multiracial consciousness. Other research suggests that some individuals tend to deny or deemphasize the Black aspect of their identities because of the continuing stigma attached to Blackness in America society and culture (Arnold, 1984; Gibbs, 1989; Poussaint, 1984).

Based on these checkered indicators, the assumption that the recognition of multiracial identity will steer U.S. race relations in the direction of the inegalitarian integrationist model of Brazil is not unjustifiable. To suggest that such recognition will move the United States toward the inegalitarian pluralist model of South Africa seems extreme, since even the trajectory of the Pretorian government's policy in the dismantling of apartheid appears to be moving toward what it has sometimes called the "Brazilian option" (Sparks, 1990).

What should be pointed out in this matter, however, is that the mere recognition of multiracial identity is not in itself inherently problematic. The critical question is whether the dynamics of race relations, be they integrationist, pluralist, or both, for that matter, are to operate horizontally (that is, in an egalitarian manner in which equal value is attached to differences) or vertically (that is, in an inegalitarian manner, in which differences serve as the basis for perpetuating inequalities). Being multiracial in a hierarchical system simply means being just a little less Black and thus a little less subordinate, but does not assure equality with Whites (Daniel, 1989).

Considering these facts, it seems clear that while we must cease denying multiracial individuals their rightful place in society—a constant reminder that they do not fit in or even do not exist, a situation certainly not supportive of the development of a healthy sense of identity in children (Njeri, 1988b; Wardle, 1987)—any discussion on this topic must necessarily take into consideration its wide-ranging and long-term consequences. That is to say, we must devise a means of statistically enumerating individuals who identify themselves as multiracial in a manner that does not negatively affect the measuring of African American demographics, potentially undermining already besieged policies designed to redress the continuing effects of past racial inequities. Otherwise, we may very well reverse even further those gains achieved by the civil rights movement that now make the recognition of multiracial identity a possibility (Rajs, 1991). Most important, we must nurture this identity without rearticulating racism in some mutant form by simultaneously and unequivocally concentrating on undermining racially hierarchical thinking—in the media and particularly in the classroom—through a comprehensive antibias curriculum, as well as through a curriculum exploring racial and cultural diversity (Daniel, 1988; Derman-Sparks, 1989; Lynch, 1984; Verma, 1984; Verma & Bagley, 1984; Wardle, 1987).

By according equal worth to all racial and cultural groups, it may become possible to nurture an ambience of both egalitarian pluralism (Marger, 1985) and egalitarian integration. That is to say, increased contact will, one hopes, not only result in a better understanding and appreciation of differences as well as of commonalities (Pettigrew, 1988; Triandis, 1988), but may, in turn, also help to steer the trajectory of American race relations beyond the one-way vertical process of assimilation toward a bilateral and horizontal process of transculturation (Ortiz, 1940/1947). By so doing, we shall ensure that multiracial individuals are not impelled to surrender the Black aspect of their identities in order to qualify as first-class citizens, and enhance the possibility that these individuals, likened to that liminal dimension between day and night, will successfully absorb all colors, as does black, while at the same time reflecting them all, as does white.

Acknowledgment

I would like to acknowledge Nina Moss for the feedback and moral support she provided in shaping revisions of this chapter.

26

From Shortcuts to Solutions

MARIA P. P. ROOT

This volume has been dedicated to confronting the limitations and assumptions of the construct of race by examining the phenomenology of the multiracial experience in history, theory, and contemporary findings. In contrast to the assumptions underlying social identity models of assimilation (see Phinney, 1990), it is possible to reconcile divergent values, customs, and cultures associated with different heritages—in this case, race. However, we have developed some habits or shortcuts for understanding our environment that are difficult to change. These shortcuts are at the root of the oppression of persons who occupy some form of "other" status, and, by definition of "other," are unclassifiable by the prevailing classification schemes. In Paulo Freire's (1970) words, "Marginality is not by choice, [the] marginal [person] has been expelled from and kept outside of the social system" (p. 10). These shortcuts will be examined and suggestions offered for how change might be accelerated.

Shortcuts

Most of the contributors to this volume have made the point that at the root of the oppression of multiracial people have been the tendencies to classify people ordinally and to resist changing the classification system if only a few people do not fit. Rules of hypodescent and subsequent evidence of the internalization of these rules has allowed America's racial classification system to remain largely unchallenged until recently. Thus oppression does not reside in our observations of phenotypic differences but in the deep imprint left by hierarchical thinking that, unfortunately, has also been internalized by people of color.

All classification schemes represent shortcuts, as they summarize general characteristics or qualities of the category, person, or group. These schemes are more reliable when they are based on very concrete physical attributes that yield little variation (such as in the sciences). However, once variability is introduced, and we insist on shortcuts, we increasingly risk creating classification systems that perpetuate the oppression of certain groups of people because these systems are created in a way that assuages the fears of the people who benefit most by them. In the case of race, not only is there variability in what we see, but as Spickard (Chapter 2) notes, there is more variability within racial groups than between racial groups and tremendous overlap between the physical attributes associated with each group. In order to retain our classification schemes, we have had to move away from relying solely on physical schemata to understand the sociopolitical construct of "race." Many biracial children's cognitive understanding of multiraciality reflects the irrationality of our system. Some young children look at halves of themselves to see if they are different colors to reflect parts of each parent; some African American children must engage in cognitive and perceptual distortions to arrive at "correct" racial identification of themselves and family members (see Jacobs, Chapter 14). We subsequently assume much about how and who a person is and what he or she represents and who he or she will be or can be in relation to us (see Nakashima, Chapter 12; Nash, Chapter 24). The shortcut we have assumed in the racial classification scheme, however, has primarily benefited "White America"; it has been a means of "keeping people in their place." People of color have had to struggle to expand and claim or reclaim place and space.

The increasing presence of multiracial persons visibly challenges the irrationality of this shortcut. If we hope to abandon this vehicle of oppression, at least three things need to be understood: First, we must understand how and to whom this classification system is harmful in the short term and the long term; second, we must understand how it has resulted in inequities; and, third, we must acknowledge the propensity we have toward ranking people and things rather than just naming them, and try to understand why we need to engage in such rank ordering. Unless we understand the process of oppression, we may not be able to detect it in a new form. Thus I worry that, unless we have a firm grasp on what this "vehicle of oppression" is, simply to advocate the abolition of the construct of race would lead to a similarly insidious means of ordering our society that perpetuates dispossession of people who have held "other" status.

Because it is natural to notice physical differences, I worry that our racial structure might be replaced by another ordinal system, "colorism," in which social status is associated with the lightness of one's skin. Several people have conducted research exploring this issue in different ethnic populations in this country, for example, among Chicanos and Latinos (Arce, Murguia, & Frisbie, 1987) and among African Americans (Neal & Wilson, 1989). Noted writer Alice Walker (1983) observes, "Unless the question of Colorism—in my definition, prejudicial or preferential treatment of same-race people based solely on their color—is addressed in our communities and definitely in our black 'sisterhoods' we cannot, as a people, progress" (p. 290). It is likely that if we are able to move beyond race, we will be confronted with the class structure of America, which is integrally intertwined with race. Understanding this structure is critical to our ability to recognize the invisibility to which many members of our society have been assigned.

Solutions

Accomplishing the synthesis of different heritages into a dynamic whole requires that the ordinal nature of hierarchical notions about race to which we have been socialized must be replaced by both simpler models (such as naming without rank ordering, or nominal categorization) and more complex models (such as ecological and multidimensional models for understanding social order and human behavior). Many of the contributors to this volume believe that if it is possible for a single person to accomplish this synthesis for her- or himself, it might be very possible for us to accomplish it as a society.

What might we have to do to accomplish such a synthesis? On the personal level, we might first increase our consciousness of the stereotypes we hold about people, such as how they look, where they live, what their level of education is, what their family structure is—and then examine our reactions when these stereotypes are contradicted. Do we still insist on taking the shortcut? Second, we must examine how hierarchical classification pervades our attitudes and relationships. A related type of process is either/or thinking. Both processes lead us to be very judgmental in the service of assuaging our fears, insecurities, and egos, which is a definition of oppression itself. For example, why do we judge someone to be better, more attractive, or more desirable? Third, we must move away from assuming that our classification schemes and values are universal truths. To what degree do we seek experiences that expose us to people, cultures, and ideas that expand our worldview and help us come to know other realities? Finally, we must examine the life-styles, communities, families, and friends that surround us and explore the ways in which they might maintain the shortcuts that short-circuit our understanding of people and relationships we do not understand. Unfortunately, as the pace of life becomes faster, we are increasingly drawn to shortcuts.

Whereas we may have to search for the ways in which we perpetuate and support hierarchical thinking unnecessarily, academia trains us to internalize a hierarchy, with the stepwise progression of degrees, methods of evaluation, and means of distributing honors. To what degree have we generalized this mode of thinking to research questions, interpretations of historical data or contemporary findings, or the judging of our colleagues? Seeking interdisciplinary collaboration may expand our "academic worldviews" and challenge us to synthesize divergent training experiences and perspectives. Subsequently, race might be a window through which we can examine our uncritical internalization of classification schemes. For example, in order to understand better the difficulties of many groups of people who are disenfranchised members of our society, we might focus on variables that have been associated and at times confounded with race, rather than study race solely as a summary, independent variable. These "other" variables have been the mark of oppression, not race; socioeconomic status, educational opportunities, English-language comprehension, ethnicity, health care, housing, and gender are all interrelated. These variables represent the insidious cumulative traumas sustained by many disenfranchised communities and persons (Root, in press-a).

At a societal level, several changes can be made, from government policies for collecting demographic data on heritages to the education we provide our children about differences and intergroup relations. For example, texts for primary and secondary education can discuss race and ethnicity more dynamically. Such a change would have implications for the subjects of history, literature, and the social sciences at the least. Without such changes we are left with the enormously difficult task of trying to educate people in their adult years to understand oppression and internalized oppression, and to unlearn well-practiced ways of organizing their worlds.

Another poignant societal example relates to the reporting of population statistics. Demographers have recently been alerting us that there will be a significant shift in the racial composition of the United States at the beginning of the next century. These projections are offered in a way that is still ensconced in a White/non-White duality, and they subsequently provoke an "us versus them" factionalization that only perpetuates hostility and fear. This duality also perpetuates rules of hypodescent and the rigidity of racial categories by ignoring the implications for the population of a growing number of multiracial people who are partly of European ancestry and do not neatly fit into this category. Given the increasing commonality of interracial couples and Thornton's (Chapter 6) conservative estimate that one-third of immigrating spouses are likely to be involved in interracial relationships, a lack of attention to the "multiracial baby boom" can end up being significant omission in understanding the changing face of America.

The census to be taken in the year 2000 will provide an opportunity for the U.S. Census Bureau to take a count in a way that will allow a more accurate understanding of who lives in the United States. Rather than perpetuating the forced-choice nature of most forms—as Hall calls it in Chapter 18, the "Please choose one" dilemma—the census might reveal a very different-looking population if people are allowed to choose more than one category under race and under ethnicity to indicate multiple heritages. Yes, this type of categorization would be complicated, but it would also be more accurate. The data collected in this manner would not necessarily be any more difficult to interpret than the data yielded by the current system's classification scheme, because of the computerized data analysis methods now available. This process of data gathering would also allow for flexible boundaries and counting for different purposes.

The accomplishment of complex identities by racially mixed persons gives us hope that if individuals have been able to resolve conflicting values, claim identities, synthesize multiple heritages, and retain respect for individual heritages in a less than embracing environment, perhaps it is possible for us eventually to do this as a nation. Those who would reconstruct the social order would do well to observe the results of the studies presented here, both historical and social analyses, and join in an effort to look at how we can avoid reconstructing more of the same by learning from the past.

References

Aboud, F. (1988). *Children and prejudice.* Oxford: Basil Blackwell.

Achenbach, T. M., & Edelbrock, C. E. (1982). *Manual for the Child Behavior Checklist and Child Behavior Profile.* Burlington: University of Vermont, Child Psychiatry.

Achenbach, T. M., & Edelbrock, C. E. (1987). *Manual for the Youth Self-Report and Profile.* Burlington: University of Vermont.

Adams, P. (1973). Counseling with interracial couples and their children. In I. Stuart & L. Abt (Eds.), *Interracial marriage: Expectations and realities.* New York: Grossman.

Adelson, J., & Doehrman, M. J. (1980). The psychodynamic approach to adolescence. In J. Adelson (Ed.), *Handbook of adolescent psychology.* New York: John Wiley.

Adler, P. (1974). Beyond cultural identity: Reflections on cultural and multicultural man. In R. Brislin (Ed.), *Topics in culture learning* (Vol. 2). Honolulu: East-West Center.

Ahern, F. M., Cole, R. E., Johnson, R. C., & Wong, B. (1981). Personality attributes of males and females marrying within vs. across racial/ethnic groups. *Behavior Genetics, 11,* 181-194.

Aiken, L. R. (1971). *Psychological and educational testing.* Boston: Allyn & Bacon.

Alba, R. D., & Chamlin, M. B. (1983). A preliminary examination of ethnic identification among whites. *American Sociological Review, 48,* 240-247.

Alba, R. D., & Golden, R. M. (1986). Patterns of ethnic marriage in the United States. *Social Forces, 65,* 202-223.

Alejandro-Wright, M. N. (1985). The child's conception of racial classification: A socio-cognitive developmental model. In M. B. Spencer, G. K. Brookins, & W. R. Allen (Eds.), *Beginnings: The social and affective development of Black children* (pp. 185-200). Hillsdale, NJ: Lawrence Erlbaum.

Allen, P. G. (1983). *The woman who owned the shadows.* San Francisco: Spinsters, Ink.

Allen, P. G. (1988). Who is your mother? Red roots of white feminism. In R. Simonson & S. Walker (Eds.), *Multicultural literacy: Opening the American mind.* Saint Paul, MN: Graywolf.

Amerasians coming "home" at last. (1988, May). *Refugees: Concern and Response, 3,* 1-2.

Amerasian Update. (1989, April). No. 5.

Amerasian Update. (1989, August). No. 9.

Amerasian Update. (1989, October). No. 11.

Amerasian Update. (1989, December). No. 13.

Amerasian Update. (1990, February). No. 15.

Amerasian Update. (1990, September). No. 22.

Amerasian Update. (1990, October). No. 23.

Amerasian Update. (1990, November-December). No. 24.

Amerasian Update. (1991, January). No. 25.

Anderson, N. (1989). Racial differences in stress-induced cardiovascular reactivity and hypertension: Current status and substantive issues. *Psychological Bulletin, 105*, 89-105.

Antonovsky, A. (1956). Toward a refinement of the "marginal man" concept. *Social Forces, 44*, 57-67.

Anzaldua, G. (1990). En rapport, in opposition: Cobrando cuentas a las nuestras. In G. Anzaldua (Ed.), *Making face, making soul (haciendo caras): Creative and critical perspectives by women of color* (pp. 142-148). San Francisco: Aunt Lute Foundation.

Arce, C. H., Murguia, E., & Frisbie, W. P. (1987). Phenotype and life chances among Chicanos. *Hispanic Journal of Behavioral Sciences, 9*, 19-32.

Armsden, G. C., & Greenberg, M. T. (1987). The inventory of parent and peer attachment: Individual differences and their relationship to psychological well-being in adolescence. *Journal of Youth and Adolescence, 23*, 45-52.

Arnold, M. C. (1984). *The effects of racial identity on self-concept in interracial children.* Unpublished doctoral dissertation, Saint Louis University.

Atkinson, D. R., Morten, G., & Sue, D. W. (Eds.). (1979). *Counseling American minorities.* Dubuque, IA: William C. Brown.

Atkinson, D. R., Morten, G., & Sue, D. W. (Eds.). (1989). *Counseling American minorities: A cross-cultural perspective.* Dubuque, IA: William C. Brown.

Baird, W. D. (1990). Are there "real" Indians in Oklahoma? Historical perceptions of the five civilized tribes. *Chronicles of Oklahoma, 68*, 4-23.

Baker, J. R. (1974). *Race.* New York: Oxford University Press.

Bandura, A., & Huston, A. C. (1961). Identification as a process of incidental learning. *Journal of Abnormal and Social Psychology, 63*, 311-318.

Banton, M. (1983). *Racial and ethnic competition.* Cambridge: Cambridge University Press.

Barnett, L. (1963). Research on international/interracial marriages. *Marriage and Family Living, 25*, 105-107.

Barth, F. (1969). *Ethnic groups and boundaries: The social organization of culture difference.* London: Allen & Unwin.

Bartholomew, J. C. (1982). *World atlas* (12th ed.). Edinburgh: Bartholomew.

Barzun, J. (1965). *Race: A study in superstition* (rev. ed.). New York: Harper & Row. (Original work published 1937)

Beaulieu, D. (1984). Curly hair and big feet: Physical anthropology and the implementation of land allotment on the White Earth Chippewa reservation. *American Indian Quarterly, 7*, 281-313.

Beck, M., with Gibny, F., Jr., et al. (1985, April 15). Where is my father? *Newsweek*, pp. 54-55.

Bem, S. L. (1974). The measurement of psychological androgyny. *Journal of Consulting and Clinical Psychology, 42*, 155-162.

Berlin, I. (1976). *Slaves without masters: The free Negro in the ante-bellum South.* New York: Vintage.

Berndt, T. J., & Perry, T. B. (1986). Children's perception of friendships as supportive relationships. *Developmental Psychology, 22*, 640-648.

Berry, B. (1963). *Almost White: A study of certain racial hybrids in the eastern United States.* New York: Macmillan.

Berry, B. B. (1988). *Black-on-Black discrimination: The phenomenon of colorism among African Americans* (University Microfilms No. 88-27, 158). Ann Arbor, MI: University Microfilms.

Berry, J. W. (1980). Acculturation as varieties of acculturation. In A. M. Padilla (Ed.), *Acculturation: Theory, models and some new findings*. Boulder, CO: Westview.
Berzon, J. R. (1978). *Neither white nor black: The mulatto character in American fiction*. New York: New York University Press.
Biddess, M. D. (1970). *Father of racist ideology: The social and political thought of Count Gobineau*. New York: Weybright & Talley.
Blacks blast Japanese racism. (1988, July 26). *Pacific Stars and Stripes*.
Blalock, H. M., Jr. (1967). *Toward a theory of minority-group relations*. New York: John Wiley.
Blau, P. M., Becker, C., & Fitzpatrick, K. M. (1984). Intersecting social affiliations and intermarriage. *Social Forces, 62*, 585-605.
Blau, P. M., Blum, T. C., & Schwartz, J. E. (1982). Heterogeneity and intermarriage. *American Sociological Review, 47*, 45-62.
Blauner, R. (1972). *Racial oppression in America*. New York: Harper & Row.
Bloch, J. H. (1965). *The child-rearing practices report: A set of Q items of the description of parental socialization, attitudes and values*. Berkeley: University of California, Institute of Human Development.
Blu, K. I. (1980). *The Lumbee problem: The making of an American Indian people*. New York: Cambridge University Press.
Blumenbach, J. F. (1973). *The anthropological treatises of Johann Friedrich Blumenbach*. Boston: Milford House. (Original work published 1865)
Bogardus, E. S. (1925). Social distance and its origins. *Journal of Applied Sociology, 9*, 216-226.
Bogle, D. (1989). *Toms, coons, mulattoes, mammies, and bucks: An interpretive history of Blacks in American films* (rev. ed.). New York: Continuum.
Bone, R. A. (1965). *The Negro novel in America* (rev. ed.). New Haven, CT: Yale University Press. (Original work published 1958)
Bouscaren, A. (1963). *International migrations since 1945*. New York: Praeger.
Boxer, C. R. (1963). *Race relations in the Portuguese colonial empire, 1415-1825*. New York: Oxford University Press.
Boykin, A. W. (1982). *Triple quandary*. Unpublished manuscript, Howard University, Washington, DC.
Boykin, A. W. (1985). The triple quandary and the schooling of Afro-American children. In U. Neisser (Ed.), *The school achievement of minority children*. Hillsdale, NJ: Lawrence Erlbaum.
Boykin, A. W., & Toms, F. (1985). Black child socialization framework. In H. P. McAdoo & J. L. McAdoo (Eds.), *Black children: Social, educational, and parental environments* (pp. 33-51). Beverly Hills, CA: Sage.
Bradshaw, A. (1989, July). Amerasians left behind. *Geographical Magazine*, pp. 25-28.
Bradshaw, C. K. (1990). A Japanese view of dependency: What can Amae psychology contribute to feminist theory and therapy? In L. Brown & M. P. P. Root (Eds.), *Diversity and complexity in feminist therapy*. New York: Haworth.
Brand, E. S., Ruiz, R. A., & Padilla, A. M. (1974). Ethnic identification and preference: A review. *Psychological Bulletin, 81*, 860-890.
Bronfenbrenner, U. (1977). Toward an experimental ecology of human development. *American Psychologist, 32*, 513-531.
Bronfenbrenner, U. (1979). *The ecology of human development*. Cambridge, MA: Harvard University Press.

Brues, A. (1977). *People and races.* New York: Macmillan.

Buck, P. S. (1930). *East wind, west wind.* New York: John Day.

Burkhardt, W. R. (1983, May). Institutional barriers, marginality, and adaptation among the American-Japanese mixed bloods in Japan. *Journal of Asian Studies, 42.*

Burman, S., & Reynolds, P. (1986). *Growing up in a divided society: The contexts of childhood in South Africa.* Johannesburg: Ravan.

Buttery, T. J. (1987). Biracial children: Racial identification, self-esteem and school adjustment. *Kappa Delta Pi Record, 23,* 20-23.

Calloway, C. G. (1986). Neither white nor red: White renegades on the American Indian frontier. *Western Historical Quarterly, 14,* 43-66.

Cannon, P. (1952). *A gentle knight.* New York.

Capra, F. (1982). *The turning point: Science, society and the rising culture.* New York: Simon & Schuster.

Castle, W. E. (1926). Biological and social consequences of race crossing. *American Journal of Physical Anthropology, 9,* 145-156.

Castro, A. (1971). *The Spaniards: An introduction to their history.* Berkeley: University of California Press.

Cauce, A. M., Ptacek, J. T., Smith, R., & Mason, C. (1991). *The Social Support Rating Scale-Revised: Validation studies of a measure for adolescents.* Unpublished manuscript, University of Washington, Seattle.

Chabran, M., & Hirabayashi, L. (1987). The cloak and the shroud: On the dual nature of ethnic and family secrets among Third World people in the United States. *Images,* pp. 42-62.

Chang, T. S. (1974). The self-concept of children of ethnically different marriages. *California Journal of Educational Research, 25,* 245-252.

Char, W. F. (1977). Motivations for intercultural marriages. In W. S. Tseng, J. F. McDermott, Jr., & T. W. Maretzki (Eds.), *Adjustment in intercultural marriage* (pp. 33-40). Honolulu: University Press of Hawaii.

Cheek, D. K. (1972). *Black ethnic identity as related to skin color, social class, and selected variables.* Unpublished doctoral dissertation, Temple University.

Chew, K., Eggebeen, D., & Uhlenberg, P. (1989). American children in multiracial households. *Sociological Perspectives, 32,* 65-85.

Christian, J., Gadfield, N. J., Giles, H., & Taylor, D. M. (1976). The multidimensional and dynamic nature of ethnic identity. *International Journal of Psychology, 11,* 281-291.

Clark, K., & Clark, M. (1939). The development of consciousness of self and the emergence of racial identification in Negro preschool children. *Journal of Social Psychology, 10,* 591-599.

Clark, K., & Clark, M. (1940). Skin color as a factor in racial identification of Negro preschool children. *Journal of Social Psychology, 11,* 159-169.

Clark, K., & Clark M. (1947). Racial identification and preference in Negro children. In T. M. Newcomb & E. L. Hartley (Eds.), *Readings in social psychology* (pp. 169-178). New York: Holt, Rinehart & Winston.

Clark, K. B. (1980, October 5). The role of race. *New York Times Magazine,* pp. 25-53.

Clark, M., Kaufman, S., & Pierce, R. (1976). Explorations of acculturation: Toward a model ethnic identity. *Human Organization, 35,* 231-238.

Cleeland, N. (1988, August 7). Reclaiming the children of war. *San Diego Union,* 1A, 10A.

Clifton, J. A. (Ed.). (1989). *Being and becoming Indian: Biographical studies of North American frontiers.* Homewood, IL: Dorsey.

Clifton, J. A. (Ed.). (1990). *The invented Indian: Cultural fictions and government policies.* New Brunswick, NJ: Transaction.

Coddington, R. D. (1972a). The significance of life events as etiologic factors in the diseases of children: I. A survey of professional workers. *Journal of Psychosomatic Research, 16,* 7-18.

Coddington, R. D. (1972b). The significance of life events as etiologic factors in the diseases of children: II. A study of a normal population. *Journal of Psychosomatic Research, 16,* 205-213.

Cohen, R. (1978). Ethnicity: Problem and focus in anthropology. In B. J. Siegel (Ed.), *Annual review of anthropology* (Vol. 7, pp. 379-403). Palo Alto, CA: Annual Reviews.

Coie, J. D., & Dodge, K. A. (1983). Continuities and changes in children's social status: A 5-year longitudinal study. *Merrill-Palmer Quarterly, 29,* 261-282.

Coie, J. D., Dodge, K. A., & Coppotelli, H. (1982). Dimensions and types of social status: A cross-age perspective. *Developmental Psychology, 18,* 557-571.

Collins, G. (1984, March 20). Children of interracial marriage. *New York Times,* p. 17.

Condrill, J. (1990, December). Amerasians standing up to be counted. *Overseas Brats, 5.*

Cooley, C. H. (1902). *Human nature and social order.* New York: Scribner.

Coon, C. S. (1965). *The living races of man.* New York: Alfred A. Knopf.

Cooper, R., & David, R. (1986). The biological concept of race and its application to public health and epidemiology. *Journal of Health Politics, Policy and Law, 11,* 99-116.

Cordova, F. (1973). The Filipino-American: There's always an identity crisis. In S. Sue & N. Wagner (Eds.), *Asian Americans: Psychological perspectives.* Palo Alto, CA: Science & Behavior Books.

Cornell, S. (1985). *Communities of culture, communities of interest: On the variable nature of ethnic groups.* Unpublished manuscript.

Cotter, J. S. (1990). The mulatto to his critics. In J. S. Cotter, *Complete poems.* Athens: University of Georgia Press. (Original work published 1918)

Cottrell, A. (1975). Outsiders' inside view: Western wives' experiences in Indian joint families. *Journal of Marriage and the Family, 37,* 400-407.

Cottrell, A. (1978). Mixed children: Some observations and speculations. In E. Hunter & D. Nice (Eds.), *Children of military families* (pp. 61-81). Washington, DC: Government Printing Office.

Cottrell, A. (1990). Cross-national marriages: A review of the literature. *Journal of Comparative Family Studies, 21,* 151-169.

Crester, G. A., & Leon, J. J. (1982). Intermarriage in the U.S.: An overview of theory and research. *Marriage and Family Review, 5,* 3-15.

Criswell, J. H. (1939). A sociometric study of race cleavage in the classroom. *Archives of Psychology, 235.*

Cross, W. E., Jr. (1978). The Thomas and Cross models of psychological Nigrescence: A review. *Journal of Black Psychology, 5,* 12-31.

Cross, W. E., Jr. (1981). Black families and Black identity development. *Journal of Comparative Family Studies, 19,* 341-350.

Cross, W. E., Jr. (1985). Black identity: Rediscovering the distinction between personal identity and reference group orientation. In M. B. Spencer, G. K. Brookins, & W. R. Allen (Eds.), *Beginnings: The social and affective development of Black children* (pp. 155-172). Hillsdale, NJ: Lawrence Erlbaum.

Cross, W. E., Jr. (1987). A two-factor theory of Black identity: Implications for the study of identity development in minority children. In J. S. Phinney & M. J. Rotheram

(Eds.), *Children's ethnic socialization: Pluralism and development.* Newbury Park, CA: Sage.

Crowe, C. (1975). Indians and Blacks in white America. In C. M. Hudson (Ed.), *Four centuries of southern Indians.* Athens: University of Georgia Press.

Csikszentmihalyi, M., Larson, R., & Prescott, S. (1977). The ecology of adolescent activity and experience. *Journal of Youth and Adolescence, 6,* 281-294.

Daniel, G. R. (1988). A view from the bridge: The new multiracial consciousness. *Spectrum* (Newsletter of Multiracial Americans of Southern California, Los Angeles), *1*(2).

Daniel, G. R. (1989). *Converging paths: Race relations in Brazil and the U.S.* Paper presented at the Winter Colloquium Series, Center for Afro-American Studies, University of California, Los Angeles.

Daniels, B., Plomin, R., McClearn, G., & Johnson, R. C. (1982). "Fitness" behavior and anthropometric characters for offspring of first cousin matings. *Behavior Genetics, 12,* 527-534.

Davenport, C. B. (1917). The effects of race intermingling. *Proceedings of the American Philosophical Society, 56,* 364-368.

Daws, G. (1968). *Shoal of time: A history of the Hawaiian Islands.* Honolulu: University Press of Hawaii.

Day, C. B. (1932). *A study of some Negro-white families in the United States.* Cambridge, MA: Peabody Museum of Harvard University.

Dearborn, M. V. (1986). *Pocahontas's daughters.* New York: Oxford University Press.

Degler, C. N. (1971). *Neither Black nor White: Slavery and race relations in Brazil and the United States.* New York: Macmillan.

Derman-Sparks, L. (1989). *Anti-bias curriculum: Tools for empowering young children.* Washington DC: National Association for the Education of Young Children.

Deschamps, J. (1982). Social identity and relations of power between groups. In H. Tajfel (Ed.), *Social identity and intergroup relations* (pp. 85-98). New York: Cambridge University Press.

Diaz, R. M. (1985). Bilingual cognitive development: Addressing three gaps in current research. *Child Development, 56,* 1376-1388.

Dien, D. S., & Vinacke, W. E. (1964). Self-concept and parental identification of young adults with mixed Caucasian-Japanese parentage. *Journal of Abnormal Psychology, 69,* 463-466.

Doi, T. (1973). *The anatomy of dependence.* Tokyo: Kodansha International.

Dominguez, V. (1986). *White by definition: Social classification in Creole Louisiana.* New Brunswick, NJ: Rutgers University Press.

Dornbusch, S. M., Ritter, P. L., Leiderman, P. H., Roberts, D. F., & Fraleigh, M. J. (1987). The relation of parenting style to adolescent school performance. *Child Development, 58,* 1244-1257.

Dorris, M. (1987). *A yellow raft in blue water.* New York: Henry Holt.

Douglas, R. (1988, November/December). Sociopolitical consequences of racial classification in the U.S. *Interracial/Intercultural Connection* (Newsletter of the Biracial Family Network, Chicago), pp. 1-3.

Drake, S. C., & Cayton, H. R. (1945). *Black metropolis.* New York: Harcourt, Brace & World.

Dryfoos, J. G. (1990). *Adolescents at risk: Prevalence and prevention.* New York: Oxford University Press.

Duffy, L. K. (1978). *The interracial individuals: Self-concept, parental interaction, and ethnic identity.* Unpublished master's thesis, University of Hawaii, Honolulu.

Edmunds, R. D. (Ed.). (1980). *Studies in diversity: American Indian leaders.* Lincoln: University of Nebraska Press.

Elfenbein, A. S. (1989). *Women on the color line: Evolving stereotypes and the writings of George Washington Cable, Grace King, Kate Chopin.* USA: University Press of Virginia.

Elkin, F. (1983). Family, socialization, and ethnic identity. In K. Ishwaran (Ed.), *The Canadian family.* Beverly Hills, CA: Sage.

Endo, R., & Hirokawa, D. (1983). Japanese American intermarriage. *Free Inquiry in Creative Sociology, 11,* 159-166.

Erdrich, L. (1984). *Love medicine.* New York: Holt, Rinehart & Winston.

Erikson, E. H. (1959). Identity and the life cycle. *Psychological Issues, 1,* 18-164.

Erikson, E. H. (1963). *Childhood and society* (2nd ed.). New York: W. W. Norton.

Erikson, E. H. (1968). Race and the wider identity. In E. H. Erikson, *Identity, youth and crisis.* New York: W. W. Norton.

Fanon, F. (1967). *Black skin, white masks.* New York: Grove.

Faulkner, J., & Kich, F. (1983). Assessment and engagement stages in therapy with the interracial family. *Family Therapy Collections, 6,* 78-90.

Felsman, K. J., & Johnson, M. C. (1989, January 23). For Amerasians, a welcome mat is not enough. *Los Angeles Times.*

Felsman, K. J., Johnson, M. C., Leong, F. T. L., & Felsman, I. C. (1989). *Vietnamese Amerasians: Practical implications of current research.* Unpublished manuscript, Office of Refugee Resettlement, Washington, DC.

Ferguson, M. (1980). *The Aquarian conspiracy: Personal and social transformation in the 1980s.* Los Angeles: J. P. Tarcher.

Festinger, L. (1957). *A theory of cognitive dissonance.* Stanford, CA: Stanford University Press.

Fielding, N. G., & Fielding, J. L. (1986). *Linking data.* Beverly Hills, CA: Sage.

Fields, B. J. (1982). Ideology and race in American history. In J. MacPherson & M. Kousser (Eds.), *Region, race and reconstruction* (pp. 143-177). New York: Oxford University Press.

Fleming, R. M. (1930). Human hybrids. *Eugenics Review, 21,* 257-263.

Fleming, R. M. (1939). Physical heredity in human hybrids. *Annals of Eugenics, 9,* 55-81.

Foner, P. S. (1975). *History of Black Americans* (Vol. 1). Westport, CT: Greenwood.

Forbes, J. D. (1988a). *Black Africans and Native Americans: Color, race and caste in the evolution of red-black peoples.* Oxford: Basil Blackwell.

Forbes, J. D. (1988b). Undercounting Native Americans: The 1980 census and the manipulation of racial identity in the United States. *Storia Nordamericana, 5,* 5-47.

Forbes, J. D. (1990). The manipulation of race, caste and identity: Classifying AfroAmericans, Native Americans and red-black people. *Journal of Ethnic Studies, 17,* 1-51.

Forbes, S. (1984). *Southeast Asian refugee resettlement report.* Washington, DC: Office of Refugee Resettlement.

Frazier, E. F. (1948). *The Negro family in the United States.* Chicago: University of Chicago Press.

Frazier, E. F. (1949). *The Negro in the United States.* New York: Macmillan.

Fredrickson, G. M. (1971). *The Black image in the White mind.* New York: Harper & Row.

Fredrickson, G. M. (1981). *White supremacy: A comparative study in American and South African history.* New York: Oxford University Press.

Freire, P. (1970). *Cultural action for freedom.* Cambridge, MA: Harvard Educational Review Press.

Furlong, W. B. (1968, June 9). Interracial marriage is a sometime thing. *New York Times Magazine*, pp. 44, 45, 137, 139, 142, 144, 147.

Furman, W., & Buhrmester, D. (1985). Children's perceptions of the personal relationships in their social networks. *Developmental Psychology, 21,* 1016-1024.

Gardner, R., Robey, B., & Smith, P. (1985). Asian Americans: Growth, change and diversity. *Population Bulletin, 40*(4).

Garmezy, N. (1978). Children at risk: The search for antecedents of schizophrenia. *Schizophrenia Bulletin, 8,* 14-90.

Garza, R. T., & Lipton, J. P. (1982). Theoretical perspectives on Chicano personality development. *Hispanic Journal of Behavioral Sciences, 4,* 407-432.

Gaskins, P. (1979). Eurasians: Strength in coping. *Asian Directions, 2,* 1, 4, 7-8.

Gay, K. (1987). *The rainbow effect: Interracial families.* New York: Franklin Watts.

Gibbs, J. T. (1985). City girls: Psychosocial adjustment of urban Black adolescent females. *SAGE: Journal of Black Women, 2,* 28-36.

Gibbs, J. T. (1987). Identity and marginality: Issues in the treatment of biracial adolescents. *American Journal of Orthopsychiatry, 57,* 265-278.

Gibbs, J. T. (1989). Biracial adolescents. In J. T. Gibbs, L. N. Huang, & Associates (Eds.), *Children of color: Psychological interventions with minority youth* (pp. 322-350). San Francisco: Jossey-Bass.

Gibbs, J. T., Huang, L. N., & Associates. (Eds.). (1989). *Children of color: Psychological interventions with minority youth.* San Francisco: Jossey-Bass.

Gibbs, J. T., & Moskowitz-Sweet, G. (in press). Clinical and cultural issues in the treatment of biracial and bicultural adolescents. *Families in Society: The Journal of Contemporary Human Services.*

Gist, N. P. (1967). Cultural versus social marginality: The Anglo-Indian case. *Phylon, 28,* 361-375.

Gist, N. P., & Dworkin, A. G. (1972). *The blending of races: Marginality and identity in world perspective.* New York: Wiley-Interscience.

Gist, N. P., & Wright, R. D. (1973). *Marginality and identity.* Leiden, Netherlands: E. J. Brill.

Glazer, N., & Moynihan, D. P. (1970). *Beyond the melting pot* (2nd ed.). Cambridge: MIT Press.

Glick, C. E. (1970). Interracial marriage and admixture in Hawaii. *Social Biology, 17,* 278-291.

Glick, P. C. (1988). Demographic pictures of Black families. In H. P. McAdoo (Ed.), *Black families* (2nd ed., pp. 111-132). Newbury Park, CA: Sage.

Gobineau, J. A., comte de. (1967). *The inequality of races.* New York: H. Fertig. (Original work published 1915)

Goldberg, M. M. (1941). A qualification of the marginal man theory. *American Sociological Review, 6,* 52-58.

Goodman, M. E. (1964). *Race awareness in young children.* New York: Collier.

Goose, S., & Horst, K. (1988, August). Amerasians in Vietnam: Still waiting. *Indochina Issues*, pp. 1-7.

Gordon, A. (1964). *Intermarriage: Interethnic, interracial, interfaith.* Boston: Beacon.

Gottman, J., Gonso, J., & Rasmussen, B. (1975). Social interaction, social competence, and friendship in children. *Child Development, 46,* 709-718.

Grant, M. (1970). *The passing of the great race.* New York: Arno. (Original work published 1918)

Greeley, A. (1971). *Why can't they be like us? America's white ethnic groups.* New York: Dutton.

Green, A. W. (1947). A re-examination of the marginal man concept. *Social Forces, 26,* 167-171.

Greenwald, W. J., & Oppenheim, D. B. (1968). Reported magnitude of self-identification among Negro children: Artifact? *Journal of Personality and Social Psychology, 8,* 49-52.

Griffith, J. (1984). Relationships between acculturation and psychological impairment in adult Mexican-Americans. *Hispanic Journal of Behavioral Sciences, 5,* 431-459.

Grosz, G. (1989). From sea to shining sea . . . : A current listing of interracial organizations and support groups across the nation. *Interrace, 1,* 24-28.

Gulick, S. L. (1914). *The American Japanese problem.* New York: Scribner.

Gunthrope, W. (1978). Skin color recognition, preference and identification in interracial children: A comparative study (Doctoral dissertation, Rutgers University, 1977). *Dissertation Abstracts International, 38* (10-B), 3468.

Hagan, W. T. (1985). Full blood, mixed blood, generic, and ersatz: The problem of Indian identity. *Arizona and the West, 27,* 309-326.

Hagedorn, J. (1990). *The dogeaters.* New York: Random House.

Hall, C. C. I. (1980). *The ethnic identity of racially mixed people: A study of Black-Japanese.* Unpublished doctoral dissertation, University of California, Los Angeles.

Halliburton, R., Jr. (1977). *Red over black: Black slavery among the Cherokee Indians.* Westport, CT: Greenwood.

Hanke, L. (1970). *Aristotle and the American Indians: A study in race prejudice in the modern world.* Bloomington: Indiana University Press. (Original work published 1959)

Hare, N. (1965). *The Black Anglo-Saxons.* New York: Macmillan.

Harris, M. (1964). *Patterns of race in the Americas.* New York: W. W. Norton.

Harris, M. (1971). *Culture, man and nature.* New York: Thomas Y. Crowell.

Harter, S. (1982). The perceived competence scale for children. *Child Development, 53,* 87-97.

Hartup, W. W. (1970). Peer interaction and social organization. In P. H. Mussen (Ed.), *Carmichael's manual of child psychology* (Vol. 2). New York: John Wiley.

Hartup, W. W. (1978). Children and their friends. In H. McGurk (Ed.), *Childhood social development.* London: Methuen.

Hartup, W. W. (1979). Peer relations and the growth of social competence. In M. H. Kent & J. E. Rolf (Eds.), *Primary prevention of psychopathology: Social competence in children* (pp. 150-170). Hanover, NH: University Press of New England.

Haselkorn, J. (Producer), & Lu, J. (Director). (1988). *America's children of war* [Video] (Christian Science Monitor Reports). Boston: Christian Science Monitor.

Haskins, J. (1975). *The Creoles of color of New Orleans.* New York: Thomas Y. Crowell.

Helms, J. (1990). What's in a name? *Focus, 4,* 1-2.

Henggeler, S. W., & Tavormina, J. B. (1980). Social class and race differences in family interaction: Pathological, normative, or confounding methodological factors? *Journal of Genetic Psychology, 137,* 211-222.

Henriques, F. (1974a). *Children of Caliban.* London: Martin, Secker, & Warburg.

Henriques, F. (1974b). *Children of conflict: A study of interracial sex and marriage.* New York: Dutton.

Hirabayashi, L. R. (1985, December). On being Hapa. *Pacific Citizen,* sec. B.

Ho, F. C., & Johnson, R. C. (1990). Intraethnic and interethnic marriage and divorce in Hawaii. *Social Biology, 37*, 44-51.

Hoetink, H. (1971). *Caribbean race relations: A study of two variants.* London: Oxford University Press.

Horowitz, R. (1939). Racial aspects of self-identification in nursery school children. *Journal of Psychology, 7*, 91-99.

Hughes, L. (1954). Cross. In L. Hughes, *Selected poems by Langston Hughes*. New York: Alfred A. Knopf. (Original work published 1926)

Hughes, M., & Hertel, B. R. (1990, June). The significance of color remains: A study of life chances, mate selection, and ethnic consciousness among Black Americans. *Social Forces, 68*, 1105-1120.

Hunter, F. T., & Youniss, J. (1982). Changes in functions of three relations during adolescence. *Developmental Psychology, 18*, 806-811.

Hutnik, N. (1986). Patterns of ethnic minority identification and modes of social adaptation. *Ethnic and Racial Studies, 9*, 150-167.

Imamura, A. (1986). Ordinary couples? Mate selection in international marriage in Nigeria. *Journal of Comparative Family Studies, 17*, 33-42.

Irwin, W. (1979). *Seed of the sun*. Salem, NH: Ayer. (Original work published 1921)

Isaacs, H. R. (1975). *Idols of the tribe: Group identity and political change*. New York: Harper.

Jacobs, J. H. (1977). Black/white interracial families: Marital process and identity development in young children (Doctoral dissertation, Wright Institute). *Dissertation Abstracts International, 38*(10-B), 5023.

Japan's rejected: Teenage war babies. (1967, September). *Ebony.*

Jedlicka, D. (1975). *Ethnic serial marriage in Hawaii: Application of a sequential preference pattern.* Unpublished doctoral dissertation, University of Hawaii at Manoa, Honolulu.

Jenkins, L. (1934). Mental conflicts of Eurasian adolescents. *Journal of Social Psychology, 34*, 48-55.

Johnson, D. J. (in press). Racial preference and biculturality in biracial preschoolers. *Merrill-Palmer Quarterly.*

Johnson, G. D. (1970). Common dust. In A. Lomax & R. Abdul (Eds.), *3000 years of Black poetry.* New York: Dodd, Mead.

Johnson, R. C. (1984). Group income and group size as influences on marriage patterns in Hawaii. *Social Biology, 31*, 101-107.

Johnson, R. C., & Nagoshi, C. T. (1986). The adjustment of offspring of within-group and interracial/intercultural marriages: A comparison of personality factor scores. *Journal of Marriage and the Family, 48*, 279-284.

Johnson, R. C., & Nagoshi, C. T. (1989). Asians, Asian-Americans, and alcohol. *Journal of Psychoactive Drugs, 22*, 45-52.

Johnson, R. C., & Nagoshi, C. T. (1990). *Intergroup marriage in Hawaii.* Unpublished manuscript.

Johnson, R. C., & Ogasawara, G. M. (1988). Within and across group dating in Hawaii. *Social Biology, 35*, 103-109.

Jordan, W. D. (1969). *White over Black.* Baltimore: Penguin.

Jordan, W. D. (1974). *White man's burden.* New York: Oxford University Press.

Kaneko, K. (1951). *Emi yo.* Tokyo.

Katz, D., & Kahn, R. L. (1978). *The social psychology of organizations* (2nd ed.). New York: John Wiley.

Katz, W. L. (1986). *Black Indians: A hidden heritage.* Westport, CT: Greenwood.
Kazdin, A. E. (1980). *Research design in clinical psychology.* New York: Harper & Row.
Keegan, A. (1987, May 13). Children of Vietnam find few fathers at U.S. doors. *Chicago Tribune,* sec. 1, p. 1, sec. 2, p. 2.
Keely, C. (1979). The United States of America. In D. Kubat (Ed.), *The politics of migration policies* (pp. 51-64). New York: Center for Migration Studies.
Kerckhoff, A. C., & McCormick, T. C. (1955). Marginal status and marginal personality. *Social Forces, 34,* 48-55.
Kich, G. K. (1982). *Eurasians: Ethnic/racial identity development of biracial Japanese/white adults.* Unpublished doctoral dissertation, Wright Institute Graduate School of Psychology, Berkeley, CA.
Kim, B.-L. C. (1977). Asian wives of U.S. servicemen: Women in shadows. *Amerasia Journal, 4,* 91-115.
Kim, E. (1984). Sex Tourism In Asia: A Reflection of Political and Economic Inequality. *Critical Perspective: Women Race and Class in Culture Context, 2,* 290-291.
King, J. C. (1981). *The biology of race.* Berkeley: University of California Press.
Kinloch, G. C. (1983). Racial identity among mixed adolescents in Hawaii: A research note. *Explorations in Ethnic Studies, 6,* 38-41.
Kitano, H. H. L. (1974). *Race relations.* Englewood Cliffs, NJ: Prentice-Hall.
Kitano, H. H. L., & Daniels, B. (1988). *Asian Americans.* Englewood Cliffs, NJ: Prentice-Hall.
Kitano, H. H. L., & Kikumura, A. (1973). Interracial marriage: A picture of the Japanese American. *Journal of Social Issues, 29,* 66-81.
Kitano, H. H. L., Yeung, W., Chai, L., & Hatanaka, H. (1984). Asian-American interracial marriage. *Journal of Marriage and the Family, 46,* 179-190.
Kodani, M. (1989, February). [Speech presented at the annual installation dinner of the Japanese American Historical Society of Southern California], Marina Del Rey, CA.
Kohlberg, L. (1966a). A cognitive-developmental analysis of children's sex-role concepts and attitudes. In E. Maccoby (Ed.), *The development of sex differences.* Stanford, CA: Stanford University Press.
Kohlberg, L. (1966b). Cognitive stages and preschool education. *Human Development, 9,* 5-17.
Kosakai, S. (1982). *Kore wa anata no haha: Sawada miki to kon'ketsujitachi.* Tokyo: Shuueisha.
Kovacs, M., & Beck, A. (1977). An empirical-clinical approach toward a definition of childhood depression. In J. Schacterbrandt & A. Raskin (Eds.), *Depression in childhood: Diagnosis, treatment, and conceptional models.* New York: Raven.
Kraly, E. (1979). Sources of data for the study of U.S. immigration. In S. Couch & R. Bryce-Laporte (Eds.), *Quantitative data and immigration research* (Research Institute on Immigration and Ethnic Studies Occasional Paper No. 2, pp. 34-54). Washington, DC: Smithsonian Institution.
Krauss, W. W. (1941). Race crossing in Hawaii. *Journal of Heredity, 32,* 371-378.
Lacey, M. (1985). *In our father's land: Vietnamese Amerasians in the United States.* Washington, DC: Migration and Refugee Services of the United States Catholic Conference.
Ladner, J. A. (1977). *Mixed families.* Garden City, NY: Anchor/Doubleday.
Lambert, W. E. (1969). A social psychology of bilingualism. *Journal of Social Issues, 2,* 91-109.
Lambert, W. E. (1977). The effects of bilingualism on the individual: Cognitive and sociocultural consequences. In P. A. Hornby (Ed.), *Bilingualism: Psychological, social and educational implications* (pp. 15-27). New York: Academic Press.

Lehrman, S. (1967). Psychopathology in mixed marriages. *Psychoanalytic Quarterly, 36*, 67-82.

Lewis, G. (1987). *Between the wire and the wall: A history of South African "coloured" politics*. New York: St. Martin's.

Lewontin, R. C. (1972). The apportionment of human diversity. In T. Dobzhansky, M. K. Hecht, & W. C. Steere (Eds.), *Evolutionary biology* (Vol. 6). New York: Appleton-Century-Crofts.

Lieberson, S., & Waters, M. (1985). Ethnic mixtures in the United States. *Sociology and Social Research, 70*, 43-53.

Lind, A. H. (1980). *Hawaii's people* (4th ed.). Honolulu: University Press of Hawaii.

Lipsitz, J. (1977). *Growing up forgotten*. Lexington, MA: Lexington.

Littlefield, D. F., Jr. (1977). *Africans and Seminoles: From removal to emancipation*. Westport, CT: Greenwood.

Littlefield, D. F., Jr. (1978). *The Cherokee freedmen: From emancipation to American citizenship*. Westport, CT: Greenwood.

Littlefield, D. F., Jr. (1979). *Africans and Creeks: From the colonial period to the Civil War*. Westport, CT: Greenwood.

Littlefield, D. F., Jr. (1980). *The Chickasaw freedmen: A people without a country*. Westport, CT: Greenwood.

Lofgren, C. A. (1987). *The Plessy case*. New York: Oxford University Press.

Logan, S., Freeman, E., & McRoy, R. (1987). Racial identity problems of biracial clients: Implications for social work practice. *Journal of Intergroup Relations, 15*, 11-24.

Lorde, A. (1990). Between ourselves. In G. Anzaldua (Ed.), *Making face, making soul (haciendo caras): Creative and critical perspectives by women of color* (pp. 139-141). San Francisco: Aunt Lute Foundation.

Lui, B., Cauce, A. M., Kwak, D., & Mason, C. (1990). *Family relationships and child-rearing practices: An examination of Caucasian-, Chinese-, Korean-, and Japanese-Americans*. Unpublished manuscript, University of Washington, Seattle.

Lykins, R. (1989, December). Children of the "Third Culture." *Overseas Brats, 4*.

Lyles, M. R., Yancey, A., Grace, C., & Carter, J. H. (1985). Racial identity and self-esteem: Problems peculiar to biracial children. *Journal of the American Academy of Child Psychiatry, 24*, 150-153.

Lynch, J. (1984). Using a multicultural context as a basis for a core curriculum: Cultural difference as educational capital. In G. K. Verma & C. Bagley (Eds.), *Race relations and cultural differences: Educational and interpersonal perspectives* (pp. 143-162). New York: St. Martin's.

MacLachlan, C. M., & Rodríguez O, J. E. (1980). *The forging of the cosmic race: A reinterpretation of colonial Mexico*. Berkeley: University of California Press.

Mann, E., & Waldron, J. A. (1977). Intercultural marriage and childbearing. In W. S. Tseng, J. F. McDermott, Jr., & T. W. Maretzki (Eds.), *Adjustment in intercultural marriage* (pp. 88-92). Honolulu: University Press of Hawaii.

Marger, M. N. (1985). *Race and ethnic relations: American and global perspectives*. Belmont, CA: Wadsworth.

Mark, D., & Chih, G. (1982). *A place called Chinese America*. New York: Organization of Chinese Americans.

Mathews, J. J. (1989). *Sundown*. Norman: University of Oklahoma Press. (Original work published 1934)

Matsumoto, G. M., Meredith, G. M., & Masuda, M. (1970). Ethnic identity: Honolulu and Seattle Japanese-Americans. *Journal of Abnormal Psychology, 1*, 63-76.

Mbiti, J. (1970). *African religions and philosophy*. Garden City, NY: Anchor.

McCall, G. J., & Simmons, J. L. (1966). *Identities and interactions*. New York: Free Press.

McDermott, J. F., Jr., & Fukunaga, C. (1977). Intercultural family interaction patterns. In W. S. Tseng, J. F. McDermott, Jr., & T. W. Maretzki (Eds.), *Adjustment in intercultural marriage* (pp. 81-92). Honolulu: University Press of Hawaii.

McFee, M. (1968). The 150% man: A product of Blackfeet acculturation. *American Anthropologist, 70*, 1096-1103.

McRoy, R. G., & Freeman, E. (1986). Racial identity issues among mixed-race children. *Social Work in Education, 8*, 164-174.

McRoy, R. G., Zurcher, L. A., Lauderdale, M. L., & Anderson, R. E. (1984). The identity of transracial adoptees. *Social Casework, 65*, 34-39.

Mencke, J. G. (1979). *Mulattoes and race mixture: American attitudes and images, 1865-1918*. Ann Arbor: University of Michigan Institute of Research Press.

Migration and Refugee Services of the United States Catholic Conference. (1988, October). *To welcome the Amerasians*. Washington, DC: Author.

Miller, R., & Miller, B. (1990). Mothering the biracial child: Bridging the gaps between African-American and White parenting styles. *Women and Therapy, 10*, 169-180.

Mills, G. B. (1977). *The forgotten people: Cane River's Creoles of color*. Baton Rouge: Louisiana State University Press.

Mitchell-Kernan, C. (1985). Foreword. In P.-M. Fontaine (Ed.), *Race, class, and power in Brazil* (pp. ix-xi). Los Angeles: University of California, Center for Afro-American Studies.

Moerman, M. (1965). Who are the Lue? Ethnic identification in a complex civilization. *American Anthropologist, 7*, 1215-1230.

Momaday, N. S. (1969). *The way to Rainy Mountain*. Albuquerque: University of New Mexico Press.

Monahan, T. P. (1976). An overview of statistics on interracial marriage in the United States, with data on its extent from 1963-1970. *Journal of Marriage and the Family, 176*, 223-231.

Moore, J. (1990, July 12). Amerasians provide an exit. *Far Eastern Economic Review*, p. 55.

Moos, R., & Moos, B. (1981). *Family Environment Scale manual*. Palo Alto, CA: Consulting Psychologists Press.

Morishima, J. (1980). *Asian American racial mixes: Attitudes, self-concept, and academic performance*. Paper presented at the annual meeting of the Western Psychological Association, Honolulu.

Morland, K. (1958). Racial cognition of nursery school children in Lynchburg, Virginia. *Social Forces, 37*, 132-137.

Morland, K. (1962). Racial acceptance and preference of nursery school children in a southern city. *Merrill-Palmer Quarterly, 8*, 271-280.

Morland, K. (1966). A comparison of race awareness in northern and southern children. *American Journal of Orthopsychiatry, 36*, 22-32.

Morner, M. (1967). *Race mixture in the history of Latin America*. Boston: Little, Brown.

Morner, M. (Ed.). (1970). *Race and class in Latin America*. New York: Columbia University Press.

Moses, L. G., & Wilson, R. (1985). *Indian lives: Essays on nineteenth- and twentieth-century Native American leaders*. Albuquerque: University of New Mexico Press.

Mrazek, R. (1987, July). *Analysis of the Vietnamese Amerasian situation and the need for congressional action*. Washington, DC: Government Printing Office.

Muñoz, C., Jr. (1989). *Youth, identity, power: The Chicano movement*. London: Verso.

Murayama, M. (1983). Cross-cultural perspectives on social and community change. In E. Seidman (Ed.), *Handbook of social intervention* (pp. 33-47). Beverly Hills, CA: Sage.

Murphy-Shigematsu, S. L. (1986). *The voices of Amerasians: Ethnicity, identity and empowerment in interracial Japanese Americans.* Unpublished doctoral dissertation, Harvard University.

Murphy-Shigematsu, S. L. (1988). Addressing issues of biracial/bicultural Asian Americans. In G. Y. Okihiro, S. Hune, A. A. Hansen, & J. M. Liu (Eds.), *Reflections on shattered windows: Promises and prospects for Asian American studies* (pp. 111-116). Pullman: Washington State University Press.

Muse, D. (1986, May/June). Interracial children speak out. *Children's Advocates*, p. 5.

Nagaoka, M. (Producer and Director). (1988). *Half (nibun no ichi) beings: A beautiful race* [Film]. New York: Half Beings Films.

Nagata, J. A. (1974). What is a Malay? Situational selection of ethnic identity in a plural society. *American Ethnologist, 1*, 331-350.

Nagoshi, C. T., & Johnson, R. C. (1986). The ubiquity of *g*. *Personality and Individual Differences, 7*, 201-207.

Nagoshi, C. T., Johnson, R. C., & Honbo, K. A. M. (1990). Assertive mating for cognitive abilities, personality, and social attitudes: Hawaii family study of cognitive offspring. *Behavior Genetics.*

Nakashima, C. (1988). Research notes on Nikkei Happa identity. In G. Y. Okihiro, S. Hune, A. A. Hansen, & J. M. Liu (Eds.), *Reflection on shattered windows: Promises and prospects for Asian American studies* (pp. 206-213). Pullman: Washington State University Press.

Narikiyo, T. A. (1987). *Ethnic stereotyping in Hawaii: Change and persistence over time.* Unpublished master's thesis, University of Hawaii, Honolulu.

Neal, A., & Wilson, M. L. (1989). The role of skin color and features in the Black community: Implications for Black women and therapy. *Clinical Psychology Review, 9*, 323-334.

Njeri, I. (1988a, April 24). Colorism: In American society are lighter-skinned Blacks better off? *Los Angeles Times*, pp. F1, F10, F12-F13.

Njeri, I. (1988b, June 5). A sense of identity. *Los Angeles Times*, pp. F1, F8-F9.

Njeri, I. (1991, January 13). Call for census category creates interracial debate. *Los Angeles Times*, pp. E1, E9-E11.

No place for mankind. (1989, September 4). *Time*, p. 17.

O'Crouley, P. (1972). *A description of the kingdom of New Spain in 1774.* San Francisco: John Howell. (Original work published 1774)

Oesterly, L., Conrad, C., Darvill, T., Johnson, R., & Higa, W. (1989). *What is local? How local is "local"?* Unpublished manuscript, University of Hawaii, Behavioral Biology Laboratory.

Offer, D. (1969). *The psychological world of the teenager.* New York: Basic Books.

Office of Refugee Resettlement/U.S. Department of Health and Human Services. (1987, December 18). Southeast Asian refugees: Estimated cumulative state population from 1975-Sept. 1987. *Refugee Reports, 11.*

Okamura, J. Y. (1981). Situational ethnicity. *Ethnic and Racial Studies, 4*, 452-465.

Old black stereotypes find new lives in Japan. (1988, August 4). *Pacific Stars and Stripes.*

Omedo, E., Martinez, J., & Martinez, S. (1978). Measure of acculturation for Chicano adolescents. *Psychological Reports, 42*, 159-170.

Omi, M., & Winant, H. (1986). *Racial formation in the United States: From the 1960's to the 1980's*. New York: Routledge & Kegan Paul.

Ortiz, F. (1947). *Cuban counterpoint* (H. de Onis, Trans.). New York: Alfred A. Knopf. (Original work published 1940)

Ortiz, V., & Arce, C. H. (1985). Language orientation and mental health status among persons of Mexican descent. *Hispanic Journal of Behavioral Science, 6*, 127-143.

Pacheco, G. K. (1990). On native Hawaiians: Lost in the shuffle? *Focus, 4*, 6-7.

Paris, J. (1921). *Kimono*. London.

Park, R. E. (1928). Human migration and the marginal man. *American Journal of Sociology, 33*, 881-893.

Park, R. E. (1931). Mentality of racial hybrids. *American Journal of Sociology, 36*, 534-551.

Park, R. E. (1937). Introduction. In E. V. Stonequist, *The marginal man: A study in personality and culture conflict* (p. xvii). New York: Russell & Russell.

Payne, R. (1977). Racial attitude formation in children of mixed black and white heritage: Skin color and racial identity (Doctoral dissertation). *Dissertation Abstracts International, 38* (6-B), 2876.

Páz, O. (1961). *The labyrinth of solitude: Life and thought in Mexico* (L. Kemp, Trans.). New York: Grove. (Original work published 1950)

Perdue, T. (1979). *Slavery and the evolution of Cherokee society, 1540-1866*. Knoxville: University of Tennessee Press.

Pettigrew, T. F. (1981). Race and class in the 1980s: An interactive view. *Daedalus, 110*, 233-255.

Pettigrew, T. F. (1988). Integration and pluralism. In P. A. Katz & D. A. Taylor (Eds.), *Eliminating racism: Profiles in controversy* (pp. 19-30). New York: Plenum.

Pettit, A. G. (1980). *Images of the Mexican American in fiction and film*. College Station: Texas A&M University Press.

Phinney, J. S. (1990). Ethnic identity in adolescents and adults: Review of research. *Psychological Bulletin, 108*, 499-514.

Phinney, J. S., Lochner, B. T., & Murphy, R. (1990). Ethnic identity development and psychological adjustment in adolescence. In A. R. Stiffman & L. E. Davis (Eds.), *Ethnic issues in adolescent mental health*. Newbury Park, CA: Sage.

Piaget, J. (1954). *The construction of reality in the child*. New York: Basic Books.

Piaget, J. (1973). *The child and reality*. New York: Viking.

Pinderhughes, E. (1989). *Understanding race, ethnicity, and power: The key to efficacy in clinical practice*. New York: Free Press.

Piskacek, V., & Golub, M. (1973). Children of interracial marriages. In I. R. Stuart & L. E. Abt (Eds.), *Interracial marriage: Expectations and realities* (pp. 53-61). New York: Grossman.

Ponterotto, J. G., & Casas, J. M. (1991). *Handbook of racial/ethnic minority counseling research*. Springfield, IL: Charles C Thomas.

Porter, F. W., III. (Ed.). (1986). *Strategies for survival: American Indians in the eastern United States*. Westport, CT: Greenwood.

Porter, J. (1971). *Black child, White child*. Cambridge, MA: Harvard University Press.

Porterfield, E. (1978). *Black and White marriages: An ethnographic study of Black-White families*. Chicago: Nelson-Hall.

Posadas, B. M. (1989). Mestiza girlhood: Interracial families in Chicago's Filipino American community since 1925. In Asian Women United of California (Ed.), *Making waves: An anthology of writings by and about Asian American women* (pp. 273-282). Boston: Beacon.

Poussaint, A. (1984). Study of interracial children presents positive picture. *Interracial Books for Children, 15*, 9-10.

Provine, W. B. (1973). Geneticists and the biology of race crossing. *Science, 182*, 790-796.

Quinn, W. W., Jr. (1990). The southeast syndrome: Notes on Indian descendant recruitment organizations and their perceptions of Native American culture. *American Indian Quarterly, 14*, 147-154.

Radcliffe, E. (1988, Fall). Round one lost. *Communiqué* (Newspaper of the Interracial Family Alliance, Houston), *3*, 1-3.

Rajs, E. (1991, May-June). Pros, cons of ethnic labels: Standard categories don't fit multiethnic population. *UC Focus* (published for the faculty and staff of the University of California by the Office of the President of the University of California, Oakland), *5*, 1, 8.

Ramirez, M., III. (1983). *Psychology of the Americas: Mestizo perspectives on personality and mental health.* New York: Pergamon.

Ramirez, M., Castaneda, A., & Cox, B. G. (1977). *A bicultural inventory for Mexican-American college students.* Unpublished manuscript.

Rankin, D. C. (1978). The impact of the Civil War on the free colored community of New Orleans. *Perspective in American History, 9*, 379-416.

Reed, T. (1969). Caucasian genes in American Negroes. *Science, 165*, 762-768.

Reimers, D. (1985). *Still the golden door.* New York: Columbia University Press.

Reuter, E. B. (1969). *Race mixture.* New York: Negro Universities Press. (Original work published 1931)

Rex, J. (1983). *Race relations in sociological theory.* London: Routledge & Kegan Paul. (Original work published 1971)

Rickel, A. U., & Biasatti, L. L. (1982). Modification of the Bloch Child Rearing Practices report. *Journal of Clinical Psychology, 38*, 129-133.

Riggs, F. (1950). *Pressures on Congress: A study of the repeal of Chinese exclusion.* New York: King's Crown.

Ringer, B., & Lawless, E. (1989). *Race-ethnicity and society.* London: Routledge, Chapman & Hall.

Root, M. P. P. (1990). Resolving "other" status: Identity development of biracial individuals. In L. Brown & M. P. P. Root (Eds.), *Complexity and diversity in feminist theory and therapy* (pp. 185-205). New York: Haworth.

Root, M. P. P. (in press-a). The impact of trauma on personality: The second reconstruction. In M. Ballou & L. S. Brown (Eds.), *Theories of personality and psychopathology: Feminist reappraisals.* New York: Guilford.

Root, M. P. P. (in press-b). Mixed race women. In L. Comas-Diaz & B. Greene (Eds.), *Women of color and mental health: The healing tapestry.* New York: Guilford.

Rosenberg, M. (1965). *Society and the adolescent self-image.* Princeton, NJ: Princeton University Press.

Rosenberg, M. (1981). The self-concept: Social product and social force. In M. Rosenberg & R. H. Turner (Eds.), *Social psychology: Sociological perspectives.* New York: Basic Books.

Rotheram, M. J., & Phinney, J. S. (1987). Introduction: Definitions and perspectives in the study of children's ethnic socialization. In J. S. Phinney & M. J. Rotheram (Eds.), *Children's ethnic socialization: Pluralism and development* (pp. 10-28). Newbury Park, CA: Sage.

Salk, J. (1973). *Survival of the wisest.* New York: Harper & Row.

Sandoval, C. (1990). Feminism and racism: A report on the 1981 National Women's Studies Association Conference. In G. Anzaldua (Ed.), *Making face, making soul (haciendo caras): Creative and critical perspectives by women of color* (pp. 55-71). San Francisco: Aunt Lute Foundation.

Scheick, W. J. (1979). *The half-blood: A cultural symbol in 19th-century American fiction.* Lexington: University of Kentucky Press.

Schermerhorn, R. A. (1978). *Comparative ethnic relations: A framework for theory and research* (2nd ed.). Chicago: University of Chicago Press.

Schwitters, S. Y., Johnson, R. C., McClearn, G. E., & Wilson, J. R. (1982). Alcohol use and the flushing response in different racial-ethnic groups. *Journal of Studies on Alcohol, 43*, 1259-1262.

Sears, R. R. (1957). Identification as a form of behavioral development. In D. B. Harris (Ed.), *The concept of development.* Minneapolis: University of Minnesota Press.

Sebring, D. (1985). Considerations in counseling interracial children. *Journal of Non-White Concerns in Personal Guidance, 13*, 3-9.

Seidman, E. (1983). Introduction. In E. Seidman (Ed.), *Handbook of social intervention* (pp. 11-17). Beverly Hills, CA: Sage.

Seller, M. (1977). *To seek America: A history of ethnic life in the United States.* Englewood, NJ: Jerome S. Ozer.

Semaj, L. T. (1979). Racial identification and preference in children: A cognitive approach (Doctoral dissertation, Rutgers University, 1978). *Dissertation Abstracts International, 39*(11), 5661-5662.

Semaj, L. T. (1980). Reconceptualizing the development of racial preference in children: A socio-cognitive approach. *Journal of Black Psychology, 6*, 59-69.

Semaj, L. T. (1985). Afrikanity, cognition and extended self-identity. In M. B. Spencer, G. K. Brookins, & W. R. Allen (Eds.), *Beginnings: The social and affective development of Black children* (pp. 173-184). Hillsdale, NJ: Lawrence Erlbaum.

Shade, J. A., Jr. (1981). *America's forgotten children: The Amerasians.* Perkasie, PA: Pearl S. Buck Foundation.

Shibutani, T., & Kwan, K. (1965). *Ethnic stratification.* New York: Macmillan.

Sickels, R. J. (1972). *Race, marriage and the law.* Albuquerque: University of New Mexico Press.

Silko, L. M. (1977). *Ceremony.* New York: Viking.

Silverman, A. R., & Feigelman, W. (1981). The adjustment of black children adopted by white families. *Social Casework, 62*, 529-536.

Simon, R. J., & Alstein, H. (1977). *Transracial adoption.* New York: John Wiley.

Smith, T. W. (1980). Ethnic measurement and identification. *Ethnicity, 7*, 78-95.

Smith, W. C. (1939). The hybrid in Hawaii as a marginal man. *American Journal of Sociology, 39*, 459-468.

Smither, R., & Rodriguez-Giegling, M. (1979). Marginality, modernity, and anxiety in Indochinese refugees. *Journal of Cross-Cultural Psychology, 10*, 469-477.

Smits, D. D. (1987). "Abominable mixture": Toward the repudiation of Anglo-American intermarriage in seventeenth-century America. *Virginia Magazine of History and Biography, 95*, 157-192.

Snipp, C. M. (1986). Who are American Indians? Some observations about the perils and pitfalls of data for race and ethnicity. *Population Research and Policy Review, 5*, 237-252.

Sotomayor, M. (1977). Language, culture, and ethnicity in developing self-concept. *Social Casework, 58*, 195-203.

Sparks, A. (1990). *The mind of South Africa*. New York: Alfred A. Knopf.

Spencer, M. B. (1983). Personal group identity of Black children: An alternative synthesis. *Genetic Psychology, 106*, 59-84.

Spencer, M. B. (1984). Black children's race awareness, racial attitudes and self concept: A reinterpretation. *Journal of Child Psychiatry and Psychology, 25*, 433-441.

Spencer, M. B. (1985). Cultural cognition and social cognition as correlates of Black children's personal-social development. In M. B. Spencer, G. K. Brookins, & W. R. Allen (Eds.), *Beginnings: The social and affective development of Black children* (pp. 215-230). Hillsdale, NJ: Lawrence Erlbaum.

Spencer, M. B. (1987). Black children's ethnic identity formation: Risk and resilience of castelike minorities. In J. S. Phinney & M. J. Rotheram (Eds.), *Children's ethnic socialization: Pluralism and development* (pp. 103-116). Newbury Park, CA: Sage.

Spickard, P. R. (1983). *Mixed marriage: Two American minority groups and the limits of ethnic identity, 1900-1970*. Unpublished doctoral dissertation, University of California, Berkeley.

Spickard, P. R. (1989). *Mixed blood: Intermarriage and ethnic identity in twentieth-century America*. Madison: University of Wisconsin Press.

Spielberg, C. (1973). *State-Trait Anxiety Inventory for Children: Preliminary manual*. Palo Alto, CA: Consulting Psychologists Press.

Stanton, M. (1971). A remnant Indian community: The Houma of southern Louisiana. In J. K. Moorland (Ed.), *The not so solid South: Anthropological studies in a regional subculture* (pp. 82-92). Athens: University of Georgia Press.

State of Hawaii, Department of Health. (1987). *Statistical report*. Honolulu: Author.

State of Hawaii, Department of Health. (1988). *Annual report, statistical supplement, vital statistics*. Honolulu: Author.

State of Hawaii, Department of Planning and Economic Development. (1989). *Data book: A statistical abstract*. Honolulu: Author.

Stedman, R. (1982). *Shadows of the Indian: Stereotypes in American culture*. Norman: University of Oklahoma Press.

Steinberg, S. (1981). *The ethnic myth*. Boston: Beacon.

Stepan, N. (1982). *The idea of race in science*. Hamden, CT: Archon.

Stephan, C. W. (1991). Ethnic identity among mixed-heritage people in Hawaii. *Symbolic Interaction, 14*, 261-277.

Stephan, C. W., & Stephan, W. G. (1989). After intermarriage: Ethnic identity among mixed heritage Japanese-Americans and Hispanics. *Journal of Marriage and the Family, 51*, 507-519.

Stephan, W. G. (1985). Intergroup relations. In G. Lindzey & E. Aronson (Eds.), *Handbook of social psychology* (Vol. 3, pp. 599-658). Reading, MA: Addison-Wesley.

Stephan, W. G., & Stephan, C. W. (1971). Role differentiation, empathy, and neurosis in urban migrants and marginal residents of Santiago, Chile. *Journal of Personality and Social Psychology, 19*, 1-6.

Stephan, W. G., & Stephan, C. W. (1985). Intergroup anxiety. *Journal of Social Issues, 41*, 157-176.

Stephan, W. G., & Stephan, C. W. (1991). Intermarriage: Effects on personality, adjustment, and intergroup relations in two samples of students. *Journal of Marriage and the Family, 53*, 241-250.

Stephenson, G. T. (1910). *Race distinction in American law*. New York: Appleton.

Stevenson, H., & Stewart, E. (1958). A developmental study of racial awareness among young children. *Child Development, 29*, 399-409.

Stone, G. P. (1962). Appearance and the self. In A. M. Rose (Ed.), *Human behavior and social processes* (pp. 86-118). Boston: Houghton Mifflin.

Stonequist, E. V. (1937). *The marginal man: A study in personality and culture conflict.* New York: Russell & Russell.

Strong, N. (1978). *Patterns of social interaction and psychological accommodations among Japan's Konketsuji population.* Unpublished doctoral dissertation, University of California, Berkeley.

Stryker, S. (1980). *Symbolic interactionism: A social structural version.* Menlo Park, CA: Benjamin/Cummings.

Swearingen, E., & Cohen, L. H. (1985). Measurement of adolescents' life events: The Junior High Life Experiences Survey. *American Journal of Community Psychology, 13,* 69-85.

Szapocznik, J., & Kurtines, W. (1980). Acculturation, biculturalism, and adjustment among Cuban-Americans. In A. M. Padilla (Ed.), *Acculturation: Theory, models and some new findings* (pp. 139-159). Boulder, CO: Westview.

Tajfel, H. (1978). *The social psychology of minorities.* New York: Cambridge University Press.

Takeshita apologizes for racist remarks. (1988, August 18). *Pacific Stars and Stripes.*

Tautfest, P. (1990, September). An immigrant of our time. *World Monitor,* pp. 31-33.

Taylor, D. M., Bassilli, J. M., & Aboud, F. E. (1973). Dimensions in ethnic identity: An example from Quebec. *Journal of Social Psychology, 89,* 185-192.

Taylor, D. M., Sinard, L. M., & Aboud, F. E. (1972). Ethnic identity in Canada. A cross-cultural investigation. *Canadian Journal of Behavioural Science, 4,* 13-20.

Teicher, J. (1968). Some observations on identity problems in children of Negro-white marriages. *Journal of Nervous and Mental Disease, 146,* 249-256.

Teitelbaum, S. (1990, April 1). Making everything perfectly fuzzy. *Los Angeles Times Magazine,* pp. 24-42.

Thornton, M. C. (1983). *A social history of a multiethnic identity: The case of black Japanese Americans.* Unpublished doctoral dissertation, University of Michigan.

Thornton, R. (1987). *American Indian holocaust and survival: A population history since 1492.* Norman: University of Oklahoma Press.

Tinker, J. N. (1973). Intermarriage and ethnic boundaries: The Japanese American case. *Journal of Social Issues, 29,* 49-66.

Tofler, A. (1980). *The third wave.* New York: Alfred A. Knopf.

Tomkins, T. (1981). *Yokosuka: Base of an empire.* Novato, CA: Presidio.

Tragedy of Korea's mixed-race war babies. (1975, June). *Sepia.*

Transit center for Amerasian children opens. (1990, January 17). *Foreign Broadcast Information Service* (EAS-90-011), p. 9.

Trautfield, M. T. (1984). America's responsibility to the Amerasian children: Too little, too late. *Brooklyn Journal of International Law, 10*(1), 54-82.

Triandis, H. C. (1988). The future of pluralism revisited. In P. A. Katz & D. A. Taylor (Eds.), *Eliminating racism: Profiles in controversy* (pp. 31-50). New York: Plenum.

Tucker, B., & Mitchell-Kernan, C. (1990). New trends in Black American marriage: The social structural context. *Journal of Marriage and the Family, 52,* 209-218.

U.S. Bureau of the Census. (1957). *Statistical abstract of the United States.* Washington, DC: Government Printing Office.

U.S. Bureau of the Census. (1980). *1980 census questionnaire reference book* (Publication No. D-561). Washington, DC: Government Printing Office.

U.S. Bureau of the Census. (1990). *The Hispanic population in the United States: March 1989* (Current Population Reports, Series P-20, No. 444). Washington DC: Government Printing Office.

U.S. Bureau of the Census. (1991a, March 11). *U.S. Department of Commerce news* (Publication No. CB91-100). Washington, DC: Government Printing Office.

U.S. Bureau of the Census. (1991b). *Statistical abstract of the United States, 1990* (110th ed.). Washington, DC: Government Printing Office.

U.S. Congress, House Subcommittee on Immigration and Naturalization of the Committee on the Judiciary. (1948). *Providing for equality under naturalization and immigration laws* (Hearings, 80th Congress, 2nd session). Washington, DC: Government Printing Office.

U.S. Department of the Interior. (1872). *Population of the United States: Ninth Census, 1870.* Washington, DC: Government Printing Office.

U.S. Department of Justice, Immigration and Naturalization Service. (1945-1977). *Annual reports.* Washington, DC: Government Printing Office.

U.S. Department of Justice, Immigration and Naturalization Service. (1978-1985). *Statistical yearbook of the Immigration and Naturalization Service.* Washington, DC: Government Printing Office.

U.S. Department of Justice, Immigration and Naturalization Service. (1980). *Our immigration.* Washington, DC: Government Printing Office.

Unrau, W. E. (1989). *Mixed-bloods and tribal dissolution: Charles Curtis and the quest for Indian identity.* Lawrence: University of Kansas Press.

Useem, R., Useem, J., & Donoghue, J. (1963). Men in the middle of the third culture: The roles of American and non-Western people in cross-cultural administration. *Human Resources, 22,* 169-179.

Uyeki, E. S. (1960). Correlates of ethnic identification. *American Journal of Sociology, 65,* 468-474.

Valdes, G. (1988). The language situation of Mexican Americans. In *Language diversity: Problem or resource?* New York: Newbury House.

Valverde, C. C. (1988). *From dust to gold: The Vietnamese Amerasian story.* Unpublished manuscript, University of California, Berkeley.

Valverde, C. C. (1989a, June 2). *Advocacy and legislation for Amerasians.* Paper presented at the Sixth National Conference of the Association for Asian American Studies, New York.

Valverde, C. C. (1989b). *What are you thinking? Attitudes toward the Amerasians.* Unpublished manuscript, University of California, Berkeley.

Valverde, C. C. (1990). *The Vietnamese mothers and their Amerasian children: A story of exploitation and neglect.* Unpublished manuscript, University of California, Berkeley.

Valverde, C. C. (1991, Winter). Belonging: A country opens its doors to Amerasian youth, a community shrugs. *Across the Sea, 2,* 18-19.

van den Berghe, P. L. (1967). *Race and racism.* New York: John Wiley.

van den Berghe, P. L., & Primov, G. P. (1974). *Inequality in the Peruvian Andes: Class and ethnicity in Cuzco.* Columbia: University of Missouri Press.

Vander-Zanden, J. V. (1963). *American minority relations.* New York: Ronald.

Vasconcelos, J. (1979). *La raza cósmica* (D. T. Jaen, Trans.). Los Angeles: California State University, Centro de Publicaciones. (Original work published 1925)

Vaughan, A. T. (1982). From white man to redskin: Changing Anglo-American perceptions of the American Indian. *American Historical Review, 87,* 917-953.

Vaughan, G. M. (1987). A social-psychological model of ethnic identity development. In J. S. Phinney & M. J. Rotheram (Eds.), *Children's ethnic socialization: Pluralism and development* (pp. 73-91). Newbury Park, CA: Sage.

Verma, G. K. (1984). Multiculturalism and education: Prelude to practice. In G. K. Verma & C. Bagley (Eds.), *Race relations and cultural differences: Educational and interpersonal perspectives* (pp. 57-77). New York: St. Martin's.

Verma, G. K., & Bagley, C. (1984). Multicultural education: Problems and issues. In G. K. Verma & C. Bagley (Eds.), *Race relations and cultural differences: Educational and interpersonal perspectives* (pp. 1-11). New York: St. Martin's.

Vietnam Veterans of America Foundation. (1989). *Report on the Amerasian issue*. Washington, DC: Author.

Vinacke, W. E. (1949). Stereotyping among national-racial groups in Hawaii: A study of ethnocentrism. *Journal of Social Psychology, 30*, 265-291.

Vizenor, G. (1981). *Earthdivers: Tribal narratives on mixed descent*. Minneapolis: University of Minnesota Press.

Vizenor, G. (1984). *The people named the Chippewa: Narrative histories*. Minneapolis: University of Minnesota Press.

Vizenor, G. (1990). *Crossbloods: Bone courts, bingo, and other reports*. Minneapolis: University of Minnesota Press.

Wagatsuma, H. (1967). The social perception of skin color in Japan. *Daedalus, 96*, 407-441.

Wagatsuma, H. (1973). Some problems of interracial marriage for the Japanese. In I. R. Stuart & L. E. Abt (Eds.), *Interracial marriage: Expectations and realities*. New York: Grossman.

Wagatsuma, J. (1976). Mixed-blood children in Japan: An exploratory study. *Journal of Asian Affairs, 2*, 9-16.

Walker, A. (1983). If the present looks like the past, what does the future look like? In A. Walker, *In search of our mothers' gardens*. New York: Harcourt Brace Jovanovich.

Wardle, F. (1987, January). Are you sensitive to interracial children's special identity needs? *Young Children*, pp. 53-59.

Wardle, F. (1990). *Research on interracial families: Some recommendations*. Unpublished manuscript.

Washington, J. (1970). *Marriage in black and white*. Boston: Beacon.

Waters, M. C. (1990). *Ethnic options: Choosing identities in America*. Berkeley: University of California Press.

Weber, M. (1961). Ethnic groups. In T. Parsons, E. Shils, D. Naegle, & J. R. Pitts (Eds.), *Theories of society*. New York: Free Press.

Weinberger, A. D. (1966). Interracial marriage: Its statutory prohibition, genetic import, and incidence. *Journal of Sex Research, 2*, 157-168.

Welch, J. (1974). *Winter in the blood*. New York: Harper & Row.

Welch, J. (1979). *The death of Jim Loney*. New York: Harper & Row.

Wheat, L. (1906). *The third daughter*. Los Angeles: Oriental.

White, J. M. (1971). *Cortés and the downfall of the Aztec empire*. New York: St. Martin's.

Wilkins, M. (1989). *The triracial isolates*. Unpublished manuscript.

Williams, J. E., Best, D. L., Boswell, D. A., Mattson, L. A., & Graves, D. J. (1975a). Preschool racial attitude measure II. *Educational and Psychological Measurement, 35*, 3-18.

Williams, J. E., Best, D. L., Boswell, D. A., Mattson, L. A., & Graves, D. J. (1975b). *PRAM II and CMT II: General information and manuals of direction*. Winston-Salem, NC: Wake Forest University.

Williams, J. E., & Morland, J. (1976). *Race, color and the young child.* Chapel Hill: University of North Carolina Press.

Williamson, J. (1984). *New people: Mulattoes and miscegenation in the United States.* New York: New York University Press.

Wilson, A. (1984). "Mixed race" children in British society: Some theoretical considerations. *British Journal of Sociology, 35,* 42-61.

Wilson, A. (1987). *Mixed race children: A study of identity.* London: Allen & Unwin.

Wilson, J. R., McClearn, G. E., & Johnson, R. C. (1978). Ethnic variations in use and effects of alcohol. *Drug and Alcohol Dependence, 3,* 147-151.

Wilson, T. P. (1981). Osage Oxonian: The heritage of John Joseph Mathews. *Chronicles of Oklahoma, 59,* 265-293.

Wilson, T. P. (1984). Chief Fred Lookout and the politics of Osage oil, 1906-1949. *Journal of the West, 23,* 46-53.

Wilson, T. P. (1991). People of mixed race descent. In Y. I. Song & E. C. Kim (Eds.), *American mosaic: Selected readings on America's multicultural heritage.* Sacramento, CA: Ethnicus, Center for Multicultural Studies.

Wilson, W. J. (1980). *The declining significance of race* (2nd ed.). Chicago: University of Chicago Press.

Winterson, J. (1987). *Oranges are not the only fruit.* New York: Atlantic Monthly Press.

Wolff, P. (1972). Ethnic differences in alcohol sensitivity. *Science, 175,* 449-450.

Wolff, P. (1973). Vasomotor sensitivity to ethanol in diverse mongoloid populations. *American Journal of Human Genetics, 25,* 193-199.

Woodbridge, H. C. (1948). Glossary of names in colonial Latin America for crosses among Indians, Negros and Whites. *Journal of the Washington Academy of Sciences, 38,* 353-362.

Wright, G. C. (1985). *Life behind a veil: Blacks in Louisville, Kentucky, 1865-1930.* Baton Rouge: Louisiana State University Press.

Wright, R. D., & Wright, S. N. (1972). A plea for a further refinement of the marginal man theory. *Phylon, 33,* 361-368.

Yoshimura, E. (1986). [Holiday issue]. *Rafu Shimpo.*

Young, M. (1989). Racism in red and black: Indians and other free people of color. *Georgia Historical Quarterly, 73,* 492-518.

Zurcher, L. A. (1977). *The mutable self.* Beverly Hills, CA: Sage.

Index

About the Authors

Tanya Aguilar recently completed her B.S. degree in psychology at the University of Washington, at which time she traveled to Mexico in order to further her understanding of the Mexican culture and language. Her research interests include identity development in biracial adolescents and the influences of different ethnic cultures on peer and family relationships. She plans to pursue a graduate degree in psychology in the near future. Her mother is White and her father is Mexican American.

Carla K. Bradshaw, Ph.D., is a clinical psychologist in private practice in Seattle, Washington, and a graduate of the University of Washington. Her clinical, teaching, and publishing interests include marriage and infidelity as well as multicultural and cross-cultural issues. She holds a clinical faculty appointment at the University of Washington in the Department of Psychology, is a member of the Washington State Psychological Association's Task Force on Ethnic Minorities, is on the steering committee for the Feminist Therapy Institute, and is a board member for the Center for Prevention of Domestic and Sexual Violence (Seattle) as Chair of the Pacific Rim Advisory Committee (which specifically targets for study and intervention the abuse of indigenous women through domestic violence and prostitution in the Pacific Rim Asian nations as a result of American military presence). She is Amerasian, born of a native Japanese mother and Caucasian, North American father. She has resided in Japan as well as in the

United States, and brings to her work the experiences of both cultures.

Ana Mari Cauce, Ph.D., is Associate Professor of Psychology at the University of Washington. Her research has focused on family and peer relations, social support, and competence in ethnic minority and "at-risk" adolescents. She is currently principal investigator of a study titled "Ecological Correlates of Well-Being in Ethnic Minority Adolescents," funded by a grant from NICHHD, and one titled "Intensive Case Management for Homeless Adolescents," funded by a grant from NIMH. She is active in numerous professional organizations, including the Society for Community Research and Action (APA, Division 27) where she cochairs the Ethnic Minority Concerns Committee and is Member-at-Large to the Executive Committee. She also serves on the editorial board of the *American Journal of Community Psychology* and has recently started a peer-mentorship network for that journal aimed at increasing the representation of research on ethnically diverse populations. She was born in Cuba and was brought to the United States by her parents when she was 3 years old. Her formative years were spent in Miami, Florida.

G. Reginald Daniel, Ph.D., received his degree in Hispanic languages and literatures and is a Lecturer in Latin American and Afro-American Studies at the University of California, Los Angeles. His teaching and research focus on comparative issues of race and identity in the Americas, particularly as this relates to multiracial individuals of partial African descent. Since 1989, he has taught "Betwixt and Between: Multiracial Identity in Global Perspective," one of the first university courses to deal specifically with the question of multiracial identity comparing populations in diverse parts of the world. Along with his numerous television and radio appearances, and his participation as a panelist at various conferences dealing with multiracial identity, he is a member of the Advisory Board of AMEA (Association of Multiethnic Americans), Education Committee Chair of MASC (Multiracial Americans of Southern California), and Coordinator of MASC's Forum on Multiethnic Identity and Intergroup Relations. His own multiethnic ancestry includes African, French, Native American, Irish, and East Indian origins.

Carlos A. Fernández, J.D., is an attorney in private practice and a writer. While a student at Berkeley High School, he was appointed by the Superintendent of Schools to serve on the Berkeley School District's Bilingual Bicultural Task Force. He is a graduate of the Mexican American Legal Defense and Education Fund Leadership Program, and he was appointed by the Alameda County Board of Supervisors to the Community Health Services Advisory Committee. He has been a board member of Interracial Intercultural Pride, Inc. (I-Pride) since 1986; he has served as Secretary (1986) and President (1987-1988, 1990-1991) of that organization. He is a founding member and current President of the Association of Multiethnic Americans, a nationwide confederation of local interracial groups that includes I-Pride. He is married and has two children. His mother is predominantly mixed European American, and a descendant of a signer of the American Declaration of Independence. His father, now deceased, was a Mexican psychiatrist of mixed Native American and Spanish ancestry; he was a direct descendant of the first president of the Mexican Republic. Both parents were active in civil rights, especially the farm workers movement, from 1965 on.

Jewelle Taylor Gibbs received her A.B. degree cum laude from Radcliffe College and her M.S.W. and Ph.D. degree in clinical psychology from the University of California at Berkeley, where she is currently a Professor in the School of Social Welfare. She has served on the Board of Directors of the American Orthopsychiatric Association and the National Center for Children in Poverty, and is a Fellow of the American Psychological Association. She is the editor of *Young, Black and Male in America: An Endangered Species* (Greenwood Press, 1988) and the coauthor of *Children of Color: Psychological Interventions with Minority Youth* (Jossey-Bass, 1989).

Nancy Gonzales is in her final year of doctoral study in child clinical psychology at the University of Washington, where she worked with Dr. Ana Mari Cauce. Her clinical and research interests include ethnic minority mental health, family interaction, and adolescent development. After completing her clinical internship at Children's Hospital at Stanford in June 1992, she hopes to pursue clinical research within an environment supportive of ethnic minority mental health.

Christine C. Iijima Hall, Ph.D., is Assistant Vice Provost for Academic Affairs at Arizona State University West. She is the third child of Roger and Fumiko Hall. Her Black father (a master sergeant in the U.S. Army) met her Japanese-born mother (a registered nurse) during the military occupation of Japan after World War II; they are still married and live in Southern California. She has two older siblings, Juanita and Roger. She received her Ph.D. in social psychology from the University of California, Los Angeles, in 1980. She was determined to conduct her dissertation research on the identity decisions and experiences of racially mixed individuals, and she persevered, although many faculty members tried to talk her out of conducting such esoteric and difficult research. Her study became one of the pioneering works in the area of ethnic identity of biracial people. She has given interviews that have appeared in magazines and newspapers and on radio and television. More than 150 copies of her dissertation have been sold.

Alice M. Hines received her B.A. from Marymount College and her M.S.W. from the School of Social Welfare at the University of California at Berkeley, where she is currently a doctoral candidate. Her research interests include adolescent development and psychosocial adjustment, the effects of separation and divorce on children and families, cross-cultural and cross-ethnic issues in research, and combining qualitative and quantitative methods in research. She is also currently a predoctoral fellow at the Center for the Family in Transition in Corte

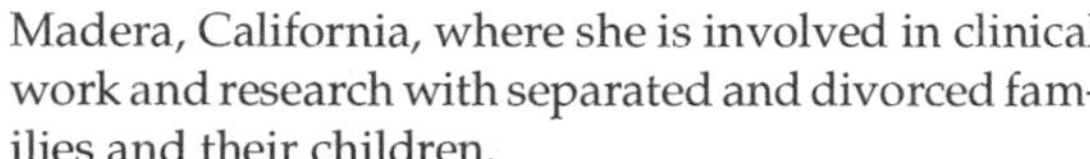
Madera, California, where she is involved in clinical work and research with separated and divorced families and their children.

Yumi Hiraga received her B.A. in psychology and East Asian studies from Harvard University. She is currently a graduate student in the Clinical Psychology Program at the University of Washington and is working as a research assistant with Dr. Ana Mari Cauce. Her research interests include mother-daughter interactions, moral development in children, and the influences of ethnic minority cultures on adolescent development. She is a Seattle native.

James H. Jacobs, Ph.D., is a graduate of the Social-Clinical Psychology Program at Wright Institute in Berkeley, California, where he continued his affiliation as a Research Consultant and Clinical Supervisor. He conducted some of the first contemporary dissertation research on biracial children's identity development. He continued his research interests at UC Berkeley's Institute of Human Development, working on a longitudinal study investigating children's development of competence within the family. A practicing clinical psychologist for 15 years, he has also been a psychologist with Alameda County Superior Court, Family Court Services, for the last nine years, providing child custody mediation and evaluation. He has provided workshops and talks on interracial families and biracial children to clinics, schools, and the media. He is a founding member of I-Pride (1979) in the San Francisco Bay Area. He has two biracial children, a son and a daughter who are in high school and college, respectively.

Deborah J. Johnson, Ph.D., is an Assistant Professor of Child and Family Studies at the University of Wisconsin—Madison. As a developmental psychologist she has primarily been interested in identity formation, socialization, and biculturality in early and middle childhood. Recently, she has embarked on a research project that focuses on the normative experiences of biracial teens in school and at home.

She is continuing to investigate these issues internationally, with ongoing work with young children in Zimbabwe. Other research on families and schools stems from her dissertation, which focused on the development of racial coping strategies among African American children. This project received an award and a commendation from the Phi Delta Kappa organization and the American Psychological Association's Board of Ethnic Minority Affairs. She is coeditor, with Diana T. Slaughter-Defoe, of *Visible Now: Blacks in Private Schools.*

Ronald C. Johnson, Ph.D., grew up in rural northern Minnesota. He served in the U.S. Navy during World War II, and then entered college in 1946; he received a B.A. in psychology in 1949, an M.A. in sociology in 1950, and a Ph.D. in child development in 1959. The long gap between obtaining his M.A. and Ph.D. was largely a result of years spent working in construction in Alaska. He has been a member of the faculty at San Jose State University (1957-1962), the University of Hawaii (1962-1965), the University of Colorado (1965-1970), and again at the University of Hawaii (1970-present). His research interests focus in the area of measurement of individual differences and their bases. He has been involved in research aimed at assessing genetic and environmental influences on individual and group differences in such areas as cognitive abilities, personality, attitudes toward and use of alcohol, and marital choice. He is currently researching Native Hawaiian beliefs concerning the nature of and most effective treatment for psychological problems in an effort to understand the treatment procedures used by Native Hawaiian health practitioners.

George Kitahara Kich, Ph.D., is a clinical psychologist in private practice and Associate Professor at the California Institute of Integral Studies. He received his degree from Wright Institute in Berkeley, California, where he conducted some of the first contemporary dissertation research on biracial identity development. He was a cofounder of I-Pride and its first President. He provides education to the public on multiracial people through talks, publications, workshops, and media interviews. He has actively introduced the issue of biracial identity at the conferences of the Center for Japanese American Studies and the Association for Asian American Studies. Most recently, he has been working to develop an international network of multiracial Asians.

Craig Mason received a B.S. in psychology from Brigham Young University and is currently a graduate student in the Child Clinical Psychology Program at the University of Washington. He is currently working as a Research Assistant with Dr. Ana Mari Cauce and has just completed teaching an undergraduate course in statistics. He is also on the Student Editorial Board of the *American Journal of Community Psychology*. His research interests include adolescence and problem behavior. His wife, Shihfen Tu, was born in Taiwan and is completing her Ph.D. in cognitive psychology. At the time of this writing, the couple are expecting their first child.

Amy Iwasaki Mass received her B.A. from the University of California, Berkeley, her M.S.W. from the University of Southern California, and her D.S.W. from UCLA. She is currently an Associate Professor in the Department of Sociology, Anthropology and Social Work at Whittier College. As a licensed clinical social worker and licensed marriage, family, and child counselor in California, she specializes in working with Asian Americans in her clinical practice. She has published on the subject of the psychological effects of the World War II concentration camp experience on Japanese Americans and on clinical social work with Asian Pacific children and families. She is married to Howard Mass, a Euro-American, and they have two biracial children.

Robin L. Miller, M.A., has conducted workshops and seminars concerned with biracial parenting for professional and mutual-help organizations in the Northeast. She is an adjunct faculty member at New York University's School of Continuing Education and at Empire State College, teaching courses on human diversity. She is also the Assistant Director of Education for the Gay Men's Health Crisis, an AIDS service organization in New York City. She received her B.A. from Sarah Lawrence College and her M.A. from New York University's Center for Community Research and Action, where she is currently completing her Ph.D. She is a descendant of Scotland, Sweden, England, France, and Black Africa.

Cynthia L. Nakashima is the daughter of a German and English American mother and Japanese American father who met in graduate school and married in 1965. She holds a B.S. in sociology from Santa Clara University, an M.A. in ethnic studies from the University of California, Berkeley, and is currently working on her Ph.D. in ethnic studies at UC Berkeley. Her research focus is interracial families and multiracial people; she has conducted fieldwork in Hawaii, California, and Vietnam. She has been very active in many of the organizations for people of mixed race that have formed in the San Francisco Bay Area, and is on the Board of Directors of the Multiracial Asian International Network (MAIN) and the Vietnamese Amerasian Family, and is the graduate student adviser to the UC Berkeley group MISC (Multiethnic/Interracial Students' Coalition). She wishes to thank her entire family for their fierce and interminable support and love.

Philip Tajitsu Nash was born in New York City to parents of Japanese American and Irish and English American ancestries. Among the early influences on him were three unique siblings; a maternal grandmother, Risu Tajitsu, who reinforced the importance of his Japanese American roots; loving Nash and Tajitsu relatives; and parents who taught respect for people of all backgrounds. He has worked as a teacher, lawyer, journalist, radio program producer, and community organizer in the New York area, and as an advocate for Japanese Americans who were interned in concentration camps in the United States during World War II. He currently lives near Washington, D.C., with activist and writer Emi Ireland and boys Matthew and Devin, while working on issues related to human rights, free speech, Wauja land rights, and Native American perspectives on the Columbus Quincentennial in 1992.

Nydia Ordonez has recently completed her B.A. degree in psychology at the University of Washington. She is currently working as a research assistant with Dr. Ana Mari Cauce. Her research interests include the psychological assimilation of ethnic minority families into the American culture and the psychosocial development of biracial children. She plans to pursue a graduate degree in psychology at some later date. She was born in Managua, Nicaragua, and came to the United States at the age of 15.

Maria P. P. Root, Ph.D., is a clinical psychologist in private practice in Seattle, Washington, and Clinical Associate Professor at the University of Washington. Her expertise lies in the areas of addiction, post-traumatic stress syndrome, sexual abuse, Asian American mental health, and biracial and bicultural individuals and families, areas in which she has also published. She serves on several regional and national boards affecting issues relevant to minority mental health and women, such as the American Psychological Association's Board of Ethnic Minority Affairs, which developed *Guidelines for Psychological Practice with Ethnic and Culturally Diverse Populations*. She is a fellow of the American Psychological Association and recipient of the Washington State Psychological Association's Distinguished Psychologist Award. She was born in Manila, Philippines, and is of Filipino, Spanish, German, Portuguese, Chinese, and Irish heritage.

Paul R. Spickard is the author of *Mixed Blood: Intermarriage and Ethnic Identity in Twentieth-Century America* (1989) and other books and articles on race and ethnicity. He was educated at Harvard University (A.B.) and the University of California, Berkeley (Ph.D.), and has taught at several universities in the United States and abroad. Currently, he is Associate

Professor of History at Brigham Young University—Hawaii and Research Director for the Cultural Development Institute. He is a mongrel European American, married to a Chinese American woman, and the father of two bicultural children. He is currently at work on an interpretive history of Japanese Americans.

Cookie White Stephan earned a Ph.D. in psychology from the University of Minnesota in 1971. A social psychologist, she has taught most of her career in departments of sociology. She has published in the disciplines of both psychology and sociology. Her research interests in intergroup relations include ethnic identity, intergroup anxiety, and cross-cultural communication barriers.

Michael C. Thornton, Ph.D., conducts work as a sociologist that has as its foundation his own ethnic heritage: Black, American, and Japanese. Aside from issues of multiracial heritage, he focuses on interracial relations, racial and ethnic group identity among Blacks and Asian Americans, and how various ethnic groups create networks of care among family, friends, and neighbors. He is trying to identify which factors predict feelings of closeness among Blacks toward various groups of color (e.g., Asian, Native, and Hispanic Americans). He and his colleagues have also distinguished several components of group identity among Blacks and how they overlap with those among Asian Americans. An underlying theme to all his work is how people of color might build interracial coalitions.

Kieu-Linh Caroline Valverde has played a prominent role in educating the public to the needs of Vietnamese Amerasians through community work and presentations at professional conferences. She worked on California's Senate Bill 55, which gave extra state funding to resettlement programs for newly arrived Amerasians. She is a cofounder of the Multiracial Asian International Network (1989) and is on the Board of Directors for Vietnamese Amerasian Family, based in Santa Clara County, a major resettlement site for Amerasian immigrants. She received her undergraduate degree in political science and Asian American studies at the University of California, Berkeley, where she is also credited with initiating Vietnamese language classes as part of the curriculum. She is attending graduate school in the fall of 1992 to study Southeast Asian politics.

Teresa Kay Williams was raised in the Kanto area of Japan. Her Japanese mother is from Tokyo, and her Irish and Welsh American father is from Beckley, West Virginia. She holds a B.A. in Japanese studies and a certificate in ethnic studies from the University of Hawaii. A member of Phi Beta Kappa, she holds M.A. degrees in Asian American studies and sociology from the University of California, Los Angeles, where she is also currently a doctoral student researching bilingualism and ethnic identity. She has appeared on several television and radio programs concerning international and intercultural issues. She is Education Co-Chair for Multiracial Americans of Southern California, and is cofounder of The Amerasian League. She teaches courses in sociology and ethnic studies at the University of California, Santa Barbara, including a course titled "The World of Amerasians"; Santa Monica College; and California State University, Northridge.

Terry P. Wilson is currently Professor of Native American Studies and Ethnic Studies at the University of California. Himself an Indian mixed blood, he has been offering an undergraduate seminar titled "People of Mixed Racial Descent" since 1980. He is also the faculty sponsor for Miscellaneous, a student group composed of individuals who are racially mixed. Much of his published Native American history work focuses on mixed bloods. He is currently researching and writing a historical analysis of Indian mixed bloods in U.S. society.